Judaism and Its History

IN TWO PARTS

By

Dr. Abraham Geiger

Rabbi of the Israelite Congregation at Frankfort on the Main

Translated from the German

By

CHARLES NEWBURGH

The Bloch Publishing Co.

New York

Preface to the First Edition.

The following pages owe their origin to a Course of Lectures before a limited audience of educated persons. As they met with friends among those, so they seek them now among an educated public at large.

Ought subjects of such serious, profound importance as those considered in these pages to venture into the vast market of life, if their treatment claims to present new results gained from new points of view? It can not be contested that the results which science has apparently established with the aid of all the means at her command, should be made the property of all educated people. But as long as such proof has not been furnished in full, would it not be preposterous to drag them before the public at large? I have seriously considered these doubts. For the views expressed herein differ in important points from those generally prevailing, and I have thus far not had the opportunity to substantiate all of them so fully as to be able to refer to works previously published. I can only refer to my book, "The Original Text and Versions of the Bible," to my essay, "Sadducees and Pharisees," and a few other shorter articles published in my "Jewish Review for Science and Life" and in other periodicals. Notwithstanding those doubts, I could not resist the temptation presented by a finished manuscript. Considering that life is short and time is fleeting, I think myself to have the permission of saying with the wise Hillel, "Praise to God, day by day." It is not always advisable to defer and repress that which we deem useful until, perchance, it might become more useful. It shall remain the literary task of my life to elaborate, in closer connection and more exhaustively, the historical views presented in these pages. In the mean time I trust that they may in their present form disclose the background, afford an insight into the serious studies upon which they are based, and make them sufficiently clear for those acquainted with the subject-matter and the original sources.

On the other hand, the very importance of the questions

treated upon, as they require on the one side a thorough and cautious consideration, may on the other side even involve the demand not to withhold too long our own views gained by honest research. The questions are, after all, on every lip, and the man can least be exempted from answering them of whose official and literary position such answers may pre-eminently be expected and demanded. Historical facts must be explained for everyone, because they are the sources whence convictions, rules for belief and practice are derived. How then under such circumstances, and especially in our time, characterized by mental and spiritual commotion, could the impulse to a publication of one's own attempted solution be repressed? May, then, my views also mingle with the crowd of diverging opinions and testify for themselves.

To provide them with a passport in the form of extensive proofs and citations would be entirely out of place in a preface. Yet *one* thought I desire to recommend to the consideration of my readers. Just because the events treated upon herein have exercised a lasting influence, views have been formed of them which are regarded as completely settled, so that any deviation from them appears as highly extraordinary. Most men find it difficult to transpose themselves, regardless of the later conceptions, into the very time of the events and tendencies then prevailing, and to consider with open eyes that which then actually existed, and not that which it became in the views of a later period. Men are so accustomed to identify the present mode of thinking, which has been developed in the course of two thousand years, with that then existing; words and terms which at the time when first used, had quite a different meaning, are now taken in a sense which was gradually attributed to them and is now prevailing. Hence, when we read the ancient writings containing those expressions, according to the modern use of language, we must necessarily arrive at gross misconceptions; nevertheless, resistance is made, whenever the original meaning is demonstrated and the whole mode of thinking at that time elucidated accordingly. The terms *Pharisees*, *this world*, *the world to come*, *the kingdom of God*, and the like, belong, according to my settled conviction, to that class of words whose meanings have undergone an important change. I appeal therefore, to impartial examination, in order that it may gain the strength to wean itself from traditional prejudices and acquire the insight to view properly into historical events long past. If it be conceded that two thousand years have not vanished away without leaving their traces in the entire process of thought of mankind, it is absurd to allege that ideas and words which throughout such a period have exercised a decisive influence upon thought and practice, had no other meaning in former times and were not changed as to their significance with the change of external conditions and sentiments. Yet, if we desire to comprehend Antiquity, we must understand its mode of thought and speech, and not measure it by our own standard.

How far my views will meet with approval, time naturally will show; I am prepared for opposition from some quarters. Whenever it shall be presented to me with quiet and soberness, I shall examine it with all candor and willingly confess all errors proven; but I shall also persist in the truth of my conviction and, if need be, defend it whenever I regard it as well founded. Irritation can not affect me. Through labors of many years in the domain of the life and science of Judaism I have acquired the experience that opposing scorn to many an unaccustomed expression could not prevent its extensive general recognition at a later time. If I have also entered the domain of Christianity as far as the subject of these lectures required it, and have unhesitatingly presented convictions which may be now and then in sharp conflict with those ordinarily current, every fair-minded thinker will soon recognize that I have not done so wantonly nor from insidious hostility, but because I was forced into it by the necessity for authentification of my own conviction, while laboring in the cultivation of my own soil. It is high time that Jews should openly declare how they understand events from the very consideration of which comes the difference of the two religions. If free expression of opinion is both a right that must not be denied, and a duty that must not be neglected, an opponent should even be glad when contradiction presents an open front, so that he may know whither to direct his mental weapons during the contest, and is not compelled to grope in uncertain darkness in warding off hidden attack from the ambush of silence. With zealots who regard every contradiction as blasphemy, every view different from their own as damnable, and who would therefore close its mouth; who love to strengthen the weakness of their arguments by the violence of their proceeding—with such zealots, considerations like those mentioned will have no weight; with calmness, I look forward to condemnation by them. And for their use, I say: *I alone and exclusively* bear the responsibility of all I have said in these lectures. How many or how few of my co-religionists share my views, I do not know. Hence, I make exclusive claim to the *entire* honor of being attacked. My words must not afford a pretext for an accusation against Jews and Judaism. But should that, nevertheless, be done under the hypocritical pretence of piety, a new, sad example would be shown of the value placed in certain circles—I will not say upon the vaunted word of love, but in general—upon justice and fairness.

If I have here added a few words to what I have declared in the lectures, I owe yet an explanation for all omissions. Originally it had not been my intention to give such scanty review, as is contained in the twelfth lecture, to the long period from the destruction of the Second Temple to the present time. The narrow limit of time only, and the numbers of the lectures ultimately made that brevity a necessity. But I trust that I shall meet no serious blame on that account. The earlier period remains the foundation and could not yield to a shorter consideration than has been given to it. For the present, the survey of that later period may be regarded as a preliminary account of the transition to the present time. To be able to present this period also according to its fundamental ideas and decisive events in a similar manner, in a new course of lectures, is a hope to the realization of which I look forward with delight.

May these leaves, then, borne by favorable breezes, reach the hands of appreciative readers.

GEIGER.

Frankfort on the Main, March 11, 1864.

Preface to the Second Edition.

Faster than I had expected, the demand for a second edition has appeared. The fact is to me a glad guaranty that the book has not lacked notice in wider circles of educated persons, and probably found attention and approval, too. If the organs of criticism have so far kept silent about it, I am far from interpreting their silence as intentional in a demonstrative sense, neither does that give me reason to assume that the book made no impression. Besides a few short notices, three notable papers have published lengthy discussions last year; viz., Die Grenzboten (No. 41), Die Augsburger Allgemeine Zeitung (Supplement No. 321), and Steinschneider's Hebrew Bibliography (No. 42). Their verdict was not an agreement in all parts with the views of the author, yet at any rate such a one as is declared upon something worth noticing. The reviewers differed widely among themselves, so that their verdicts often mutually cancel each other in surprising manner. It appeared to one of them that my remarks on Renan and Strauss touched them but very little, while the other one found that I had thrown strong light upon their central points. If this one thought proper to designate my review of some sayings of Jesus as subtle, the third was of the opinion that just that view would meet with most approval. The last one again emphasized the doubt expressed by myself, whether views ought to be offered in popular presentation to the public at large before being scientifically authenticated by all parties; and this with a certain amount of reproachful aside. In contradiction to that, the first one declares that whoever knows my other scientific labors, would find nothing new in the book. The reviewer of the Allgemeine Zeitung seems to enjoy, relative to that point, a naive ignorance which behaves in the manner of self-admiration or arrogance, belonging to that mental plane.

Considering those contradictions in which the preliminary representatives of public opinion are moving, and considering the mere indicatory manner by which, notwithstanding greater detail, they rather touch the results, without entering deeper into examination of those and the investigations leading to them, I have no cause for making essential changes in the book. From the surprise expressed by the Christian reviewers at my giving to Judaism both in Antiquity and in relation to Christianity, continuous justification of existence as a religious force and a future and a mission for the future —from that surprise they will gradually recover. To be shaken out of a prejudice in which one has been comfortably rocked, is inconvenient. But that can not induce me to cease from designating the prejudice, spread ever so far, as prejudice, and I feel neither desire nor need of working over a book which has proceeded out of the author's inmost mental and spiritual life, as long as my presentation has not been proven erroneous. I have therefore limited myself in this edition to smoothing occasional crudities in expression. I can now point more definitely to a supplement, because a course of lectures which I am delivering this winter is continuing the consideration of the history into the Middle Ages and will be published later.

Meanwhile, may the book begin its journey for the second time, and gain new friends in addition to the old ones.

GEIGER.

Frankfort on the Main, January 15, 1865.

First Part

Closing with the Destruction of the Second Temple
In Twelve Lectures, with an Addition
"Renan and Strauss"

Contents.

Judaism and Its History.

I.

On the Nature of Religion.

If I ask your attention for a series of Lectures on Judaism, its essence, formation, development, its relation to similar appearances in history, on the mission which it undertook to fulfill and the manner in which it has fulfilled it, on the mission which still remains to it, both for the present and a long future—the subject, presenting a grand world-historic phenomenon, may well demand your sympathy. A grand, world-historic phenomenon—not conveying the idea that Judaism, like many other historic phenomena, entered upon the world's stage for a certain time, and during that time exerted great influence, but as something finite, disappeared again and has become merely a subject for historical consideration. No, we may call it a world-historic phenomenon as an institution reaching back into that period whence historical knowledge began for the world, having not only existed for thousands of years and still existing, but because passed, as it were, as an immortal traveler through history, continuously accompanying history and co-operating with history from its very beginning to this day. A world-historic phenomenon, because it had given birth to kindred phenomena, Christianity and Islam, and projected them into history as grand energies which exerted their transforming, vivifying effect upon great multitudes, ruled the whole tendency of their mind and affected the entire development of the conditions and of Judaism too, through them. And notwithstanding Judaism presents such a world-historic phenomenon—may claim such great importance—notwithstanding, or perhaps on that very account, the opinions expressed concerning it are most conflicting; the importance of Judaism is denied out and out, or it is asserted that it has lost all importance a long time ago, or at least for our time.

Judaism, such is the first assertion, is a *Religion*, is one of the various forms in which religion presents itself in the life of man, in history; but religion itself is something beyond which we have progressed. Obscure, blind belief, hypotheses that can not be proven and should not be proven, which the human mind can not master, but which take possession of it and subjugate it—such conceptions have been relegated to the rear, long ago. Such ideas may have been very appropriate for a time when mankind was yet in its earliest infancy, groping its way in attempts to understand its environment, while the premises were lacking by which it might have arrived at knowledge. But we are the knowing ones, we have already reached such an eminence as affords us the means to pronounce the most decided judgment so that we are no longer fit subjects for blind belief and submission. But granted even that religion may still claim in our time some authority, that it embraces higher truths which man evolves from his own mind, higher truths concerning God, the human soul, freedom of will, immortality, virtue, etc., and that those truths, arranged in compact order may be designated as a System of Religion; what validity can be adjudged to the claim pre-eminently asserted by Judaism and after its manner also by other religions, the claim to *Revelation*, through the medium of which those truths have reached the mind without being produced by it; the claim that those truths made their appearance within mankind in an extraordinary manner and have thus been handed down without being reproduced anew by each and every generation. We have conquered for ourselves the autonomy of the mind; all claims raised against it, such as Judaism raises, are unjustified, and still more so when the turbid admixture of tradition is added to be also received as a truth. Or does Judaism perchance repudiate revelation and tradition? Does it want to be satisfied with the glory of having first proclaimed those sublime truths that have become common property of mankind—that it was the first to clearly enunciate ideas which are destined for all mankind and have completely taken possession of it? Be it so! Let it rejoice in that glory! But so runs the further assertion, even this glory can not be granted to it undiminished. The truths, as enunciated by Judaism, are *imperfect;* other, later religions have given them proper profundity and made them perfectly clear, on one side filling all gaps in magnificent manner, and on the other side, removing all superfluous matter and correcting all errors. Accordingly, Judaism is *antiquated,* is a ruin which has been preserved for a small circle, but which is no longer a determinative energy, its spiritual life became stunted and has fallen to the rear, while other religions have gone forward and extended their power over the world. Judaism remained within a small circle for which, it is still further asserted, it may perhaps still have had some importance in a period likewise passed away during the Middle Ages; for those professing it, it was a medium of spiritual and moral life. At a time when barriers of separation were the rule and fashion, when every small group existed as a close corporation and the members of each one of those had their growth and development only within such narrow confines, Judaism also had its authoritative and beneficent influence. But now we, especially those who think and have attained to a higher plane of culture, have progressed far beyond that point. Mankind has become a unit; mental and spiritual life, thought and feeling, though manifesting themselves in many forms, are nevertheless one and the same in essence, all mental treasures have become a common inheritance of humanity; the individual is satisfied with being a man. Those occupying a higher point of view among all parties and associations constitute a unit; Judaism has lost its importance for the *present age* for those who stand on the summit of our time.

Those are powerful and weighty objections. Let us approach them. The thinking man must unswervingly face all doubts, must not cowardly hide himself before them, and even when such doubts are presented in the form of assertions, he must not at once despair and surrender to them.

We are the knowing ones. This assertion is put forward with proud consciousness by our age in opposition to a sage of whom it is said that he had brought wisdom from heaven to earth by announcing that the highest degree of knowledge consisted in knowing that we know nothing. During the two thousand years since that saying was given to the world, we have made immense progress, and results of which there was then not the slightest presentiment are now either common property of all, or at least of those who more seriously devote themselves to research. Natural science has made giant strides. It now knows how to dissolve substances which were formerly considered indissoluble. It understands how to follow up the forces which bind and dissolve; it knows how to come at the volatile and evasive elements, how to fathom their laws deeper and deeper and reduce them to higher laws. How far it may progress, who can foresee? What depths it may yet penetrate, who can foretell? It has watched the secret ways in which growth and decay proceed, and has arranged them in a system of rules and laws. And yet, however farther and farther it may penetrate, for we can put no limits to its progress, will it not meet individual matters which can not be dissolved? Will it not ultimately come up with original substance that will ever remain original substance? With an original energy that will ever remain intangible and inexplicable? Will it not everlastingly be compelled to imagine laws and rules which must be supposed as existing, without being able further to prove them? Grant even one law is established, one order is arranged. The human mind will not quiet down at the point of blind force, will not be satisfied with standing still upon arrival at a certain point. With a presentient glance it will always perceive the ordering mind that must have put it up in such manner. Man, conscious of his own reason, can never resist that impulse.

Nature presents herself to us in a great variety of beings

according to classes and species; they are different and distinct; though they touch each other, they do not pass over, one into the other. Modern investigation has made the bold advance to search out how from the lower orders the higher ones might have evolved, how from the most imperfect organisms, the higher ones gradually shaped themselves. Whether it will succeed in clearing up also that mystery, whether such production of one from the other shall prove to be the truth—that is the business of the naturalists to decide, now or in the future. But this much we see: species do exist, they do not change one into the other, they are apart and they remain apart. The same force which created them at the beginning, one out of the other, as alleged, should necessarily continue the same process, should even at this time produce an animal out of the plant and perfect it to the higher organism. But the present world does not present to us such a phenomenon, each kind remains within its fixed limits, it continually begets only individuals of its own kind, and not one is transformed into another. Hence it is not a necessarily propelling force, but an ordering one which puts up each kind according to its peculiarity and preserves it, one that is not blindly rushing ahead without stopping, but which preserves nature as a whole, composed of different parts, so that it is unchangeable both as a whole and in its variety. Nature is ordered according to a definite *will*, according to an *independently ruling reason*, and is preserved in that arrangement; the whole universe is one structure, united notwithstanding its great variety, forming a harmonious whole, notwithstanding its various parts. That is *wisdom*, arrangement according to purpose and plan, so that even destroying forces present themselves as transforming ones, in order to cause the rising of new and nobler creations. That can be only the work of conscious reason—no, never that of a force propelling without purpose. It is a bold word which a great astronomer once uttered when he presented his work upon the mechanism of the heavens to his sovereign. The monarch expressing surprise at not finding God mentioned in the book, the man of science said,

"I do not need that hypothesis." Of course, it was not necessary for him in his explanation of the laws and their operation, at the same time to state how those laws originated and who fixed them everlasting and unchangeable; but what a man in a certain specialty may put aside, that a thinking man can not avoid, he is compelled to seek a higher cause that works according to rational principles.

Man has to explain not only nature surrounding him—he himself must be explained together with it; he is part and parcel of nature, and to know himself is a task which he can not avoid. But just to himself man becomes the greatest enigma, the more he reflects upon himself. It has been attempted to connect man very closely with similar creatures; species of apes have been mentioned as being but very little apart from man. Some kinds of apes, so it was said, have the appearance of being sunk in melancholy, as if pervaded by a longing desire to get out of that close restraint of mind. A contemplative sentiment, such as man attributes to the animal, but simply attributes, if he regards and conceives animal stupor as melancholy. The distance between the most highly organized animals and man remains a gap that can not be filled. To draw the most remote parallel between man who, despite his inconsiderate bodily strength, notwithstanding he is in many ways with regard to corporeal qualities inferior to other animals which are stronger and swifter, has nevertheless become lord of the earth, of all creation, who more and more gains dominion over everything in inanimate and animate nature, who accommodates himself to every place and knows how to control all conditions; to draw even the most distant comparison between man and any animal which leads an unprogressive life, which continuously remains on the same plane and is limited to a certain part of the world; which, without exercising any influence upon the rest of creation, perishes and leaves no trace behind—such a comparison, it must be admitted, looks like childish behavior, throwing away and destroying its own valuables.

No, man is of an entirely different genus. Man who is bound to time and space like all other corporeal and earthly creatures; individual man who is tied to a certain locality, who lives and moves within a small particle of time, nevertheless on the other hand overcomes time and space within him, he can transpose himself into the most distant regions, can place the past before him, presuppose the future, has a conception of what is beyond the present. Such faculty can not be the attribute of the body. The body is circumscribed by space and time. Man has the power of recollection, he bears within him that which is past, he can recall it, bring back the most various things from his memory, knowledge has become his property; secure in the possession of knowledge of one thing, he progresses step by step. Yet, where, in what part of his body is it? Let us pronounce the word which would not exist at all if the thing did not exist: it is the *spirit.* Man has a spirit, a faculty which is connected with his body in so far as it moves and animates him, but which is still far more because it leads him to rational contemplation, opens for him an insight into objects which his physical vision is unable to perceive or to grasp. That is a great word pronounced by the thinker who inaugurated the modern system of thought: "I think; therefore I am." The consciousness of the fact that I think, affords me the guaranty that I am; I might doubt all that surrounds me, might lose faith in my own existence, my physical vision is very deceptive, it assures certainty only through my consciousness. In fact, man sees all objects presented to him from without in a reverse position as they are mirrored on his retina, and his belief that he sees them as they really are, is the result of our thought, which effects the transposition with imperceptible velocity. Properly speaking, man sees no distance, the impression made of an object through the medium of ray is fixed within his sense of seeing. One object appears as near to him as another, no matter how much the one may be removed or the other brought nearer to him. It is for that reason that, at first, nothing appears distant to a blind person on gaining sight; every object presents itself to his vision as though it were close to him. Thought, habit only, teaches man to size the objects lying between, and from that he concludes that some objects are not so near as they are reflected upon his organ of sight, that they are at different distances. Sounds approach one after another; their connection is expressed only through our thought; through our mental grasp they become a unit; their harmony is within us; it is, as it were, awakened within us by the sounds succeeding each other. And the same can be proven with regard to all other senses. Thought gives shape to the perception of our senses, thought which, at the same time, furnishes man with expression for all feelings, sentiments and ideas. For language, the most faithful reflector of the spirit, constitutes the connecting link between man's inmost essence and the outer world; language most decisively marks him apart from all other creatures, language which, born as it were, of inward clearness, in its turn renders thought intelligible and gives it full and complete clearness. And nevertheless, that being upon whom the mark of dominion is so distinctly stamped, who can view the universe and all time through his spirit and its mind, that being feels himself, at the same time, limited, meets everywhere bars set up to his life and thought. An individual may advance ever so far and still remains an atom of humanity, so mankind itself is but a part of creation, and creation in its turn streams forth from the source of a greater Spirit. The limits adhere to man; being but a part, he can not arrive at a complete knowledge of the Original Cause of the whole; he must ever bear within himself the consciousness that he is but a fractional part, a fragment, incomplete.

And yet man feels that he occupies a high position in other respects according to resolutions, according to principles which he forms for himself; he proceeds according to his own will, he chooses, he is the author of his own deeds; no compulsion from without drives him on, he reflects, judges, and decides accordingly—what a boundless distinction! Oh, if he only could rejoice thereat in perfect ease! Even there, a mighty conflict arises within him. Whatever I may choose, however I may decide, I am induced thereto by certain reasons. These depend upon knowledge, and this I have derived from certain causes; aye, I am a child of my time, I suffer myself to be impelled and guided by what my time presents as truth; I am a product of my environment, I am not my own creator, I am not the author of my own actions. The desire everywhere to recognize the law of cause and effect crowds against my freedom, shows a necessary continuance of cause and effect, until I arrive at causes that are without me. And yet, man in his deepest self-consciousness feels that he is free, that his will is vested with the power to oppose and dominate all external influences. He is seized with repentance when he recognizes an action of his to be wrong; but he must reproach himself only with actions that have been prompted by himself, and not with those to which he was impelled by uncontrollable necessity. Thus, then, man is free and yet again in bonds! Here also, he perceives his limits, feels that he has not arrived at that degree of perfection for which he longs and of which he has presentiments. He is endowed with a double nature: the consciousness of his greatness and eminence, and over against that, the humiliating feeling of his dependence; on the one hand, the impulse to raise himself to that source whence has proceeded his own mental and spiritual faculty which is not self-creative even because it is dependent; and on the other hand, his inability to completely occupy that highest plane. Now, is not this true religion: the consciousness of man's eminence and lowness; the aspiration to perfection, coupled with the conviction that we can not reach the highest plane; the presentiment of the Highest which must exist as a freely acting will, of the Wisdom whence also our little fragment of wisdom proceeds, of an infinitely ruling Freedom whence also our limited freedom has sprung forth—is not that longing for the higher, that soaring up with all the strength of our soul, the very essence of religion? Religion is not a system of truths, it is the jubilation of the soul conscious of its eminence and, at the same time, its humble confession of its finiteness and limitations. Religion is the aspiration of the spirit after the ideal; the pursuit after the loftiest ideas; the desire to reach maturity in spiritual life and to dive deeper and deeper into it; to conquer the corporeal and earthly; and on the other hand, the unavoidable sentiment that we are still linked with the finite and limited. Religion is the aspiration after the Most High whom we conceive as the sole, full truth; the soaring up to the All-encircling Unity which man, through the whole nature of his spirit, presupposes as a whole, as the foundation of all that exists and shall be, as the source of all earthly and spiritual life, of which he bears within him the vivid conviction, though he be unable to completely know it. All that may be designated as an ancient conception; nothing but presentiment, longing, assumption, which can not be satisfactorily proven. But such is the very nature, the very essence of man, and it must be so, because he is a disconnected being, a fragment torn from the whole spiritual life to which he feels himself attracted without being able to perceive it in its entirety and perfection. The great saying of Lessing: "If God, holding in one hand complete truth, and searching after truth in the other, were to say to me, 'Man, choose!' I should ask God and say, 'The whole truth is not for me, searching after truth is fit for me,'" is a saying of the most profound and truest religiousness. Yea! longing after the Highest, attachment to the Whole, striving toward the Infinite despite our finiteness and limitations—that is religion. Therein we have also the guaranty for the Highest and Infinite, because we long to rise up to it; for the Eternal Wisdom, for the Free Agency that encompasses and produces everything out of itself, because we aspire thereto, because we bear the longing after it within ourselves. It can not be a fiction, the offspring of our imagination; it is the noblest reality within us. Religion is not an invention of idle priests; it existed and exists in mankind, and every good and noble aspiration—when man, putting aside his seclusive selfishness, lovingly and fervently attaches himself to his country and gives to it his own life and welfare and gladly labors for all and is filled with the desire to strive toward the Highest—is the work of religion. Though religion may present itself according to its rise in various outward forms, religion, as such, is a necessity, the noblest feature within man. It will cease only *with* man, not among men.

As long as the spirit's yearning for the Spirit of All remains, as long as that must remain, so long religious life will exist. Religion is life. All actions of man, as far as they are prompted by and are striving toward higher views, are the work of religion, and the results of religion. Religion will become purer, more enlightened, its essence and function will be better understood, and it will always remain in existence, because man's longing and imperfection will always remain. The more he advances, the more he will feel this distance from the Infinite and Eternal Wisdom; but he will also the more devotedly look up to it, draw from it, bow to it with fervency and humility. If Judaism did and still does work such an effect as a religion, it is one of the noblest animating forces among mankind.

II.

Religion in Antiquity, and Religion in Judaism.

The preceding considerations do not lay claim to establishing new foundations confirming truths thereby. That would be in conflict with the essence of religion; it would divest it of its very peculiarity of being the inheritance of humanity. Religion is an eternal, self-containing force, not a fragile thing which, soon breaking down, is put up again in an altered manner. Nor did our essay mean to adduce new, decisive evidences for religion, to prove its existence. Religion is not philosophy, the slowly progressing thinking power of man; it is an inborn longing of a whole man who thinks, feels, and wants to act morally and right. Our intention was merely to invite you to again examine whether science, especially natural philosophy and the knowledge of man, had now so far progressed as to have so clearly solved the enigma of existence, of the nature of man, and to have so thoroughly explained all antagonism that man's desire for looking beyond, for breaking through finiteness, for seeking some explanation which may satisfy the wants of his inmost soul, even if it may not afford the most perfect evidence—that such a desire ought to be repudiated as something foolish and uncalled for. Religion is not philosophy; it is rather the manifestation of the force of attraction spread throughout all nature. Wherever we turn, we discover in the separate parts of the life of nature a propulsion of one toward the other, a sensation of one part being attracted by another, that every being is invested with the desire of one for another. The same force of attraction moves man, but with this difference, that he is conscious of it; he feels the desire to associate, to step out of his finiteness and to connect himself with the

Infinite, to nestle himself lovingly, with all the fervency of his soul, near the Source of Wisdom and Love. Philosophy, like every other science, is the toilsome conquest of individuals, of those endowed with faculties of a higher order. Religion is a common property of humanity, it is a peculiar susceptibility of man, which irresistibly develops itself within him, more or less clearly illuminating him with its truths. Hence, religion has existed from eternity and will exist unto eternity.

While religion is thus the most individual element which appears to man as his deepest, innermost quality and distinguishes him as an individual in his belief and practice, constituting the inmost motive power of his whole being, it forms, on the other hand, the bond of all mankind, just because it is something common to all, the connecting link between the several parts, as well as between them and the whole. Everything in each man is vested with the desire of union with all men; mankind has the desire that all individuals, while completely preserving their independence, may put aside their distinct exclusiveness and co-operate together as a united whole. Such mingling of the separate individual with the common interest is primarily manifested in the tribe and the nation. A nation appears as a unit, distinct from other nations, and yet as a conglomeration of a large number of widely differing human beings. Thus also, religion primarily presents itself as the religion of a tribe, but with the instinct to conquer all mankind, to gather all under its banner. If that instinct is powerful enough, if religion, though presenting itself as a tribal or national religion, yet rises superior to its nationality, if it continues its existence after the fetters which national life had put upon it have been broken, if it does not die when the people among whom it lived have lost their existence as a nation, then indeed, it has successfully passed the trial of its reliability and its truth. Judaism has proved itself a force outliving its peculiar nationality and therefore may lay claim to special consideration. But the fact of enduring existence alone should not sway our judgment; an examination into its intrinsic worth alone can afford us a true measure for our estimate. A comparison between Judaism and other religions at a time when they had not yet come into contact with it and had not yet been affected by its influence, will furnish us the surest conviction of its superiority over the other religions of Antiquity.

Without doubt, the most talented nation of Antiquity which was distinguished by noble culture and which exerted the most profound influence upon the development of the whole human race, whose art and science have had the most vivifying and quickening effect upon all times, so that when they were again dug up from under the rubbish that had covered them so long, they appeared as a refreshing well from which humanity drank with greedy drafts—that nation was the Greek nation. As Pallas Athene comes forth armed and equipped from the head of Zeus, thus also the Greek nation appears on the stage of history completely furnished with the noblest weapons of the mind, decked out with the loveliest bloom of life. Even in its first authors and poets, it displays its whole inner being, presenting, though not yet grown out of its infancy nor fully emerged from semisavagery, a harmonious, complete nature. Its most ancient poet, *Homer*, has remained an unequaled pattern for all time. He exhibits an imagination which boldly soars up and yet is not unbridled, a taste for the beautiful and harmonious expressed in the noblest euphony. How much joy we derive from beholding the beautiful, noble forms of his creation! Men of giant strength and yet sobered and moderated by an innate feeling for the decorous; figures that, though high and sublime, move and affect us by their childlike traits. Nausicaä in her maiden modesty, Penelope's touching faithfulness, the stalwart, bold Hector affectionately bidding farewell to his wife and playing with his child—those are everlasting, noble, human figures to which we return again and again with heartfelt elation. And what strange religious belief did that richly endowed nation bring forth! How imperfect and childish is its belief concerning the Divine, its mythology! Its gods—for of an only God there is no mention—are a set of powerful turbulent aristocrats presided over by a more powerful one. A more powerful one, but by no means an All-Powerful One; for his power is not effectual everywhere, is barely able to execute what his will had resolved to accomplish. Why, the other gods at one time ventured to bind him; of which he was once reminded by Thetis, who saved him:

> "When the other Olympians did once threaten to bind him"

she called Briareus to her assistance,

> " . . for his strength is greater than even his father's."

His power being thus limited, that of the other gods is still more so. It is true, they surpass man; but after all, they are but greater, more exalted men whom even mortals can resist, and who are even wounded by bold heroes. Why, Cypris and Ares, the god of war, receive wounds at the hand of the impetuous Diomedes! And when Venus complains of her disgrace, her mother consoles her with the reply:

> "Many of us who inhabit Olympian houses have suffered
> Grief at the hands of men . . . . ."

Above the gods there stands a mysterious, unconquerable power, before which even the gods must bow. Ate, the goddess of mischief, dements them, so that Agamemnon refers to her in order to clear himself from responsibility, saying,

> "What then, indeed, could I? All things are done by the goddess,
> Jove's all-powerful child, Ate, dementing all mortals.
> She allures them to sin, and one at least, she misguided;
> Jove himself, she seduced, though he surpasses supremely
> Men and gods in power . . . ."

and then relates how she deceived him:

> " . . . . . . Jove did not suspect her deception,
> Uttered the fatal oath and sustained deep grief for his rashness."

Jove has no power to control unavoidable Fate, Moira, and breaks into this lament:

> "Woe me! Woe me! Fate now wills that Sarpedon, of mortals
> Dearest, should fall by the hand of Patroclus, the son of Menoetius."

The same doctrine resounds centuries thereafter, out of Sophocles:

> "The pow'r of Fate supremely rules indeed,
> No Ares can, nor courage bold,
> Nor towers, nor the blackened ship
> Borne by the waves, escape its blows."

Thus even Ares, the god of war, must yield to that mysterious power.

That an omniscience of the gods, or even of the highest god, can not be even imagined, is evident from the idea that they are ruled by Ate, are demented and deceived by her, because they are ignorant of what is to happen. Therefore, we must not be astonished to hear very strange statements concerning the life of the gods, how they indulge in sweet slumber:

> "Now all beings, the gods as well as the warriors gallant
> Slept all night; but slumber would flee from the eyes of
> Jove, who pondered within his soul . . . . ."

He was awake, not because he never sleeps nor slumbers, but because reflections in which he indulged drove sleep away. Those imperfections, those ideas unworthy of God, are deeply rooted in moral defects to which the gods are heirs, in foibles exhibited with the most open naivety. We have seen that Ate dements them and causes them to do wrong; they also revel in repasts, indulge in the most sensual pleasures, break faith and promises, perpetrate fornication, dispute and quarrel in the most intolerable manner, so that even Jove can not help complaining to Thetis:

> "Fatal, indeed, it is, that strife and contention with Here
> Thou wilt excite, who will upbraid me with gibes and reproaches.
> Why, she quarrels already with me in the midst of th' immortal
> Gods, unceasing . . . . . "

They are cruel and arbitrary, envy men their happiness and welfare; and if they now and then protect the cause of justice, it is merely the whim of the moment, which at another time is frustrated by all sorts of causes.

If then, the gods are such, it is but natural that the men who have produced such divine ideals and looked up to them, can not aspire to true perfection. Man, it is true, is often better than his principles, and the Greeks may also have been better than their mythology would lead us to suppose them to have been. Nevertheless, the ideal of the divinity above us and the ideal of the morality within us is too close, that the defects of the former should not make an impression on the latter. Let us consider how that is shown in Hellenism. It is emphatically man's limitations and evanescence: All must die and pass away; man has no power to contend against the gods, and whenever he ventures to do so, guilt and horrible ruin will pursue him. Therefore man should put off all pride, abstain from all bold aspirations, move within certain limits. Moderation—*Sophrosyne*—is the true virtue, the taste for the proper and decorous, for harmony, the intelligence for judging and limiting; virtue is the middle of the road between all extremes, preventing all excesses. Accordingly, to the Greek, virtue is the Useful, the Agreeable; but the inner striving for higher purity, the desire to put off human moral defects, and to lean on the Divine as the source of all purity, had not come clearly to the surface with the Greeks. The consciousness of our sinfulness, of the disposition of our nature which is limited also as to purity; the consciousness of the continual struggle which we have to make against sensuality, in order to be able to follow our impulse toward the good and perfection—a struggle which ennobles and elevates man, which through repentance even leads him to worthy victory—such ideas were almost completely hidden from Greek perception. If the later poets who drew from the noblest elements of Greek nature, if the tragic poets preeminently emphasize guilt as the cause of the most difficult entanglement in human existence, the guilt is almost always brought over upon the sufferer, not the result of his own doings, but inherited from sire to son down to succeeding generations. Because someone would not honor the gods, scorned them, dared to contend against them, defiled himself by heavy guilt, that guilt passes over upon a succeeding generation which suffers and perishes by it, without taking an active part in the matter. It is not a really moral struggle, not a guilt from which man has to cleanse himelf; it is blind Fate that throws the sin, posterity is laid in chains by the cruel decree of ancient guilt. Of course, we are moved at seeing such a struggle, when great strength shakes its fetters; we feel our weakness, we bow in reverent fear, it is a taming of passions, as Aristophanes expresses it, but not a moral elevation. But how different it is if man, though conquered physically, gains the victory within himself by his moral exertions, by his struggles against external adversities; if noble thoughts give support to him; when profound ideas gain the ascendency within him in spite of the actuality without which does not permit their execution; if the individual as the representative of a higher idea must yield, but nevertheless rises a hero, a victor even in defeat:—that higher conception we find but little exhibited in Hellenism.

Greek philosophy is not blind to those shortcomings and defects; it did not hesitate to express its censure. In the sixth century before the Christian era, Xenophanes, the founder of the Eleatic School, severely inveighs against a belief in such gods. Their plurality is an objection to him; only a unity agrees with a true conception of Deity. He censures also the idea that, even if the gods are not mortal they had a beginning, as if

> "It were not so wicked to believe they had been born,
> As to present them vested with mortality."

When sacrifices and dirges are part of the worship of the goddess of the sea, Leucothea, he denounces the contradiction:

> "If she be mortal, sacrifice should not be offered to her;
> If she be goddess, funeral dirges should not be sung for her."

Thus also, he inveighs against the fancy that the gods occupy certain localities, that they have certain forms, and especially the sensual qualities that are attributed to them without hesitation:

"Hesiod and Homer attribute unto the gods
Whatever disgraces the mortals and calls for censure,
Robbery, and adulterous practice, and cunning deception."

Here we perceive a full and clear acknowledgment of the imperfect idea of Deity in Hellenism, a severe censure pronounced by one of the more ancient Greek philosophers, but one which was hardly repeated with such scorching emphasis. Later philosophers have not entirely abstained from censure, but they preferred an attempt to idealize, to teach purer ideas of Deity and man's relation to it, without undertaking such a distinct fight against the current belief. Such action on their part undoubtedly proceeded less from fear of the issue of a conflict between their conviction and error, it rather seems as though they felt that such a conflict would involve the very essence of the nation, that it would cut the nerve of national life by openly assaulting the history of their gods. They sought to remain more or less in agreement with the popular belief, either by ignoring it, or by attempts to explain it. But if, nevertheless, a bold expression now and then ventured out among the people, such a decided opposition arose that the critic was soon forced into silence. Anaxagoras and Protagoras were compelled to go into exile; Socrates, who treated the popular belief with great discretion, had to drink the poisoned chalice. The popular belief of the Greeks was not susceptible of transformation or reformation; it had to remain such as it was, or cease altogether. A religion which bears within itself a more powerful idea than it can exhibit in the transient imperfection of the time, may, in the course of its development, cast away many a side-shoot, efface many antiquated expressions and produce new ones by its creative energy. But a religion that has completely exhausted itself by its very appearance, whose stem, blossom, and fruit, fully correspond to its root and have taken all available substance out of that, must perish down to its very root, when its blossom and fruit are injured. Such was the case with Hellenism.

Considering that one of the most talented nations of Antiquity produced such crude religious conceptions, we need hardly cast an examining glance at the multitude of other nations that have passed away without leaving any vestige of culture; nations that lived in rude savageness must naturally have had rude notions concerning the Deity and man's relation to it. And when we contemplate the groups of nations surrounding the Jews, nations that far surpassed that little people in power and kept it encircled, some of which for a time exerted decisive influence upon the destiny of the world, we shall feel horrified at the savage cult that prevailed among them, at the excesses presented as divine worship: human sacrifices offered up to Moloch, who robbed mothers of their children to consume them in his red-hot embrace, degenerate debaucheries as pleasing worship of their gods. The standing expression of the bible, "to go a-whoring after the gods of the nations," may be taken in its most literal meaning. A horrible picture!

Now, in the midst of such surroundings, Judaism appeared, and, like the witch of Endor at seeing Samuel, we may well exclaim, "I see God ascending out of the earth;" out of the earth that is defiled, given up to sensuality, desecrated by low practices, out of that earth I behold the Divine arise in lustrous purity. The name attributed in Judaism to God was afterwards most significantly considered as ineffable, because no name can comprise Him, is adequate to His being; the very sounds of that name have been lost, and we do not know its true pronunciation. But its meaning is certain. "He is" is that meaning; as God, speaking of Himself, proclaims in holy writ, "I am who I am," so man says of Him, "He is!"—the Only Existence, the All-comprising, both for nature and for the life of man. *He is* and as such All-comprising naturally also absolute Unity. That term of unity resounds through all the writings of Judaism and the fundamental axiom of Israel is: "Hear, O Israel, *He is* is our God, *He is* is one." That Existence which comprises all, is the Sole, fully living Individuality, but at the same time, as the Most Universal One, indivisible. "Ye saw no manner of form," you heard only utterances, you observed only the brilliant light beaming forth from Him, sounds proceeding from Him; those are merely effects; but to represent Him by an image, Judaism had avoided as a great monstrosity, as the greatest abomination. For that *Infinity*, the Jews have at all times sacrificed their lives. It was this that at first appeared as something curious in the eyes of heathendom: a religion without idols. Even Juvenal still refers to it, saying:

> "*Nil praeter nubes et coeli numen adorant*"
> Nothing but cloud and a God of heaven they worship.

"There is no image in the Temple of the Jews!" Tacitus scornfully writes—a queer religion without images. And just that was its very core, the conviction of the All-comprising—"the whole earth is full of His glory." And to this Unity, to this idea of the All-comprising One, naturally omnipotence is joined. Should there be anything impossible for God? "Is God's hand, perchance, waxed short?" Nor are the pages of Judaism less full of the conception of God's omnipotence, of that supreme wisdom which penetrates and searches everything; of the eyes of God that see through everything, not merely beholding the outward appearance, but looking into the heart, into the innermost mind of man. No man can fully grasp true wisdom which is so sublime and can be found only with God. Thus Job teaches, taking his beautiful poetical comparison from the science of mining:

> "There is a vein for the silver, and a place for gold where they fine it. Iron is taken out of the earth, and brass is molten out of the stone. Man setteth an end to darkness, and pierceth down to the bottom, to the stones of darkness and the shadow of death. The flood breaketh forth before him, which runneth about there, forgotten by the foot, removed from men. The earth, out of which cometh bread, is turned up under it as by fire. There is a place of sapphires and precious stones, and it hath dust of gold. That path no fowl knoweth and the vulture's eye hath not seen it. . . . Man cutteth out rivers among the rocks, and he seeth every precious thing. . . . But where shall wisdom be found? Where is the place of understanding? Man knoweth not the price thereof, it is not found in the land of the living. The depth saith, It is not in me, and the sea saith, It is not in me. . . . Destruction and death say, We have heard the fame thereof with our ears. God understandeth the way thereof, and He knoweth the place thereof."

A grand presentation of wisdom, hidden from the eyes of men, and seen through only by God!

But all that is surpassed by the conviction of God's Holiness, of the purity that can not bear the sight of evil, nor tolerate wrong. "Of pure eyes, so that He can not behold evil, nor look on iniquity."

God is pure, holy, He alone, and no other being besides Him. In His holiness, He is all-kind, gracious, merciful: "Self-existent, eternal, almighty, gracious and merciful, long-suffering, and abundant in goodness and in truth," that is the keynote running through all doctrines and convictions of Judaism. He is the Loving One, who though He also awards punishments, loves the repentant and extends His hand to him, that he may turn from his evil ways, for He rejoices in all His works and accords His love to all of them.

Guilt is not fate irretrievably clinging to man: "I have no pleasure in the death of the sinner, but that he may turn from his ways and live," that he may attain the true and pure, higher life. The certainty of His justice, of His boundless love for man, is based upon such immovable foundation in Judaism, that even the saddest experiences can not shake the conviction thereof. Poets and prophets complain of sufferings and trials; they present the riddles of human experience; they can not understand why many fare well or ill on the earth contrary to their practices; they confess, too, that they are unable to find the full explanation of such facts. But they are far from uttering any doubt of the justice of God on that account; their conviction remains unshaken, that His proceeding is based on supreme justice.

The relation of men to God and to each other tends toward the same ideal. Man is a finite, limited, dependent being; that thought is often repeated in Judaism.

But the complaint about it is by no means as predominant as in Hellenism. The fact is accepted with quiet resignation, together with the consciousness of man's high position, and that consciousness breaks forth everywhere as with jubilation. At the very beginning it is said: "Let us make man in *our image*, after our likeness," a likeness to God, which is soon explained as referring to the spirit. "He breathes into his faculties the spirit of life." Endowed with that likeness, man is soon represented in his greatness. The psalmist says: "Thou hast crowned him (man, who is so insignificant and puny) with glory and honor. Thou madest him to have dominion over the works of Thy hands." Everywhere man is presented to us in that high position which advantage actually gives him the impulse for further development and aspiration to higher eminence. For man has the capability of higher development:

"Yea, there is a spirit in mankind and the inspiration of the Almighty giveth them understanding."

Reason being a ray from Divine Reason, ennobles man, awakens within him the desire more and more to rise toward the Supreme Reason. But the most essential element in him is the consciousness of his moral power, which is innate in man and is the foundation of his real nobility; and which, even because it awakens his aspiration to perfect purity, makes him feel his limitations along that line, and the bars to moral life so much the more. He feels that sensuality accompanies him from his infancy, that it is a part of his nature, so that a conflict is started between his sensuality and his spiritual ideals: "the desire of man's heart is evil from his youth." That sentence expresses the imperfection which is also manifested in the moral life, an appetite the allurements of which we have the power to resist. In ancient time the question was raised, why the bible begins with an account of the beginning of time instead of the first commands, and why all that introduction. The answer runs: "He hath showed to His people the power of His works," and though commandments do not occupy the first space, yet the pages contain considerations replete with religious element. The question was prompted by a narrow, literal view. But when *we* read that beginning of the bible, we discover a deep significance in the naive and simple presentation which even at this day not only fascinates us, but furnishes material for reflection. Not only that creation is presented in its well-constructed order, the conflict within man is brought in too. We behold man first in his innocence, then soon in struggle with craving that is, of course, part of his nature; he must control it if he does not want to become a prey to sin. Physical desire did not allure the first man only, it is part of the nature of all men and in that way the mother of sin which is not an involuntary inheritance from father to son but is committed by every one individually. Sin proceeds also from selfishness, from the narrowminded separation of man from his fellow-man; it is the product of envy and manifests itself as discord; Cain is filled with ill-will against his brother. There we meet the great word: "Sin lurketh at the door, unto thee is its desire, *but thou canst rule over it.*"

At the entrance into the outer world, in our connection with it, sin is lurking; but thou art a man, endowed with the sublime power of the will, who is not bound to yield to sin, to whom sin is not an external, invincible power, but a desire within, which can be kept down by using thy better force. The doctrine of man's striving for self-ennoblement, of the conflict from which he can and should proceed as victor, is presented to us everywhere. With that moral conviction, connected as it is, with the consciousness of his limitations on that point, he moves toward Eternal Purity and seeks its aid in loving devotion. *Love* of God is an idea which paganism did not know, which Judaism presents with such sublime simplicity, as though it were a matter of course: "Thou shalt love the Lord, thy God, with all thy heart, with all thy soul, and with all thy might." "Though my flesh and my heart faileth, God is the strength of my heart and my portion forever." "It is good for me to draw near to God." "Whom have I in heaven but Thee? And there is none upon earth that I desire besides Thee."

Those are expressions found scattered about in great numbers. The full devotion, the intensity of feeling, wherewith moral man attaches himself to the Highest Moral Purity, to God's holiness, the expression of such a relation to the Most High, determines also the relation of men to each other, produces the mutual attachment of men to each other in love: "Thou shalt love thy neighbor as thyself" is an admonition which in like manner is treated as a matter of course and is not especially accentuated; it bears its own emphasis within itself, because it runs through the whole law, whose every provision breathes love. I shall point only to one noble moral flower, the like of which is probably not to be found in the law books:

"Thou shalt not respect the person of the poor in judgment."

That the person of the rich and respected should not be given advantage is also emphasized, of course; and such admonition appears natural against the temptation of favoring the rich man, in view of the benefits that his good will might afford, or of violating justice in favor of the influential one on account of his power. But Judaism presupposes also sympathy, commiseration with misfortune as such, a profound fundamental trait, that it apprehends justice might be violated in suit-at-law in favor of the poor, who might be favored even if in the wrong, just because he is in distress. Beware also of such an act! Sympathy and pity are emotions that have their proper place and use, but even those noble feelings must be silent before justice. In that scriptural command, there is a height of conception, a sublimity of moral view, which we can but reverence.

And this Religion has also in its very nature the impulse to offer its blessings as the religion of humanity. It is an exalting strain resounding from all prophets and poets in the idea that the acknowledgment of God will spread over all the world; it is not to be a narrow nationality but a complete humanism. Because God is the Sole Father of all men, because Love turns toward all men and should bring its quickening and consecrating power to all:

'God shall be king over all the earth: in that day there sha be one God, and His name one.

"They shall beat their swords into plowshares and their spears into pruning hooks, nation shall not lift sword against nation, neither shall they learn war any more."

A time shall come when all nature is transformed, when

enlightened mankind will so prevail that savagism exists no more and even the wild beasts' havoc ceases, "and the suckling child shall play on the hole of the adder, and the weaned child shall put his hand on the basilisk's den; they shall not hurt nor destroy in all my holy mountain: for the earth shall be full of the knowledge of God, as the waters cover the sea."

The religion shall be a light to all people: "My house shall be a house of prayer unto all nations." At the consecration of the Temple, Solomon prays also for the stranger who cometh out of a far country: "Hear Thou him, O God in heaven, Thy dwelling place, and do according to all that the stranger calleth to Thee for." That is a grand sweeping look beyond oneself, beyond the barrier, an aspiration manifesting that the idea in Judaism is mightier than the vessel in which it first appeared; it seems as if from every side we hear the ancient teacher's words: "Let the vessel be broken, but preserve the precious contents," the contents that cannot be contained by the physical outside matter.

In such manner, Judaism presents itself to us, and its very simplicity and originality reveal its inexhaustible glory. Even the foregoing short outlines show the vastly different form in which that religion entered the world, how it was the only one of its kind, unlike all other religions in Antiquity. Besides, it must be considered that it arose among a nation that did not develop a finished logical system of philosophy, that is not distinguished by works of other sciences or of art, and yet brought forth such conceptions and views unaided, as if prompted by some inner force. How did it happen that such a people, a mere tribe surrounded by so many mightier nations, which had no opportunity of having an unobstructed view of the great events in the world, which had to fight many battles for its bare existence, which was confined within a limited territory, and had to employ all its resources to defend itself against its powerful enemies—how did it happen that such a people rose to those sublime conceptions? It is an enigma in the world's history. Who will give us a complete solution?

III.

Revelation.

There are facts of such an overwhelming power that even the most stubborn opinion must yield to them. Such a fact is the origin of Judaism in the midst of rude surroundings, like a vigorous growth out of a barren soil. We have essayed to draw, in a few scanty outlines, a comparison between the convictions, presentiments and assertions that prevailed in Antiquity in general, and those presented by Judaism. Even that incomplete sketch must convince the unprejudiced mind that we behold an original energy which has preserved its significance for all times and has proven to be a creative force. Let us for a few more moments, dwell upon the principal representatives, the organs of that religious idea, upon the *Prophets.* In them we perceive characters of quiet greatness, of simple sublimity; of fervor with moderation; of boldness with humble submission—traits that are imposing and make us feel the very breath of a higher spirit. Our ancient teachers observe: "No two prophets deliver the prophetic message in the same strain and expression. Each one of them is complete within himself, each has a peculiar, distinct character of his own, and yet all have the same general characteristics and are animated by one great idea. *Isaiah,* bold, noble, severely serious, and yet lovingly indulging in the most joyful and glorious hopes, full of the most cheerful confidence; hence hurrying from gloomy predictions and threats of severe chastisement over to a description of a most brilliant future. *Jeremiah,* tender-hearted, looking sad into the tangled and desperate condition of his time; hence plaintive and reproving his contemporaries with severity, yet never despairing, yet full of cheerful conviction that the idea he proclaims must prevail, if not in his time, certainly in the future. *Ezekiel,* as if overwhelmed by the idea that animates him, as if dazzled by the light surrounding him, indulges in bold figures in the effort to represent the glory of his visions, yet clearly and fully conscious whenever moral precepts are to be distinctly emphasized to his people; and withal, endowed with that clear, comprehensive vision which penetrates the very heart of man and calls attention to his faults and virtues." Our ancient teachers finely describe that difference: "Isaiah appears as a man of the palace, familiar with the manners and the pomp of a court, with the divine appointments, speaks only in general terms of its brilliancy; standing on an eminence, he draws the sublime in his own light. Ezekiel appears as a villager who is suddenly brought into brilliant city life, and in his excitement does not know where to stop in his picturing of both the detail and the whole of his impressions." They differ, but all are devoted to one great idea, all are sustained by the same higher spirit.

They love their country with intense fervor; their speeches and admonitions are addressed to the people at widely different times, to uplift them, to strengthen and encourage them, to support their country and the national life. They love their country, take profound pleasure in describing it as a land flowing with milk and honey, a land in which a man "may eat bread without stint," "whose stones are iron, out of whose hills thou mayest dig brass"; joyfully they describe it as a land that has been favored by God with the most various blessings, but the most essential matter to them always remains: "For from Zion goeth forth the Law, and the word of God from Jerusalem." "Mountains around about Jerusalem, but God round about His people."

And with naivety and affection, the condition of that land in comparison with Egypt is described: "The land whither thou goest in to possess it is not like the land of Egypt from whence you came out, there ye sowed seed and watered it with your own labor, as a garden of herbs: but the land whither ye go to possess it, is a land of hills and valleys, and drinketh water of the rain of heaven: a land which God forever careth for: His eyes are always upon it, from the beginning of the year even unto the end of the year."

Egypt, it is true, is a garden of God in the eyes of the Israelites, a land which, by the annual overflowing of the Nile and by canals, carries water everywhere; which may be cultivated with the sure hope of success; which exhibits, with but rare exceptions, its fertility from year to year and offers its rich treasures in abundance; but nevertheless, Palestine is prized more highly: a land of valleys and mountains, needing rains, depending upon Nature's moods, so that the eye of God has to be upon it from the beginning of the year to its end: and therein consists the glory and the excellence of the country.

They glorify that land as an especially favored and gifted one; and even when it has vanished from them, when it has been taken from them, their strength is not broken, they are not bound to its soil; their love for their earthly country rests upon their love for a higher one from which a ray descends upon the former. The poet, after bewailing the destruction of the city, the banishment of its inhabitants, after having indulged in lamentations, exclaims: "Thou, O God, remainest forever; Thy throne, from generation to generation"—a thought which runs through thousands of years, even after the national life has disappeared. Can it be wondered at that such a cheerful confidence exerted a powerful influence also on later generations? You hear the same words centuries thereafter. The state was destroyed a second time, every hope blasted, the last flickering light, kindled by Ben Kosiba, was put out, and Roman oppression lay heavy upon the people. Rabbi Akiba with some friends visited Jerusalem, and they saw a jackal running out from where formerly the Holy of Holies had been standing. Akiba's companions wept and rent their clothes; Akiba remained quiet, almost cheerful. His friends asked, "Since when have you become so indifferent to the misfortunes of our people? Do you not see the second fulfillment of the words: 'Yea, for this do we weep, because of the mountain of Zion, which is desolate, jackals walk about upon it?'" "Well, my friends," replied

Akiba, "indeed those words have again been verified; but the other will also come true: 'Thou O God, remainest forever, Thy throne from generation to generation.' I live in unshaken, firm confidence."

That the prophets did not look for security of their persons when the interests of the cause demanded their devotion; that they labored with entire unselfishness, regardless of appreciation or glory or praise, is attested by every word uttered by them. It appears as though the words spoken by one of them resounds through all their sermons:

"I gave my back to the smiters and my cheeks to them that plucked off the hair, I hid not my face from the shame and spitting, for God the Lord will help me; therefore shall I not be confounded, therefore have I set my face like a flint, I know I shall not be ashamed."

And though from different sides they heard cries such as these: "Prophesy to us of wine and strong drink," "Foolish is the prophet, the man of the spirit raveth," they did not yield, they did not desecrate their lips, they did not keep silent: "The Lord God hath spoken, who can but prophesy?" A higher force impelled them, would not suffer them to keep silent, to grow weary of preaching; it was a moral and spiritual enthusiasm that placed them on an eminence to which we, in later days, must ever look up.

Thus Judaism is a grand phenomenon in history; and thus its representatives and organs are men of such dignity and spiritual greatness that we must pay them the tribute of our admiration. They entered the lists without being encouraged, without having patterns before them; on the contrary, in a discouraging environment, encircled by nations addicted to idolatry, amidst priests and proclaimers of other nations who did homage to sensuality which degraded human nature. Whence, then, came that force which all at once enters the scene as something original? We arrive here at the consideration of the very depth and bottom of the human soul, beyond which it can not go, of an energy creating of its own apprehension, without being impelled thereto by any external impulse.

We discriminate, in general, a two-fold intellectual operating ability in man, a two-fold distinguishing endowment —we discriminate *talent* and *genius*. They touch upon each other in many points, so that a distinct line of demarkation can not be drawn between them; yet they preserve each its own particular peculiarity; they are not only separate, but they differ in their whole nature, in their foundation. Talent is an endowment with the ability of easily and quickly receiving, digesting, and reproducing with taste and skill; but talent leans upon something that has been achieved, upon results that are present before it, upon treasures already acquired—it creates nothing new. Genius works quite differently. It is independent, it creates, it discovers truths heretofore hidden, it discloses laws heretofore unknown; it is as though the forces that work in the depth of nature bared themselves to it in greater clearness according to their connection and legitimate co-operation; as though they presented themselves to it to be grasped, as though the mental and spiritual movements in the individual as well as in mankind as a whole, unveiled themselves before it, that it may behold the deepest foundation of the soul and may be able to dissect the motives and impulses hidden away there. Talent may be practiced, it may even be acquired by laborious application; genius is a free gift, a gift of grace, a mark of consecration stamped upon man, that can never be acquired, if it be not in the man. Talent, therefore, can not overcome impediments and obstacles if they present themselves with overwhelming force, it can not thrive under unfavorable circumstances. Genius, on the other hand, advances its conquering force against the most untoward conditions, it opens a way, it must expand its force, for it is a living impulse, a power that is stronger than its possessor, a touch of the energy dispersed into nature but condensed in him, linking him with the Spirit of all spirits who manifests Himself to him by higher illumination. Talent propagates the knowledge which has been stored up, perfects it also now and then, and makes it the common property of all. Genius enriches humanity with new truths and perceptions, it gives the impulse to all great things that have come and are still to come to pass in this world.

When Columbus discovered the New World, he had not been specially prepared for it, nor fitted thereto by superior geographical knowledge, by greater experience gained on his voyages; nor could those justify any conclusion that India was to the west of Spain. It was the light of genius that caused him to see the surface of the earth, he was favored with a look into the nature of the globe and to feel that the land must be across the ocean which had been thought to be boundless; and thus what had been as knowledge, but imperfect, in him, turned into living conviction whose truth he made every effort to prove. Copernicus was probably not the greatest astronomer of his time; others may have made more correct calculations and may have been far superior to him in the science, but it was as if the whole working of the natural forces of attraction and repulsion and the entire movement of the world had been revealed to his vision; as though the veil which dark tradition had thickened, had been drawn aside from before him; as though he had looked with bold eye into the mechanism of the universe and held fast to what he had seen as a rapidly grasped truth which he afterwards with deep insight tried to substantiate, in which he did not fully succeed, because it had to be more clearly explained and more firmly established than he was able to do then. Newton is said to have been induced to establish the law of gravitation by the falling of an apple observed by him while sitting near an apple tree. Many people before him had seen apples falling, but not with the eye of genius; for that beholds in the single phenomenon the great, comprehensive law which causes that phenomenon; it looks through that external manifestation into the invisible working from which everything proceeds.

Such instances could be added to by others from every field. The historian who deserves the name as such, is not made by the profundity and care in research, the full knowledge of all incidents; he is perhaps often compelled to refuse a mass of burdensome material in order not to be perplexed and crushed by crowd of details. But this affords him his favored position, that his vision is sharper and sees into the character of the time, that the entire working of the wheels of the ideas moving in the depths of the period, is laid bare before him. It is as if the period as a whole with its deepest foundations uncovered, stood before his mental vision, as if he had actually listened to the most secret intentions of its chief actors. In that way, all that was before known is put into its proper place, because the connection between the events and the actors has only become perfectly clear. You may perhaps call that good sense, acumen, a happy faculty of combination. When the acute thinker does not run into error, when his combination knows how to connect the proper parts, then it is the work of genius. And what is it that enables the poet to look so deep into the soul that he recognizes the temperament, the desires, the passions so clearly, as though the chambers of the heart were opened for him? What enables him to grasp and present all complications and combinations in the most various relations and conditions, however much they may be entangled and hidden to ordinary vision, and to fathom and picture a character in its unity? Is it the great experience he has had? Is it that, perchance, he himself has passed through all that? Certainly not! It is the vision that more surely and sharply receives the picture of the whole life of the human soul from the individual phenomenon and knows how to represent it. In fact, it is only genius that enables an individual to interfere with might in the movements of the mind and spirit and to give them a forward impulse for centuries to come—and as it is in individuals, so it is in whole nations as well.

The Greeks boasted of being autochthons, of having risen and sprung from their own soil. We shall not examine whether that claim is justified; but another claim, which is the real meaning of it, will surely be admitted; namely, the autochthonic character of their mind, the aboriginal nature of their national talent. The Greeks had neither pattern nor teacher in art or science, they were teacher and master to themselves, they speedily attained such perfection in art as makes them instructors of mankind almost for all time. It is as though a higher living sense for the Beautiful, the Harmonious, the Symmetrical, and the Pleasing had been innate in that nation—we observe a National Genius through the possession of which masters in every art and science made their appearance. Therefore, even later centuries willingly listened to the words of that nation, hastened thither, where they could see the works of the plastic art, where they could enjoy, as it were, a rejuvenating bath in the spiritual fountain that parts thence and runs through the centuries. Is not the Jewish people, likewise, endowed with such a genius, a Religious Genius? Is it not, likewise, an aboriginal power that illuminated its eyes so that they could see deeper into the higher life of the spirit, could feel more deeply and recognize more vividly the close relation between the spirit of man and the Supreme Spirit, that they could more distinctly and clearly behold the real nature of the Moral in man, and then present to the world the result of that inborn knowledge. If this be so, we may speak of a close touch of the individual spirit with the Supreme Spirit, of the light thrown into individual spirits by the Power that fills everything, so that they could break through their finite barrier; it is—let us not hesitate to speak the word—it is *Revelation*, and that too, as manifested in the whole nation.

The Greeks were not all artists; each one of them was not a Phidias or a Praxiteles, but yet the Greek nation alone was capable of producing such great masters. The same was the case within Israel. Surely not all its men were prophets, and the exclamation, "Would that all the people were prophets" was but a pious wish; the other: "I shall pour out My spirit upon all flesh," is a promise, it had not become the reality. Nevertheless, Israel is the people of revelation within which the favored representatives appeared; it is as if the sparks of light had been scattered and had been gathered into a blaze in the more favored ones. A thorn-bush produces no grapevine; a neglected people produces no prophets such as the Jews gave to the world. The historical books of the bible are full of reproach about the morals and the depravity of the people of Israel at the time of their kings; the authors want to prepare us for the devastation that came on later as a punishment for their sins. Yet, noble forces in great number must have existed within that nation; there must have been a native endowment and disposition, when men of such significance could rise and develop out of the people. Judaism was not a mere voice crying in the wilderness, and though it did not prevail in all, it was still an energy which existed, though weaker in many, yet to such an extent that, concentrating in individuals, it could produce such heroes of the spirit. Nor does Judaism claim to be the work of individuals, but that of the whole people. It does not speak of the God of Moses or of the God of the prophets, but of the God of Abraham, Isaac, and Jacob, of the God of the whole race, of all the patriarchs who were equally endowed with the gift of prophetic vision, the genius of revelation which was latent in the whole people and found concentration and expression in individuals. The fact that the greatest prophet left his work unfinished contains a great truth: he must not be regarded as the Atlas who bears the world on his shoulders, who completes the work without the co-operation of others from beginning to end. "No man knoweth of his sepulchre unto this day" and our ancient teachers remark, "His grave should not serve for a place of pilgrimage whither people go to do honor to *one* and thus raise him above the level of man." Moses did his part of the work according to his great capacity as one of the whole people. Judaism arose within the people of revelation. And why then should we not use the word where we touch bottom rock, an illumination proceeding from a higher mind and spirit, which can not be explained; which is not a compound produced by a process of development even if it is further developed afterwards; which all at once appears in existence as a whole, like every new creation proceeding from the Original Spirit? We do not want to limit and define the word in any dogmatic manner; it may be understood in different ways, but as to its essence it remains the same: the point of contact of human reason with the Fundamental Source of all things. High as the ancient teachers estimated revelation, they never denied that it is connected with human ability. The Talmud teaches: "The spirit of God rests only on a wise man, on a man possessing moral power, who is independent because he is frugal and contented by having conquered all ambition, greed, and desire;" a man who bears his importance within him, who feels the divine within him. Only such a one is capable of receiving the Divine, not a mere speaking trumpet through which the spoken word passes without his being conscious of it; no, a man in the true sense of the word, who touches close upon the divine and is therefore susceptible of it. A deep thinker and great poet of the Middle Ages, Juda Ha-Levi, emphatically designated revelation as a disposition that was present in the whole people. Israel, he says, is the religious heart of mankind which in its totality always preserved its greater susceptibility, and its individual distinguished men were the heart of that heart. Maimonides speaks of a flash-like illumination as which revelation must be regarded; to one the light lasted but for a short time, to another it occurred repeatedly, and with Moses, it was a lasting one, an illumination which lights up the darkness, affords man a look into the hidden recesses, which reveals to him what remains concealed for others.

Judaism is such a religion, has grown out of such divine visions and has connected into a whole all that it did behold; Judaism is a religion of truth, because the view into the essence of things is infallible, beholding the Unchangeable and the Everlasting: That is its everlasting message.

IV.

Nationality, Slavery, Woman's Position.

Every new birth is attended with painful labor; every new idea which, creative and transformatory, enters into the mental world, must expect a hard and obstinate fight with all those mental powers which insist on their right of custom and well feel that they are threatened with destruction by a mightier force; they contend against it with all the bluntness and rudeness of inert possession, with all the violent arrogance of mental shallowness which easily works itself into bitter harshness. An idea which endeavors to create a new mental and spiritual life, must of course fight with mental weapons, it bears within itself the guaranty of certain victory, it sees in it something imperishable which is equal to all emergencies and can defy all obstacles. But though it enters the mental world light-winged, it will, by the protracted contest, be compelled to put on coarser material arms and harness, in order not to be crushed at the very outset. Young David enters a glorious fight and comes out of it victorious. Saul, on hearing of his bold resolution, armed him with his armor, and put a helmet of brass upon his head; also he armed him with a coat of mail. David tried to go, but he takes them off again, saying, "I can not go with these, for I am not accustomed to them." He enters the contest with Goliath, armed only with his shepherd's staff and smooth stones—and conquers. It is the confidence of bold youth that objects to constraint and will not be fettered; it is the assurance of victory, manifested in the shepherd boy whose mind has grown up and gained vigor in contact with nature. But can you suppose that David, after having passed on into the serious struggles of his life, would then also refuse helmet and armor? As he became more deeply engaged in life's battling, he was forced to also adopt life's usages, though full of the bold spirit of youth. And the same is the case with an idea, if it is to assume real life, that, though it be conscious of its mental and spiritual existence, it must also bear arms and enter the bloody contest of opposition, offered to it from all sides.

Judaism's doctrine of revelation has not been spared its battles. By struggle, individual man gains strength, he needs it; but here and there it will cover him with dust. Judaism also needed such a struggle against the world, and in consequence, many a dust from the earth has settled upon it. In opposition to the whole world, possessed by other conceptions, there arose a small nomadic tribe that had just emerged from a great empire addicted to idolatry. It must needs keep closely together, lest it be crushed beneath the weight of the outside powers. With the divine spirit that had been fanned into life within it, it intended to proclaim a new faith, preserve it, and make it victorious throughout the world. A beautiful, grand, sublime, but difficult task! Every contact with the outside world was a snare; every word exchanged with a person outside of its own pale contained a temptation; every friendly meeting, every meal taken with the outsider was profanation, because it was dedicated to his idols. Thus every closer association was a sin, a temptation offered by the outside world. And could it be avoided that many in Israel cast eager looks at the brilliant pomp surrounding them everywhere? Of course, a living spirit was present in the whole people, not only in the individual, distinguished representatives who were the implements of shaping and firmly setting the new thoughts in corresponding expressions, it was present in the whole people, even if in lower and weaker degree. But would there not also be many who suffered themselves to be seduced by the material pomp, by the alluring prevalence of superior numbers? The entire history of Israel during the period of the first Temple, covering the very establishment of the faith, offers innumerable instances of apostacy, of energetic battling, which the truly enthusiastic, the great men, had to carry on against their wayward ones.

The closer the seductive influence approached to Israel,

the more the danger increased that the worm of corruption might gnaw into the body of the sound trunk, so much the more had the glowing zeal of the better-minded to increase for keeping that danger at a distance; they were compelled to contend against the inroads of the corruption with all possible determination, with a fire of energy that would not only produce heat, but consume the evil itself. Considering that condition, should we then be surprised, if we find here and there a harsh, severe expression against other nations, that implacable opposition to them is preached and practiced? Should we marvel that in a contest wherein not a bit of territory or some other earthly territory is at stake, but wherein defense is made for an idea which the combatants reverence as their highest treasure; which raises them above the nations, which is destined to be spread over the whole earth by the people chosen for that purpose—should we marvel if the fire of devotion and enthusiasm burns in them in mighty flames and puts them into glowing heat, so that now and then they uttered sentiments which did not always express the purest benevolence, the most friendly consideration for those that wanted to rob them of their most valued treasure by their allurements? We fail altogether to transpose ourselves into that time and its conditions if we gauge, with the large-hearted idea of tolerance appropriate to an age of considerate mutual recognition and appreciation, a time in which two antagonistic convictions were engaged in a struggle of life and death; if we want to judge every harsh word with superior tenderness, if we talk of hostile nationality and national pride (which, by the way, make their appearance even nowadays for vastly less valuable possessions), while the stake was by no means something merely national, but was the protection of freedom of the mind and spirit and the safety of the very foundation of truth, as well as the neutralization of all destructive influences. No, it must not appear strange if we meet many a severe expression, with many a harsh precept; on the contrary, it must ever be a proof of the mental and spiritual vigor with which the people were endowed, that in those struggles the conscious impulse for holding all mankind in its embrace and laboring for it has not disappeared out of Israel; that, notwithstanding that hostile attitude which could be but mutual, there always prevailed the word: that this religion came into existence for the benefit of the whole world, that the whole earth should be comprised within its fold. It affords a testimony of the profound spiritual life of Judaism, that the purity and clearness of that idea were never dimmed. We are uplifted indeed when, despite all outbursts of passion engendered by the heat of the conflict, we can again breathe the refreshing spiritual air as it flows from the words of the prophets: "Let not the son of the stranger that has joined himself to God speak, saying, 'God has utterly separated me from His people,' neither let the eunuch (the eunuchs of the Persian court are here referred to) say, 'Behold, I am a dry tree.' For this saith the Lord unto the eunuchs that keep my festivals, and choose the things that please me, and take hold of my covenant; even unto them I will give in my house and within my walls a place and a name better than of sons and of daughters, an everlasting name that shall not perish. And the sons of the stranger that join themselves unto God to serve Him and to love His name, that keep the Sabbath from polluting it, and take hold of my covenant: even them I will bring to my holy mountain and make them joyful in my house of prayer, their burnt offerings and their sacrifices shall be accepted upon mine altar; for mine house shall be called a house of prayer for all people." "It is not sufficient," thus we read elsewhere, "that thou alone shouldst be my servant: I will also give thee for a light to the gentiles." And again we read: "And I will also take of them for priests and Levites." All mankind is to be united in the one true service of God.

It is mere nonsense to assert that Judaism teaches the doctrine of a national god, a god belonging exclusively to the one people. Such an assertion is even childish, made in the very face of the passages quoted and in plain contradiction of the oft-repeated vision of the future when God will be One and His name one. It is true that here and there an expression can be found, apparently attributing some importance to idols, such as, "Greater is our Lord than all gods" and others like it. But how does the prophet so often characterize them? "One breath and there is nothing good in them." And with what fine irony does he show how the gods are made, how the workmen work with their hammers and assist each other, how one portion of the material is used to prepare food with, while the other is employed to fashion a god from it! How can that refer to a national god? Yes, a God is spoken of who was first recognized among that people; nay, was first acknowledged by that nation alone, but who is the God of the whole world, the God whose throne is the heavens and His footstool is the earth? That surely is the God of the world, the God who fills all time and space, the God who shall be acknowledged by all nations. We perceive here the traces of a struggle in which, of course, many expressions must occur that do not wholly and perfectly correspond to the spiritual idea, but lucid clearness is gradually developed. We behold ancient Jacob as he must wrestle in the darkness with a man, they are covered with dust, and he limps because the hollow of his thigh gets out of joint, but yet he prevails, prevails according to both the human and the divine idea, and becomes a blessing to all mankind.

But Judaism was not intended simply to introduce a new idea concerning God into the world, but also to dignify and ennoble all human relations. The men who taught in ancient time, "The true foundation and the nerve of the Law, Whatever displeases thee, do not unto others, that is the essence and the root of the Law, all the rest is commentary which thou mayest learn at thy leisure," or, "Thou shalt love thy neighbor as thyself, that is the great comprehensive principle of the Law," or, "This is the book of the generations of man, is still a greater principle, conveying the lesson to be a man and to recognize under all conditions, all men as equals and peers"—the men like Hillel, Akiba, and Ben Soma, who taught such lessons, are the props and pillars of Judaism, and we must well take to heart their words. Judaism, I repeat, did nor enter into this world to simply present to it a new idea of God, but to illumine and ennoble all human relations and to teach the proper recognition and estimate of man. But just with regard to the relation between man and man it is so much the more incidental that the idea must at first appear with limitations, must accommodate itself to existing conditions, if it is to have any success. An individual, if he stands separated from his fellow-men by his eminence, does not share their lives, takes no part in their endeavors, will be without influence and will labor without effect, however superior he may be; men may look up to him with reverence, but they will not be influenced by him. If a man wants his work to be effective, he must enter into the existing conditions; there must be mutual accommodation. Of course, on the point of the idea of God, there is no compromise, no accommodation possible; there can be no agreement between the Pure Spirit and Corporeality; where the fundamental principle is at stake, Judaism could not choose half-way measures, the opposition had to be contended against with unswerving determination. Not so, concerning the relations between men; there the idea may, even must, perform its work of education and transformation by the process of gradual solution until the hard shell crumbles and falls off.

The nations of Antiquity believed that the state could hardly exist without slavery being firmly established within it as irrefutable right. A free citizen should do no labor, that was left to the slave; the slave was the property of his master, a chattel, a mere thing completely subject to the pleasure of his owner. Judaism enters with the idea that every man is called to labor: God places the first man into paradise, the Garden of Eden, but even there, to work it and keep it. Yet, man soon enters into more prosaic conditions and is told: "In the sweat of thy face shalt thou eat bread." But all men are created in divine image, not the forefather of one nation or another one only, but the progenitor of all, and from him the whole human race has descended, *endowed with equal rights*. Of course, the complete abolition, the annihilation of slavery by Judaism, at its first entrance into the world, would have been in direct conflict with nature and the historical development of human relations; it would have proved an undertaking without the intended salutary results either for the people or for mankind who can be gradually educated but not transformed at one stroke. Hence, slavery was not entirely abolished, but it really existed only in name without its essential substance; the new wine which, poured into the old vessel, must burst it in time. Among the race, within the people itself, real slavery was out of the question; for the slave served only six years, or regained his freedom even sooner, when the year of jubilee arrived; he then returned to his former civil conditions, of fully equal standing and rights with his brethren. But the slavery of aliens, for that was tolerated—how were alien slaves treated? The smallest injury to the body of a slave, smiting out his tooth, was not regarded as a mere blemish caused by the owner in his property; no, the slave was free. And the killing of a slave was punished, even if done by the master. And what beautiful precept is this, removing the very sting of stings of slavery: "Thou shalt not deliver unto his master the slave that is escaped from him unto thee: he shall dwell with thee in thy cities which he may choose. Do not deceive him."

With those words a problem was solved thousands of years ago, which in our day left its bloody traces on a whole continent, and came near rending it in twain. And yet, the inhabitants of that country are professors of the dominant religion, some of whom cleave to that branch which claims to be the sole and only saving Church, and others cling to the form of tenacious puritanism, and both with the missionary fever of making converts. The fight had in its beginning nothing to do with the nature of slavery, whether or not it should be permitted to exist; one section had repudiated it for itself, but had hitherto found it altogether right to preserve it as a constitutional institution in the other. The whole question was mainly narrowed down to this: whether a slave who had fled into the Free States must be delivered to his master, whether it was not theft to allow him to remain away from his master; whether, in that case, rights were not violated and the very idea of justice shaken. That question of a punctilious conscientiousness was settled by Judaism three thousand years ago; and when Judaism shall have prevailed, when its spirit shall animate all men, when the spirit proceeding from it, undiluted and in full, shall have spread everywhere, then that question will be finally decided. Truth and real right, humanity and recognition of the human dignity of every individual will then, and only then, prevail over that sham-justice which boasts the more insolently, the shallower it is itself.

The regard in which domestic life is held by a nation is of still higher moment. A dark shadow rests on the Greek nation, otherwise so finely gifted and beautifully developed, that the sanctity of matrimonial life comes so little to the front, that the unity of the family finds so little expression; the worth of woman according to her true character has not been properly appreciated in Hellenism. How different that is in Judaism! At the very beginning we find the idea expressed: A man leaveth his father and his mother, and cleaveth unto his wife, and they shall be one flesh—an essential unity. The reverence due to parents, however diligently taught, however fervently cultivated, is secondary to that ardent attachment that should bind husband and wife together in domestic life. The wife shall follow her husband: "To thy husband is thy desire, though he rule over thee," yet in full equality; he joins himself to his wife, they become one being, one house.

And what noble pictures of woman we find throughout the Jewish literature! What noble relation within the families —simple, unpretending, yet great and heart-refreshing! The wives of the patriarchs occupy almost the same position with their husbands. Later generations regard them both alike. And what a picture of life is presented to us when, for instance, we contemplate Rebekah as at first she appears in the unrestraint of maiden innocence, friendly and kind-hearted toward the stranger, readily complying with his request to give him water to drink, and caring even for his camels. She steps with him into the house of her folks, and behold! he has been sent hither by a highly respected kinsman from a distant land to ask for the daughter. Rebekah is asked; free choice is left to her—"Wilt thou go with this man?" Her heart tells her that yonder is the place where she will attain full development and she replies, "I will go." She starts upon her journey; without restraint she looks all around; all at once she observes the man to whom she is destined to be a companion for life and she asks, "What man is this that walketh in the field to meet us?" The servant replies, "It is the son of my master." Maidenly blushes mantle her face, and she covers herself with a veil. "He brought her into his mother's tent, and he loved her." Jacob takes his wife, Rachel, home; he had served for her seven years, "and they seemed unto him but a few days, for the love he had to her." Farther on, we read the history of the great Liberator; his infancy is beset by great dangers. Moses was born when dark clouds hovered above Israel. They put him in an ark of bulrushes and lay it among the flags by the river's brink; his sister Miriam cannot endure remaining at home; she hurries near to the place, to know what would be done to him. The king's daughter comes down to wash herself, she notices the ark, opens it and sees the child. The girl, generally timid and embarrassed, but courageous now when her brother's life is in the balance, steps out and asks, "Shall I go and call thee a nurse of the Hebrew women?" We do not find it strange that Miriam who, while young, exhibited such devoted courage, appeared later as prophetess. And our ancient teachers say of her indeed: "Miriam was for Israel like a fresh fountain whence refreshing waters pour forth"—she had glowing enthusiasm for truth, joined with the devotion of a woman's heart. And again our ancient teachers say with profound insight: "Through the merits of their women, the Israelites were delivered from Egypt." The men were given over to oppression, they were forced to hard labor. Who guarded their homes, who attended to the morals of their children, who watched over the domestic hearth, who held up the standard of purity and chastity? It was the mothers in Israel who attended to those matters, it was their work that Israel was made worthy of deliverance from the dangers that surrounded them. We proceed still farther, we enter upon the period which appears to be a dim, confused age of heroes, the time of the Judges when the loose tie of the tribes was dissolving and their union was to all appearances breaking up. Now in one place, then in another, a Judge appeared, a light was started; and again a beautiful figure rises before us, Deborah the prophetess and Judge, a brave and courageous woman, an enthusiastic leader, and yet fully conscious of her womanhood. She does not want to go into battle, amazon-like, and says to Barak, "It will not be unto thy honor that thou shalt gain the victory through the hand of a woman." But since he will not undertake to fight without her, she consents to go with him, and gains the victory; and afterwards she announces it in a song, chastising and praising like a true prophetess of God. And later, after that period, when matters appear as settling down into more tranquil conditions, at the very threshold of this new epoch, we meet again with a woman who demands our reverence; it is Hannah, the mother of Samuel. With the yearning of a genuine woman who laments that children are denied her and fervently, from the very bottom of her heart, she prays to her God, "for I am a woman of a sorrowful spirit." And Elkanah, her husband, comforts her: "Hannah, why weepest thou? Am I not better to thee than ten sons?" What profound affection those few words express! And Ruth—what a lovely picture! A Judean has emigrated into a foreign land where his two sons get them wives. The man dies, and both sons also pass away without leaving children. The mother, Naomi, is returning to her native country and the second daughter-in-law—the other one is too much a Moabite to go with her and turns back at the last moment—Ruth, goes with Naomi, saying, "Entreat me not to leave thee, or to return from following after thee: for whither thou goest I will go, and where thou lodgest, I will lodge; thy people shall be my people, and thy God my God;" and she follows her as an obedient child, remains her daughter, lovingly cares for her and is her devoted companion—is she not worthy to be the ancestress of David?

All that is told with childlike simplicity, without embellishing pomp, because it is part of the very nature of Israel, and it *must* come to the surface, although we often see it come in only as insignificant shading in the picture. Can you then wonder that among that people—a rare example in Antiquity—woman was not treated with disregard, can we wonder that the scanty remains of the literature of that people, the whole compendium of which is almost exclusively devoted to religious life and historical narrative, nevertheless contains a booklet which is designated as the Song of Love? At a time when the pressure from without weighed them down, when not the consecration of the senses, but their suppression, when not the glorification of natural life, but its deadening, were regarded as piety, it was impossible to conceive that the little book, taken in its plain, natural meaning, was intended to extol a fine, pure love. Granted even that it contained also a so-called deeper meaning, this much is at all events certain: a picture must be true if it is to mirror a higher relation. However—as a recent ingenious scholar observes—when the poet was singing, the language had not yet died the agonizing death of its holiness; fresh, natural vitality coursed through it then, and the song that glorifies love flowed quick and alive from the poet's heart. And as a consequence, we find in the booklet many a sensual embellishment. But with what depth is the higher, nobler nature of love depicted, what fervor do even these few lines express: "I sleep, but my heart is awake." A world of feeling is shown, and we may well say without further commenting on its contents, that whoever reads the little book with a pure mind will find that profound emotions are described in it in noble expression.

It is but natural that a later poet also indulges in the consideration of the virtuous woman, and the conclusion of his proverbs and lessons of wisdom is devoted to her glorification. "Who can find a virtuous woman? for her price is far above pearls." "Who can find her?" does not mean that she is rare; no, he describes her in full, and he that has found her has obtained a precious treasure. And he concludes with, "Her children arise and call her blessed, her husband also, and he praiseth her. Favor is deceitful and beauty evanescent, but a God-fearing woman, she shall be praised." Only the subtle, melancholy Ecclesiastes who can find hardly one tolerable man among thousands, can not find in a thousand women one that is not treacherous and cunning. But that is not the general view running through the literature of Judaism, and if isolated Oriental opinion mingles in, the pure estimation of woman, the moral eminence of matrimonial life, remain the fundamental principle.

Judaism teaches the marriage of *one* wife to *one* man, monogamy. Although exceptions are now and then met with, they are simply exceptions which are explained by the fact that the tendency could not at once take full effect by formulating a law at a time when the opposite practice ruled among the nations all around; but monogamy alone is in agreement with the fundamental principle of Judaism, and with thorough union of husband and wife. It is therefore but natural that in later times, when external influences became different, a teacher appeared in Europe who put the ban on every one that should violate the natural law of Judaism. And even in such countries where polygamy is the rule, Judaism had repudiated it, and though not prohibited there by a distinct law, practice, which is always the living spirit in Judaism, had ruled it out long ago, even if legally permissible. By such fruits Judaism is known, and a noble family life has at all times been cultivated in Israel. Of course, courts of love, love's tournaments, and playing at love, were unknown to Judaism, just as it was unable to fathom the mystery of unconscious virginity coupled with the feelings of a mother. Healthful and energetic, pure and fresh was the clear fountain flowing forth from their homes over all their relations in life; pure domestic life has at all times kept Israel fresh and vigorous. Having supported them during the days of oppression, it will not disappear from among them in better times, and the exclamation of Balaam at the sight of Israel encamped according to its tribes will ever remain true: "How beautiful are thy tents, O Jacob, thy habitations, O Israel!"

V.

Sacrificial Service and Priesthood. Divided Nationality.

The conception of Deity by a nation is also the gauge for its views of morality, and vice versa. The higher or lower moral culture of a people is an infallible index of its more or less enlightened religious convictions. As the savage individual, so also does an uncivilized people, living in a state of nature, respect and honor superior force only. The power which it exercises over others or which others can enforce against it, affords the measure of the estimation with which it claims, or in which it holds others. Neither justice nor moral worth nor purity of moral sentiment is of any value in its eye, but pre-eminently and essentially, brute force, worldly power. A man without education and culture, just as an uncivilized people, bows before his superior who can make him or it feel his power; and on the other hand, they are rude and tyrannical towards their inferiors. A people which as yet has but a religious instinct and has not yet worked its way towards a clear conception of religion, which is not yet permeated by a higher idea, recognizes in God at first a mighty being and fears the power that shows the ability to crush it. It bows before that power just as it bows before a man of superior force, but on the other hand, its treatment of others whom it regards as its subordinates shows what low position it occupies with regard to morality. Therefore, the very views concerning slavery and the treatment of the weaker sex, is a true gauge for the high or low plane of their religious ideas. Judaism—as we have shown by the preceding considerations—establishes itself as a religion that adores God as the Holy One, as the ideal of moral purity, by the fact that it invariably emphasizes moral worth also in its human relations, that it does not recognize the mightier ones as possessing exclusive rights, but grants them power only so far as they are justly entitled thereto. Justice, the pure, moral relation between man and man, is its highest consideration, the gauge wherewith to measure the conditions.

That difference in the plane of culture occupied by various nations must eminently manifest itself in their divine worship, in the manner in which God is approached it is bound to show, whether men have a presentiment of God only as a higher power, whether they tremble before Him and seek to conciliate Him, or whether they worship Him as the Holy One, look up to Him as the pattern of highest morality, the purest expression of mercy and benevolence. Wherever, above all, only the power of God is recognized, the tendency predominates of courting His favor, men will bow before Him that He may not pour His wrath upon them; they will try by some act or other to win His good graces, to procure His kind consideration, to ward off His displeasure by offering to Him gifts and undergoing privations. That is the origin of sacrificial worship. Sacrifice expresses the endeavor to win favor or soften the possible wrath of God, or at least to show Him in what deep subjection one is to Him, by offering to Him and depriving oneself of something, be it even the dearest object, if it may be pleasing in His sight. The crudest manifestation of such a feeling exhibited at the lowest stage of religious life is human sacrifice, especially the sacrifice of those nearest and dearest to us. Rude heathenism sacrificed its children to the gods. The dearest and most priceless treasure—that is the meaning of such sacrifice—I offer unto my God, and He will be pleased therewith because I do not hesitate to deaden every feeling and emotion within me and to give up to His pleasure the dearest treasure I possess. That lowest religious sentiment is a complete misconception of the Divine Being, that He is to be conciliated by slavish self-degradation and self-imposed cruelty; it is fear of the cruel and arbitrary element as Deity, and cruelty and arbitrariness in man is nurtured by it. That was the religion all around Israel, the worship of God or gods among those nations that now and then ruled over Israel and were at all times in such close contact with Israel, that the sentiment necessarily became known to the people and here and there had its influence. The worship of Moloch is well known to have been one that demanded human sacrifices; to burn one's own children was the terrible sacrificial service designated as the worship of God.

Judaism carried on an energetic war against that degradation of the Divine Being; for that kind of sacrificial service, it knows no mercy. It is true, traces of it are imprinted also in its history; it influenced weak minds that believed to perceive in the self-suppression of the tenderest emotions an act of devotion to God; but with what indignation do the prophets inveigh against that eruption of the most brutal heathenism! At its very threshold, Judaism makes the individual patriarch go through that struggle in his mind and gain a glorious victory. "*Elohim* tempted Abraham." Various names of God are used in Holy Writ, and our ancient teachers give us an ingenious explanation: "Elohim" represents God as the Mighty One, the Rigorous One, which attribute is also reverenced in God, as the other nations likewise recognize him in some manner, but the other name, "He is"—the Ineffable, as we have become acquainted with it—the Eternally Existent, underlying all earthly and spiritual existence, "the God of the spirits for all flesh," is the God of mercy, of benevolence, of ardent love and kindness toward man. *Elohim* tempted Abraham. The old conception of God, as it then predominated, was uppermost also in the mind of Abraham, the recognition of that Divine Power has possession of him to such a degree that he wants to show himself as its obedient servant. "Offer thine only son, whom thou lovest!" What greater treasure hast thou acquired, wherewith canst thou better manifest thy submissiveness? He is ready for the sacrifice, everything is prepared for its consummation; then a messenger of the God "He is" calls from heaven: "Lay not thy hand upon the lad!" The higher knowledge of God awakens in him: God is mighty, but is He not also all-kind? God is all-powerful, but is that power a tyrannical one? Does it demand of man that he should not ennoble his feelings, but that, on the contrary, he should deaden them? Is it worship of God to mutilate myself, or to mutilate or immolate the only child I call my own? No, "Lay not thy hand upon the lad"—that is the true worship of the All-merciful one, and Abraham did not sacrifice his child. Not his readiness to offer that sacrifice constitutes the true piety of Abraham, but his *omission* of it; not the will of offering his son, but the deed of preserving him; not that he shows blind submission to the Divine Power by tearing his child from his heart, but that he recognizes God in His sublime and true nature, constitutes his true, enlightened piety. Therefore it is not proper to always point to Abraham's willingness to offer his son as an act of extreme piety—he was and is an example of piety because he omitted that sacrifice.

Thus we find at the very outset the picture of that struggle, together with the victory of pure moral conviction, and that victory runs through the whole of Judaism. The service of Moloch is detested as an abomination which God abhors, which deeply degrades men; and whenever a horrible place is to be mentioned, the Valley of Hinnom is named, the location where sacrifices were offered to Moloch. "*Ge Hinnom*," the Valley of Hinnom, Gehinnom, Gehenna, later became the designation of the place where all evil is concentrated, where the severest punishment is dealt out, where damnation dwells; in one word, it became the name for hell. Human sacrifice was thus most energetically contended against in Judaism; no compromise was possible on that point.

But animal sacrifice is no less the expression of a low religious sentiment. Animal sacrifice, too, has for its object the winning of favor by giving up some property without tending to moral reform and furthering moral ennoblement. Nor did animal sacrifice spring from the soil of Judaism, it was tolerated, and only tolerated; it was continually inveighed against by Israel's best and noblest men, the prophets, who point out its low degree in the most emphatic terms. The prophet Micah says: "Wherewith shall I come before God, bow myself before the High God? Shall I come before Him with burnt offerings, with calves of a year old? Will the Lord be pleased with thousands of rams, with ten thousands of rivers of oil? Shall I give my first-born for my transgression, the fruit of my body for the sin of my soul? He hath showed thee, O man, what is good, and what doth God require of thee but to do justly and to love mercy and to walk humbly with thy God?" That is the manifesto of prophetism against sacrifice, and that manifesto is often repeated, is authenticated everywhere in the same manner, though differently worded. "'To what purpose,' saith the Lord, 'is the multitude of your sacrifices unto me, I am full of the burnt offerings of rams and the fat of fed beasts, I delight not in the blood of bullocks or of lambs or of he-goats'." "Wilt thou offer sacrifices unto me," says the psalmist, "am I hungry? If I were hungry, need I tell thee? Is not the cattle upon a thousand hills mine?" Away with sacrifice!—And Jeremiah pronounces with dry soberness and really with almost surprising directness: "I spake not unto your fathers, saith the Lord, nor commanded them when I brought them out of the land of Egypt concerning burnt offerings or sacrifices." More clearly and emphatically, it cannot be expressed. Yet, the institution of sacrificial service was so deeply rooted in the universal conviction, was to such an extent the expression corresponding to the natural religious promptings, that it made its way also into Israel. And as everything corporeal occupies space, whereas the spiritual, being in mind and heart, is not visible in space, the regulations and laws concerning sacrifices may, of course, occupy a very great space; but nevertheless it is but the expression of something tolerated. And if you desire another strong proof of that, examine the Repetition of the Law, in Deuteronomy, and notice how the provisions concerning sacrifices have dwindled down, are merely indicated as something customary, but are not elaborated with the extensiveness which such an important branch of divine worship, if it were a direct command, could properly claim. Sacrifice was a tolerated institution in Judaism, and speedily it vanished away. During the period of the Second Temple, numerous Houses of Prayer arose as a victorious power, rivals of the

Temple at Jerusalem, where sacrifice was still retained and which as a symbol of unity of the Commonwealth, preserved its significance while those Houses of Worship actually rose above that Temple in spiritual importance. And when the latter was destroyed, sacrificial service also was buried beneath its ruins. We have before emphasized the idea that whatever is truly fundamental in a religion can not be separated from it, however unpropitious the circumstances surrounding it may be: the very spirit contends against the separation, and seeks the preservation of the matter; if it can not be preserved in the old form, transformation is resorted to. It is as though the whole foundation were injured; hence this dilemma presents itself: either complete dissolution or preservation with proper natural expression. When paganism perished in its forms, its very spiritual foundation fell with it. If the sacrificial idea had been a necessary element in Judaism, sacrificial service would certainly have outlived the destruction of the Temple, and attempts were made to continue it. But the very idea had become completely exhausted. Sacrifice had lost its hold upon the hearts and minds of the people; it was an inherited custom, an institution upon which some political offices were based, upon which the authority of so many leaders and their employees rested, and which, therefore, could not have been overthrown all at once. But as soon as the storm burst upon the Commonwealth, the disrooted tree became a sport for the winds, and sacrifice *is* vanished from Israel, and will forever remain vanished. Every establishment of religion on the basis of sacrificial worship, of a sacrifice that was offered once upon a time, be it animal, human, or even divine, every longing, retrospective glance at the ancient sacrifices as being manifestation of a fuller and loftier life, every assertion that sacrificial service had vanished for the present and must therefore be represented by a certain prayer —every such acknowledgment attributing spirituality to sacrifice is a relapse into heathenism. Together with the animal which is offered up as a sacrifice unto God, the loftier religious knowledge is immolated; from the ashes, with the smoke of the sacrificial animal curling towards heaven, rises an idol.

Sacrificial worship, wherever it is practiced, requires also an especial method of operation. It demands special employees for its management; there must be specially designated persons who understand how to offer the sacrifices, who are consecrated in order to be better prepared to appear before their gods, or God. The worship of God through sacrifice is the mother of Priesthood; priests are necessary as officers to conciliate the gods, to approach them in an appropriate manner. Priesthood in its connection with sacrifice, is not a straight growth out of the native soil of Judaism. Even at the outset, before the Ten Commandments had been proclaimed, God commanded Moses to tell the people, "Ye shall be unto me a kingdom of priests, and a holy nation. These are the words which thou shalt speak unto the children of Israel." All shall be priests! In the religion of Judaism there is no need for mediation by particular persons, every one shall be his own priest, his own mediator between himself and God. Priesthood was merely tolerated in Judaism, and again a continued war against it runs through the whole history. Tales of the discontent against their priesthood, both in the first time of its establishment, and at later periods, are not isolated instances, they are a characteristic element of the national life of the Jews. On the one hand, the want of it exists; the people have not yet passed beyond the stage of sacrificial worship, hence there must be priests; but since they have to be on hand, they must exhibit special purity, must not be priests of idols, but priests of the True God, so that they might be leaders to the people in purity of morals and in honest endeavor of self-improvement. But, after all, every institution which arises from a mere yielding to human weakness, carries along with it the defects of its low origin. The priests did not come up to that standard during the first period of Judaism. The prophets continually contended against the priests. "The priests that despise my name." "Both priests and people, all are alike full of sin." They are inveighed against for the selfish motives that they joined and carried out along with their prominent office. Thus, then, priesthood is a tolerated institution, not an integral part of Judaism. When idolatry was subdued by means of the *one* Temple, and those of the priestly estate who belonged to that Temple gained greater respect thereby, priesthood was highly honored for a time, so that after the return from the Babylonish captivity the descendants of those priests became also rulers. But they preserved their authority only for a brief period; even then, during the time of the second Temple, they did not come up to the expectations entertained of them. Therefore again a struggle was carried on against them with all energy, and again we read in one of the later books: "God hath given *unto all* the inheritance, the priesthood, and sanctification." Equality for all! And again, all the earlier writings of that second period state that the priests had not proven true, that they were selfish, poor in religious knowledge. As during the existence of the first Temple alongside of the priests of lower degree, there had arisen the great men of God, the prophets, men who performed no priestly function, who were no descendants of the priestly caste, so we find during the period of the second Temple, alongside of the priests, the teachers, the men of the law and of knowledge, men who rose from the humblest classes of the people, but were permeated by the spirit of God.

Priesthood, too, fell with the Temple, and though isolated fragments of the disintegrated structure remain, although certain arrangements connected therewith still continue a feeble existence, they are nothing but fragments which may retain a significance as reminiscences of Antiquity, but they are not in line or touch with the essence of Judaism, or true Jewish piety.

Thus the world-reforming Idea of Judaism manifests itself. I have essayed in a few outlines, to present to you its innate power, its substance as well as several of its important practical manifestations. The world-reforming and world-moving Idea of Judaism naturally required for its practical introduction a ready host bearing its arms; it required a numerous, united multitude raising high the banner of their idea, ready for victory or death. A compact nationality, a thoroughly united community was necessary, if the Idea would claim recognition as a legitimate power. Right here enters the conflict manifested in all phenomena of history. The idea is comprehensive, but it requires its standard-bearers, and those must be compactly organized, lest they be scattered. The Idea of Judaism is a world-comprising one, but it required an individual nation for its first introduction into the world. That thereby contradictions arose, that universal humanity and nationality came into conflict with each other, we have already endeavored to show in several instances.

But another thought suggests itself in that connection. It is the lot of all culture-historic nations which have exercised a profound influence upon the whole world, that with all their spiritually powerful unity, they are not able to attain to a perfect political unity. A nation that has not such a brilliant mission to fulfill, unites more closely and easily for the performance of the task allotted to it. Every nation consists of various tribes, but the more cultured, powerful one rises above the rest and gathers them under its sway, and unity results. But nations permeated by a more profound spirit, borne by a mightier idea can not so easily arrive at unity. Look at the Greek people! The Doric, the Ionian, the Attic, the Lacedemonian tribes—all of the Greek type and character, in all of them the power of the Greek spirit crops out—but that spirit was too vast not to be formed in different expressions; each tribe had its own clear-cut peculiarity, and none of those peculiarities would suffer itself to be effaced by the other ones. The Greek people did not attain a political unity; each tribe would preserve its own distinctiveness. Of course, a unity of spirit did exist among them; and that spiritual unity was indeed powerful enough to resist hostile assaults. History does not record how Persian diplomats might have regarded the small nation with silent contempt, and many a statesman may have expressed the opinion that Hellas was but a geographical term comprising but individual tribes which could be easily subdued. But the powerful Persian Empire stumbled against that geographical term and had a great fall that came near breaking it, and we would hardly know anything of the Persians and their mighty empire if the same Hellas and despised and enslaved Judea had not furnished us with information about them. The unity of the Greek people was strong, the national consciousness was its living tie and bond, yet they never attained to a really compacted political united state. Only when its vital energy flagged and its peculiarity began to vanish, a ruder tribe, the Macedonian, came to the surface, forced them together into a unit, and spread the shallow remnants of Grecian culture all over the world—but it was no longer true Greek genius, genuine Hellenism. Yet, for all that, Hellenism has not perished, it revived repeatedly to refresh the world; its spirit did not die, although the nation itself perished and had never presented a real political unity. In the same manner, although not to the same extent, the Italian states of the Middle Ages appear in history. They were states small in territory, but great in their characteristic peculiarities which are so sharply marked and so deeply graven into the culture and historic development of their people that each was determined to preserve its own type, and thus a union into one state was not possible. Whether Piedmont is destined to become the Italian Macedonian, the future will show. Does Germany present the same picture? Does she, too, occupy a culture-historic position in history? And is each one of her races for that reason intent upon preserving its independence so that they may never attain to that unity which they crave with their whole heart? Is the German nation destined not to become a greater state but a great mental factor in mankind? Well, it is not the worst destiny that may be allotted to a people, though it is painful and sadly grievous to the patriot who desires not its mental and spiritual importance only, but also its full directive power.

Be that as it may, Israel was such a people. Israel too, had an Idea which went beyond its national existence, and for that very reason, that idea assumed different forms of expression in the several tribes, so that a thorough unity of their political life could not be arrived at. The ancient history of the Jewish people has reached us in very fragmentary form, conceived and rendered by its writers from their several and individual points of view only; a great part presented by its conception by that tribe which, in the end, remained the victor; namely, the tribe of Judah. Furthermore, that history is always written from the point of view as to whether the people were sinful or not, as to whether the kings were devout or remiss. Besides, there are, in the history of a state or nation many other factors; and although the working out of the true conception of God was its proper task, there was also a more general history of the Jewish state which has come down to us in fragments only, and we have to guess at it together again by ourselves. The people lived in tribes, that the whole history shows; each individual tribe remained rather independent for a long time; the tribes joined themselves together into several unions. Of that grouping, we have various information: a grouping into four divisions represented by descent from four mothers, which indicated a certain dividing line between the tribes, and marked each division as belonging together by itself. Besides that division, we find another grouping of the tribes as they were camped in the desert, three invariably march under the banner of one chief tribe, but upon that arrangement into four parts we are also informed very little. On the other hand, another division is exhibited as decisive from the earliest time. I say, from the earliest time, for it is a very significant remark made by our ancient teachers: "The history of our patriarchs, the first founders of Israel, is of great significance for the history of later times." The traits which determine the history of the later time, are pointed out. Now, from the very beginning, Reuben, Ephraim, and Judah, are presented as the chief tribes.

Reuben, the first-born, who has the legal claim of primogeniture which is not acknowledged, is the first tribe to settle down, to acquire territory, and thus to gain importance beyond the other tribes, yet fails to get their confidence. Reuben claims leadership, he seeks—so it is told of the patriarch Reuben, and it forms the characteristics of the tribe—to take possession of his father's concubine and thereby to acquire dominion. With rare exceptions in the most ancient times, we find among the Jews concubines only with kings; whoever took possession of them indicated thereby that he claimed the dominion. Therefore the prophet Nathan in his sermon to David on account of his misdoings with Bathsheba said that he should have been satisfied that God had given him the wives of his former master, Saul. When Absalom sought to usurp the dominion of his father David, his cunning counsellor Ahitophel saith to him: "Go in unto thy father's concubines which he hath left to keep the house, and all Israel shall hear that thou hast broken with thy father; then shall the hands of all that are with thee, be strong." Another rebellion threatened David by the Benjaminite Sheba, the son of Bichri whom all Israel joined, with the exception of Judah. Then David "took the ten women, his concubines, whom he had left to keep the house, and put them in ward, and fed them, but went not in to them, and they were shut up unto the day of their death, living in widowhood." The reason for that proceeding is not that he abhorred intercourse with the women that had been violated by Absalom, but rather because he wanted to protect them against another attack, and himself against the usurpation of another pretender, and thus, while his throne was tottering, he voluntarily resigned his royal prerogative. When Adonijah, who had also unsuccessfully sought to usurp the reign during the life-time of David, received after the king's death, permission to remain in the country, he goes to Bathsheba, the mother of Solomon, and tells her: "Speak, I pray thee, to Solomon, the king, that he give me Abishag, the Shunamite"—who attended David in his last years—"to wife." Which appears to her a harmless request, and Bathsheba innocently conveys that request of Adonijah to Solomon, but Solomon takes offense and says: "Ask for him the kingdom also." To the writer of the Books of Kings, the connection between the request for Abishag as the concubine of David, and an attempt at usurpation of the crown, is something very serious, and to justify Solomon's suspicion, he has the tale of Abishag's reception by David, and Adonijah's rebellion during David's lifetime quite close together, as if to illustrate that second attempt. You see that the intercourse with the concubines of the father and ruler involved also a claim to the acquisition of dominion; and thus the pretension of the tribe is mirrored in the proceeding of its progenitor Reuben. Reubenites, Dathan and Abiram, revolted against Moses; the whole of them appear almost as seceders, and the other tribes of Israel do not trust them. When a national war was being fought, the prophetess Deborah exclaims: "Reuben, why bodest thou among the sheep-folds? to hear the bleatings of the flocks? for as to the divisions of Reuben there were serious doubts." Thus Reuben is pushed into the background, is blamed, though he has his claims which, however, find no favor. He wants to save Joseph, but he is not listened to; he is ready to offer himself as hostage for Benjamin, but receives no answer; he afterwards complains that he had not been obeyed, but no attention is paid to his complaint. When Jacob blesses his sons before his death, he says: "Reuben, thou art my first-born, my might, and the beginning of my strength, destined for the excellency of dignity and the excellency of power; but unstable as water, thou shalt not excel." Moses says in his blessing: "Let Reuben live, and not die, although his men be few"—and nothing more. The tribe of Reuben was the first to disappear. Even before the other tribes were carried into exile, his land was conquered and the inhabitants carried into captivity. That is one tribe that aspired to prominence, but could not obtain it for any length of time.

Another tribe, more powerful, is that of Ephraim. The history of Ephraim from his earliest time, or rather, that of Joseph, his father, is overcast with real charms; it is a prototype of the later time, of the history of the tribe itself. Joseph is also a first-born son—he is the first-born son of the beloved wife, of that wife who was *the* wife of Jacob, whom he had beheld first, for whom he had served, whom he loved, and whom he bore in his heart as long as he lived. Joseph himself, a lovely, beautiful youth, how noble is his conduct everywhere! Dreaming, he peers into the future, but just therein appears the aspiring disposition, a profound presentiment of his future importance and greatness, and not only that he is great and becomes great in authority, but he is also great morally. His purity is proven by his resisting all temptations, he remains guileless and cheerful by the innocence of his heart amidst the heaviest trials. But he removes to a strange land; his greatness is exhibited in extension of power outside, rather than within. Such are the indications about the tribe of Ephraim. We do not know enough about him to demonstrate his importance fully; the accounts have all a Judean coloring, have reached us through Judean channels, and yet his prominent position shines through them everywhere. Out of Ephraim is he that first enters Canaan: Joshua is an Ephraimite, and he is the successor of Moses. Ephraim is the first to establish the power of Israel. The first prophets arose in Ephraim and proclaimed the noble, high-minded spirit reigning there. Of course, it has the temptation and impulse to become a great power; it is not satisfied with occupying an important position within Israel, and often attempts conquests. The chief power in Israel wants to be a Great Power in Asia, and yet fails to attain its purpose of ruling all Israel.

By the side of Ephraim we meet Judah. Judah, gloomier, less attractive, is in his whole appearance more self-contained and secluded, more austere, and through that austerity, more tenacious and impelled to develop the idea farther. Judah saves Joseph from death; Judah offers himself as surety for Benjamin, when Joseph wants to detain him. Out of Judah is one of the messengers, Caleb, the son of Jephuneh, who is also full of enthusiasm for the conquest of Canaan, and rejects the hesitancy of the other tribes as unworthy. Judah preserves his tribal independence and, for a short time, attains dominion over all Israel. That dominion was certainly not an absolute one, the independence of the tribes was surely distinct enough, so that also David's and Solomon's time does not show a really consolidated monarchy, although Judah's hegemony was fully, even if unwillingly, acknowledged. A story which is really more of a parable, significantly discloses the very ideal of the popular movement:

David was dead, and Solomon succeeded him; he was a wise king, and of his wisdom one instance is related, which at the same time reveals the principal issue of that time. Two women appeared before him, one with a living child, the other with a dead one, but each one asserted that the living child belonged to her and must be adjudged to her. Then Solomon said: "Bring me a sword and divide the living child in two, and give half of the child to each." One of the women was satisfied with the division, but the other exclaimed: "Let the child live, give her the living child, and in no wise slay it." Then Solomon decided: "She is the true mother of the child"—she would rather give him up than see his life put in jeopardy. A beautiful thought, of genuine sagacity. But it is more than that, it is a complete designation of the tribal condition at that time. Division of the realm was the issue, and the animosity which one tribe nursed against the other appeared when the strong arm of Solomon was palsied in death. The kingdom was divided; the desire of each individual tribe to assume the supremacy could no longer be repressed. "Mine is the living child; mine is the whole people!" was the cry of either tribe, and division followed. The division surely displeased the true patriots, yet neither one of the rivals could bring himself to the point of saying: "Give him the whole kingdom, but do not divide it!" Solomon's word may have flashed as an admonition, but it failed to kindle in their hearts the proper enthusiasm; the division of the kingdom was consummated, and mutual animosity between Judah and Ephraim ensued; Ephraim was the Great Power, Judah a small state of second or third rank.

Do you want to listen to a significant expression of that condition? There was a king in Judah, Amaziah, a valiant, gallant man, who had humbled and chastised many a neighboring ruler. Encouraged by these victories, he sent word to Jehoash, the king of Israel at that time, saying: "Come, let us look one another in the face!" And Jehoash, the king of Israel, sent to Amaziah, the king of Judah, saying: "The thistle that was in Lebanon sent to the cedar that was in Lebanon, saying, 'Give thy daughter to my son to wife,' and there passed by a wild beast that was in Lebanon, and trod down the thistle." You can easily hear in that speech the overbearing manner of a Great Power towards a smaller state. Ephraim treated Judah as such, and it came so far that Ephraim allied himself with foreign nations to humble Judah. Pekah entered into an alliance with Syria against Judah, and through such measures Ephraim, the kingdom of Israel, sealed its own destruction; thinking it had grown beyond the Israelite Idea, it aspired to be an Asiatic Great Power, and to achieve that project, it believed itself at liberty to betray the true interests of Israel, its spiritual life and ideal, under the pretense of serving larger and more general interests. But a greater power, Assyria, came in and crushed Israel. Judah maintained its ground on the battle-field, the Assyrian Power was compelled to retreat, preserved its political existence for some time thereafter, and during the short time allotted to it, the great men arose who gave vigor to the ideal of the people. Judah knew how to preserve its more austere unity within, and that manifested itself in the unity of divine service at Jerusalem as well as in all its religious institutions. Judah developed that spirit to an imperishable, intrinsic strength. It had also to submit to the force of arms and was swallowed by the Babylonian Empire, but not consumed. Its political existence perished, but the mental and spiritual life was preserved, despite the exile; Judah was compelled to emigrate, but it was only an emigration of citizens, the fellow-members of the faith continued their connection and union. The ten tribes had disappeared; a part of them mingled and blended with the population of other nations, the other part went over and joined the people of the Kingdom of Judah which continued longer and remained the standard-bearer of the spiritual life, and from that is derived the name that is now borne by the religion that for thousands of years has victoriously maintained itself in the world's arena.

VI.

Exile and Return, Tradition.

Let us for a few moments more dwell upon the consideration of the various political groups which in their time corresponded to the religious tendencies in the process of development in Israel. We observed that the tribe of Reuben was the first that changed its nomadic life into a permanent settlement. It was the first that had become the element in Israel which led to the organization of a state, to the establishment of a nation, but in later times it was pushed to the rear and did not receive the consideration which its pioneer establishment of nationality perhaps deserved. Nor is there any doubt as to its having been laggard in religious development. It is true that the foundation of the doctrine of revelation was laid on the other side of the Jordan in the territory which belonged to the tribe of Reuben and those that were allied with it. Moses never passed beyond that territory, he remained within it and he died there; there revelation had its first habitation and was first entrenched and elaborated according to the varying conditions of life but yet it evidently remained in a stage of arrested development, immature, and passed by higher evolution, it finally sank into oblivion. At a very early date, we learn that Reuben and those tribes that followed its leadership built an altar unto the One Living God, and that such proceedings had excited suspicion, as they had manifested idolatrous intentions, so that the other tribes came near making war upon them. Reuben went down, unsung and unremembered, and its land came into possession of Ammon, Moab, and Edom, nations which are described as especially hostile to Judaism. There is no trace of a continued existence within that territory of a spiritual life such as had come down through the remaining tribes. At a very late period, the land was again annexed by conquest as belonging geographically to Judea, and then no difference appeared, because Judaism, spreading far and wide, penetrated there, too. The ancient religious condition of the territory had completely passed out of existence.

Next, it was the tribe of Ephraim that came to the front, both by political power and by spiritual eminence and ennoblement. In Ephraim, distinguished alike by intellectual qualities and noble, refined manners, the prophets arose, the men who bore within themselves the full, pure knowledge of God, who proclaimed the Doctrine according to its profound conception and full development. 'Tis true, it did not grow within the entire people to its full, vigorous vitality, and Ephraim is also laid low; its political life, and with that, the soil for further religious development disappears, but yet it does not waste away altogether. The kingdom of Israel was destroyed by Assyria, and its inhabitants were carried into captivity; however—as in Antiquity generally, only partial expatriation but not total extermination of nations took place—a portion of its people remained in their native country. That part was increased by settlers sent into the country by the conqueror, with the view of saving the territory from desolation. And here the power of intellectual culture proved its superiority; the conquerors had to yield spiritually to the conquered. As in later times, savage hordes destroyed the Roman Empire and, as victors, crushed the ancient nationality, but had to yield to its higher culture, were civilized by it and thus transformed into a humanizing element of the world, so it happened also in the conquered land of the ancient Kingdom of Israel. The settlers who were sent to share the land with the remainder of its native inhabitants, themselves gradually changed into Israelites, or rather, Ephraimites. They called themselves Shomronim, Samaritans, after the ancient capital of the Kingdom of Israel, Shomron (Samaria). They were people who accepted Israelite belief at first with an admixture of their own Assyrian customs, and gradually grew more and more into the Ephraimite ideas, hence into the fundamental principles of Judaism, taking hold of the pure idea of God and together with it of the practices of life as they had come forth out of that idea, both in moral action and in ceremonial form. That is the origin of the Samaritans; and they occupied a stage of development beyond which the Idea had then progressed. The Kingdom of Israel had lagged in the rear in religious knowledge and although it possessed the foundation, it had neglected the living spirit which ceaselessly continued to work ahead and was cultivated in the Kingdom of Judah. The Samaritans had only the law of Moses; but the great prophets that had arisen in Judah, who regarded Jerusalem as their center, who looked upon the house of David as the representative of the political, social, and religious conviction of its people—those great prophets, they repudiated from motives of jealousy. Thus they had the letter of the law, but the full spirit was not alive in them to mature nobler fruit, and therefore they clung with tenacity to their ancient holy places. Shechem, which already in ancient times had been a place for the cultivation of religious life, continued to be their holy city; Mt. Garizim, at the foot of which Shechem was situated, was venerated as the place of Revelation, and both as localities of peculiar sanctifying influence; to offer their sacrifices there was considered an act of loftiest piety. The Samaritans of later times adopted much of Jewish doctrine; poor in knowledge, living only on isolated ancient recollections and traditions, they had to draw out of the living, spiritual stream running through Judaism; they adopted from Judaism parts only, and only such parts and only so much of those as did not endanger their own separate existence. Thus they remained a sickly religious community, and yet maintained themselves a long time. Such is the power of even a crippled idea, that, after all, it proves to be a life-imparting agency. They maintained themselves a long time; they exist even to this day, but their existence was a sickly one, their religious life morbid. Their spiritual development could not rise farther, because they clung to weather-beaten ruins on which moss may start, but no healthy, vigorous plant can grow and develop there. Even at those times when fresh starts were made in the march of events and they touched also those regions, some slight quiverings became perceptible in those benumbed members and a few individuals gave signs of awakening, but they did not get fully out of their sleep, and their community sank deeper and deeper into spiritual atrophy and political decay. Their members diminished more and more; they could not tear themselves away from the little spot which alone continued to afford them new nourishment. The idea within them was not an idea comprising all mankind, one that might be carried unto all the world; they must cling to their home city. There they would live, there they live even unto this day, dwindled down to about a hundred families; and there they are waiting for extinction, living on the memory of a great time of youth which, because it was not able to rise into vigorous manhood, was arrested while in the midst of its course.

It was the tribe of Judah that took upon itself and completely carried out the development of the Divine Idea. In Judah, in its austere union, permeated by the belief in the One in Unity who as the Pure and Incorporeal One was represented as "He is," that belief had fully taken hold of the people. And as the belief bears unity within itself, it produces also unity in all the institutions of the tribe, in the uninterrupted succession within the same royal family, in its Temple and all the institutions connected therewith, and in the harmony of a living, civilizing spirit in all the forms and expressions resulting from that belief: it was Judah that ripened into true manhood and developed the Revealed Doctrine into a full life-power. There those great men arose whose comprehensive works—but why call them works?—whose comprehensive words of life and deeds of life have been handed down even to this day as a life-giving fountain. In Judea, the Idea had been developed to such power that it had no further need for being confined within a certain country. The establishment of a nationality was not Israel's mission; Israel's mission was not accomplished by the establishment of its nationality.

Nations which the World's History commissions only to establish and preserve commonwealths for a time, in order that they may do their allotted share in the world's work, are cut asunder, their lives and works cease, they move toward their destruction, as soon as they are disengaged from their commonwealth. But a nationality which is only a means for a higher object, an external form for a great Idea intended to comprise all mankind must, for a time, gather its forces, until a serried host is prepared, among whom the Idea may obtain its full manifestation, so that it may, fully strengthened, spread all over the world. Such a nationality may cease as a commonwealth, and yet is not broken up as far as its essence is concerned. The Kingdom of Judah fell, but Judaism did not fall with it. Judaism is the name which thenceforward the Revealed Doctrine bore and still does bear; Judaism alone is the full and mature expression of it. Let us bear and keep that name as a name of honor. Much ignominy has been heaped upon that name and the name of those that hold that faith; ignominy has settled upon it, and therefore it has often been regarded by those that bear it, with a certain nervousness; they would willingly exchange it for another: Israelites, Professors of the Mosaic religion, etc. But taking the term in its more limited sense, we are by no means Israelites. We are Israelites as descendants from Jacob-Israel, but not Israelites as citizens of the Kingdom of Israel. We are not professors of the Mosaic religion exclusively, because we do not cling to the letter of the law only, even if it is our symbol, that comprehensive book which contains from its beginning to its end the Doctrine of God. Let us not repudiate the great men who appeared in Judah, the Isaiahs and Jeremiahs, the poets of the Psalms and Job; they are part of the quickening spirit, part of the spiritual stream that flows through the whole; and if we, as the Ephraimites did, would hold only to the dead letter of the law without accepting the spiritual stream, then indeed, we are no Jews, nor do we deserve to bear the name.

Judah fell, but Judaism continued to exist even after Judah had been carried into captivity. For Judah was not spared that fate either, it succumbed to the power of Babylon. But it had become firmly established in mind and it now proved to be permeated by a higher spiritual energy. True, in their exile, the Judeans hanged their harps upon the willows, they would not sing the songs of Zion, lamentations flowed from their hearts, yet together with those, there also arose the conviction that their greatest possession had come along with them and had not been left behind to decay. They had gone to Babylon, and as everything in the history of that people is providential, as everywhere the direction of a higher power is manifested, so it appears also in the destiny that awaited them there. They did not remain long under Babylonian rule; Babylon was forced to surrender to another empire; the recollections of Babylon are buried; another nation took her place—Persia—which was animated by milder manners and higher knowledge. It was also an Asiatic nation, moved in the mental environment of that time, and yet had a peculiar higher culture of its own. Judah, or rather the believers in Judaism living in Persia, had to adopt nothing of Persian teachings, they carried their specialty within themselves and developed it independently; but the fact that they had no longer to contend against crude idolatry, was of powerful effect upon them. Life in Persia was of a purer kind; the Religion of Light, the worship of Light (Fire) as the purest emanation of the Deity, afforded peculiar religious satisfaction to the Persians. The Jews adopted nothing of the Persian views, at all events, nothing important. The assumption that a transformation was effected by the influence of the Parsees, is not justified by any facts, nor is there anything in sight that would show a need or cause for such action; isolated, subordinate conceptions may, as even our ancient teachers tell us, have crept into Judaism, but they remained secondary. Our ancient teachers report: "The names of the angels migrated with the Jews at their return into their home country," and that means nothing else than that the whole belief in angels had crept into Judaism from Babylon, from Persia. That belief in angels, that grand court, or state council gathered around God, as the rulers of Persia had it around them, the assumption of seven Archangels who, as the highest princes near the king, are assembled around Ormuzd as his most immediate serving ministers, may have passed into Judaism. Judaism also had adopted in many places the theory of angels and their ministrations; but that conception never rose to the dignity of an influential belief, to a dogma, that would have had any decisive effect upon the development of Judaism. On the contrary, we find a determined struggle against Parseeism, insofar as it was antagonistic to the fundamental principles of Judaism.

Parseeism recognized a Dualism: *Ormuzd* as the creator and god of light and every good thing, *Ahriman* as the creator of darkness and every evil. Now, the prophet writing from the standpoint of that time, especially that great seer who by no means shows hatred of Parseeism nor raises his voice against its rule; who, on the contrary, glorifies Cyrus and his deeds in exulting strains, that same prophet proclaims: "I am the Lord, and there is none else, there is no God besides me; I girded thee (Cyrus) though thou hast not known me; that they may know from the rising of the sun and from the west, that there is none besides me: I am the Lord, and there is none else. I form the light and *create darkness;* I make peace and *create evil.* I the Lord do all these things." There are not, as the Persians assume, two creating spirits; no, the same God is the creator of dark and evil. The assertion that God is the very creator of evil, is here announced with such trenchant directness as we do not find it elsewhere, and it does not even correspond fully to the spirit of Judaism, but the antagonism had then to be emphasized with all directness. In the course of time, when the influence of Parseeism offered no longer any danger, and when the authorities introduced that verse into the prayer-book, they changed it into: "who formeth and createth darkness, who maketh peace and safety and createth *the whole*"—not, "the evil."

Thus the Jews lived under Persian sovereignty in general without oppression, as it seems, zealously attending to their own peculiar spiritual life. Then there appeared in that nation a man entrusted with a civilizing mission, with a grand, world-historic task. Every hero, every great conqueror is an instrument in the hand of Providence, and whatever his ambition undertakes, becomes a seed of blessing for many centuries. Cyrus undertook to destroy many kingdoms and to make great conquests, and he succeeded in founding a great Persian empire. He certainly also was a noble man, permeated by a lofty spirit. Everything which ancient historians report of him, bears the character, not of a cruel conqueror, but of a noble, high-minded man, and as such he showed himself also to the Jews who lived in his domains. He seems to have understood the character of that closely connected band, the Jews, who preserved their union even in a strange land, and he proclaimed to them: "Who is there among you of all his people, whom God urges to go up again to Jerusalem, which is in Judah, and build the house of the Lord God of Israel? And whosoever remaineth in any place where he sojourneth, let the men of his place help him with money and with goods and with beasts." And many went thither, not all—a great part of the Jewish population remained in Persia; nor were those that remained the worst of them. Even then, fervent attachment to their faith was united with love for their new home, although but a short time, hardly two generations, had elapsed since they had settled in their new country. Many remained, a considerable number returned to Palestine, and they were followed by several separate emigrations, and thus they established, for the second time, their national existence, the Jewish commonwealth. Another phenomenon is thus presented, the like of which is hardly found in history. Whenever a people has left its country, when its commonwealth is destroyed, its citizens are dispersed, State and Nation can not be restored; when the nerves of a nation are severed, its bond of union rent asunder, its inner life deadened, it is a difficult task to breathe new life into the same material. To the attempt of renewing the circulation in the dead members, hardly any people has shown itself equal; the example of the Jews is almost the only one in the world's history.

The Jews returned and established a nationality a second time, and how could *they* succeed in that? Because they were more than a nation, they were a Community united by the bond of an idea. Greek mythology relates of the giant Antæus, that he had been invincible as long as he stood upon the ground, but that it was an easy task to conquer him when he was raised up from it; and when Hercules was set to kill him, he was unable to overcome him while on the ground, but as soon as he had lifted him up, it was an easy matter. The same is the case with almost every nation. Upon its parent soil, it continually receives fresh energy; as long as it abides there without interruption, its life is assured for a long time, but when it is removed from that soil, its vigor has vanished. But Judah was not merely a people, it was the depositary of an Idea, permeated by a living thought of which its nationality was one mode of expression only, and which could therefore be repeated a second time.

True, the real, direct, creative agency of revelation was at an end. Nevertheless, at that restoration, men arose in Judea who, in a measure, are the seal or the conclusion of prophecy: above all, that seer who with exulting strain greets the beautiful time of restoration and rejuvenation, that great seer who, as one of the noblest and far-seeing, penetrates all conditions with comprehensive glance and loftiest view, and forcibly describes the mission of Judah to all mankind. He hails that time, and Cyrus, the hero of that time, with enthusiastic word, saying: ". . . That saith to Cyrus, my Shepherd! Let him perform all my pleasure, that he may proclaim, Let Jerusalem be built; let the foundations of the Temple be laid. Thus saith the Lord to his anointed, to Cyrus, I have seized his right hand, to subdue nations before him, I will go up before thee, and make the crooked places straight, break the gates of brass, give thee the treasures of darkness, and hidden riches of secret places, that thou mayest know that I am the Lord who call thee, the God of Israel." And then the prophet continues: "That they may know from the rising of the sun and from the west . . . I form the light and create darkness," etc. (as quoted above). In those words we hear the enthusiasm of a richly endowed bard who, permeated by the living idea of Judaism, greets with fervor and highest delight the time in which it could again display a living activity through a living nation. Several other prophets, Haggai, Zechariah, Malachi, appeared at the beginning of the enterprise and greeted the time in the spirit of revelation. But yet the time was to arrive when the stream of Divine Revelation was to cease running, the Revealed Doctrine was finished, Israel and Judah had become thoroughly imbued with it.

Revelation was at an end, but as a sequence, a living spirit was yet to continue and animate the whole if it was not to become stagnant; the spirit that formerly prepared men by direct effect and created the Doctrine must needs continue its work in order to preserve and quicken it. As in nature, the creative energy called forth the entire existence in a marvelous manner and then, when things settled down, rested in a certain measure, ceased to produce new formations, but still manifests itself as a force of preservation and advancement; as the same force that created, still lives in the laws which regulate nature in her freshness and continuance, forming a living stream that ever fertilizes her anew—so it is also in the spiritual life which was created by Revelation, and was to be preserved and quickened by *Tradition*. The creative spirit had not altogether vanished from Judaism, there was no complete conclusion, so that nothing could be renewed, nothing improved—the living spirit continued to flow through the times. Though the complaint is heard, "There is no more prophet among us"—yet the same holy, ennobling spirit continued to work. Tradition is the developing power which continues in Judaism as an invisible, creative agent, as a certain ennobling something that never obtains its full expression but ever continues to work, transform, and create. Tradition is the animating soul in Judaism, it is the daughter of Revelation and of equal rank with her. Tradition never did, and never will, vanish from Judaism; it is the fountain that ever fertilizes the times and must make transformations according to the changing wants and necessities of life arising from the contact with the outside world. It was the spirit that laid the foundation of the renewed national existence, the new religious life. If ever a time should come

—but it will never come—when the stream of Tradition will be dried up, when Judaism may be regarded as something completely finished and closed, when men turned backwards, look at the creations of former times and, without inquiry, want to preserve them, while others will not readily conform with the past and yet look with romantic reverence, with a sort of antiquarian affection upon Judaism as upon ruins which must be preserved in their fragmentary shape, or when others pass by those ruins with aristocratic indifference, when no living energy, no transforming force, shows its appearance anywhere—whenever such a time should come, then indeed, you may prepare a grave for Judaism, then it will be dead, then its spirit will have vanished altogether, it has then become a walking skeleton that may continue a little while but must surely move towards dissolution. But Judaism is not constituted that way; Judaism has a continuously advancing Tradition. Let us give due honor to that word! Tradition is, like Revelation, a spiritual energy that ever continues to work, a higher power that does not proceed from man, but is an emanation from the Divine Spirit, a power that works in the community, chooses its own ministers, manifests itself by its ever purer and riper fruits, and thus preserves vitality and existence itself.

With Tradition, the second popular and political life, the second epoch of the existence of Judah was developed. But that political life had to be established by a hard struggle, and notwithstanding the intense delight felt at first by all, sadness soon crept into their hearts on account of the scanty means at their command and the small results gained. For it was a second birth that had to be effected, and it soon became evident that the work went on with a certain nervousness, that it was not guided by the living, creative spirit, but that with painful consideration, ancient custom was preferred, though it no longer suited the time. Again, priesthood and sacrifice appeared in the foreground; the more so because in Judah the Davidian dynasty and the priests who had remained faithful, the sons of Zadok, had attained to high authority and were regarded as the natural leaders around whom all gathered, and in fact, the first leaders of the returned pilgrims were descendants of those two families; one a descendant of the House of David, and the other, one of the sons of Zadok. Now, as the new state was merely a province under the sovereignty of Persia, it was but natural that the reigning descendant of David was of less importance and that the High Priest obtained a greater honor and thus formed around himself a priest-court, a nobility, which soon boasted of their sanctity, a family which identified their personal claims with those of the sanctuary and clothed their human passions with the garb of holiness. The same great seer, therefore, uttered his severe strictures against those who boasted of their inherited holiness, who prided themselves of their aristocratic descent, and who derided the servant of God, although he was the only faithful one, the man of the middle class who clung to what he had inherited as sacred but who did not belong to the set in authority, yet constituted the core and body of the political and religious life in Judah. We hear complaints about oppression, about internal decadence; and another circumstance added its burden; namely, that the political life could not gain vigor; it had not been produced by growth, it was a gift by the grace of the king of Persia. A given liberty is a broken reed which is not in connection with the soil, and withers and dies. Thus, sadness had seized upon the people, it was a kind of despair of themselves. Many gloomy, despair-breathing words uttered by the Preacher-Prophet are the production of that very time. They are expressive of the sense of insecurity which takes hold of the popular mind when its inner and outer life is attacked, when culture has reached an advanced stage and yet can not proceed to its full development. It was a state of things which the prophet expresses thus: "Children have come to birth, but there is no strength to bring forth." There is no advance or development, nothing but dissension and disruption, the feeling of impotence gnaws upon all. That is the worst disease of a people, its heart breaks thereby and its spiritual power dies of it. And yet, that was not to happen in Judah; even if heavy burdens settled upon it, it was to be roused up and rise again. There is a point which no people suffers to be injured, for which it struggles with all the energy of its soul, for the defense of which it awakens all its powers —that point is its vital center. Judah was assailed at its vital center: it was its faith that was to be broken up by the inroads of Hellenism. Then a struggle ensued for its very life, and Judaism came out of it with new-born strength.

VII.

Hellenism, Sadducees and Pharisees.

The history of the world lazily and quietly passed over the new Jewish commonwealth and Society for several centuries without recording any particular results. "Shall a country bring forth anew in one day, shall a nation be born at once?" Thus exclaims the great prophet of that time, and we repeat his words. Many centuries pass away in history with apparent stillness while yet, in the deepest parts of the popular life, lasting work is accomplished to become manifest in due time; even great mundane events pass by certain sections quite unnoticeable, and it seems as if hardly any traces had been left upon them, and yet impressions were made, and they become visible through their fruits and results as soon as air and light are favorable, as soon as impulses from within are pressing forward. Alexander the Macedonian established his vast empire in which portions of three continents were united. In consequence of that enterprise, Hellenism was spread far and wide, seeds of the Grecian spirit all over his great empire. It is true, Hellenism as it was carried over the world by the armies of Alexander, was already exhausted and faded; Alexander himself, though a disciple of Aristotle, was to a certain extent a wild graft upon the olive tree of Hellenism; and whatever he intended to achieve by the force of his arms, was undoubtedly less the dissemination of the Grecian spirit than the subjection of nations under his rule. At any rate, a Grecian culture went along with him, which, even if approaching senility, was new to those countries. His empire did not outlast his life; it broke to pieces after his death, but Grecian states maintained their existence in those regions of which Palestine formed a part. The visit of Alexander among the Jewish people is pretty well wrapped in legend. His presence shook the whole Orient; his name shone everywhere and for a long time; nor did the Jews forget him. They remembered him as a ruler who was not unfriendly to them, who even met the reigning High Priest with humble reverence. How much of truth there may be in all that, or how much embellishing legend may have added to it, we are now unable to determine clearly. This much is certain, that Alexander's campaigns and his reign did not influence the development of Judaism or the Jewish people, but the states that were formed out of his great empire and were also founded on Grecian culture, did exert their influence in various ways.

Whenever two spiritual powers meet, such as Hellenism and Hebraism, Greek culture and Jewish religion, when two such spiritual world-transforming powers come into contact with each other, that contact must necessarily cause new formations; something new will grow out of it, be it the result of antagonistic struggle or of their spiritual interpenetration. New creations will be evolved, bearing either the character of both, or pre-eminently that of one of them, yet in a certain measure impregnated by that of the other. The clashing of Hellenism and Judaism produced effects in two ways. In Egypt, and especially in Alexandria, which had been founded by Alexander as a city of refuge and which soon became a free center of Grecian culture in Egypt, a country that offered a field deeply furrowed by elements of culture, ancient Grecian culture sprang forth, even if not in rejuvenated form, as a kind of aftermath, and spread mainly among the higher class, among those endowed with higher intellect. Grecian culture became there a new element of life, yet without being able to show creative effects or result in new, sound productions. In that new Grecian home, dependence upon the ancient mental achievements predominated, learned critical research and investigation, an endeavor to adopt and reproduce the external form of ancient science and learning, a pedantic, would-be scholasticism which was not impregnated with inborn, scientific impulse. The remnants of the science of that time which have been preserved, and whatever other information on that subject is available to us elsewhere, exhibit no fresh living spirit, but merely an endeavor to punctiliously investigate the ancient literature, to squeeze its letter and to gnaw at its bone. And yet, Alexandrianism spread manifold culture.

Here again, we behold a remarkable trait in Judaism, guaranteeing its importance. Wherever a new culture springs up, where the mind develops itself untrammeled, where a fresh nationality or a fresh spiritual development is manifested, there Judaism quickly joins the movement and its professors soon adopt the new culture, digest it, and regard the country which offers them the highest boon of life, mental and spiritual liberty, as their home. As a healthy plant longs for air and light and winds, and climbs up to them through all kinds of obstacles, so also does Judaism. It requires air and light, and wherever those are granted to it, there is its home, there it feels as in its own native land, as though it had been naturalized there for centuries past. Such is man's superiority over the brute creation that he is not limited to certain spots of the world for the selection of his abode, that he may establish himself wherever life may be developed, wherever organic beings may exist; he is the lord of the earth, unlike the brute that is confined to a certain region. Judaism, in that respect, shows its comprehensively human character; it can acclimatize itself everywhere, carry its seeds and participate in the popular life everywhere, and especially where higher culture can spiritually transform also the substratum.

In a word, the Jews had soon established a new home in Egypt. Whether they emigrated thither with Alexander, or whether some refugees had already gone there with Jeremiah after the dissolution of the Jewish commonwealth and came then more into prominence by reason of freer opportunity for development, we will not investigate; they were there, fully nationalized and naturalized. Soon the Grecian language was their speech which they used, not only in their daily life, but also the language of their religion, the Jewish religion. They went so far that they erected at Leontopolis, a city in the district of Heliopolis, a temple which was a copy of the Temple at Jerusalem, not with the intention of seceding from Jerusalem and breaking off connection with their mother country, but moved by the full consciousness that they belonged entirely to the country in which they lived and desired to fully gratify their religious wants there. That temple was called after its founder, the temple of Onias, and it was considered perfectly proper, and even in Palestine it was not pronounced idolatrous. The temple was the visible housing, but far above that was the spirit, the doctrine; and that too must needs be made accessible to them in Hellenism, in the Grecian language. That a translation of the bible and the pentateuch was made for a Greco-Egyptian prince, one of the Ptolemies, is but legendary glorification. The people felt the urgent necessity of becoming fully possessed of the bible, their written sanctuary, in the Grecian language. Although they had not yet altogether been estranged from the Hebrew, when the translation was made, they were no longer so much at home and versed in it that they could have readily read and understood the book which was to furnish them the bread and water of life; the Grecian language was to bring it home to them.

We have here the first instance in history of the translation of a book. The Hebrew bible was translated into the Grecian language, and that translation is still extant under the name of The Septuagint Version (70). Embellishing legend tells us that seventy elders had translated the book, each one of them separated from the others, yet all agreed completely, and it was thereby shown that the translators had worked under inspiration. In such manner, legend glorified that version, not only among the Greco-Egyptians, but the same story is given to us in the writings of Palestine and in the Talmudic accounts; proof sufficient, to show what authority and reverence that work enjoyed, even outside of Egypt. Yet, that version could not escape the influence of the local spirit; it clings closely to the letter of Holy Writ, fully rendered its meaning as the translators understood it, but it has also alterations such as were demanded by the conditions of that country. Aside from such variations as were due to local conditions, due consideration was given to religious and philosophical views. In order to afford a glance into the manner of variation of the first class—influence of the local spirit—we may adduce as an example, how the translators took care not to give offence to the reigning dynasty or to popular prejudice. Among the animals prohibited as food, the hare is named. The Hebrew term would have required the equivalent word *lagos* in the Grecian version; but as the royal family was called "the Family of the Lagi," the mention of that name as that of an unclean animal in the law-book of the Jews would have given offence. They changed it and used a word which signifies "hairy-footed" or "thick-footed," a word which they coined to avoid giving offence. Asses for riding were used by the lowest classes only; in the bible they are often mentioned as the customary riding animal. The translators did not use the word, fearing to excite scorn and derision. But also with regard to law and religion, they carefully avoided all expressions that might give offence to the critical mind of those Grecians, especially all figurative expressions for God, which are permissible in Holy Writ as innocent, poetical terms, but would have appeared strange in the eyes of those sober-minded critics.

Such infiltration of Grecian language and culture proceeded more and more, without shaking the Jewish-religious views of the community. Knowledge of the Hebrew language gradually decreased; that language which is the depository of the Jewish religious conviction, which breathes forth the religious idea in its freshness, was gradually neglected and forgotten by the Greco-Egyptian Jews, so that even their most distinguished scholars, such as Philo, had but a schoolboy knowledge of it. Even at a later time, during the second and third centuries after the Christian era, when a large portion of the Grecian Jews had changed into another religion, while the faithful remnants of them more firmly embraced the Hebrew, Palestinian Judaism, the want of a Grecian version of the bible was felt. Then it was noticed that the ancient version corresponded too little to the original text, a more faithful, closer adherence to it was demanded—but yet, a translation could not be dispensed with. Hence, new Grecian versions had to be essayed, although the Hebrew was then again more generally known among them. Such translations were not undertaken in ancient times with the view to furnishing a work of art to be handed down to posterity, but because the demand for them proceeded from the very soul and heart of the time. Three bible translators of that time are mentioned: Aquila, Theodotion, and Symmachus; fragments of their versions are still extant. Even the teachers of the Talmud praised them for their work, and the bible verse, "God shall enlarge Japhet and he shall dwell in the tents of Shem," was expounded according to the manner of paraphrasing then usual, to mean, "The beauty of Japhet shall dwell in the tents of Shem, the grace of Hellenism shall acquire a home also in the tents of Semitism," a verse which has been perverted and misused also by others in various ways. For when Christianity became predominant at a later day, the verse was interpreted to mean, "God shall enlarge Japhet so that he shall dwell in the tents of Shem, Japhet is the heir of Shem and will become the new Israel"; and in our day it has been asserted with more checkered ornament than plain truth that the ancient Shem must be polished by the culture of the race of Japhet. But enough of that! Grecian life and spirit entered deep into Jewry, and out of later periods yet, it is reported that a teacher of the Talmud heard congregations using the Grecian language when reciting the *Shemang* portion of the prayers [the confession of the Divine Unity. Deut. vi, 4-9.] You perceive from such examples of Antiquity that an enlightened nationality which exerts its mighty influence upon the minds of men, leaves its traces also upon the religious life of Judaism, and that the professors of Judaism, though remaining faithfully attached to their religion, nevertheless identified themselves with the manners and the language of the country in which they lived.

While Alexandrianism, as a scholastic science of Antiquity, exhibits neither freshness nor vigor, it is the more significant that it acted within Judaism as a motive power, as a germ for new creations. The desire arose to blend the Jewish inheritance with the newly acquired knowledge to heighten the truths of Judaism by the addition of Grecian culture, to harmonize both possessions so that each should make the lustre of the other shine the more clearly and brightly. The most various literary productions were the result of that desire, although there is not one of them of special value. A fruit of an earnest, spiritual struggle, was the "*Alexandrian Jewish Philosophy.*" In the domain of philosophy, a severe spiritual struggle and peculiar results were bound to be produced by the clashing of Judaism and Hellenism. Directly antagonistic as they were to each other, a compromise must needs be effected between them. Judaism starts with self-evidence, with inward experience and living conviction for which no proof is required, which can not be fully proven. On the contrary, Hellenism starts with investigation, with human research, rising from the physical to reach by analysis and combination, the Higher Idea. Those are two different processes diverging not only in their progress, but in their whole conception! And those two directly antagonistic views clashed against each other. But there was also in Hellenism a philosophical school which, though born of the Greek spirit, nevertheless endeavored to apprehend by a certain prophetic-poetic effort the Higher, thence to descend to the Lower, and assumed that in similar manner, the former descended into lower planes. It also attempts to directly conceive the Divine, the Ideal, by intuition, by higher perception. By such bold flight, *Plato* conceived the everlasting Good, the everlasting Beautiful, whence individual ideals evolve themselves, which as archetypes—we are not told whether they have an actual existence or must be regarded as mere pictures of the spirit—are expressed in real objects, perfect in themselves, while the several visible objects represent them only in their limitations. That was a system which especially suited the philosophizing Jews. It afforded them a bridge between the purely Spiritual and the physical objects. How does the Highest Spirit, the eternally Perfect One, enter into the finite world? He creates ideals from Himself, says Plato —He introspects Himself, and thus Perfection is produced; and that Perfection impresses itself in more subordinate existences and thus it descends from intermediate causes to intermediate causes, until the real objects spring into existence and Creation becomes manifest to us. God, the Eternal Existence, the eternally Perfect, is the highest cause; but the eternally Pure One does not immediately come into contact with the impure—only by means of manifold emanations and concatenations, the earthly grows into existence.

Such views were agreeable to the Grecian Jews who had enjoyed a philosophic education. They afforded them a happy means of preserving the incomprehensibility and unrepresentability of God, and yet of accepting the different figurative expressions concerning God in the bible, because they could refer those to the subordinate existences. Hellenism of that time, stiff and sober as it was, was unable to descend into naive poetical imageries and to admit them as poetical expression, without marring the sublimity of the thought. The letter was tenaciously clung to, and whenever it was too sensible and corporeal, it had to yield to forced interpretation. And by such the narratives and commands of the bible, too, were forced from their natural simplicity into artificial philosophical propositions, in the belief that their value would thus be enhanced; the symbolic method of interpretation is the product of the Jewish-Alexandrian spirit. The figurative expressions and events in connection with God were referred to such subordinate spirits as had evolved themselves from God. In the writings of Philo, the most distinguished philosopher of the Jewish-Alexandrian period, and perhaps also in those of all earlier authors whose works have been lost, that doctrine is comprised in the "*Logos*." Philo is a believing, zealous Jew; he is fully convinced of the truth of Judaism which, for him, requires no proof; with the most intense love, he devotes himself to an examination of the doctrines of Judaism, he conceives its moral spirit in the noblest purity, but he is just as completely possessed by symbolical interpretation, and the fudamental character of the Jewish-Alexandrian philosophy converges, in his system, in the "Logos." That term means, in Greek, both "*thought*"—as Philo understands it—and "*word*." The Logos is the *demiurgos*, the creator of the world; it was the first creation of God, emanating from

Him as thought, as a pure idea; as a force emanating from God, it then produces the world and sustains it as animating and transforming energy. Such was the compromise which Judaism made with Hellenism. The Jewish-Alexandrian philosophy is the mother of numerous systems of philosophy that prevailed throughout the Middle Ages; it is one of the factors in the creation of a new Religion, at the very beginning of which it exerted a highly important influence upon its formation, and surrounded it with a certain halo, illuminated it with a certain mystic-philosophic lustre.

That was one way in which the contact of Judaism and Hellenism produced new effects.

But in another country also, Hellenism clashed with Judaism, and that was in Palestine itself. While the Egyptian Commonwealth was filled with true civilization, the Syrio-Grecian Commonwealth seems to have been at a much lower stage of culture. Only a purely outward civilization existed there, a mere varnish without affecting the inside; not a trace remains to show that a purely Grecian mode of thinking, or any product thereof existed there. But the more half-refinement, the more fanaticism, the less inner worth there is, the more will outward forms be valued. Whenever religion is not a true inward power, wherever national life is not actually borne by an idea, the people will be seized with the zealous desire to establish an apparent outward unity, and one of the ways to effect that is the attempt to bring about apparent religious unity within the commonwealth. As we find in later times, that desire expressed as endeavor for a German-Christian State, so we meet in Asia with the design to establish a Pagan-Hellenic Realm. Palestine was under Syrian sovereignty, it should now become part of that Pagan-Hellenic State. Judaism had thus far, in the course of its second political existence, suffered many trials and tribulations—it endured them quietly, now and then with a shriek of complaint, yet there was never a forceful popular endeavor to throw off the oppression. But now, its very innermost heart had been touched, the time had arrived that called for answer to the question: To be or not to be?

Not all showed a readiness to enter upon the contest. Those who stood at the head of the people, the priests, the Sons of Zadok, are said not to have been filled with glowing zeal to undertake the contest; they thought to be able to cast a spell upon the approaching storm by subterfuges. The statue of Jupiter should be placed in the Temple; it was put up there. Contributions should be paid to the Temple of Hercules; they were paid. Gymnasiums, that is to say, not schools for instruction, but places for the peculiar Greek athletic games, should be established in Judea in order to introduce and exhibit Grecian manners and amusements; that was done. In every way, obedience was yielded to the ruler, perhaps to ward off the storm from cowardice and lack of spirit, with the sole aim of self-preservation. But the heart of the people could not endure it; and being deserted by its leaders, it was compelled to undertake from its own ranks its defense against foreign oppression which designed not only to destroy its earthly home, but to rob it also of its spiritual realm. A small band collected under the leadership of the Hasmoneans, a high-minded, priestly family, made resistance, found adherents; the enthusiasm spread, the oppressor had to retreat, and in consequence of the insurrection, there arose from the distracted little commonwealth a valorous, independent State which lasted much longer than could have been expected under the circumstances. Hellenism and Judaism had measured their strength against each other—it is true, it was faded and enervated Hellenism against Judaism not yet grown to its full strength—and yet the latter gained the victory and survived, whereas the Syrian Empire perished after a short and morbid existence.

In such times, when the innermost parts of the popular heart are stirred up, the popular energies also are roused from their deepest hiding places, spiritual life is mightily and speedily developed. Quiet reigned for centuries; all at once a noisy bustle appears, the stirring motive power is perceived producing new creations, or rather driving freshly invigorated tendencies. Even at the establishment of the Second Commonwealth, various parties had sprung into existence. At the head of the people, as leader of the first band of returning emigrants from the captivity, there was a descendant of the family of Zadok, a branch of the priestly race. The ancestor of that family had enjoyed high honor as High Priest of the Temple of Solomon; his descendants had uninterruptedly exercised the priestly function in that Temple at Jerusalem. By the side of that descendant of the family of Zadok, Joshua, the son of Jozadok—there was also a descendant of the House of David, Zerubbabel, the son of Shealtiel. These two together were at the head of affairs, and they and their immediate descendants remained at the head of the nation. But the nation was neither then nor afterwards independent; at first it was under the sovereignty of Persia, then of Egypt, and later of Syria, till the contest began. By those sovereigns, satraps were sent, and they were the actual rulers of the land. A native king or prince directing the administration of the civic and political affairs of the people, was scarcely tolerated, and if tolerated at all, his power was so insignificant that his authority soon vanished. It was otherwise with the High Priest who represented their religious life; his office being the only homesprung one with the holiness of his functions superadded, his authority increased more and more, and he soon united with power, all that remained of native, secular authority. That time was the only period in the history of Judaism when, to a certain extent, there existed a hierarchy, when a real priestly rule prevailed, and it proved itself pitiful enough. The family of the priests was that of the Zadokites. The people that had returned were full of enthusiasm to restore their nationality, clung with all their might to those whom they regarded as their chiefs, especially the religious representatives of the nation: they reverently attached themselves to the priests. The determination to preserve their ancient customs was uppermost in their minds at that time. The Temple and Temple service, the priesthood connected therewith, the contributions to the Temple and priests constituted the center of their religious life and occupied the mind of the zealous part of the people. But they found in the territory of Palestine, various elements that had in the meantime settled there and who were either not at all in sympathy with the Jewish faith, or were only lukewarm in their support. The more zealous portion of those that had returned and their adherents separated themselves from those of mixed descent, and were on that account called "Separatists," or "men separating from the nations of the country and their uncleanness," and they stuck closely to their chiefs and leaders. The other portion of the people were called "the People of the Country"; they were the inhabitants who had either not accepted the Jewish faith, or had only ancient, dim recollections of it, or were converts, proselytes, strangers. For such were readily accepted, even if they would not rigorously adhere to all the precepts which the Separatists regarded as binding upon themselves.

It is a current phrase that Judaism is opposed to proselytism. That is partially true but only so far as the phrase is understood in its true meaning. Every religion which is convinced of its truth not only for a limited circle, but for all mankind, must exert itself to spread over the whole human race. If it would confine itself within the narrow limits of the ground it occupies for the time being, address itself only to those that are born to it, who belong to a certain country, who have a distinct history of their own, then it ceases to bear the characteristic attribute of true Religion; then it has become a mere sect, it is no longer that breath of life, which, intended for all men, should spread over all humanity. Judaism, on the contrary, was the very first to speak of proselytism; it was the first that recognized the strangers that join themselves to the Lord and who were received into all its rights and privileges, whereas Antiquity elsewhere recognized only that citizen who was in the country and had grown up on its soil. The stranger remained always a stranger until perhaps he became identified with the nation in succeeding generations or citizenship was especially conferred upon him. Judaism broke down the barriers of narrow nationality; it is not birth that makes the Jew, but conviction, the profession of faith, and he also who is not born of Jewish parents but accepts the true faith, becomes a Jew, fully entitled to all rights and privileges. Proselytism in the more exalted meaning of the term, conveying the idea that the conviction of those hitherto strangers is accepted, because they have declared to be in agreement with the principles—that kind of proselytism is an offspring of Judaism. Of course, "making proselytes," mere change of form, use of violence to force affectation of belief without conviction by means of the innate power of truth—such a kind of proselytism is an abomination in the sight of Judaism—it is opposed to it.

Accordingly, strangers or proselytes constituted a large portion of the people at that period.

Even at the beginning, long before the outbreak of the Syrian war, some disagreements arose between the several portions of the people. The Zadokites, the princes, and priests became—as it naturally is in the character of such hereditary dignity and especially when joined with the attribute of holiness—more and more narrow-minded, sought to identify the whole range of religion with themselves, they gradually ceased to be the ministers and servants of religion, religion was to serve them. On the other hand, the Separatists, the sound and vigorous body of the citizens, regarded the priests and ruler their representatives only insofar as they truly watched over their religious and political life; but as soon as they made their own personal interests paramount to the claims of Religion and the Commonwealth, the Separatists, the best body of the citizens, were in opposition to the Zadokites. Then, when the great struggle began, and the reigning families showed themselves lukewarm, while the middle class resisted with all strength and enthusiasm, such disagreements grouped the people in distinctly separate parties. The Zadokites, the *Sadducees*, the descendants of the priest estate in connection with the families of rank, constituted one party; the Separatists, the *Pharisees*, as they were designated in the Aramaic vernacular, were the other party. The Hasmonean or Maccabee family, supported by the citizens, crowded the Zadokite dynasty from the throne and took possession of both the throne and the altar. The Hasmonean family attained to the office of princes and high priests, partly through their own merits as leaders, but chiefly by their close alliance and action with the solid mass of the middle class of the people. But here too, we see a general historic phenomenon repeated. A new dynasty makes every effort to rally the ancient nobility around it. The Sadducees were the old nobility; the differences between the new kings and priests and the descendants of those who had formerly held those offices, were soon reconciled; the Sadducees became the courtiers, the nobility of the new royal court, and that clung to the noblemen as the party powerful through its hereditary dignity. And that produced a still more serious struggle between the Sadducees and the Pharisees; the reigning dynasty tried to please first one party and then the other, but on the whole yielded to the designs of the nobility.

It was a religio-political fight that had started between the Sadducees and the Pharisees, so that the chasm widened more and more; a religio-political fight in which, so far as that period is concerned, it is hard to discern which element predominated, the political or the religious. On the religious side, the chief point of difference of the Pharisees is this, that they objected to having the sanctity of the priesthood placed so much in the foreground. A sentence in the Second Book of the Maccabees, which belongs to that period, most distinctly expresses that sentiment, saying: "Unto *all* are given the heritage, the kingdom, the priesthood, and the sanctuary." All the people should be regarded as priestly and holy, was the contention of the Pharisees; of course, there were especial priestly functions and rules that could not be disputed, but the whole people was to be raised to sanctification, should be formed into a holy, priestly establishment. In that way, burdens were made for the whole people, ordinances which were to make them priests as much as it could be done. If certain precepts concerning cleanness and uncleanness were observed by the priests, all the people should observe them with equal care; if certain ablutions at the holy sacrificial ministrations were prescribed for the priests, all the people were to eat their ordinary meals after the same preparation: "every-day fruit with the holiness of the sanctuary." If the Temple was the place for the priests where they performed the sacrificial service and if the sacrificial repasts constituted a religious act affording to the body of the priests an opportunity of assembling together, in like manner the people got their side-temples, their synagogues, which, though not intended to supplant the Temple, should serve as people's temples at which they also had their communion repasts that were to be considered a sacred function. The repast was prepared for by ablution which consecrated the meat, wine was a substitute for the drink offering, and frankincense was not wanting, either. The holiness of those repasts was yet heightened by prayers, and thus every man became a priest to a certain extent. Thus the design of the Pharisees to acquire the character of priests called the great institution of Houses of God into existence. The institution of Prayer is a fruit of that design which now and then was rather one-sided and unbalanced, but yet contained many sound and vigorous creations. But there were also many arrangements fixed that were burdensome, and of which some are still observed and others are flitting about as the shadows of the past. For instance, the ceremony of bidding farewell to the departing Sabbath with wine and spices, is a survival out of that period of popular desire to observe priestly practices.

In all matters where religious or secular matters called for a decision, the Sadducees and the Pharisees came into collision. The Pharisees succeeded in getting into their hands the management of all the institutions that were of great importance in the popular life. The arrangement of the calendar and the judiciary were taken out of the hands of the priests, and the People, the Learned, attended to all that. The "People," the "Learned," we say; for the names "Pharisees" and "Sadducees" were used more by the respective opponents than by the parties themselves. The Sadducees called themselves "the Sons of the Noble Families," or "the Sons of the Priests," while their opponents called them "Zadokites," "Sadducees," which conveys no idea of contempt, but was intended to designate them by a mere family name as denial of any special nobility. In like manner, the

Separatists called themselves "the Learned" or "the Fellows of the Society," who advocated self-sanctification; their opponents called them by their ancient name "Pharisees," which was no disgracing expression, but simply ignored their claims to especial learning and holiness. Only later times sought to asperse ignominy upon that appellation.

Thus a great division had arisen within Judah; and that division increased and produced mighty internal transformations.

VIII.

Sadducees and Pharisees, The World to Come, Hillel.

The difficulty of presenting and looking at a past age according to its inner motives and impulses is great enough in itself, but it is very much increased when we are without contemporary records which might by their mere existence reveal to us what the people of that time thought and what they strove for, and how certain events came to happen. Even the most faithful accounts given by a later time view the conditions and events from their own standpoint, involuntarily or intentionally color them with their partisanship, or misrepresent things from want of a true conception of the past. If unimportant periods of time are hidden behind a misty veil, we might pass by them with indifference and leave them to the industry of the antiquarian curiosity seeker or to bold, combinative criticism. But just such periods are sometimes the very ones that have shaped a long line of succeeding centuries. Although we may know little of them, they have left deep traces behind; their creations and events have exerted an influence lasting for all times; and if we wish to gain a clear understanding of ourselves, of what we are, and how we became such, it can not be a matter of indifference to us, thoroughly to understand the source from which we have sprung, to know the very foundation whence the Present has grown. The ideas entertained, the events that happened in Judea two thousand years ago, the conflict of the Sadducees and Pharisees, and the results produced by that conflict, exerted their effect upon later centuries, are of great importance in the world's history, and exert their influence unto this day. That very influence is it to which we sometimes yield, against which we struggle at other times, which is now the foundation on which we stand, and then again is the barrier the limit of which we feel and strive to break down.

If we desire to gain a conclusive judgment concerning the most important questions of the Past as well as of the Present, we must cease to grope in uncertain darkness while explaining the events within Judaism during the period of the Second Temple. It is high time that all fable and fiction about Sadducees and Pharisees should cease. On one hand the Sadducees have been represented as Philhellenists who had placed themselves beyond the pale of Judaism, who had embraced new Grecian refinement and had thus become entirely denationalized; they were made to appear as Epicureans, Sensualists, Worldlings, who neglected all religious interests. Others on the contrary, misled by the similarity of the sound in the name, went so far astray as to take them for Stoics. But for a time, they were the very representative men of the Jewish national life, and *their* exertions likewise were directed towards fathoming the foundation of Judaism; they were the first priest-nobility vested with power, and formed, at the time, the center around which the people gathered, but which later degenerated and went down, as is often the end of those who, elevated above the masses, strive to rise still higher, make their own persons and personal interests paramount to all others, and therefore, making but very little effort to promote the advancement of the welfare of the people, are at last pushed aside by the people.

The name of the Pharisees, too, has assumed a false meaning in the memory of later generations. It was especially by the influence of another religion that the Pharisees were regarded as petty, narrowminded men, who strain at a gnat, indulge in outward worship, without being animated by true inward piety, as men devoid of more exalted religious ideas. The Jews did not judge them thus severely, yet that worth which was actually innate in them was not attributed to them. For, in reality, they were the very core, the brain and the brawn of the nation; their exertions were directed toward the establishment of equal rights for all—their fight was the fight that was repeated in all times when great interests are at stake, the fight against priestcraft and hierarchy, against privilege of individual classes, the fight for the very truth that not outward qualities alone, but inward religious conviction and consequent moral conduct constitute the proper worth of the man. The means which they were in many respects forced to employ, seem at first sight not to bear out such a view, but when examined more closely, they fully correspond to it. To oppose the priests they were compelled to claim for every man everything that distinguished the priesthood; they would not assign higher duties to others lest they were obliged to yield them also special rights. We are—thus they said—just as holy, and occupy the same exalted position as you. Let us suppose a case, that some later period received the superficial account, that once upon a time a dispute had arisen as to whether it should be the duty of all classes of the people to defend their country, and that even those who in former times had been exempt from military service now were foremost in their determination to leave that duty no longer to the nobility, the knights, who alone had hitherto staked their lives and fortunes for the security of their common country; might not some persons think that those who were so anxious to do the fighting were ruffians, dissatisfied because others fought the fight to a finish? Would such an opinion be just? Certainly not! The classes who enjoyed that negative privilege, the privilege of having no share in the activities of the country, now come forward with the claim: "We are equally children of our country, we shall perform the same duties and demand the same rights; you shall perform no higher duties, to claim in consequence superior privileges and represent yourselves as the pillars of the Commonwealth; we are equally ready to bring the same sacrifices." The same sentiment brought forth the struggle of the Pharisees against the Sadducees, and was the motive of their readiness to submit to the same priestly burdens.

That serious, bitter fight was sometimes carried on with insufficient means—a phenomenon which is often repeated in history. The aspiring party bear within themselves the full power of the idea but can not put it into practice. The stubborn fact was that the Sadducees were the nobility; they held all offices; they were either priests and therefore commanded respect, or noble families connected with the priests; they basked in the favor of the Court, which occasionally, when it could not help itself, grasped the hand of the Pharisees, but felt comfortable only in the atmosphere of the Sadducees. As it was, the Sadducees were in actual possession of the administrative affairs and were sure to retain a part of them. The Pharisees might be ever so determined in their fight against the special privileges of the priestly families, as far as they touched civil and political life and legal rights, yet they could not abolish priesthood altogether because history had established its right of existence, and as long as the Temple with its sacrificial service remained, their ministers could not be dispensed with. In such times when the result of a struggle appears dubious and undetermined, when the combatants struggle with full determination, behold their victory close by and yet begin to despair of its results, men will then turn their eyes to the future.

Healthful times, healthy nations are thoroughly conscious of their spiritual power, they feel their infinity and eternity of the spirit even in the present; vigorous spiritual energy is so strong, superior as it is to all that is finite, it requires no additional guaranty for itself. Healthful times, healthy nations will never arrive at the conclusion that the spirit is but a weak decoction, a mixture of changing matter, of nervous fluid and blood-globules; they are conscious of their spiritual independence, of the convincing power wherewith it is endowed—of the distinct and separate existence of the spirit. And for that reason they do not continually think of the future, do not indulge in dreams as to what may be in times to come; in the very present they bear within themselves the strength of the spirit with its convincing power; to them every minute is an infinity containing the germs of development for all later times. Such times and such nations look upon the future as upon the natural result of the present, well knowing that whatever moves and animates it, will and must be realized at some time to come, being to them as something already present in the spirit. Morbid men, morbid times or religions, incessantly think of the future, place it upon the foreground. From the present, in which they lack the energy to effect their ardent wishes, they take refuge into a future to which they are unable to find a natural transition, and for which they long the more fervently, and which they picture to themselves with embellishments so much the more brilliant. "It will be otherwise" is their continual consolation; the weaker their present confidence, the bolder the poetic imageries of a brilliant future.

Judaism knows no such weakness, it is deeply and fully convinced of an independent spiritual life; it regards man's likeness to God impressed upon him by Divinity Himself, as none other than a spiritual attribute. The directness with which it speaks of a spiritual power, both of the spiritually living God and of man as living through the spirit, that profound conviction permeating all its writings, is a guaranty for the belief within Judaism, that the spirit is everlasting and can never be cut off. But it does not place that belief in the foreground, it has not designated this earth as a vale of tears, nor pictured the reward to come beyond the grave in brilliant colors; it has never commanded us to destroy this earth as something vain and sinful; it has never demanded that joy in life on earth should be crushed, because this life is but a time of probation. Judaism does not know such morbid sentimentality.

That it contains the belief in the immortality of the soul and further develops it is proved even by the subtle author of Ecclesiastes; he expresses his doubts about that subject the same as with regard to other matters, but the very fact that he utters such doubts, proves that the belief had been generally adopted: "The spirit of man goeth upward." "The dust returneth to the earth as it was; and the spirit returneth unto God who gave it." In that manner, the belief affords strength, elevation and inspiration without deadening and crushing the present. But times had arrived when the present was very gloomy, when men could not feel satisfied with what it afforded. They beheld their own efforts and the contrast exhibited in the actual conditions; they considered their means to carry their endeavor into effect, and saw their insufficiency. It is but natural in such times men will take comfort by saying to themselves: "Never mind! Whatever can not be accomplished in the present, will assume form in a better time. Another time is bound to come in this world, and then conditions will be changed at once." In such mental condition, the Pharisees said: "The priesthood will go down, a descendant of the House of David will reign, the people will be invigorated, the national life will mature the fruit which we so much long for; *another* world will come, and we, too, shall participate in it." They were not satisfied with the hope that the future would develop what the hot air of the present had germinated; they themselves desired to participate in the enjoyment of that future, because they had enjoyed nothing in the present. That is the origin of a belief in a future *Resurrection of the body.* That belief was part of Parseeism, and the Jews may have become acquainted with it during their sojourn in Persia. Traces of its existence among them at an earlier period can not be discovered; the book of Daniel is the first that makes mention of it, and that book dates from that very time in which the internal severe battle was raging. Granted even that such belief, prevailing among the Parsees, affected the Jews there, Judaism would never have adopted it if it had not been impelled thereto by circumstances in its internal development. Just as the Pharisees, the men who struggled for a change of conditions and could not bring that about, could not help creating for themselves a future as the realization of their present desires: so the Sadducees who were satisfied with their power, who did not wish for a change and even opposed it, for that very reason repudiated the belief in the resurrection of the body. Whether they can be condemned on that account as infidels, is a question which I may confidently leave to your own decision rather than to that of many another tribunal.

The fight between the Sadducees and the Pharisees grew hotter and hotter, both in the domain of civil life and in that of religious affairs, and dominated all thought and sentiment. The more serious and gloomier the aspect of affairs became, the more intense became the differences; the threatening crisis into which the nation was thrust, challenged all healthy popular energy. Just as the people arose at the time of the Maccabean War, when foreign oppression wanted to crush them, so it also happened in the subsequent history of Judaism. Conflicts of the most various kinds raged within, even in the royal family; the several sons of a deceased king, the succession not being fully regulated, made rival claims to the throne and contended against each other; foreign nations were appealed to for their decision, for their assistance to one or the other. That increased the discontent with the present and its representatives. That, for all that, true religious sentiment was not extinct in the heart of the noble-minded during those strifes, may be shown by the following incident. During the contest of two rival claimants, Hyrcanus and Aristobulus, the adherents of one, and the officiating priests with them, had fortified themselves in the Temple, and their opponents laid siege to the building. Both crowds were full of the most rabid party spirit. A man of great reputation, Onias, known in the Talmud as *Honi Ha-Meaggel*, to whose prayer especial efficacy was ascribed, was called for by the besiegers and requested to pray for their victory and the defeat of the besieged. But he made this prayer: "Lord of the universe, our Father in Heaven! within Thy Temple are Thy priests, sons of Thy people; out here are likewise sons of Thy people; they are enraged against each other, do not hearken unto the prayers of those against these, nor unto the imprecation of these against those." The crowd stoned him to death. That man was the child of true Jewish spirit, who can be numbered among the noblest martyrs. Inspired by true love of man and country, he remains faithful even in the very face of death. He would not desecrate his speech in spite of the wrath and rage boiling around him. Whether that noble martyr, when he breathed his last, did or did not utter the prayer, "Father, forgive them, they know not what they do," legend does not inform us; for it is only legend that can tell such things—the words of a dying man are heard by no one —his sentiments are surely of that character.

But the fierceness of those conflicts was soon to mount and be merged into a question of existence. A nation entered upon the world's stage which soon gained the greatest power and exerted the most decisive and authoritative influence everywhere. Rome came in like a lion among the weaker animals, and in cat-fashion, like the lion, it at first approached cunningly and pleasantly, acted the part of a mediating ally, then to pounce upon those friends, usurping supremacy over them, and then reducing them into complete subjection. When Rome began its cat-lion game with Judea, the people felt that a mighty foe was approaching; alarming restlessness seized upon their minds; the party conflicts grew more violent and more general. Herod was hated, feared as a foreigner and a tyrant, yet his good qualities might, in the eyes of the people, perhaps, have covered those two objections, and his native energy might have acted as a bond of union. But what constantly brought him to mind as a foreigner and put fuel to the flame of hatred against him, was the fact that he appeared as a satellite of Rome, that his face was incessantly turned toward Rome and that he always earned favors from Rome.

In times like those, men appear who reflect the very soul of the nation and who mean to give it shape and form. I shall mention to you a name which is not circled in history with the halo that is attached to many other names, although it well deserves it and that his great importance should be recognized and appreciated. As the Revealed Doctrine is connected with the name of Moses, Tradition with that of Ezra, so Regenerated Judaism is identified with the name of *Hillel.* The Talmudists have well understood and, in the naive expression of their time, have characterized the importance of Hillel in the saying: "The Torah had been forgotten, then Ezra came from Babylon and established it anew; and again the Torah fell into oblivion and Hillel arrived from Babylon and established it anew." It was not forgotten, but it was paralyzed, it was about to lose its vital energy and influence upon later development, if Hillel, the man of profound understanding and true religious life, had not effected its regeneration. It may be that the Babylonian Gemara emphasizes with especial pleasure the fact that Ezra and Hillel had come from Babylon—for the men of the Babylonian Talmud were proud of Babylon, despite the oppression they had to suffer there—and that very fact may contain a truth; viz., that just such men who had not been mixed in and were not wholly saturated with the momentary conditions of Palestine, who had breathed a different atmosphere and perhaps viewed wider fields, were especially fit to awaken a new popular spirit. At any rate, Hillel was a man who exerted a decisive influence upon Judaism.

Hillel is a fully historical person. The records concerning him may surround him with some embellishing legend but those legends only draw some lines more distinctly, they do not cover or blur his portrait. Legends accompany every distinguished man, even in the most historical ages; anecdotes, piquant tales and incidents are related of him, which can not stand the test of historical investigation, but they emanate from his character, so that we must acknowledge that, even if they did not actually come to pass, they are yet in full harmony with his character. Legends of that kind are no fiction, they are the product of true poesy: the inmost depth of such a man's heart is fathomed, pearls are brought up thence which are to be found there and only accident had not started them out into the light of day before; the sharp contour of his picture becomes more perceptible by them. As a poet, although he does not render history with complete fidelity, nevertheless must portray his hero faithfully, even if adding a line here and changing another there, in order to throw a clearer light upon his entire character, so also does healthy and sound popular tradition treat persons who have taken a well-defined part in history, so that legend must fit closely to them, unable to obliterate their physiognomy. It is true that with others, legend changes their whole character, ornaments them with miracles and covers them with a full stock of tinsel, but the more miraculous legend appears, the less credible it is and the more does it veil the real character of the person. The glorification leaves so much less of the actual historical man. If such a man would have presented a sharp, well-marked outline, legend could not have surrounded it with direct contradictions and could not have obliterated the distinct traits. It did not do so in Hillel's case. Some legends may have become affixed to his life, but they are so completely in accordance with his character, no miracles are attributed to him, that he continues a man, a sound, whole human being; he is not claimed to be more, and for that very reason he is the greater.

He is designated as a disciple of Shemaya and Abtalyon. While a poor youth, so it is related, he was once unable to pay to the janitor the small fee which was demanded of those desiring admission. It was a cold winter evening; he climbed up to the window of the lecture room, in order to hear the discourses of the teachers, and there he lay, regardless of what happened around him; the snowflakes fell upon him thick and fast and covered him entirely. Stiffened with the cold, he passed the whole night there and when, in the morning the lecture room was opened and daylight would not enter by that window, on examination being made, Hillel was discovered, unconscious and half frozen; he was carried into the house and resuscitated. We will pass no judgment on the truth of the tale; if it be but a legend it keeps within the bounds of probability and nature, intended to depict both his extraordinary zeal for study and his great poverty. Of his poverty we are informed also in other ways; but although he had no abundance of the good things of this life, he preserved his independence, and because he was of the common people, he had the more heart for the people and their wants.

Of all his virtues, his meekness is especially praised. That trait of his was so well known that it has passed into a proverbial saying. Two men entered into a wager, one of them taking the side that he could arouse Hillel to anger. One Friday evening when people were preparing for the Sabbath he went three times to him and asked him the most trivial questions. Hillel admitted him and answered the questions in the most quiet manner. When the man, upon his third attempt, perceived that he had failed, he exclaimed violently: "May there not be many in Israel like thee!" which caused Hillel to ask the reason. "Why?" replied the questioner, "through thee, I have lost a large bet." "Well," said Hillel, "it is better that thou shouldst lose thy bet than I my calmness and humility." Persons desiring information upon Judaism with a view to joining, applied to him as well as to Shammai. Shammai was older and his superior; clinging more to inherited custom and following old, beaten tracks, he was the leader and was first addressed. Such an inquirer came to Shammai, saying: "I desire to join Judaism, but I make the condition that I shall be made high-priest." Shammai sent him rudely away. He then applied to Hillel, who said to him: "My son, let us try." He gave him instruction; soon they came to a passage treating of the priests where it was said of those not descended from priests that they could not enter certain parts of the Temple under penalty of death. And the man said to himself, "If not all native Israelites are permitted to assume priestly functions, how could I do it?" And he withdrew that condition. Another came scoffing and wanted to be taught the tenets of Judaism during the brief space of time that he could stand on one leg. Shammai drove him away; he went with the same request to Hillel, who said to him, "Whatever is displeasing unto thee, do not unto another; that is the foundation and root of Judaism; the rest is commentary which you may learn at your leisure." The scoffer was changed into a convert. A third one came, saying, "I should like to join with you; I have read the Written Law, the Bible, and accept it; but I do not want to observe another law which has been but orally transmitted." Shammai repulsed him, but when he applied to Hillel, the latter received him kindly, at once commenced his instruction, and taught him on the first day the letters in their usual order, but on the second, he read them to him in reversed order. "How is this?" asked the pupil, "Yesterday I heard the letters in a different order." "Behold!" replied Hillel, "Yesterday you believed in the order of the letters adopted by me; follow me further in that which is not written down, but which is only a natural development of the other." Those men became ardent disciples of Judaism and once upon a time, meeting each other, observed, "The harshness of Shammai well-nigh drove us away from the sanctuary, but the suavity of Hillel has kindly initiated us into it."

Such tales afford us a full insight into the character of the man. If it should be supposed from the fact that he pointed to passages of Holy Writ for certain privileges of the priests, that he was favorable to the priests, it would be a great mistake. He accepted what could not be changed by him, but he was the very man who carried on the contest against the priests with all possible determination and narrowed down the limits of their prerogatives most closely. His presentation of the foundation and essence of Judaism fully discloses the sentiment of the man; the essence of Judaism consists in love of man and mutual regard, in the respect of the dignity of man and the equality of all men; the rest is commentary. Do you perchance suppose that Legend has attributed to Hillel in that story a trait out of the life of the founder of another religion? It would be in itself unnatural to adopt from another religion, and especially from a hostile daughter religion, a maxim of which it boasts as its exclusive property; it would rather be contended against and its value denied. Besides, that maxim was not so much in keeping with the rigid legalism of a later time that it should have invented the story which was really an obstacle in their way. But aside from that, as you gain a better knowledge of our Hillel, you will see that the maxim is in full accordance with his character. At an earlier date, the canon had been established: "Whoever believes God to be all-merciful and all-gracious, regards also benevolence and love towards his fellow-men as a fundamental duty." Listen now how our Hillel thinks of God. There are three different classes of men; namely, the fully pious, the intermediary, and the fully wicked. On some future day, there will be a day of judgment for men; the fully pious will at once enjoy their reward, the fully wicked will receive their punishment, but what will become of the intermediary? Of them the School of Shammai says, "They will first be sent into hell, given up to punishment, but will longingly look up and wail and gradually ascend."—"Not so," says Hillel, "as regards the intermediary, He who is abundant in mercy will incline the scale unto mercy." Whoever entertains such an idea of God, holds also higher opinion of man and teaches love for all mankind. Accordingly, that maxim is quite in agreement with his character. As regards a third point, that he defends Tradition, his very character affords the clue: he is a man of living, continuous development, he demands that actual practical life in its freshness should decide upon measure and form.

Hillel knows man according to his inner being but no less, according to the demands of life. He is wont to consult with his soul. He hastens, a tale beautifully relates, from the house of learning, in order to attend to a dear guest. His disciples ask him, "Master, who is the dear guest whom thou keepest in thy house from day to day?" "That guest," he replied, "is my own soul—during my intercourse with the world, it must always be pushed back, but it claims its right nevertheless." That is true, profound introspection. But he was, withal, far from sentimentality and transcendentalism; he apprehends life rather in its freshness, beauty and importance. A long-drawn-out dispute existed between the Schools of Shammai and Hillel. The adherents of the former maintained in perfect accordance with their gloomy ways, that it would be better for man never to have been born than to be born; the followers of the latter asserted that it is better for man that he has been created; he is born for action and the earth is the place of his activity. They had to yield in a manner, because the others had the greater authority, but their whole yielding amounted to this: "Well, we are created; let us be active, and examine well our action." "Make the most of life and its day," was the motto of Hillel. Whenever Shammai came across anything good and nice during the week, he said, "Let this be kept for the Sabbath." Hillel said, "Praise to God day by day; this is a day on which I may rejoice through the goodness of God; another day will bring its own." He recognized the claims and the mission of every period, and the difference of the times gave him the rule for his labors. He used to say, "At a time of gathering in when they love to see everything clothed in religious garb, you may spread and scatter, let ceremonies and formalities grow in luxurious abundance; but at a time of casting off, when ceremonies and formalities are dropping out, then pull up, be ready to yield, desist from forcible preservation and enlargement."

That was the fundamental idea along the lines of which Hillel proceeded, as attested by all his works and words. He presents the picture of a genuine reformer; that word will not do him any harm; it ought to raise him in our estimation. He was confronted by the difficulties that present themselves to rejuvenation and revival at all times; some may have told him, "Why wilt thou make changes? Stand by that which is authoritative now. How canst thou usurp the right of making innovations?" The saying of his: "If I work not for myself, who will work for me?" is probably the answer to such objectors. If only that which former times have produced, beyond which we have already passed, shall be binding, and I do not make timely regulations for myself, who is to make them for me?—Others may have said, "Well, keep it to thyself; think and act accordingly; but why wilt thou interfere by introducing changes and reforms for the community?" As if an idea were for one individual only, as if it could be locked up in a box, to be looked at, at an opportune time, while it is in fact a vital energy ruling and impelling man, as the prophet expresses it: "It was in mine heart as a burning fire, shut up in my bones, and I was weary with forbearing and I could not stay." And Hillel's saying replies to those: "If I am for myself alone, what am I then?"—Do I ask anything for myself? The community wants its burden made lighter. "Desist, dear friend," others may have cautioned him, "thou art too hasty." His maxim, "If not now, when then?" is probably the reply to those conservatives. Every age labors and must labor, and if we mean to creep along in indolence, the future is killed in its very germ. Such was

Hillel, and that he labored in that manner, that he was the man who dared to make determined resistance to all aggravations, that he never feared the name of mitigator, all will clearly perceive who have once cast a glance into the history of Judaism. I shall not trouble you with details; but I shall adduce a few examples to show how he understood his time.

There is a biblical precept that, when a house situated in a city surrounded by a wall has been sold, it can be redeemed by its former owner within a year; if he has neglected the redemption, the house remains the property of the purchaser (mortgagee). Usually the grantor (mortgagor) waited till the last day of the term, when he would use every effort to raise the money for the redemption. But often the purchaser (mortgagee) went away on the last day for redemption and locked the house, in order to make it impossible for the former owner (mortgagor) to repay him the purchase money and regain his property. The law existed, its letter was binding. "No," said Hillel, "the letter is not binding—in case the man in possession is not at home, let the door be forced open, or the money be deposited in the Temple treasury; the lawful owner shall not lose his property in consequence of the cunning used by the other party." Another much more far-reaching example is the following: Every seventh year there was a release of debts, a precept born of the tender spirit of Judaism, but naturally intended only for the simple times when the people's life moved within the plainest conditions. In such a period, only those borrow money who are in actual want and the sums are small—to assist such persons is an act of pure charity—and under such circumstances the law of the year of release is a very beautiful one; the time has expired, the debt is canceled. But in later times, borrowing and lending were no longer merely the result of want on the one side and of pure generosity on the other; men borrowed for business purposes, to have ready means for carrying on trade; nor did people do the lending from a sentiment of charity, perhaps as a favor, but mainly to share in the profits. Now, if the debtor had an opportunity in the seventh year to get rid of his debts, what would follow as the consequence? That which Holy Writ apprehended; there was no longer any one willing to lend money, because it was known that at a definite time the right of collecting the loan would lapse, because the year of release canceled all debts. How could that be remedied? "What do I care?" said conservatism, "*it is written;* the law must stand." "No," said Hillel, "shall business be stopped because the defrauder covers himself with the mantle of the law? Shall the poor starve, because fear of loss ties up the hand of the wealthy —and all in the cause of religion? No, this thing must be remedied. Henceforth the contracts may be executed at court, with the stipulation that the year of release shall not cancel the debt; and that stipulation shall be valid."—"But that is clearly against the law as it is written."—"Maybe; but when we stick to its letter, all morality will be lost; written or not, practical life decides." And Hillel's announcement was accepted and prevailed.

Such was the man and thus he became a restorer or reformer of Judaism, and his influence continues to this day. He did not believe in seclusive piety, as his saying, "Separate not thyself from the community or thy fellow-men," plainly expresses. To assume to be pre-eminently devout, to forsake others as backsliders and bask in a lustre of seclusive piety, is immoral. He had no respect for hermitical piety—he was a man of social practical life and he invigorated and elevated the life of Judaism in all possible manner. How that period might have further shaped itself, if the quiet development of Judaism had thus continued its course, is superfluous to conjecture. Quiet development was not granted to it. Great events came to pass; two events which, taken together, do not constitute the heart and central point of the world's history, but which produced great revolutions; I mean the origin of Christianity and the dissolution of the Jewish Commonwealth.

IX.

Parties and Sects, Origin of Christianity.

If it is a difficult task to show how the spirit of Religion has entered the human mind and become rooted therein, to disclose the mysterious ways through which its development has passed, to point out the various formations by which it manifested itself amid the chances and changes of external historic life, and yet, at the same time not to lose sight of the Unity of the religious idea: the difficulty of such a task is greatly increased when, in reviewing history, we have arrived at a turning point which is followed by most searching consequences and with which a world-historic transformation begins. Even the various impelling and moving forces which co-operate, as it were, to introduce a new creation into the world, are at work at such a depth that they are concealed from our view and manifest themselves only through their external effects. From insignificant beginnings, limited at first within a narrow circle, a new spiritual power has all at once developed itself; and we must track it into its various starting points, examine how its paths are entwined with and met by circumstances and conditions which favored that development. And here, still another difficulty presents itself. Historical events which have turned into deepest convictions, which are regarded by some as the very life's nerve of their own minds and also of the spiritual movement of the world's history, in fact, as the very aim and center of man's existence, which are reverenced as the Holiest of Holies, challenge our attention; whereas, by the other side, the protest now raised aloud and then again by intentional silence, is no less determined, and also has its root in the idea and conception of human life and destiny. Every one who perceives the moving of the Divine Spirit in the grand course of the world's history, will reverence also God's work in a world-historic event that produced such important transformations in all relations; will see His disposing hand in a faith that has kept for nearly fifteen centuries the civilized world under its sway; he will with reverence examine a religion by which millions have been, and still are, quickened and comforted. And, though he does not share the belief that this historical event should be venerated as the spiritual center of the entire historic existence of the world, that an entirely new spiritual creation had occurred which had illuminated the world with ideas that had never before been felt or conceived; that henceforth it had become the prop and pillar of a new world-structure as well as the only source of a new spiritual life: he will feel himself pressingly called upon to justify his opposition and to explain his interpretation of the peculiarities of those events. But he must also be permitted to utter, though modestly, yet without repression, his own opinion, without fearing that a word might escape his lips which would sound unpleasantly to one side or the other. Whoever respects in himself free, honestly acquired convictions, and claims the right to freely express his own opinion, honoring true manly courage therein, will not, it is hoped, deny the same right to others, but will quietly receive the utterance of an independent conviction, however much it may militate against his own.

A great world-historic movement approaches; and before we proceed, we must once more vividly place before our eyes the state of the world at that time, especially the conditions in Judea. There was a strong, in part very healthy movement of the spirits in that country. The reformatory labors of Hillel had partly turned the minds from the tactical error of assuming priestly garb in the fight against the priest-caste. Phariseeism had entered upon a phase of development wherein it gave the true spirit of Judaism free rein, although, as is the case with all such movements towards reform, only a sort of halfway station had been reached. Priesthood and Temple-service still retained their importance, although that was on the decline; but the elevation of man to free and independent religiousness had not yet reached that high point, from which the sight can behold, free and untrammeled, the

Divine in man ruling the conviction and transforming and creating the outward form. Transformation was ardently striven for, but effected only by closely leaning upon existing forms, and in that manner it succeeded. Continual working along those lines would surely have carried Judaism to higher development. Phariseeism was a sound limb on the body of Judaism, and proved itself as such also at that time. Its adherents were zealous patriots, and at the same time seriously devoted to the study and practice of their religion. Yet, with all their efforts to preserve the national and political life, to fortify the customs and independence of their country, they were men who were opposed to every revolutionary enterprise and exerted themselves to moderate all inconsiderate zeal. They had entered into the heart of political life, their leaders had gradually acquired enough importance to have a weighty voice in the council of the nation by the side of the high-priests, the chiefs of the Sadducees, to pronounce their decisive judgment concerning both political and civil affairs. And it could now be seen that they themselves, formerly the men of violent opposition, weighed with prudent circumspection the means at their command, and well estimated the forces in their hands. Even Josephus, the fawning and partial historian of that time, is forced to acknowledge, when speaking of the man who stood at the head of the Pharisees during the period of the Jewish war—Simon Ben Gamaliel, grandson or great-grandson of Hillel, who was no friend of Josephus but rather opposed him in his measures because he probably had suspicions about him—even Josephus is forced to concede that Simon Ben Gamaliel was a man of determined energy joined with the most circumspect prudence, a man who studiously sought to keep the people from committing excesses, who by no means approved the foolhardy enterprises which shall yet present themselves to our attention. Thus the Pharisees, though powerfully impelled by religious hopes for the future, lived nevertheless chiefly in their present, and their energies and activities were directed towards improving conditions in their own time.

But in such times as we have under consideration, men of

that stamp might in a measure preserve their authority, but they could never satisfy the people. Rome was knocking at the gates of Jerusalem with an iron hand, to lay it heavily on the neck of the nation; the distant roll of the thunder was heard long before the storm burst forth in its full fury. There is a saying of our ancient teachers still extant: "Forty years before the Temple was destroyed, its gates opened and could no more be closed." Be that as it may, at all events the words convey the idea that even a generation before the catastrophe actually occurred, all eyes were turned towards it with alarm, and people settled down to the conviction that a desperate struggle was coming, that the battle would have to be fought even if it should turn out barren of results. In such times, the mass of the people will not regard prudent moderation as a virtue. It chooses quite different men for its favorites, men who come forward with burning zeal, with a fervor of faith and patriotism bordering on raving madness, to whom every means appears fair as long as it seems to lead towards the accomplishment of their object; men who, without reflecting whether or not their means are sufficient and without regarding what the result may be, will attempt anything to give vent to the vehemence of their emotions, even if it should accelerate the catastrophe. Such men did appear, and even their contemporaries designated them by the fully characteristic name of Zealots (*Kannaim*). With their zeal for their faith, they nurtured an implacable hatred against the tyrannical rule and influence of the foreigners. On account of the insufficiency of the means at their command, many of them had no scruples against employing such means as would have been indignantly rejected in more quiet times. They were also called *Sikarioi*, because they carried a dagger concealed beneath their cloaks and secretly stabbed everyone who advocated moderation and, by that, appeared to them suspicious, as a traitor hired by the enemy. They were so numerous and well-connected together, they were in such favor with the population, that the legal authorities dared not lay hands upon them. With such ideas, revolts occurred. Judah of Gaulonitis, a Galilean, proclaimed it as a crime, as a denial of religion, to obey the empire or to yield in any manner to the secular rule imposed by a foreign country. "There is but one kingdom," so ran his dictum, "and that is the kingdom of Heaven, the Kingdom of God. When the country's God-believing power is broken and is to bow down before the heathen unbelief, then is the world moved from its foundation. Our duty, first and last, is not to yield to that worldly power." In his eyes it was a sin to touch a piece of money which had the picture of the Roman Emperor on it; to pay taxes to a foreign power was a crime; to date contracts according to the Roman custom, under this or that Consul, or under this or that Procurator, was blasphemy as well as treason against the country. The words of another one of those Galilean zealots are related as follows: "How can you Pharisees make any claim to piety? You write in contracts the name of the foreign ruler by the side of that of Moses, beginning them with 'In the . . . year of the Emperor . . . .' and conclude with 'according to the law of Moses and Israel.' If the name of the unbeliever is in such manner incorporated in contracts of marriage and the like, that have any religious significance, can you call that piety?" The Pharisees of course rejected and rebuked such exaggerations, but among the population at large, they reverberated to such an extent that they led to isolated revolts and the formation of new sects. To such an importance had the party of the Zealots risen that Josephus actually represents the adherents of Judah of Gaulonitis as a fourth sect, by the side of the Pharisees and the Sadducees, and a third one, the Essenes, which last one we shall also consider. Theudas, another Zealot leader, acted on the same ideas somewhat later; he too came from Galilee, stirred up revolts, and found many enthusiastic adherents. That the leaders were crucified by the Romans, did not injure the respect paid to them; their sentiment spread only the more rapidly.

The feeling which prevailed in Judea, bursting forth in deeds of wild fanaticism, rested on an old spiritual foundation which increased more and more in strength and intensity. Already during the time when the Maccabean war had started, an idea had general circulation which was firmly rooted in the assurance of the faith in themselves, though joined with the certainty of despair that it could not come to pass just then. The idea took form in the exclamation: "The world is breaking up; the future world must soon come." In the book of Daniel which describes those matters in the form of a vision, the mighty powers who rise against the saints of the Most High are described in their full terror; but at the same time he encourages the timid, saying, "A son of man shall then arise, hidden in the clouds of heaven; all empires shall bow to him, all peoples shall yield in obedience to him, and many of them that sleep in the dust of the earth shall awake and rise up, some to everlasting life and some to everlasting shame." This world is in itself completely ruined and destroyed; a future one, not beyond, but here on this earth, shall appear, in which also the ancient saints, rising up, shall participate. The Kingdom of God, or the Heavenly Kingdom, as it is also called in Daniel, shall come. Of course, the Maccabees did not appear as such sons of men, hidden in clouds of heaven; they were warriors and ended as victors; nor was the position pointed out in the visions reached; the nations did not obey them, the empires did not yield to them, but Judea had become independent. A position had been reached sufficient for the considerate and energetic; and those hopes for the future fell to the rear into the background. But again a time had come which witnessed spoliations and devastations, and betokened yet greater evils; again, a still more powerful enemy pressed upon Israel with far more effective opposition; again it was intended to break not only the power of the nation as an independent state—for that was already broken—but also their spiritual life was to be crushed out. The worship of images and idols was again to be introduced in Judaism, the Emperors were to be adored as gods, as *Divi*, their statues were to be set up in the Temple. Even the Roman standards, adorned with the eagles as the emblem of the Roman Empire, the flight of the bird being observed and interpreted, appeared to the Jews as of idolatrous significance. And those eagles were ordered to be affixed to the

Temple, and their removal to be punished with death! Then despair again seized the minds of the people; their religious sentiment was so powerful, ruled all conditions of life, had grown in intensity, and yet was to be crowded down. Then it was that the ancient idea, which had fallen to the rear for awhile, came again with full force to the front: The Kingdom of Heaven will and must come, this world is given up to evil, it is a world of heathenism and doomed to destruction; let it perish, the future world will soon succeed it; the Kingdom of Heaven appears, the pious will rise up again, and theirs will the kingdom be then. Will you hear the words of a zealot, or rather the disciple of a zealot of a later day, as it has been preserved for us by our ancient teachers? He announces: "Whoever takes upon himself the yoke of the Law, shakes off the yoke of the empire and the yoke of civil authority; but whoever shakes off the yoke of the Law, upon him shall be the yoke of the kingdom of this world and the yoke of all civil ordinances." Only the Law, the faithful observance of the religious statutes shall and must rule, and when the Law rules, the whole artificial political structure will fall; all those organizations that keep political life together, unless Religion prescribes them, are superfluous and will vanish; but as soon as you shake off the yoke of the Law, that easy, sweet yoke, then you must bear the whole pressure of the heavy yoke of the world. Therefore away with it, and seriously cling to the Law! Such thoughts filled the hearts, such hopes were entertained with the most decided confidence.

There were also timid and tender-chorded hearts that did not join in the energetic fury or in the elated hopes, and who found satisfaction for their religious sentiment in seclusion through hermitical asceticism; they were the *Essenes*, the third sect mentioned by Josephus. They did not influence the changing conditions of the commonwealth, yet found favor and won disciples; they were regarded as having power to work miracles and were revered on account of their quiet, pious practices. The Essenes, generally speaking, did not greatly differ from the Pharisees; they were of the Middle Class, were not at all on a friendly footing with the aristocracy and the priests; they are even reported as having altogether repudiated animal sacrifices, but (far more than the most extreme Pharisees and almost in opposition to the main body of them) they shunned as much as possible all contact with the world at large, secluding themselves, as it were, in the secret sanctuary of their hearts, satisfying their spiritual wants by mystical contemplation. They regarded the world and its affairs with indifference; they are even said (but the only authority for particulars about them is the very unreliable Josephus) to have espoused celibacy, community of property, etc. All that increased their reputation and they gained reverence as healers, workers of miracles, prophets, but they exerted no influence upon the development of events.

Such was the state of feeling in Judea.

Whatever found expression and shape in and around Jerusalem, the center of the kingdom, found also not alone its echo, but even its peculiar intensified expression in the outermost limits of the country; and these outermost limits were Galilee. Galilee was separated from Judea only by Samaria, inhabited from very early times by a mixed people, whence its name, "the Land of the Nations," surrounded by Syrians and Phoenicians, and containing quite a number of settlements of those populations. You have probably read in a recent work a very glowing description of Galilee of that time. It runs about like this: "Galilee is a highly fertile, picturesque country in which pleasant plains are varied by green, wooded hills whose soil furnishes everything that man can wish for; its inhabitants are unsophisticated children of nature, harmless, ignorant men, and lovely ignorant women who follow an enthusiastic youth with innocent love." It is not exactly stated whether that love is directed more to the person or to the cause he represents. I am sorry that I have to demolish this charming idyl. It is true, Galilee was a fruitful country; it was intersected by rivers and hills, and yielded an abundance for the gratification of all physical wants; its inhabitants were ignorant indeed; their language was mixed and corrupt, having lost its purity and character and accepted many foreign elements. Hence the people stood not so high as the inhabitants of Judea. But their ignorance was by no means an idyllic life of quietude. On the contrary, it was blended with a certain amount of savageness. The revolutionists before mentioned, those who sought to do away with their opponents by fire and sword, by dagger and other secret means, hailed mostly from Galilee. Young Herod, even at a period just preceding the one under consideration, gave the first proofs of his character in Galilee. He had executed the robbers around about there without ceremony and mercy, driven to it by the exigencies of the case. He was indicted for it; but his power—although at the time he was but governor of the province of Galilee under his father Antipater, the representative of Hyrcanus—had even then become so great that the Sanhedrim did not dare to pass judgment against him, and it is certain that he had good cause for his extraordinary proceeding. For a spirit had spread in Galilee, such as generally lays hold of that portion of a people which only receives the general impetus of a movement without being able to account clearly for the reasons and causes. The Galileans were, if I may be permitted to coin the term, the *Marseillesians* of the Jewish struggle, of that commotion which surged so violently. It was in Galilee where the most violent and extreme movements found the fullest applause. In a similar way, as the Galileans were inclined to rebellion, so they were ruled and inflamed by the belief that this world was breaking down and a new world, the future world, would soon appear—an idea which visionaries who use little reflection but have strong feeling, will always readily accept. It was there probably, where John went about exclaiming, "Repent, for the Kingdom of Heaven is near at hand." That kingdom is the future world —the rule of justice on this earth, the destruction of all secular fetters and the illegitimate reign of heathenism to which the present world is given over as prey.

Thus the hearts were in full agitation, prepared for the most wonderful phenomena.

It was then that a man appeared in Galilee who still more confidently gave shape to the commotion of the times. While others before him had merely advised preparation for the Kingdom of Heaven, promising that it would come—that a son of man wrapt in the clouds of heaven would appear—that a complete transformation would take place, while others acted only as prophets and proclaimers of that belief, bearing in their imagination that hope without giving it shape, he had the courage and confidence to state, "The time *is* fulfilled, the Kingdom of Heaven *is* come, and the son of man wrapt in the clouds of heaven"—at first he did not distinctly pronounce it, but he had the belief within him and let it shine through everywhere—"that son of man, *I am*." It was not his idea to carry on a fight against the kingdom of this world; the words attributed to him by a later narrator, "My kingdom is not of this world" may have fully corresponded to that belief. It means, "My kingdom does not begin in the present heathen world; this heathen world will soon have been broken up and passed away; the future world will then come in, actually and tangibly, and then my kingdom will begin." He was fully convinced of that, and in all later times of deep oppression we meet with men who presented themselves with the same self-assurance as Messiahs. Should we wonder that at such a time of general tension and suspense, a bold and glowing enthusiasm for Judaism and its reign at large should completely possess and carry an over-anxious man to the point of faith in himself, of filling him with the courage to announce those hopes with the fullest assurance? It was such a belief that animated the first author of Christianity. He was a Jew, a Pharisean Jew with Galilean coloring—a man who joined in the hopes of his time and who believed that those hopes were fulfilled in him. He did not utter a new thought, nor did he break down the barriers of nationality. When a foreign woman came to him with request to heal her, he said, "It is not meet to take the children's bread and cast it to the dogs." He did not abolish any part of Judaism; he was a Pharisee who walked in the way of Hillel, did not set the most decided value upon every single external form, yet proclaimed "that not the least tittle should be taken from the Law;" "The Pharisees sit in Moses' seat, and whatsoever they bid you observe, that observe and do." It is true that, if the accounts are faithful, he allowed himself to be carried away to trifling depreciatory expressions concerning one subject or another, when he was opposed; but he never faltered in his original convictions. The replies which we learn from the most faithful reporter—a completely accurate report can hardly be expected, but the one styled "according to Mark" is the most reliable—the objections and tests presented to him rest all on the basis which he occupied. The Sadducees took him to task concerning the resurrection which he distinctly emphasized with his assertion of the entrance of the future world, of the kingdom of Heaven. With the scoffing question, "Moses wrote unto us, if a man's brother die and leave his wife behind him and leave no children, that his brother take his wife and raise up seed unto his brother;—now there were seven brothers, and the first took a wife, and dying, left no seed; and the second took her and died, neither left he any seed; and the third likewise, and the seven had her and left no seed; last of all, the woman died also;—in the resurrection therefore, when they shall rise, whose wife shall she be?"—with that scoffing question, cunningly calculated to meet his assertion of the speedy appearance of the future world and the resurrection, the Sadducees met him. He replied, "The future world will appear, but there will be no more marrying nor giving in marriage." When a Pharisee heard that and found that the answer was a good one, he asked, "Which is the first commandment of all?" and Jesus replied, "The first of all commandments is, Hear O Israel, God is our Lord, God is One (this beginning of his answer is found only in Mark, the other Evangelists—a very significant pointer—have omitted it) and thou shalt love God thy Lord with all thy heart and with all thy soul and with all thy mind and with all thy strength. This is the first commandment. And the second is like, namely this: Thou shalt love thy neighbor as thyself." There was nothing new in that. And the Pharisee replied, "Well, Master, thou hast said the truth: for there is one God; and there is none other but he: And to love him with all the heart and with all the understanding and with all the soul and with all the strength, and to love his neighbor as himself, is more than all whole burnt-offerings and sacrifices." The Pharisee raised no objection, for what he had heard corresponded fully to his own conviction. That reply of the Pharisee is also to be found only in Mark; the other later Gospels shape it to suit their purposes.

If the author of Christianity is represented as having taught the specific doctrine: "God is a God of love and not of anger and vengeance," it is likewise a later addition which is not found in the book of the more faithful narrator. What could be added to the saying of Hillel: "The Merciful inclineth the scale toward mercy?" If Jesus' utterances concerning the purely moral relations of men to each other are indeed faithfully reported, they either present nothing new, or whatever is new, bears such a diseased character as belongs to a diseased age. "Thou shalt love thy neighbor as thyself" was a saying to which the Pharisee gave his approval, "Well, Master, thou hast said the truth!" But in the varying reports, Jesus is said also to have praised poverty and contempt of the world and everything that proceeds from this world; to have repudiated cheerful participation in the affairs of this world. Such doctrines are not taught by Phariseeism; on the contrary, it announces this principle: "The world is an ante-chamber for the future one; prepare thyself well in the ante-chamber, that thou mayest appear properly in the reception room. One hour in the future world is sweeter than all enjoyments in this one, but also, one hour in this world spent in the study of the Law and the performance of good deeds, is better than all the pleasures in the future world." If such cheerful and energetic participation in the affairs of this world, undertaken in honor and honesty, is to be shunned and everything earthly to be despised, it must be a morbid tendency, unless it can be explained by the belief that the future world, organized quite differently, was near at hand. If an alleged morality is to suppress every sense of justice, if the doctrine is to prevail: "Whosoever shall smite thee on thy right cheek, turn to him the other also" (in other words, Do not only suffer, but lose all sense of honor) and also: "If anyone take away thy coat, let him have thy cloak also," if that be the new doctrine proclaimed by Jesus (*Jesus* is the Greek pronunciation of the name Joshua; Joshua, the son of Nun, is called Jesus by the Greek translators, and so is Jesus Sirach), then it is either the product of a diseased period which perverts all order and destroys all notions of right, or it proceeds from the transfer of an entirely different future world into the present.

Thus the movement started at first, and no new departure in religion is exhibited, although the impulse to one was contained in it. It was the belief in the fulfilment of the Messianic hopes entertained by Pharisean Judaism of that period. Whatever else is related concerning the author of Christianity belongs to that class of myths or legends which we have alluded to in a former place. Whenever legend fails to make the outlines of a person sharper and more distinct, whenever it fails to draw its matter from the distinctive character and essence of the man and thereby throws more light upon him; but when, on the contrary, it adorns him so much that he becomes unrecognizable, far exalted beyond all individual distinctness and *volatilizes* him into a mere abstraction, then the legend is a formation of the imagination which in exuberant growth shapes things out of the dim fancies of the period and wraps them in an ever deepening darkness.

That the first author of Christianity found believing adherents was the natural effect of the conditions of his time. At first, the educated and intelligent were not attracted by him. In Galilee, a small band who stood low and were despised by the bulk of the population—many of them mercenaries of the government, publicans that gathered the taxes for the hated empire, upon whom the whole weight of contempt rested, who were shunned on all sides; they, the low and vulgar, willingly listened to his announcement. "They that are whole have no need of the physician, but they that are sick," he said. And those sick ones were gathered around him. Soon he did not confine his addresses to those exiles from the population; his fame spread, and he ventured to move to the metropolis of Judea. But soon, charges were made against him. Here and there he also met approval, he was hailed with, "Hosanna, son of David." For such he must needs be, if he meant to be a Messiah. He was brought before a court, and we are not told that a large number of followers were with him, so that they would have been afraid to pronounce judgment against him. The judgment had to be executed by the procurator. Pilate asked him, "Art thou the King of the Jews?" and he replied, "Thou sayest it." He did not deny it. According to a later account, he added, "My kingdom is not of this world"—of course not, but of the future which will soon come and appear. "Verily I say unto you, there be some standing here which shall not taste of death till they see the Kingdom of God"—"there be many here who shall see it how the end of things shall be fulfilled." To Pilate, the whole matter seemed strange, unintelligible doings, not important enough to demand his rigorous interference, but the people to whom he left it to pray for his release, according to an ancient custom, giving them the right to obtain pardon for a criminal before a festival, repudiated all fellowship with him and refused their intercession. Thus a judgment was pronounced which could not have been different in a time of such commotion, which threatened to be made still more miserable by the announcement of lying hopes—for such they were to those who did not believe in him—and by the implied attempt at revolution. Imbued with the religious convictions of his time, he raised himself into a position which was not accorded to him, represented the hope of the future as fulfilled and embodied in himself, raised expectations of a complete change in all political conditions, and ignored the whole civil arrangement of the time, even if he did not start a revolt. Under such circumstances, the verdict could not have been otherwise; he was crucified, as was Judah of Gaulonitis and his followers at a previous time. The adherents of Jesus at first were stunned by that issue, but not shaken in their belief. Of course this world moves on in its course, he also dies; this world must hate him, it had power yet for a short time, but the Heavenly Kingdom comes, then he rises again, the resurrection will start with him and then become general. That faith prevailed even during his lifetime, it could not be shaken by his death; on the contrary, it was but natural that it would appear more vividly in the foreground. He must rise again—he will surely rise again—and soon the opinion was arrived at: He *is* risen—he is gone to heaven and will appear again, wrapt in the clouds of heaven at the general resurrection with the entrance of the Heavenly Kingdom. That course of development is perfectly natural, there is nothing strange about it; and his disciples see him, waiting day by day for his glorious return. That is the first disposition to the origin of Christianity, the germ out of which the mighty tree comes forth, to which the other factors become joined, to gradually transform the sect, feeble in its incipiency, into a ruling power.

X.

The Evolution of Christianity.

By the side of the various tendencies then existing within Judaism, by the side of Sadduceeism, of Phariseeism with the profound commotion within it, of Essenism, of Zealotism, of the following of Juda of Gaulonitis, and some other minor groups, all within the small territory of Judea—a proof of the deepest excitement of all forces, of a severe struggle, both spiritual and political—by the side of those various tendencies, another new one sprouted from the soil of Pharisean Judaism, that of *the fulfilled Messianism.* The Greek translation of that term is *Christianity;* Messiah, the anointed (*Christos*) was the designation of the king who was expected to inaugurate the future world, to bring about, while destroying the entire present ancient world, the conditions in which God alone shall be King, and the Heavenly Kingdom, or the Kingdom of God, proclaimed and introduced by that Messiah, shall prevail. Thus the belief in the fulfilled Messiahship, or Christianity, presented the claim that the new world was now beginning, or had already begun, that the Messiah had appeared, that he had died within the old world, in fact, had to die in it, but would rise, had even risen, and would soon reappear in the clouds of heaven, in order to completely arrange the new world, to force all mankind to submit to the Kingdom of God, and to call a new race into existence, even outside of the present disrupted and corrupted civil laws. Such was the new tendency which now came to the surface within Judaism, and starting from the very soil of Phariseeism.

The new feature was this, that the event which all, or at least the greater part of the Jewish people regarded as something to come in a far-distant time, and therefore sketched in indistinct outline, was now believed to have been fully accomplished and would soon show up in its full glory. That was the first phase of Christianity. That tendency could not make much growth within Judaism in Palestine. The old time was indeed a gloomy and hard one for the Jews there; that the old world was doomed to perish, was a belief which afforded them comfort and fortitude; but that it had already perished, that a new world had already appeared, was a great step from reality into imagination, which the facts and actual conditions most emphatically refuted. "No, the new world has not yet appeared, though we most fervently hope for it," was the general verdict. Besides, the minds were burdened with too many heavy cares to indulge in the play of the imagination that the future had actually come. Every day brought new troubles; as often as the sun arose, it shone upon new struggles and new hardships—all energies were called for, not to indulge in speculation and to strengthen a belief which stamped ideals of the future as present realities, but to give undivided attention to the actual present with its burdens and oppression. Accordingly, the belief in the actual fulfilment of the Messianic hope spread very little within the boundaries of Palestine. The historian of that time, Josephus Flavius, makes no mention of the author of the tendency and of the tendency itself, while he treats extensively of all the others, especially of those which were of a very recent date: that of Juda of Gaulonitis, that of Theudas, of the Zealots, and gives a full account of the persons and their purposes. The few lines found in the present shape of his book concerning the author of Christianity, bear the most distinct mark of a later interpolation; the brief words are in the fullest conflict with the character of the whole book, are without connection, a fragmentary patch, not the work of an author who elaborates the task proposed to himself, according to a certain plan.

Within Palestine, the tendency could not gain an extensive spread. The lower class of the people, by nature prone to believe in wonders, and greedy of miracles, who, because pushed to the rear by the better class, gladly take up something new—the lower class were the first to take and follow the new lead. That miracle-mad class creates its fulfilled prophecies and miracles with the greatest ease, in luxurious abundance. Accordingly the new doctrine was almost entirely covered with the most luxuriant creepers of the superstition of the lower class of the time. The belief in *Demons* who can be found everywhere in innumerable multitudes, as evil spirits infest the atmosphere, take possession of men and infatuate them, but can be driven out by incantation—that crude belief in demons may now and then be found in Jewish writings, but it forms by no means their center and substance. But such matters occupy a very great portion of the records of incipient Christianity; the stories of the work of the Devil, that he possesses humanity, that his hosts enter men as demons, and that the possessed are cured again, almost crowd out everything else.

Such was its course in Palestine.

It fared differently among the Jews residing elsewhere. From ancient time, Jews had been living among the Grecians, had formed congregations, and their numbers were swelled by emigration from Judea so much the more, the gloomier the conditions became there. Although those Grecian Jews felt deep sympathy with the sufferings of their brethren in their old home country; although every woe that befell Palestine, found a responsive chord in their hearts; although they looked with reverence toward the holy land which ever remained to them their parent soil, yet they did not have to go through the struggles or fight the battles themselves. While arms clashed in Judea, while all energies were called upon, day after day, to attend to the demands of the day, to endure its labors and hardships, to make front against vexations and irritations; while thus in Judea, mind and strength were directed entirely towards the present, the Grecian Jews were but passive spectators who from afar beheld with profound grief, perhaps derided as aliens with different customs and ceremonies by the nations among whom they lived, yet from a safe distance the ruin of their parent country and the probable loss of their spiritual center. Now, as they were also looking with hope and trust for the new time in which they were to be rid of those ills that were with them of rather a mental nature, they were much nearer to the belief that such hopes would soon be fulfilled, or even that they were fulfilled. They were not pressed down by the burdens of the day, they breathed more freely; hence hope had freer play. Besides, the announcements of the enthusiastic votaries were more readily believed in the distance than among those who had seen everything pass before their own eyes. Thus it happened that Messianic Judaism proclaimed as already fulfilled, found a far greater number of adherents within Grecian-Jewish colonies even in the very beginning. And among them the new belief met again a new spiritual element. The Grecian Jews possessed a Greco-philosophical trait which they had interwoven with their religious belief. The religious speculations tended towards the recognition of a divine reflex, a *Logos*, the Divine Thought which, as emanation from God, had called the world into existence and keeps up the connection with it; filled with the spiritual idea of Judaism, philosophy attempted to place God beyond all contact with the material world, to put him so far beyond all that is finite and temporal that a certain connecting link was found necessary for making it possible to deduce the creation and preservation of the world from God. The Logos, the Thought, the Reflex, the Idea emanating from God, was the *Demiourgos*, the creator of the world. Whether he was to be regarded as an individual being, or as a mere idea, remained undecided; it was a habit begun by Plato, to keep the idea suspended between something actually existing and something merely imaginary. Now, the Thought, the Idea, or the "Word," all of which meanings are in the Greek term *Logos*, was in a way, the connecting link, the medium or mediator between God and the world, and was, as Philo and others expressed it in bold poetic figure, the only begotten (*Monogenes*) of God — a bold, poetic expression, but justified by their philosophic system. The *Thought* born of God, but always remaining with God, could justly be called the one and only begotten son of God. That conception and its figure of speech had spread afar and become common property, and leaning upon expressions in Holy Writ, such as the word of God, the glory of God, and other similar terms, it did not remain confined to the Grecian Jews, but passed also into the vernacular of Palestine. Here, *Logos* was *Memra*, the "Word," the emanation from God to guide mankind, the medium or means for all that produces effects upon the senses, and the Chaldean version uses the word "Memra" when it seeks to avoid sensible, corporeal attributes to God. Now, a new world has come, the future world is becoming a reality. The world had first been created through the Logos, through its mediation. If then the ancient world, created by the Logos, passes away and a new world takes its place, if the future world becomes the present reality, can that have been created by anything else than the Logos? To be sure, the Messiah is the Logos, the Word, the only begotten son of God! The Messianic idea is thus transplanted upon another soil, the views are transformed, and the Son of Man is changed into the Son of God, at first only as an idea, as a philosophical thought; but in the belief of the multitude, he soon becomes the *real* Son of God. The Son of God creates a new world; the old one is destroyed; by his appearance, a new one is being inaugurated. By his appearance—should he indeed have been born like an ordinary man? The Palestinian Messiah is a descendant of David, is born like any other son of man, enters the world with a sublime mission from God, yet without being more than a man. But should the Logos, the Son of God, enter into the world as a child of human parents—the Logos a child? the Logos born in human manner? Are those not contradictory terms? If generation and birth can be spoken of in connection with him, they can not be understood as ordinary, natural events. He is the Son of God; of course he enters the flesh, but in a miraculous manner: a mother gives him birth, but the Spirit of God is his father. That was a transformation which necessarily grew from the contact with Grecian Judaism. And if such was his entrance, how about his exit from the world? The Messiah is a man, even if vested with divine power, yet he ever remains an instrument in the hand of God. He can die, can be killed, he appears again, he will inaugurate the new world, he rises again, he is risen again. But how can the only begotten son of God, who bears within himself the full power of God, be killed? Why of course he can not be killed by human power, but he may die, if he wills it himself—he can voluntarily give himself up an apparent sacrifice. The old world must perish, it was also begotten by the Logos—Adam represented the archetype of the human race, Adam bore within him the whole of mankind. According to that philosophic system which holds that everything is produced by a process of emanation and effluence, and that the higher contains the lower, in the first man, in Adam, lay also the whole human race. Now, if the human race has become so corrupt, if the old world has turned so evil that it must perish, such a condition must be referred back to Adam. He sinned, and through his sin the entire succeeding race became diseased, and in order to be made whole, the old world must die and a new one arise. But, if the old world must die, must not all men perish with it? No, the Logos himself, the creator of the human race, dies for it. By means of his incarnation he takes upon himself the whole punishment of humanity, sacrifices himself for the human race; but his divinity remains, and henceforward fills the new mankind.

Such were the new conceptions which developed themselves out of the Jewish-Grecian philosophy, making thoroughgoing changes in the idea concerning God and coming very near to going beyond the bounds of Judaism. And concerning man also, those new conceptions produced a mighty change. Judaism teaches that man dies for his sin, that everyone receives his punishment for his own transgressions; that God is a forgiving and merciful God who, though He allows no sin to go unpunished, yet works no universal destruction on account of sin, and least of all, visits the sin of a man upon others, even if his near relatives. Necessarily, a totally different view arose upon that point. In one man —of course in the first of all men—all men had sinned; guilt had been bequeathed, all bore the disease wrought by that guilt, it clung to them as fetters from which they could not relieve themselves. *That was the second phase of Christianity.* Such ideas are foreign to Judaism, they are merely grafted upon it. Some mystical speculative minds might have favored them, but a general acceptance could not be effected, even among the Grecian Jews.

While in the first phase of Christianity, *the Kingdom of God* as brought about the human Messiah is emphasized, in the second phase, the *Son of God* is brought to the front. Of the miraculous conception and birth connected with that transformation of ideas, the most faithful report "according to Mark" knows nothing; even if in its present form—rarely enough—here and there the expression "Son of God" occurs, it occupied pretty much the first stage of development in which there was no necessity for such an idea. Only in the second phase the miraculous generation makes its appearance, and still later, in another account, which stands wholly on Grecian footing, in the one bearing the name of John, we find the full, plain statement that the Logos became flesh and appeared on earth; that as the vicar of the whole human race he had taken their sins upon himself and expiated them by his death. Such was the second phase of Christianity, and it had thereby almost ceased to represent a tendency within Judaism, however much it kept still within its pale. For as yet we find no efforts made to break out through the barriers of Judaism, to effect changes and transformations, such as to declare that the law was abolished and that its provisions had lost their validity. Of course, an impulse thereto lay in the very root of the matter. The Messianic time—such is the expression all through ancient Judaism—is to be quite different from the present, all special statutes and ordinances will cease, all separation is to vanish. Thus there was in the very belief that the Messiah had come, that a new world had appeared, the impulse to transform all practices in life. And yet, thus far the demand is not uttered.

But the more the new tendency, the belief in the new Messiahship placed itself beyond the pale of Judaism, the more it came into conflict with its essence and fundamental principles, so much the more it must have felt the pressure to go outside of it. The belief had adopted ideas which, the farther they were developed, came in the most glaring conflict with the basic principles of Judaism; to remain standing still at that point was impossible; there was but this alternative, either to pass beyond the pale of Judaism, or to cease to exist. Compromise was out of the question. The impulse for spreading outside of Judaism was natural. If the Logos had indeed appeared, if a new world had really come, that new world must form itself out of itself through the belief in the Messiah who had come, who had risen to reform the world; through him alone, even if starting from Judaism, the new world must be built up. A man of force and decision first uttered that word, he had the courage to break down the bridge. It was *Paul*, a Grecian Jew, not a disciple of the author of Christianity, who had never been in personal touch with Jesus who had always with determination proclaimed and emphasized the continuance of Judaism in all its parts. Paul at first persecuted the adherents of the new tendency; he was a man of thoroughgoing work who could brook no half-way doing. Either to oppose the new departure with all determination, or to carry it through to its extremest consequences, such was his character. On the way to Damascus, that is, to the Grecian cities, a new idea struck him: "How, if in the tendency as it has been developed by Hellenism there be a truth, and by that truth a new order of things, a new world could be inaugurated? Judaism teaches that the Messiah is destined for all mankind; the Logos is the creator of the world, the creator of all mankind—well then, forth to all mankind! Down with all barriers! Let the new Messianic Judaism take them all!" Such was Paul's conclusion, and with that began *the third phase of Christianity.*

A new formation now arose. Paul constituted himself the Apostle to the Gentiles; he first ventured to address the people outside of Judaism, to preach the new doctrine to those who were outside of the movement and unaffected by the course of its development and must have been startled by his announcement. He carried the pure doctrine concerning God into the pagan world and made the Jewish moral and religious ideas the common property of mankind, but without the aids to their observance as formulated in clear and certain laws. That was sufficient for those people, and the general spread of those truths of Judaism was a mighty step in the advance of mankind. The various historically evolved laws were not known to them, and would have been an intolerable burden. For a declaration of their abolition or invalidity no justification was called for, for them; but for Paul's own conscience and for the believers won over from the Jews, it was necessary. Granted even that the God-given law has lost its binding force in this Messianic time, does it not remain a sanctifying power, does it not exalt those who still cling to it and observe it? Granted even that it should not be imposed upon Gentiles as a binding rule, could it be taken away from the Jews who were born into such obligations? Should it not remain at least for them as a means of higher sanctification? Should the express declaration of its invalidity not be postponed at least until the return of the Messiah and the complete establishment of the new world? Paul was undecided. Although the bold idea of uniting the whole human race under the banner of one belief had silenced all doubts within his own heart, it was not so easy to move his Jewish brethren in the faith, from their view. They had already merged the ancient practices with the new faith. Why then, should they discontinue them? Paul hesitated, and drew a distinction: "Let the Jews cling to their ancient accustomed law; for the Gentiles, the new belief is sufficient." But that brought a dangerous cleft into the new faith and Paul's entire plan would have been wrecked thereby. Such a double-headed arrangement of votaries of the same belief, producing in itself confusion, bore the germ of dissolution in its own bosom. By it, the Gentiles did not appear as citizens of equal rights in the new Empire of Religion; the Jews remained the privileged class of saints by birth and the continued observance of the law, the Gentile believers were but an unholy appendage. And just they were the main support of Paul.

Thus Paul was forced to take a further step. It was not

sufficient to designate the "Law" as superfluous, as dispensable, it must be entirely abolished, it must be declared an obstacle to holiness. The present observance of the law, such was his next proceeding, is not merely unmeritorious, it is the result of a defective faith, the true believer is not even *permitted* to practice the ordinances of the Law. How should the observance of the Law be a sin? Was it not given by God? Was it not binding in former days, and should now its observance be even sinful? Yes indeed, Paul made response, the Law was given by God, but in behalf of sinful mankind to the Jews; it is in a measure, the result of sin; it is a "yoke," but not a sweet one, it is a hard and heavy yoke. The new faith is a sweet yoke, a blessing for all mankind; the old law was a curse, a scourge for the Jewish people; the ban is removed in consequence of the vicarious death of Jesus; the whole human race, the Jews as well as the Gentiles, are now sanctified through the *Holy Spirit* which has been poured out over all mankind. And will ye be willing to remain further under the curse, under the scourge, now when a blessing, a kinder treatment awaits you? Break the Law! If you desire to be the saints, you must fully acknowledge the fulfilled salvation. Away with circumcision, away with the dietary laws! The former is a token of the old covenant, a new one has been established; the latter consider the Gentile meats as idolatrous sacrificial repasts, but they have now become feasts of love and sweet communion.

That line of thought was, on the one hand, the most logical consistency, but contained also, on the other hand, the most trenchant severity against Judaism, because not alone its forms, while appropriating its fundamental principles, were represented as worthless, but because it was violently divested of its entire profound intrinsic substance. A reconciliation of such views with Judaism, even if representing it as a divine institution but merely for the past, could be established only by the most artful dialectics, which Paul practised by both oral instruction and epistles. He created an imposing effect, but did not carry matters so easily. A violent struggle arose between the so-called Judaizing Christians and the Gentile Christians. The doctrine of Judaizing Christianity—i. e., Messianism joined to continued observance of the whole Jewish Law—was predominating; the new (Paulinian) tendency seeking to obtrude itself upon it, was contended against, not alone by the Jews, but also by the Judaizing Christians. The new Christians were called Balaamites, men who attempted to introduce idolatrous sacrifices among the Jews, as Balaam had sought to lead the Israelites astray by idolatrous practices. Violent struggles and frequent splits occurred within the various congregations; mutual concessions were made and peace was restored; only after a long time, after many ups and downs in the fight, Gentile Christianity prevailed, as it was in the nature of the case. Within Judaism, the contradiction of the ideas was too glaring—there could be no harmony of mind in an individual who attempted to be a Jew on the one side, and tried to accept for the present, Messiah and Logos ideas—to be a worshiper of the One God and to make an addition by a new element of God. The conflict did not last long; Judaizing Christianity succumbed to pagan-Gentile Christianity which was *the third phase of Christianity.* Heathendom had formerly been held to be unclean, impure, unholy; now the Holy Spirit—a genuine Jewish idea in itself—entered the new world, purifying and sanctifying it. The third phase was now complete, and with that belief in the *Holy Ghost* which pours out over all mankind and acts as a creative personality, comes into prominence. Thus there was in three phases of development which could not be parted from one another and which were bound to run together into one complete course, the belief in the Trinity. God and His Kingdom was the first phase; the Son of God to establish the Kingdom, was the second; the Holy Spirit to purify all mankind, constituted the third; their connection into a unit thenceforward formed the essence of the belief. Christianity, thus fully developed, was destined to enter heathendom.

But could it indeed enter heathendom—were the pagans prepared and inclined to adopt it? Let us now cast a glance at the pagan world. We no longer stand on the ground of ancient Hellenism. The educated classes of the time are no longer illumined by philosophy, no longer develop their ideas with an original creative energy, as at the time of the ancient Greeks—we behold a very different age. Roman spirit rules that world, everything proceeds from Rome, her hand rests heavily on all nations. Rome has a great mission to fulfill in the world's history, and is fulfilling it, somewhat in the same manner as absolutism works in the evolution of the state. Absolutism, that rule of might by one man without regard to the rights of all the rest, which is so clearly designated by the words of Louis XIV.: "*L'etat, c'est moi*"—"I am the state"—as a form of government, represents, properly speaking, no idea at all; it has no innate justification for investing one man with all possible power, and divesting all the others of their natural rights, yet absolutism has its place in the historic evolution—it was its mission to level mankind, to produce an equality of the various prerogatives that had grown up as *estates* with all their perverted phenomena; to destroy at one blow, all those prerogatives that had become an obstacle in the world's progress; to convert all into slaves first, in order that afterwards all might become free citizens, and that every one of them might have free chance according to his ability and merit. A similar mission was that of Rome in the history of the world. Rome united the world under one and the same oppression, brought all nations into servitude, forced their approach to one another, and brought them close together. Rome did not develop from within herself any peculiar native spiritual power or ideas; whatever she accomplished in the realm of the mind was imitation, was adopted, and merely adopted superficially and poorly. Philosophy dragged on a sickly life among the Romans, and was popularized in the most sober conceptions; all other mental and spiritual products that gained authority, had been received from without, borrowed, transplanted upon Roman soil, but were not sustained by creative vigor, did not originate from native excellence.

If mental and spiritual life in general did not occupy a

high plane, it was but natural that the idea of God, the doctrine concerning gods, was in a still worse condition. The mythology of the Greeks was not the strongest point of their culture, of their spiritual life, but yet there is a certain ideality in it; it bears the impress of the law of beauty; it contains ideas which, though they are wrapped in corporeal forms and as such sensible phenomena were not deeply rooted in the mind of the people, could nevertheless give the impulse to a higher conception, and philosophy deepened that conception. In Rome, mythology was something bare, a kind of home-made product. The gods of the house, the Lares and Penates, were to a certain degree the center of religious life; the boundaries of the fields received consecration; the affairs of every-day life, of the rude popular power, were personified and worshiped as gods. And when with advancing culture, with the contact with Hellenism, not alone general science, though in rather faded state, but also an acquaintance with Greek mythology entered Rome, a curious mixture took place: the Greek divinities were identified with those of ancient Rome, the former were forced down from their ideal heights, and the latter were divested of their originality. Thenceforward there were but shadows that the people adored.

Then even in Hellenism, a tendency arose to divest Greek mythology of all poetic character, and very soon Rome was ready to adopt the same. Euhemeros was the name of a Grecian author who reduced mythology to the level of most vulgar rationalism. The gods—thus he taught—were great kings who were glorified and raised into high position by later admirers. All that is related of them is but embellishment of common events which we must trace back to their plain, natural realities. If, for example, Kronos is said to have swallowed his own children and to have been dethroned by Jupiter, he makes it out to be the history of a king in ancient times, when human sacrifices were in vogue, who was dethroned by another king that abolished such immolation of human beings. In such way everything in Greek mythology was flattened out, divested of its deeper meaning; for after all, poetic thought, even if clothed in fanciful garb of the imagination, is more profound than such platitude. That conception soon invaded Rome; the book of Euhemeros was translated into Latin, and his views became predominant. The old customs still prevailed, the old priestly institution, the ancient sacrificial service, the examination of the entrails of the sacrificed animals, the observation of the flight of birds—all were still in practice, but the belief in them no longer existed. It became almost a proverbial saying that two augurs meeting had to do all in their power not to burst into laughter. If the gods were but human beings, it was naturally an easy step to make gods out of men, and it came about that the emperors with their passions and follies were adored as gods, and they demanded and received such divine worship. To such a low point all religious life had sunk in Rome and in the world in which she ruled.

But human nature is not satisfied with such a state of things. As there arose bold disbelief on the one side, so started on the other side a longing for another faith, a desire for a higher idea, for something wonderful that does not meet the eye, day after day in the natural course of events. Alongside of disbelief, superstition arose; for such is human nature that, by the side of luxuriant materialism, rapping spirits are honored. Thus Rome became full of a number of the most varying and heterogeneous ways of divine worship. The Oriental divinities which, by their novelty and their mysterious character, offered stimulation to the imagination, were in great preference. Judaism also spread in Rome to a considerable extent, but it was too serious and too earnest a religion to be accepted by the degenerate Roman world at large. Now, a new belief presented itself, which was in close touch with heathendom, and yet was altogether different. A man who was at the same time a god, was the center; but the manner and form of his appearance, the doctrine connected with the belief in him, had impressed upon that new religion a character such as had, until then, not been presented to them. It must have made a deep impression, acted as a caustic, and gave new elasticity to the enervated minds. And thus the doctrine of Christianity, in its third phase, when it had become accessible to the whole human race, made its entrance into heathendom. It went in, not as a triumphator, not as a power that strikes like a bolt of lightning illuminating the minds and overpowering, but very gradually, after being fought against for a long time, and only after centuries, raised to the throne and made dominating the religion by an event that has not yet been fully cleared up. After a long protracted struggle, it penetrated into the heathen world—it was then Christianity completely severed from Judaism. It went its own way, and we are not called upon to farther follow its history. Yet it is for us to give an answer to the question, Is there any task left to Judaism by the side of Christianity which has now become a religion of the world? Or is Judaism in a state of decay, an ancient ruin that should be abandoned? The reply to that question which forces itself upon us requires, before we follow the history of Judaism any farther, that we take yet another look at Christianity.

XI.

Christianity as an Ecclesiastical World-Power. The Destruction of Jewish Nationality.

The inspiring proclamation which the prophets of Judaism had sent into the world with the most determined confidence—namely, that a time shall come when God alone shall be acknowledged, when peace based upon justice shall unite and gladden all mankind—that glance at an ennobled future of truth and human brotherhood contained a decided energy which afforded Judaism durability and courage and conferred upon it a never-failing self-confidence going hand in hand with the very development of mankind. In direct contrast to Greek mythology, which places the golden age in the very cradle of the human race, and lets it be followed by times more and more worthless, Judaism preserves the sublime belief that mankind is the fertile soil out of which the seed of the spirit shall ripen into an abundant harvest. Hence also the mighty perseverance displayed by Judaism; and this very hope has proved its preserving energy throughout the centuries. But now, if such hope is not merely hailed as one the fruition of which yet was to be in a distant future, if it is announced as one soon to be fulfilled, if times appear when men boldly proclaim, "The present world is broken down to its very foundation—the new world, the Messianic time must and will soon take its place," then that confidence, that glance at the speedily approaching future in which a complete betterment and transformation was to take place, created a courage and a strength which could make front and battle against the greatest obstacles. We beheld that phenomenon in the time of the Maccabean wars which, although a sore trial, yet could not break the popular strength, because the sure conviction of a change of the conditions living in the minds of the people, produced an unconquerable, unshaken confidence. But now, if even the proclamation is made, "The old world has perished, is broken up, the new one has already appeared; a new human race, as it was promised, now lives and shall live henceforth"—that belief in oneself, that confidence entertained by mankind or a portion of mankind, such increased self-consciousness contains a power which naturally invested that portion of mankind, not only with an intensive elasticity to persevere even under the most trying conditions, but even to present an imposing front to the world at large.

A sublime self-confidence, the bold assertion of one's own power, bears within itself such an energy that the rest of the world is astonished and shaken thereby. We see such an effect in the history of even individuals. If a man confronts the world with the full conviction of his own worth, if he has the belief in himself, he will obtain much, his bold demand will actually compel many to yield to him; his belief in himself will beget also the belief of others in him. Review the great characters in the world's history and you will find this generally proven: they became great because they presented themselves with the claim of being great. When Caesar said, "This ship carries Caesar and his destiny," such an expression of his full conviction, that the destiny of the whole world was interlaced with his own, contained an imposing power. When the French Revolution entered into the world's history with the determined conviction, "The old times have perished, a completely new time must come," when it announced itself as a New Era with which a new computation of time must begin, its successes did not come so much from the new ideas which it created, nor from the positive truths which it proclaimed, but from its very determination, from its belief in itself. That constituted its triumphant power that gave it the impulse to spread all over the world. If it was indeed a new world, the whole earth must be subjected to it, no barrier of any nationality must impede its onward march. That constituted also the power of Christianity when it presented itself to the world.

Christianity proclaimed, "I *am* the new mankind, the new world is come, the old world is dead and broken up." That was a word making an epoch; and if the author of Christianity is represented as having said, "I am the truth, the way, and the life," the words are probably apocryphal, the idea and the claims with which Christianity represented itself to the world found their full expression in them. I am a new power, a new world, all must yield to me; before me there was nothing, before me—such was the assertion—there were but sin, decay, and spiritual perversity; all the wisdom of former times is but tinkling folly, all their virtue but shining vice. Even while it puts its structure on the foundation of Judaism, acknowledged the ancient sacred scriptures of the Jews, adopted their contents, it yet announced—and if it is not found in the earlier writings, it is the full consequence of its doctrine and is contained in the teaching of Paul—that the author of Christianity had to descend into hell in order to save all the damned souls of former times. All those patriarchs, devout men, prophets, preachers of truth and religion, were acknowledged of course, yet they were doomed to spiritual death. "For with me," such was the assertion, "the new race begins, and all that existed before is vain, and not only vain, but entirely corrupt." Such boldness contains a force which not only exerts an inspiring influence upon its adherents, but also has a startling effect upon outsiders. And if such claims happen to strike an age and a community that are really decayed and in a decline, they take them as productive of full health. Mankind at the time, had become severed from its former phases of development; it had arrived at a point where decay commences; its vigor formerly existing in Hellenism and indirectly transmitted to Rome, was exhausted, had lost its impulse. From the decay in all conditions they found but one way of salvation, and that way was disavowal of this world, in casting off everything that appeared unsound. With all that, Christianity had to struggle for several centuries before it prevailed, as it was bound to prevail in that degenerate Grecian-Roman world. Whether it would have been able to effect a reformation and new creation within the empire, is a question unanswered by history. It swept away, like a wind-storm, all the withered leaves of the ancient culture, and covered up all fragments of the ancient magnificent mental structure; but whether it would then have been able to construct new edifices on the same ground, we may just as well answer negatively, as it is claimed affirmatively by others; history leaves us without the slightest intimation on that point. We may perhaps find in Byzantinism, which represents a continued development of the Grecian world within Christianity, such an intimation of an answer to the query where the world would have been driven if the ancient elements had been permitted to develop under the rule of Christianity—that answer would not be favorable, of course.

But the new world was destined to take a different course. Antiquity was annihilated, not only in its remnants, by Christianity, it was also in part destroyed in its very elements, thoroughly riddled and mixed up with new material. The migration of nations brought a host of uncivilized new people, still possessing pristine vigor, into that ancient world. And there Christianity unfolded its special important power; there it fulfilled its great mission within mankind. There no ancient recollections were to be wiped out—those nations had no history in the true sense of the word—they possessed no peculiar culture of their own, but they were characters of primitive vigor. To meet that, and to thunder into their ears, their minds, their conscience, "Your force is nothing, your intrepidity is wickedness, your natural propensities are sin, all your creature endowments are degeneracy"—to tame those iron bodies, and make gentle those obstinate spirits, to startle those rude consciences, that was the task of a world-power, of a power that asserted of itself, "I am all in all; all your actions, all your efforts, all your boasts of your bodily strength with which you might confront an enervated world, all those are vain. You must bend your necks under my yoke." Such an autocratic edict prepared the nature of those people for a truly spiritual and moral culture, the religious and moral elements that were thrown out of Christianity into that virgin soil found a fertile ground there, receptive to produce mature fruit. This is the grand work of Christianity, that it met as a spiritual power a raw product of nature, a power that boasted merely of stalwart arms and iron strength of bodies. And Christianity executed at the same time, its grand mission by this, that it united the nations hitherto living in isolation and stupid seclusion, that it entwined the bond of humanity around those separate and selfishly closed-up elements, infused into them ideas of a common interest, and wove them together into a great human aspiration. That is the power of Christianity.

But that which was, and still is, its power, is at the same time its weakness. It made the assertion, "I am the new world, all that existed before is nothing," and accordingly smashed and destroyed everything humane, beautiful, and noble, that earlier times had produced. It is not due to Christianity, if anything has been saved out of the wrecking. For it opposed with a perfect mania for destruction, not only what was idolatrous and pagan as such, but all the mental treasures of Antiquity too—all was adjudged to be the work of the devil, all must be destroyed. The genius of mankind has ordered with more charity, has saved it from losing it all, it has saved productions of the art and the science of earlier times, some in fragments, others in full, fine form, in order that later times may be elevated and fertilized through them; the genius of mankind has protected it against such complete self-destruction, and that too, in the most determined opposition to the demands of Christianity, and has shown that it is mightier than the latter. Christianity disavowed the old world, denied both its proper existence and its right of existence—all right was to begin with itself and from thenceforth it never tolerated anything to exist by its side as long as it had the power of suppression. "There is nothing outside of me, I am mankind, I rule mankind, all the actions of the world must be under my superintendence, must be according to my rule," such is its ever-recurring demand. Every development in the human world which would take its course by the side of Christianity, was designated by it as a sin, as heresy, and fought against with all determination. When we contemplate the world's history with an unprejudiced eye, we find the assertion that Christianity is the mother of modern culture a decided error. The Christian Religion, the Church representing its body, has always fought against science, she has invariably declared every light that would shine beside her own, to be a will-o'-the-wisp, false light that must be put out.

For that reason, its power could not gain full entrance into those portions of mankind whose native character was still healthy, and which still produced from within themselves a healthy development. Even paganism made a long fight with Christianity, not because it so highly honored its idols and considered them as nearer to truth than the doctrine of Christianity. That belief had long been shaken, that struggle proceeded from the higher culture among the pagans. Their philosophic schools disputed the teachings of the new religion with an enthusiasm born of their love of science. The neo-platonic, neo-pythagorean, and other schools protested with all their might against the glorification of ignorance, against the praise given to the poor in spirit, against the lustre that was claimed to attach to the lack of wisdom. Christianity had great difficulty to force that power of a higher culture to yield. Only fire and sword, the greatest physical horrors, not the power of the spirit, finally annihilated its fragments. Yet in the ninth century such scattered remnants as had been preserved in the East, the Harranensians, asserted with full consciousness that they stood far higher than the Christians. Thabet Ben Korra, a Harranensian Syrian pagan—for even into the tenth century philosophic Hellenism had preserved its existence in those regions, until the combined fury of Christianity and Mohammedanism succeeded in destroying even those small remnants—Thabet Ben Korra says in one of his books, "When many were subjected by violence to error, our fathers persevered with the help of God, and escaped through their heroism, and this blessed city (Harran) has never been defiled by the errors from Nazareth. We are now the heirs and transmitters of heathenism which shone so brilliantly in this world. Happy is he that, with unshaken confidence, endures sufferings for the sake of heathenism. Who rendered the earth habitable, who built the cities for places of abode for families, who else than the nobles and kings of heathenism? Who constructed the havens, made the rivers navigable, who discovered hidden sciences? . . Only the renowned among the heathens have fathomed that, have caused soothing of souls to come about, shown the means for their liberation; they have also discovered and taught the healing of the flesh; they alone have filled the world with well-ordered morals, with wisdom which is the chief of excellency. Without those fruits of heathenism, the world would be void, poor, wrapped in deficiency and scantiness." That is a proud assertion, but an assertion emanating from the consciousness of the object in view, to which the latest remnants of philosophic paganism clung with perfect clearness in their struggle against Christianity. And again, when the nations attained to independence, when a new human culture grew up within them, when they awoke to a free use of their mental and spiritual powers, then also the struggle at once began against Christianity, as well as the fight of Christianity against all those new formations which it condemned as heresy and even condemns today in its consistency. For the power of Catholicism consists in this, that it most decidedly asserts the claims of Christianity in all their consequences, that it represents itself as the only power on earth vested with the prerogative of regarding the whole world as subject to its authority, that it appoints bishops *in partibus infidelium*, that it maintains, "I alone am the human race, and to those who represent me, the whole world must do homage, all consciences must disclose themselves to them, all spirits must bow to them, and all impulses and endowments of men must yield their service to me."

That assertion which constitutes the power of Christianity, contains also its weakness which is that it is not willing to work as a spiritual power within mankind, but claims to stand above mankind, and denies humanity itself in all its other relations. It would be folly joined to blasphemy, were we to deny that a religion which has exhibited such a power through eighteen centuries, has not a mission imposed upon it by God; but on the other hand, it would be no less a defiance of history if we were to deny a historic mission to that religion which is the mother and root of the new religion and which, throughout all the period that the other developed its power to its full extent, still preserved its existence despite all oppression and derision, poverty and broken conditions, aye, even when its spiritual eye was by violence covered with darkness—to that religion which has, despite all that, preserved its existence, exhibited its vitality with renewed freshness whenever it was permitted to move, and at all times retained a fund of spiritual ability, moral stimulation, and moral power. It could not have existed throughout that long period alongside of Christianity, it must have decayed, it must have died long ago or have been brought near death, if it did not have within itself a healthy vitality.

Yes, Judaism has been preserved alongside of Christianity, and despite Christianity. It has been assailed not alone with carnal weapons, with fire and sword, with expulsion and oppression, but also with spiritual weapons; all the good and noble elements accorded to Judaism before it had given birth to Christianity, were adjudged as simply a preparation for Christianity, as Christian property even before its existence. Judaism has kept alive nevertheless, has saved its eternal treasures, and has not allowed itself to be dimmed. It has not permitted its belief in God to be disfigured and combined with foreign elements. It has not allowed the doctrine of original sin to be grafted into it, though great pains were taken in the attempt to deduce that idea from the Scriptures; it has not permitted the annihilation of the title of the nobility of mankind and has clung to the conviction that man has been invested by God with the power of free self-determination and self-improvement; that despite the sensual propensity innate in man's nature, he is vested with the power of conquering it and of reaching by his own exertions the goal of elation and ennoblement. And precisely because it remained free from the doctrine of original sin and the corruption of human nature, it never had any need or desire for again attaining purification by means of an extraneous redemption. It has never exchanged its Merciful God for the God of that Love which, to satisfy its anger, requires a grand, sufficiently vicarious sacrifice. Judaism has not regarded the development of mankind towards a higher goal as a negation of itself, and therefore has never undertaken a fight against the process; it has never announced the verdict: "The time is already fulfilled; eighteen centuries ago the keystone was put in, being the keystone of one world and at the same time, the foundation stone of another—there is the whole truth; nothing can be added."

Christianity must needs look upon that time as the most important in the world's history, it is its heart and center—the person that brought it about must always remain its highest ideal. Even the most liberal-minded, who divest the author of Christianity of everything miraculous about him, can not escape the urgent necessity of creating for themselves, in order to retain some connection with their religion, a fanciful, artificially constructed ideal to which they attribute the greatest earthly perfection—a form which falls to pieces before criticism far more quickly than the old massive presentation. Judaism, on the contrary, can dispense with individualities, it can allow free play to criticism on all its great men, even if it were to go so far—which it might do only in overbold presumption—as to erase Moses out of history. We might perhaps regret such work; but is it Moses, is it any one of the succeeding elaborators, upon whom the foundation of Judaism rests? The doctrine exists; therein is its belief and it will continue its existence; the doctrine stands of itself as it entered Judaism, no matter who taught it, no matter who was the historic individual that was the means of its announcement; no matter whether he was free from sin or a man not free from human foibles. Therefore, Judaism has preserved its mission, its history is not broken by the rise of Christianity. It acknowledges in that, a great world-historic event which deserves to be appreciated in its full significance and hence the following question must suggest itself to a Jew: "Why do you not appreciate it in the same manner as a large portion of the human race do? Why do you recognize in it only a world-transforming event, and not as the sole truth, the full, whole, unclouded truth entered into the world?" Having reached in our view of the course of the development of Judaism the time of the rise of Christianity, we could not avoid the task of examining what that tendency which was started within Judaism and afterwards shaped itself into a world-power, was to us, and how we explain it and its triumphant march. It is not my intention to furnish a criticism of Christianity, and still much less to attack a faith that did and still does inspire millions, or to give offense to devout hearts. But after all, it is our duty to state clearly how those who do not profess that belief, regard it in its origin and as a world-historic event—and what justifies us in preserving, alongside of it, our own spiritual structure and even to add thereto. Whoever is not willing to listen to our defense may close his ears and shut his eyes; but he must not bear us any ill-will for it, nor deny us the free expression of our opinion.

Judaism had arrived at a period which was in the highest degree fraught with danger. Our review left it at a time when all destructive powers gnawed at its vitals, when from without, all-powerful Rome charged down upon it, and within, the parties were riotously burrowing and thereby threatening to undermine its best elements. And it was under such conditions that it commenced and continued the fight which was decided against it, or rather against its national existence. Such issue was in the very nature of things. The small nation had to succumb to Rome; it could not, for any great length of time, withstand her superior power. Besides, it was not its mission to establish a nation, its nationality was but a temporal hull, a necessary means for fortifying the belief and so deeply rooting it in the constitution of the individual members that it could continue to live with full vitality even in their dispersion. That point having been reached, the national form might be broken. Of course, the men living in that period did not see it in that light. They fought with courage and enthusiasm in defense of their national existence. I shall not place before you the sufferings endured by that little band; I shall not depict to you how slain were heaped upon slain, how destruction progressed step by step, how the men closed up breaches in the walls by their bodies, how enthusiasm sustained the waning strength of the weakened arms; I shall not detain you with the woes and lamentations that filled those times. Suffice it to say, the Temple fell, the nationality was demolished, Judah ceased from being a nation, her citizens were driven from their ancient soil, again led into exile and dispersed all over the globe. The hatred of the victor, who was deeply mortified at having been forced to a test of his fighting qualities for a long time by such a small nation, persecuted them; scorn and oppression weighed them down, especially when the daughter-religion ascended the throne of Rome. From that time on, a tearful drama unfolds itself before our eyes, the most painful sufferings without and within were not wanting; for even the minds and spirits were oppressed, and gloomy despair often took possession of the hearts; and it almost seems as if they must have been forced to lose confidence in the truths which had become part and parcel of their being. And yet, it is not a tearful tragedy; the tragic unfolded in the destiny of the Jews since that time, contains a grand idea, discloses a profound conviction which remains alive, and preserves a spiritual freshness which never suffers itself to be bent down, an original vigor which again and again expands wherever room is granted to it. The history since that time is not a mere fatal tragedy, it is more than may be guessed or felt by romance which sees in Jewish history but a continuous woe over which to shed tears in a sentimental mood, but over which the staff must be broken without mercy. No! the power of resistance in Judaism knows not alone how to suffer, but knows also how to preserve and create in the domain of the spirit. *The drama is not yet concluded*, and he only, who shall have seen the last scene of it, may pronounce a full verdict.

XII.

In the Dispersion.

The Jewish commonwealth was destroyed, dissolved, the Jewish nationality disrupted, the Temple was burnt down. Whether the tears which Titus is said to have shed at the sight of the devastation, flowed from the depth of his heart, or whether they were hypocritical—what does history care about it? What did it matter to the scattered remnants of the Jewish people? They had been struck a severe blow, and however long it may have been foreseen, however well they may have been prepared for it, they stood deeply shaken, wounded and broken in their innermost hearts.

Sadduceeism was annihilated. What was now left for the priests and the men of rank? The priests with their ministrations in the Temple, with the sacrificial service, were banished from the sacred places; they were defiled, their traces could hardly be seen any longer; what was left for the priests? Legend tells us that they threw the keys of the Temple and sacred cells toward heaven, exclaiming, "Do Thou preserve them, Heavenly Father; we have no more use for them." And the officials and men of rank, what were they to do? Not a shadow of political rule was left; there was no more struggling for office and distinction, no separation from, nor elevation above the masses; one oppression weighed upon all, all glory was buried in one grave. The Sadducees vanished from history.

The Zealots—the Kannaim—stood in sullen anger, in brooding depression; but what avails anger in opposition to superior power? For some time they nursed plans of revenge; guerilla warfare continued to devastate Judea; isolated forts, unimportant outposts, were for a time defended with foolhardy bravery—they too, fell. The fire which they kindled served only to consume them. Still two generations later, an insurrection arose, a new Messiah appeared; Bar Kosiba placed himself at the head of bold, daring men, and found adherents and confidence among even the considerate and sober-minded. He was a hero in the full meaning of that word, and succeeded with a small band in resisting mighty Rome for years. The war of Adrian assumed large dimensions, but resulted, of course, in a further destruction of the weak remnant and an increase in repressive measures. The Roman, ordinarily caring little or nothing about the religion of his enemy, felt too well that he was confronted by a mental and spiritual force which offered him greater resistance than the feeble bodies of its defenders, and his fury was kindled against Judaism and its customs and ceremonies. The observance of ceremonies and ordinances of Judaism, of everything that externally designated the Jew, was punished with death—the blood of martyrs flowed in streams. It was but natural that renewed vigor of the faith should be produced by that blood, but the demolition of independence as a nation was sealed thereby for all time. The Zealots (Kannaim) gradually disappeared, leaving but their name behind them; blind fanatics who, misjudging the holy spirit of history, fight against the power of the times, and seek violently to preserve the ancient conditions, are called "zealots."

Pharisees of the ancient strict observance still existed in large numbers—the Shammaites who had made resistance to the power of the priests by covering themselves with the garb of priestly law, who believed to effect the sanctification of the people and their equality with the priesthood by adding burdensome usages; but they would have gradually died out, for they did not possess the living energy able to preserve Israel's holy treasure for centuries. When the Temple had fallen, their gloomy sentiment, continually looking back to ancient customs and institutions, tried to assert itself; they announced: It is no longer permitted to eat meat or drink wine, now that the Temple is fallen, because animals can no longer be sacrificed in the sacred house, nor wine offered there as a drink-offering. By such asceticism, those Pharisees of the strict school would have caused the destruction of Judaism.

But the Hillelites were still alive—the men who had inherited the spirit of Hillel, who rated conviction higher than burdensome ceremonies, and consulted the times more than the old ordinances. It was they who kept the remnants together in close connection, did not permit the spirit to vanish, although the material outward bond was broken. That branch of Phariseeism as it had shaped itself out of the very core of Judaism, breathed into it the living spirit that it was able to enter upon its pilgrimage through the world at large.

Israel now started upon his new pilgrimage, full of hardships and sufferings. Thenceforth, heavy oppression was piled upon him, almost down to the present time. The Romans could not forgive him for having kept their military forces busy for such a long time, for being obliged to put forth their whole strength to break up that weak and small nation; and the triumphal march of the victors had to be raised and made more brilliant by the contumely and chains which were put upon the vanquished. Thenceforward the Romans nursed a deep hatred against the scattered remnants of the Jews, against the dispersed individuals who gradually settled down in all parts of the Roman Domain. And when the belief in the fulfilled Messianic idea ascended the throne of the Cæsars, the heritance of that transmitted hatred was joined by another factor—the weapon of humiliation was added, plunging into the very vitals and making it a meritorious work to mortify the spirits, to lacerate the hearts. Thus the poor pilgrim made his progress through the wilderness of the Middle Ages.

Is it surprising that he turned his face towards the past, which appeared to him so much the more brilliant the farther it receded, that he expected all happiness and glory from its re-establishment only, that he imagined the future as a copy of all that had been dead and buried long ago? Do you marvel that he journeyed along, panting and depressed, that he put on a rough coat of mail in order to be protected against the dagger and hostile touch from without; that he added hull upon hull to keep his limbs from shaking with the cold, icy breath that met him from every speech, from every word?

Is it surprising that he wore many a worthless amulet and kept it in sight, to deck out his joyless life and, while in its contemplation, to indulge in pleasant and cheerful dreams? Only tottering huts were permitted him. He might expect to be compelled to-morrow to tear down the hovel which he put up to-day, or that it might be torn down by others. And yet, wherever he found greater security, wherever a breath of kindness met him, wherever the new phase of his sojourn gave him an opportunity to till the mental field and sow spiritual seed in quiet, that new abode soon became to him a new and true home.

It is an affecting sight—but no! it is more than affecting; History is not merely a sentimental comedy, not merely material for tearful, romantic sentiment that it may thereby for awhile feed its agony at the world's disappointment and then give itself the more undisturbedly and indolently to worldly pleasures. It is more than affecting, it is inspiring, to behold how the Jews, wherever they were permitted to settle down for a longer time, also became deeply rooted in the spirit and character of the country, despite their love for Palestine, despite their fervent attachment to their inherited customs, notwithstanding they were full of the spirit that went forth from Jerusalem, full of the law that proceeded from Zion. Soon after the destruction of the Temple, they had again settled in numerous congregations in Babylonia. There the new Persian Empire, the empire of the Parthians, existed —a mighty empire which alone knew how to meet the Empire of Rome with an unconquerable resistance. We are not sufficiently informed of the internal institutions of that empire, of the mental and spiritual life that reigned there; at all events, the very fact that it knew how to resist the all-coveting superior power of Rome testifies to the independent energy of the people. Numerous Jewish congregations existed there, soon a mental and spiritual life began to bloom, and soon also their love and attachment to their new country became firmly founded. It is a significant declaration, handed down from a teacher of that time—viz., the third century—a declaration which truly expresses the sentiments of the Jewish population of that time and country, to wit: "He that emigrates from Babylonia to Palestine violates God's command and commits a sin." To that extent they felt themselves affiliated with Babylonia, with New-Persia. Of course, that teacher founded his decision on a verse of the Bible which he interpreted and explained according to the manner of that time, but the verse had not produced that sentiment, it is merely quoted as a support for it; the sentiment arose out of their love for their newly acquired country. Fully consonant with that declaration is that of another teacher, who decides: "The law of the land is religiously binding;" in former times, the law of the land (political and civil laws) had been declared the product of paganism, a work of ungodly, heathenish nature, and as such, not entitled to existence or recognition; and it was considered the worst stumbling-block. But now, in a new country which, though it did not afford full liberty, yet offered a firm and safe place of abode, its laws were regarded as perfectly correct and valid. Babylonia was a new home for the Jews; and its language, the Aramaic or Chaldean, became almost a sacred language to them. The Aramaeans had formerly been called idolators, and the name itself was used as equivalent to idolator; the faith of ancient Aram had been in hostile antagonism to Israel, but now the Jews lived among them, enjoyed a favorable and secure position, and thus became identified with the people in their civil policy and language. Even to this day our prayers contain Aramaic portions and they are regarded as sacred, though they are no sounds of Zion. The Aramaic version of the bible is recognized as the most authoritative, partly, perhaps, on account of its faithful and close adherence to traditional views, but chiefly because coming from a country which had become a second home to the Jews. The language of Babylonia, the Aramaic, held its own for a long time, even after Arabian literature had begun to exert an influence upon Judaism, and the Arabians had supplanted the remnants of an older culture by their own.

When that young nation entered the world's history with its young literature which for a time exerted its fertilizing influence both upon the progress of mankind in general and upon its higher development in particular; when Arabianism, growing up fast, ruled a large portion of the human race, the great number of Jews who lived in the Arabian-Islamitic territories soon identified themselves with those countries and considered themselves members of those nations. The numerous Jewish congregations in Spain which was also soon brought under the dominion and culture of the Moslems, especially show a fine example of complete affiliation with the inhabitants of the country; they revered the soil as their home, fertilized it with the sweat of their face, drew from it by their industry the most variegated fruits. Proudly they called themselves "*Sephardim*," exiled Jews who live in Sepharad, maintaining that Sepharad in the bible meant Spain. With noble pride, they regarded their Spain, glorified it in poems, clung to it with all the fervor of their hearts. The weary wanderer had found a new, beautiful abiding place and looked no longer back toward the past, he loved the present. After they were expelled from thence, their memory yet turned, and in a measure is still turning towards Spain and Portugal.—In other countries, too, wherever they had found a place of abode for a longer time, the Jews affiliated with the people in heart and spirit, loved its language, adopted its manners and diffused them farther and maintained the speech even when they were again driven away by the blind fury of the inhabitants. The German language is heard from the lips of Jews of the most distant countries, they have kept it for centuries among themselves; they love the old sounds that remind them of a home which, though irrigated with their blood and never grown into a lasting, peaceable resting place, yet for awhile had given them chance to breathe and receive a certain amount of culture. The wanderer felt that it was his task not to proceed on his pilgrimage through mankind merely with fleeting foot, but to establish lasting habitations, in order to live with and among men and work for their elevation.

He had guarded himself against intrusion by the world without; he had to walk about panting, filled only, as it seemed, with the care of the day, his countenance furrowed by wrinkles, his looks sad and careworn. But enter his frail hut and you find there:—the rough coat of mail is laid aside, the hulls are taken off, and a life of cordiality flows from his heart. He is not chilling, though he be covered with bandages and wraps; he has no thorns, though it may seem so; he carries a warm heart in his breast though he be compelled to protect himself against the icy breezes of the outside. Wherever he finds genial warmth, he is also warm and genial, and in the family, in the mutual affection and fidelity encircling the individual members thereof, the comfort and fortitude of Israel rested and persevered. He was excluded from the outside world and he protected himself against its influences and assaults as long as he had reason to fear hostile approaches; but whenever fresh mental and spiritual life awoke, whenever a breath of spring, even if often but seemingly, passed through the world, when new culture started, when the streams of the spirit traversed the land with their fertilizing waters, there he also knew to eagerly draw new life, there he also was in close connection with the spirit of the age.

In general, his spirit was never bowed down, however much depressed in his outward carriage. While in dark ages, bishops and knights were given to praised and sanctified ignorance and the art of reading and writing remained something foreign to them, that remnant of dispersed Jews retained an aspiration to mental and spiritual development, often one-sided and not always keeping pace with life as it was progressing, but still it was a mental activity which preserved their vitality. Canonization of ignorance never held sway in Israel; science took a crooked route now and then; their acuteness went astray sometimes; their mind decked itself out with worthless tinsel on occasions, but it was always active. Gigantic works from darker and brighter times stand before us, productions of thought and mental labor, that excite our reverence. I do not endorse every word of the Talmud, nor every idea of our teachers of the Middle Ages, but I would not cast away a tittle of them. They contain an acumen and power of thought which command respect of the spirit that animated our ancestors, an abundance of sound sense and salutary maxims—an originality of opinion often bursts out which even to this day exerts a vivifying and inspiring effect upon us.

A new people, hitherto untamed and wildly roaming about, entered upon the stage of history, impelled by a lightninglike idea to a new spiritual development; in Arabia, a new civilization is in process of formation. At the cradle of that new culture also, Judaism stood with its doctrines. Whatever good elements Islam contains, whatever enduring idea appears in it, it has taken over from Judaism. With the battle cry, "There is no God but the one God in Unity!" the Arabian galloped through the world on his fiery charger—but his battle cry was not heard by him on Mount Sinai, he simply took it over from those who were carrying it as their inheritance through the world. It is the only fruit-bearing and world-conquering thought contained in Islam. Islam adorned that thought and repeated it in many shallow and tautological formulas. It was garnished, and that too, with Jewish views and tales. And hardly a century after its birth, that new religion had, in a most remarkable way, conquered not only a large portion of the world but tamed the conquerors themselves, and awakened them to a new spiritual life. Those nations which were then in their early youth, which had been initiated, raw and uncivilized, into that new religion, soon listened eagerly to the word that was delivered to them from Antiquity by the remnants of Hellenism through the channel of the Syrian pagans. The latter had translated the writings of the ancient Greeks, of both the philosophers and the men of other sciences, into their own idiom, and soon the Arabians took possession of the remnants of Antiquity, accessible to them in that way; they sat at the feet of the ancient Greek teachers as industrious disciples of their doctrines in the form transmitted to them, became civilized through the discipline in the sciences and a new culture flourished, such as can not be seen at any other period of the Middle Ages. The Jews soon take part in it; they too, live right in the midst of it; they are also philosophers and translators and feel the kinship of the aspirations awakened in the youthful nation. They too, are translators of that new mental and spiritual upward movement, and to a much wider extent. They were not confined to the Arabians; they did not labor like the Arabians, only within their own limits and their own soil; they carry those Greek works everywhere, and scatter the seeds of the new culture far and wide. From the Arabic they are translated into Hebrew, and from the Hebrew into the Latin and the various languages of Europe; only through that channel, the works came to be known to Medieval Europe, and they were the only mental and spiritual seed sown during that time of drought. Jews are often mocked at as business brokers, as old-clothes men peddling cast-off clothes from house to house; as a matter of fact they have carried the cast-off garments of ancient culture into the habitations of the nations of Europe; and if these had not clothed themselves with those remnants, they would have remained naked indeed.

But the Jews were not only transmitters and middlemen, they exerted also great influence by original production. Whatever knowledge there was during the Middle Ages of botany, especially of the so-called officinal branch of botany, was gotten through a translation of the work of Dioskorides, made with the assistance and under the direction of a Jew, the physician and vizier, Chasdai Ben Isaac Shaprut. The more distinguished philosophers of the Arabian time, or at least a large portion of them, were Jews. The name Avicebron resounds through many writings of the Middle Ages as that of one of the most original minds. He was a Jew, Solomon Ben Gabirol, or Gebirol. His name Aben-Gebirol was mutilated into Avengebrol, Avencebron. He was an original thinker, and also a distinguished poet—a mind upon whose creative power I should like to dwell longer. Moses Ben Maimon, Maimonides, a pillar of the faith, a mind productive in all departments of Jewish science, was also a thinker whose works exerted a lasting influence, not only upon Judaism; he became a teacher for all Europe. Albertus Magnus appropriated to himself the best thoughts, and Thomas Aquinas has borrowed much from him. Who could count all the great minds who lived within the Arabian territory, where they developed their mental activity and issued the productions of their poetic talent? What a glorious age! What testimony it bears to the energy in Judaism, which can not be broken, which develops itself in rich luxuriance, if only time and space are granted to it. When in Italy there came a revival of poetry, a sense of the beautiful rather than the vigorous spirit of science, a Jewish poet appeared by the side of Dante, intimate friends, Immanuel, a man full of fresh humor; and we shall generally find that, despite all oppression, the Jewish mind never became weak and weary. Mathematics counts many votaries among the Jews; and in the medieval books of that science we meet another strange sounding name, "Savasorda," who is none other than Abraham Ben Chiva, a Spanish Jew residing in the Provence. He had the Arabian title Sahib al Shorta—i. e., Chief of Police—given to large landed proprietors, like lord, or prince, "Nasi" as the title is in Hebrew.

Times became brighter and everywhere we behold Jews participating with lively interest in everything that quickens the spirit. In a measure, the bible had to be again discovered for Christendom. Who saved it, the Hebrew bible? Who kept it for fifteen centuries, that it could again reappear in its original form? Canonization of ignorance would have condemned it long ago—it would have been lost if it had been under that protection only; we might perhaps find a few pieces of it under an old Palimpsest, under a breviary of some monk, and we should guess at it as at the Assyrian cuneiform inscriptions. It is owing to the care of the Jews that this part of the mental and spiritual achievement of Antiquity has not been lost—the product of Hebraism, of Revelation. The Jews have saved it, they have carried it as their treasure through the world, have explored its hidden spirit with nice understanding and transferred their own aids for instruction to the world. Proud Science, that imagines herself to-day independent and able to explain the bible in her own way, works with the very aids furnished her by the Jews—she walks about on crutches borrowed from the Rabbis. As they had punctuated and accentuated it, and in places transformed it, Science has taken it and works farther on. When the time of the awakening of culture arrived, the staff of Judaism was looked to as a supporting pillar. Reuchlin, the instructor of Germany, took hold of the two pillars of the mental and spiritual temple, Hellenism and Hebraism, and depended on them, drawing on both for support. Holy ignorance laid snares for him on that account, wanted to give his works over to the ban; her minions complained grievously because he was not delivered into their hands. He held the transmitted treasures of Judaism in great respect, perhaps some counterfeit more than it deserved. The critical works of Jews of that time, the works of Elias Levita, of Azariah de Rossi, are of great importance. As the time progressed, the Jews advanced with it.

In that land where a beautiful life had flourished for the Jews for a long time, in the land which they loved with holy fervor, blind fanaticism was mightier than science. The latter had fertilized the land as long as the Arabians occupied it; when they were crowded back, science also fled from before the serpent tongue of religious fury. The flame of fanaticism was fed by ignorance more and more; it consumed the best energies of the land, and the Jews too, were compelled to give way. It was not enough to oppress them, their very presence was regarded as a profanation; they were forced to leave a country in which they had dwelt with honor for a thousand years, in the welfare and glory of which they had most brilliantly co-operated. They were forced to emigrate. Whatever they saved of mental and spiritual culture, they carried along into Turkey, where, however, they were not able to graft a higher culture on the barren tree of the Ottomans. But also to another country which had been tributary to, and had made itself independent of Spain, to Holland, they carried, together with their love for their former Spanish fatherland, the remnants of culture and refinement of the time. Holland set the first example in Christendom of announcing and proclaiming the principle of religious liberty in its essentials, at least, if not fully; and Holland flourished for a long time, in both material prosperity and mental and spiritual superiority, and its Jewish inhabitants with it. Right there in Holland a Jewish child was born who, though he grew up a man of feeble body, became the pioneer of a new mental and spiritual era, and soon became celebrated, even to this day. Baruch Spinoza was a native of Amsterdam; he was the originator of a new line of thought which has since made its entrance into the thinking world and transformed many ideas. He did not remain a close adherent of the Jewish doctrine, yet he never severed his connection with it; he matured under the instruction of his old Jewish teachers; he had zealously studied Aben Esra and Maimonides, and rose on the support of Judah Alfakar and Chisdai Kreskas. He contended against the Jewish adherents of Aristotle, and yet he had got his education in philosophy through them. He also fought against the Cabbala, though he had received many an impulse from it; its doctrine of emanation became with him his doctrine of immanation. Baruch Spinoza laid the foundation of a new philosophy which has become the mother of many modern philosophies. He was a character of granite, and accordingly his system is of granite construction. Others have chipped little stones from that structure and fitted them into various conglomerate and thus created new systems; yet they originate in his structure. Has he found the truth? I can hardly assume it; but that he has become an instructor of mankind, that he has freed it from many errors and prejudices, has mightily stirred up the minds, was the father of a new mental and spiritual life and the creator of free biblical criticism, is an uncontrovertible fact. The poor Jewish lens-grinder of Amsterdam has not passed through the world without leaving fertile productions behind him. Let us not proceed farther into later times—let us forego the mention of many more recent brilliant names; those times are yet too near to us and their contemplation might be regarded as vainglorious self-admiration.

But now a new time is taking shape. We have not completely passed out from the Middle Ages, but their pillars are crumbling; what was their staff of support formerly, proves to be but a splinter to-day. As yet, no new mental and spiritual idea with fertilizing influence appears on the horizon of the world; as yet, no fresh breeze passes through the withered leaves of mankind. But it is getting ready for the New Age—sound science, live reason, honest inquiry shall investigate everything and clear up everything. Before sound science, that science which, despairing of itself and aware of its weakmindedness, denies the existence of the spirit, shows up with triumphant mien the apparatus of a skeleton and thereby supposes to have given an explanation of man, will retire with shame. With a sound science which respects the spirit and has a presentiment of the Spirit of All, Judaism will go hand in hand, because it has always been permeated and quickened by such ideas.

How then are we prepared for that New Age? There are many overeducated and sensual ones that would willingly throw away all ancient treasures, bend their knees before the powers that be, and divest themselves of their own character and their past as something valueless; they are frail clay vessels, unavailable as instruments for ushering in a spiritually healthy time. There are also zealots among us, who, merely looking back upon the ancient time, are in love with the shell worn during the Middle Ages and will not lay aside the rough coat of mail; who want to use the dagger of suspicion and the poison of calumny against every new aspiration; they likewise are unavailable as instruments for ushering in a new time. Neither are Pharisees of the strict observance lacking; they carefully wrap themselves up, cling devoutly to all that has been handed down from former times; they are animated by the ancient spirit, but without new, fresh, quickening energy. But where is the new Hillel, with his mild, clear eye, with his loving enthusiasm, with his sound mental and spiritual energy to co-operate in the ushering in of the new time? Whenever he shall appear—and surely he will not fail us—he will again pronounce, perhaps in another form, his old maxim: "*If I do not for myself, who will do for me?* Beloved pilgrim, do not continually look backwards," he will say, "do not continually keep your eyes on the past. Jerusalem is a tomb;

you must draw from the living present and labor in it. If we do not labor and produce from the innate spirit within us as it is linked with the spirit of Revelation, who shall do it? *And if I do for myself alone, what am I then?* If we do not identify ourselves with mankind, we do not do our duty. Beloved pilgrim, cast off your rough coat of mail, there is no longer hostility abroad; undo the wrappings that hide and disfigure you, frosty and icy winds no longer blow against you—love will blossom everywhere—you have a warm heart, and all mankind appreciates it; take them all in your embrace. Lo! the wrap is not the spirit, and the rough coat of mail is not the essence. *And if not now, when then?* If not now, while the spirit of Judaism yet animates its members, if nothing is done now, if no space is cleared whence the knowledge of ancient times may fertilize the world and new seeds be sown for the future; if indifference increases in Israel and throws away the old treasures as worthless; if the understanding of truly Jewish knowledge, the illumination of the idea of Revelation, the draft from that eternal fountain is not encouraged now—when then? Is it to be done only then when everything shall be encoffined, when on the one side there will be but dead bones, and on the other, only ashes?" With such words the new Hillel will, when he puts in his appearance, encourage the pilgrim to vigorous action, to cheerful co-operation in the spiritual sowing; he will speak it with tongue of fire, with that conquering enthusiasm which bears down all caviling hesitancy. The time will come, Judaism has not yet finished its mission. Judaism does not consider the world's history closed up, neither eighteen centuries ago, nor to-day; it moves along with mankind on its conquering march of progress, and brightens it with mild rays.

APPENDIX

Renan and Strauss.

A Glance at the Latest Works on the Life of Jesus.

About thirty years ago, Strauss accomplished the great feat of writing a critical work on the life of Jesus, and showed that the accounts of that time, as contradictory in themselves and impossible as the records are in conflict with one another, contained no actual history, but merely the legends which were formed within the circle of the first Christian Congregation about the personality of Jesus, and that those same legends were the result of the Messianic belief, were the offspring of expectations connected with the coming Messiah or with the events that were related in the bible, of the lives of other men, either by direct statement or put into it by interpretation. Thus it was very doubtful how much there would be left of real history besides the fact of the existence of the person. But Strauss had then just emerged from the School of Hegel, which, in the habit of converting historical facts into a dialectic process from within, in the habit of regarding events of the past as preparatory steps to later finished ideas, had long before viewed the facts of incipient Christianity—without, however, denying their historical character—as the hulls of higher ideas, and had asserted that those formerly veiled ideas had been brought to light and made perfectly clear in philosophy—the Hegelian philosophy, of course. That School called its philosophy the Absolute Philosophy; it represented Christianity, which it respected as a ruling religious power, as the chrysalis of its philosophy, as the popular, yet immature religious presentation, preceding the complete, clear conception, and called the Absolute Religion. In that manner, the Hegelian School had persuaded itself and others that it was not only in perfect accord with the belief of the church, but raised it even to the dignity of inviolable, philosophic certainty, it imprinted the stamp of the highest mental and spiritual perfection.

Strauss, with his love of truth, and his clear, critical acumen, destroyed that cobweb which the Hegelian had spun around itself as a saint's garment; he shook the whole foundation of the belief in the definite historical person, and on that, the entire Christian faith is based. Yet he wanted to think that in those representations which, though without being actual facts, had been shaped into history, the philosophical ideas of his School had found expression, even if immature, and that therefore the essence of Christianity, now more purely expressed in their philosophical ideas, was preserved.* With that, he not only eased his mind, but he even believed that the Church could and should be satisfied with what had thus been saved. But it very soon became evident that the Church was not at all satisfied with seeing the One Person whom she adored as her highest ideal, nay, even as a superhuman being, yield his place to the whole human race that continually develops, struggles, suffers, dies, rises again, ascends to heaven in a transfigured state, etc. Although he gallantly held his ground in the fight that was made against him from all sides, yet he thought there was a possibility of effecting a reconciliation between the traditional faith of the Church and the glorification of the individual. In his "Leaf of Peace," published a little later, he announced: "The Idea manifests itself in the fullness of its radiations only in the whole community, yet it appears in especially gifted individuals with such force that they seem unapproachable, that we look up to them as the highest possible embodiment of the Idea, and yield to them a Worship of Genius. If we behold the art of poetry, of painting, manifested in the highest possible perfection in certain persons who do not arise as the crown of a long line of development, but rather as the first ones with regard to time, and whom other, later ones try to approach, just so, an individual may have been a genius of religious sentiment as author of a religion worthy of adoration or at least, emulation."

* It followed out of that view that he preferred to designate the popular legends, as which he regarded the stories, rather as myths, because the latter are held to be ideas couched in poetic forms.

With that, Strauss let the matter rest, and turned away from the subject for a long time. Of course, such action on his part did not set at rest the commotion that had been stirred up. Some, seeing that the very center had been unhesitatingly assailed, sought to defend the more obstinately the fartherest outposts which had before been almost surrendered; others thought they could, by way of compromise, the more securely save that part which to them seemed to be the more important one, if they would yield the apparently less important and tenable branch. But soon results of criticism were again brought forward, though from a different starting point. A system came into existence which, though also the offspring of the Hegelian School, investigated the growth and development of the ideas within Christianity rather with a view to the history of the dogmas of the church; it is the so-called "Tuebingen School." In the course of the researches made for that purpose by Baur, its author and indefatigable leader, in conjunction with some gifted disciples, they were compelled to investigate the events during the first centuries of Christian history. Gradually they arrived at the result, that the manifold dogmatic differences which disturbed especially the first periods, could not be regarded as an apostacy from convictions previously settled, but presented a process of fermentation out of which Christianity only very gradually was shaped into its subsequent fixed form. Christianity—such was the result of which they became more and more convinced—is not a new spiritual system produced by *one* man and arising *suddenly*, but it is the product of a mental and spiritual commotion running through two centuries, and it was made up by a number of various factors. The person who, until then, had been adored as the creator of full, complete, and finished Christianity, was divested of that glory by the result of such researches; yet the honor of having given the impulse to that commotion was left to him. The investigators were also inclined, following the example of Strauss, to admit that he should be regarded as an overwhelming individuality on account of the ability to give such a powerful impulse, even as a religious Genius who, in advance, with the intuitive grasp of genius, had already completely apprehended all that the process of development later got into shape by laborious toil. Closely examined, the latter supposition especially is superfluous, even contradictory. To what purpose should that have existed in advance in an individual which the commotion of the minds produced out of the bitter and severe fight with one another? But still more! If the Master had indeed arrived at that high plane which was attributed to complete and finished Christianity, how was it possible that his immediate disciples who, in their immediate intercourse with him, saw his actions, to whom he gave uninterruptedly his personal instruction, who must have known the convictions held by him down to his death, to whom, as his chosen apostles he disclosed his innermost thoughts and communicated his best aims—how was it possible that they rendered his doctrine, conceived in an entirely different shape from what it afterwards assumed and was attempted to be ascribed to its author? But soon they were led to this conclusion, that during the internal conflict in the first centuries, the Apostles proper had not been the standard-bearers of the doctrine which worked its way to victory, but that theirs was gradually compelled to give way to a later tendency, as the representative of which especially Paul, the Apostle to the heathens, came into view. And thus the person of Paul made its way as the carrier of the progressive movement of the ideas more and more to the foreground, and the first author receded in proportion. That was not announced very emphatically by that School—they were satisfied with a so-called *Ideal Christ;* i. e., with the Idea of a finished Christianity. How much was left of a *Historical Christ*, they left undecided.

The clearer knowledge of that conflict of the ideas in the first Christian time brightened the view for critical investigation of the Gospels and the other earliest writings of Christianity; it even forced a more searching criticism of them. Those oldest monuments of Christianity in its formation period must be likewise speaking witnesses of that conflict which excited the minds so mightily, they must show in sharp lines the questions of those times, even the number of the records —namely, that four gospels have been handed down—and the diversity existing between their composers can have proceeded only from more or less conscious intent of carrying the shades of their own religious opinions into the efforts of the author of the faith. That knowledge has greatly promoted criticism of the Gospels and insight into the inner process of the development of Christianity; but at the same time it has brought still greater uncertainty upon what the author did, intended, and taught. If the records are legendary and mythical, as Strauss asserted, in that they had intended to see all former expectations fulfilled in the author and thus unhistorically ascribed to him their actual fulfilment, another difficulty was added, to wit, that their own later and more recently formed shape was also dressed up as act and doctrine of Jesus, and thus obscured his character still more. Accordingly, the Tuebingen School has thus far not attempted to draw a full picture of the Author of Christianity; it lacked all material for it, because the Past and the Future had worked on it to such an extent that the living character then present had become completely indiscernible. Besides, he had been reduced to a single factor in the great sum of Christianity; to know that in its entirety, in the demonstrable phases of its development, was of more importance than to trace the single, less seizable factor.

When now all at once, and that from the point of view of that School, two new works appear, which treat exclusively of "The Life of Jesus," it is really a retrogressive step. Of course, less so in the case of the French author. That process of thought had not yet been independently worked out in France. The first "Life of Jesus" by Strauss had been translated into French, the literary works of the Tuebingen School had been known, considered, and discussed within a certain circle of French theologians, but independent research and elaboration had not been attained. Mr. Renan, therefore, was fully justified in commencing again, for France, with the life of Jesus. And yet, he has not stopped there. He does not desire that his book should be regarded as a whole work completed; he publishes it as a first volume of a larger work calculated to treat upon the development of Christianity during the first three centuries, as the beginning of a full and elaborate disquisition. The German author stands worse in this respect. He regards his task fully accomplished by his book, he means to present "The Life of Jesus" exclusively, and that too, after having performed this task, thirty years ago, as far as it can be performed from his standpoint —namely, as a critical opinion upon the records on that subject—a task which may be executed now more correctly and in better shape in consequence of the new views gained, but can hardly turn out a new work intended for the general public. While now the second part of the new work is merely a recast of his former critical analysis with omission of a large portion of learned matter, Strauss means, after all, to give in the first part a positive presentation of the actual historical facts regarding Jesus—just like Renan, who, however, blends both points. And right there, the evil result of a mode of proceeding unjustifiable by science appears, and again much more so in the work of Strauss than in that of Renan. For while we must accord the palm of superiority to the German author as far as labor of criticism is concerned, it must be admitted that his historical presentation—even aside from the historical art which, with Renan, is working more in a more poetic, divinatory manner than in elaborating the material on hand—is far more untenable, much less permeated by a historic spirit than that of the French scholar. The latter has this advantage, that he intermingles criticism with his narrative, that he introduces many more portions of the records—often in a very uncritical and arbitrary manner—as genuine history and has thus far more material left him. Finally he sees in Jesus a man wrestling and struggling within himself, soaring and falling back until death relieves him at the right time, before he might turn faithless to his mission. In contrast to that, Strauss at first presents us a history, and only afterwards proves the unreliability of the records, so that when we have come to the close of his book, we look about with uncertainty for the remainder, of which the actual history must once have consisted; of a growth, of a development within the person of Jesus, which is the real object of biography, we learn nothing at all, for he presents his man finished and complete from the start.

But how does this man appear in both works? There is the rock against which the feeble bark of either was wrecked as soon as it ventured to pass from the waters of historical criticism into those of biography. Every attempt at biography is attended with danger. As soon as an individual is taken up as a fixed point in the moving fluid stream of history, he has been given a higher importance, and the temptation grows stronger and stronger to justify in the presentation, why such importance is given him; compelled to group around him the facts connected with him, the writer easily falls into the mistake of deducing them from him, and thus he becomes the center and representative of the history of which he was but a single part by the side of many others. The interest which an earnest author takes in the subject of his treatise, passes over to the appreciation of the person; he is led astray into overrating him, in emphasizing, more than unbiased judgment could permit, his bright sides, into paling the dark spots, in excusing the foibles; in short, the biographer easily turns into the advocate, into the eulogist. Such being the danger attending every biographical work, how much greater must it be when its subject is a person who is closely connected with one of the grandest events in the world's history, who has hitherto been regarded not merely as one of its impelling or co-operating factors, but as its complete and sole creator. However critically unbiased the writer may be, as soon as he disengages such an agent from all other factors, he slips into ascribing to him more than he would in a work comprising a history of all co-operating causes—he would not like to go too far out of the beaten track, he would not want to make the transition from the customary conception to his own, too steeply precipitous. And when criticism proves that very little of all that the ancient records contain can be relied upon, then the writer is left to himself, to his own combination, to the picture moving before his imagination, and in that light he will represent his hero. But critical truth suffers shipwreck thereby.

And such has been the case with both authors, with each in his own way. In the work of Renan, Jesus appears as a visionary hypocrite, greatly vascillating: now as a pronounced national Jew, and then again as a cosmopolitan; now as initiated by John the Baptist into ascetics, then rising above all outward forms; now as overcoming all obstacles by the most amiable meekness and then again in great wrath at the lack of results of his labors and losing heart, and withal, devoid of all means and efforts towards higher culture of mind and spirit;—and towards the end, after we are shown some very suspicious preparations for deceptive miracles, some very low morality which our author defends with oratorical pathos and and even praises, because he thinks it to belong to a creative, idealistic time which should not be measured by our own short standard, we finally come to a glorification of Jesus who is to be the pattern of highest religious and moral perfection for all times, an ideal which has as yet not been sufficiently understood and much less reached. Though he should not be worshiped as a God, yet he must be looked up to as an Ideal of Mankind, as a "Demigod." Thus the epos closes in a dignified manner with a surprising flash. But when we shut the book, calmly weigh its contents in our mind and render its poetry into sober prose, we find the hero has been dissolved into vapor during the course of that chemical process of thought. The demands made upon us by the historian prove to be wholly illegitimate.

Nor do we fare better with Strauss. He saves us from all flight of the imagination, from all suspense and tension that might be caused by contemplation of a wrestling mind; in his presentation, Jesus appears from the very beginning in unchangeable, unapproachable tranquility, in lofty dignity. Even in the preface (p. xviii.) he is announced as "the individual in whom the deeper consciousness of man's inner nature first appeared as an all-pervading force, determining his entire life and being," and again at the conclusion of the book (p. 625), we are assured that "among the promoters of the ideal of humanity, Jesus stands at all events in the front rank. He introduced features into it which were wanting in it before, or had remained undeveloped; he reduced others which prevented its universal application; he imparted to it by the religious aspect he gave to it a more lofty consecration and bestowed upon it the most vital warmth by its embodiment in his own person, while the Religious Society which took its start from him, provided for this ideal the widest acceptance among mankind." But when we ask for the facts underlying that picture, we are refused an answer by Strauss regarding actual facts, because he does not recognize the reported actions as historical and true; and if those reported acts were recognized as actual facts, they would in a great measure contradict his views and could find their explanation only in a relapse by the immediately succeeding age, which we shall consider farther on. Now then, actual facts do not furnish the basis for such a description of the character of Jesus; but instructions and maxims do. But many of those have to be deducted from the sum of that character, because they originated at a later time. Others are decided to be genuine and thus ought to afford the best testimony for that lofty individuality. Strauss selects (p. 253) some of "that rich collection of sentences or maxims as they are found in the gospels, of those pregnant sayings which, even independent of their religious value, are so inestimable for the clear penetration, the unerring sense of right expressed in them."

Let us consider these pregnant sayings which by themselves alone are to furnish the justification for the claim to that proud unapproachable character. "Give unto Caesar that which is Caesar's, and unto God that which is God's." If that saying is taken in that sense which a later application attributed to it, namely, that the domains of the religious and civil bonds of Church and State, should be separated, and that each should be recognized on its own soil and according to its title, then we rejoice at the tangible expression in which the idea is given. But right there, another opinion of Strauss gives us pause and doubt. Considering his admission (p. 626) that "in the pattern exhibited by Jesus in his instruction and life, some sides being shaped and worked out to perfection, while other sides were but faintly sketched or not indicated at all," and that in elaborating that idea, he continues, "his relation to the body politic appears simply passive," we soon conclude that in the first part of the cited saying the sensible idea of the rights of the State can not be contained, that Jesus did not recognize the State, but merely tolerated it. But that the meaning of that saying is altogether different from that put into it, after it was elevated into a maxim under changed conditions and altered views, is proven by its shape and the occasion that called it forth. According to the meaning now generally adopted, it should demand that to Caesar should be given what is due him, but not "that which *is* Caesar's" already, that which already fully belongs to him—for that is self-understood as a matter of course. But Jesus employed the saying for a reply to the question of the Pharisees, whether they should pay tribute to the emperor, to Rome, and only after he had made them show him a coin which bore the emperor's picture. The Pharisees, being the party of compromise, did not refuse to pay tribute; with all their attachment to their faith and country, hence with all their readiness to give unto God all that they could dispose of as a gift to God, it was their principle not to rebel recklessly against the authority of the Emperor, but rather to give to him that which under existing conditions he could justly claim. But the *Kannaim*, the Zealots, rejected such pliant weakness, condemned the payment of tribute or taxes to Rome as an apostacy from faith and country. The Pharisees and Herodians—as they are called in Matthew and Mark, i. e., the Boethusians, the priestly families and their adherents—who regarded the announcement by Jesus that he was the Messiah both as a religious presumption and as an implied dangerous political agitation, very naturally supposed that he would, like the Zealots, repudiate the payment of tribute to Rome; and that would have afforded them a cause for delivering him as a rebel over to the Roman authorities for punishment. Jesus cunningly foiled the attempt, without turning from his principles. The coin bearing the image and inscription of the Emperor showed that everything still moved within the condition of this world which, after all, "*was*" Rome's, "*was*" Caesar's—not "ought to be his"—the reply meant, give unto him that which he has already, until the world-to-come appears, when all things will be God's, and you will then pay all tribute to Him. Judging from his point of view, the reply may have been appropriate, even wise, but it can not claim authority for all times, it reveals no insight into the nature of the State, hence "peculiar, clear penetration, the unerring sense of right" is not expressed in it.

As a second example, the author quotes the saying, "No man putteth a new patch unto an old garment; neither do men put new wine into old bottles." What the sentence is intended to express is well known; but I have great doubts about its fitness and the general application. About a new patch upon an old garment, the figure is extremely puzzling. An old patch is undoubtedly less suitable for an old, torn garment than a new patch; for if a garment be still usable and have but a rent, one will certainly take a new patch for mending the damage and preserving the whole garment for some time yet. If, therefore, Matthew (ix. 16) and Mark (ii. 21) add: "for that which is put in to fill up, taketh from the garment and the rent is made worse," they commit, as far as I understand such matters, a direct error. Luke seems to have felt that, for he changes the metaphor somewhat by quoting the saying (v. 36) in this manner: "No man putteth *a piece of a new garment* upon an old; if otherwise, then both the new maketh a rent, and the piece that was then taken out of the new, agreeth not with the old." But by that turn, the truth to be embodied by the parable is entirely changed, and it evidently does not correspond to its original object. According to Matthew and Mark, Jesus, following up the observation that the disciples of the Baptist and the Pharisees, but not his, might fast, means to say, that it is of no avail to patch an old, torn system of religious views with a few new ideas; that it must be formed anew from its very foundation —that meaning fits the saying, but it can not be applied to a garment. Now, while Luke intends to improve the parable, he destroys the meaning intended to be conveyed by it. For according to him, the system of new views must have been completely established and carried into practice, to have a piece taken from it and tear it, while the new patch would not agree with the old. That does not correspond to the idea intended to be conveyed. At all events, the older form of the saying is such as is found in Matthew and Mark, and as Strauss has transcribed it from them; but in that form, the metaphor, being little to the point, seems to have roused already the suspicion of Luke. The same can be said of the second part. That new wine, being in process of fermentation, may easily break the bottles, is correct; but that old bottles, if they are at all fit for preserving liquids, are more liable to burst than new ones, I am inclined to doubt. Even the new ones are more apt to burst, on account of their untried tension, as expressed also by the author of Job (xxxii. 19), to which verse only forced interpretation could attribute the meaning from the passage in the Gospels. Thus then, the form of the saying with its simile is badly selected. But is the idea to be conveyed by it, to be adopted without any limitation? The saying, if accepted as of general application, is in conflict with all historical development, the law of which consists even in gradual transformation, in the interpenetration of the old elements by the new ones. It has an intelligent meaning only—and that, too, in a Paulinian sense—for the commotion of that time which was opposed to Judaizing Christianity, as being a mingling of ancient custom with the new Messianism. Now if it alludes to that condition—and in this sense it is still farther elaborated by Luke, who had the new system completely finished before him—it can not be ascribed to Jesus at all but belongs to the later time when the internal struggle was well under way. And in fact, the saying is very loosely, even contradictorily attached to the preceding reply. If the disciples of Jesus, as is stated in the preceding passages under consideration, do not then fast, because the bridegroom is with them, but would make up for it after the latter shall have been taken from them, the saying does not at all contend against ancient custom, but designates it as untimely only for the moment, again to become appropriate at a future period. But the added phrases occupy a different standpoint, that of a later period, which insists on having abolished all ancient custom for all time to come.

Both the expression and the idea of the saying, "If thy hand or thy foot offend thee, cut it off and cast it from thee," are of very doubtful value. The other, "Take first the beam out of thine own eye; and then shalt thou see clearly to cast out the mote out of thy brother's eye," was, as is evident from the Talmud, an adage in general use at the time. The other two sentences, "They that be whole need not a physician, but they that are sick," and "Not seven times shalt thou forgive thy brother who offends thee, but seventy times seven," are of very ordinary kind. If Strauss adds with emphasis, "These are imperishable words; for in them, truths that are every day getting fresh corroboration are enclosed in a form that exactly suits them and is at the same time universally intelligible," the otherwise unbiased thinker can have been blinded only by the frequent application that has been made of them during the course of centuries, and this too, with a partial sublimation of their original meaning. In comparison with the great treasure of pithy sentences and proverbs, the single pearls of which are scattered about in the Talmudic literature, one is tempted to say, with the lavish carelessness of a millionaire, the sentences quoted deserve very small consideration.

But Strauss is determined, at all hazards, to see in the subject of his book, the embodiment of the human ideal, even if he should be forced to assume that history had taken a retrogressive in place of an advance movement. When we read expressions such as (p. 140), "Luke and Mark undoubtedly did right when they omitted from the instructions to the twelve, the command not to turn to the Gentiles and Samaritans, as that prohibition in the account of the first gospel had probably got into it only from the ideas of rigid Judaizing Christians," when we read soon thereafter, "If we accept . . . that the first disciples of Jesus did not fully comprehend him, that the standpoint of the first congregation remained behind his own, and that our oldest Evangelists, especially Matthew, were also on the standpoint of the oldest congregation . . . and if we put up the saying in Matthew, about the indestructibility of even the smallest letter of the Law, and that in John about the worship of God in spirit and in truth, as the two most extreme points, it is very doubtful to which of those two points we are to think the historical Jesus to have been the nearest"; or when he says (p. 318) of "the phantastic mood of the most ancient congregations, that it had been in many respects a simultaneous relapse into the views of Jewish times"; or when (p. 616), the fact that Mark "names as the signs which are to characterize believers, the power to cast out devils, to speak with new tongues, to lift up snakes, to drink deadly poison without harm, to heal the sick by laying on of hands" is to show "at how early a period in the Church, a superstitious feeling directed only to signs and wonders began to smother the genuine spirit of Jesus"—when we read those and similar expressions, we no longer recognize in them an unbiased historical mind and spirit, but the violent assertions of the Apologist.

Many of the passages quoted above, show that Strauss approaches those assertions with rather unsteady and hesitating step, yet he rushed unhesitatingly into them in other places. His critical conscience must necessarily have troubled him then. For such assumptions rob all settled historical results accomplished by modern research, of their true value. If it is true that Christianity was evolved only from the struggle between an older tendency and the later Paulinian view, it is impossible that the later, more finished form had been already known, and had been taught in its complete state, and even in a higher form, by the original starter. It is impossible that all his immediate disciples and all the churches established by them, should not only completely have misunderstood the intentions of their Master, should have totally renounced his doctrines, but that they even contended against his views and purposes with the most determined and violent opposition, as soon as they were presented to them in mere tentative form by Paul, who had not known Jesus, nor even heard anything from him directly, and that those views gained the ascendency only by the pressure of events. And even Paul is made out to have only approached them; for the author is represented as having possessed a far loftier conception than that which Paul deduced by scholastic dialectics, and thus his real spirit has remained unknown to this day. Whenever a writer enunciates new views, they may be ignored for a time or be bent to the prevailing opinions and perceived more clearly by a later generation only. But when a teacher—who in personal intercourse and by oral instruction unhesitatingly and with the greatest emphasis, pronounces his convictions which are diametrically opposed to the prevailing views and "in a form that exactly fits them and is at the same time *universally intelligible*"—gives his ideas the most definite expression in all his actions, accepts the contest with the ruling powers for them, and dies for them, can he have been so totally misunderstood by the men who were unceasingly with him, who were prepared by him as his missionaries and devoted themselves to that mission with the greatest self-sacrifice, and also by the crowds and congregations that gathered around those men—can he by all of them, and however weak their mental powers may have been, have been so totally misunderstood that they repudiated all his doctrines without exception while other points which he peremptorily rejected or, at least, did not emphasize and, at best, only tolerated, were made by them the core and center of the new system? It is claimed that Jesus breaks down the national barriers between Jews and non-Jews; his disciples adhere to them with determination, call "Heathens and Samaritans" outcasts, contend against the adherents of Paul who accepts such, as apostates, as "Balaamites." It is claimed that Jesus abolishes the validity of the Jewish law and ceremonies; his disciples emphatically enforce them, assert their everlasting validity, say that "it is easier for heaven and earth to pass away than one tittle of the law to fail," are indignant at the later attempted assault upon those institutions. It is claimed that Jesus repudiates signs and wonders; his adherents cite them again and again, and on that point the greatest unanimity has existed to this day. On the other hand, there is the conviction, which comprises everything immediately succeeding Jesus and held by all as an unshaken faith, namely: that Jesus was the Messiah, commissioned as such to bring about a new epoch for the world, and that he, though he died, had soon risen again and would return with the greatest power in a short time, in order to establish the new epoch with a general, rigorous judgment of the whole world. What is the relation of the new apologetic, or the relation of Jesus as represented by it, to that faith? Strauss devotes a separate chapter (C. 39) to that subject, and we must here transcribe his own words, omitting only unessential parts. He says (p. 236, etc.):

"Jesus speaks in the Gospels . . . of the coming of the Son of Man; i. e., of his own Messianic second coming at a later, though not distant period when he will appear in the clouds of heaven, in divine glory and accompanied by angels, to wake the dead, to judge the quick and the dead, and to begin his kingdom, the kingdom of God, or of Heaven. . . . To this part of the doctrine of Jesus in the most literal conception, the older Church held fast; it is even built on that foundation because without the expectation of the early return of Christ, no Christian Church could have been established at all. . . . To a human being, no such thing as he here prophesied of himself could happen. If he did prophesy it of himself, and expected it himself, he is for us nothing but an enthusiast; as he would be a braggart and an impostor if he had said it of himself without any faith in it on his own part. . . We find the speeches of Jesus about his second coming in all four gospels; we certainly find them in the first three, which we acknowledge as the repository of much genuine historical tradition, at greater length and more definite than in the fourth. What then, is here to be done? . . . Shall we make him bear the burden of all those speeches in the full literal meaning of the words and therefore be compelled to confess that he was an enthusiast, and not of a small degree at that? . . . With our Christian habits of thought, it might be a very bitter pill for us; but if it turned out to be a historical result, our habits of thought would have to give way. Nor can it be said that an enthusiast could not have had the sound, lofty views, the historic effects that proceeded from him. . . . It is no unusual phenomenon to see high mental and spiritual gifts and excellency of sentiment tempered with a dose of exaggerated enthusiasm. . . . That Jesus, according to the Evangelical accounts, should have considered his second advent so near that he said to his disciples that there were some among those standing around him who should not taste of death until they had seen the Son of Man coming in his kingdom . . . that therefore he should have made a great mistake with reference to the time . . . all that, on our standpoint, does not make the case even worse. . . . So much the less can we feel ourselves tempted to one of the violent interpretations of the words which the theologians, in genuine rivalry, have here undertaken. . Also by the coming of Jesus himself . . . we can not, if his words are faithfully reported to us, understand an invisible and gradual development, i. e., the natural development of the effects of his action upon earth, but only a visible and sudden, a miraculous catastrophe. . . . . What Jesus says in the principal passage of Matthew (xxiv. 30, etc., xxv. 31, etc.). . . . such a description resists every attempt to give it a merely symbolical meaning . . . . of course, it is but too plain that the speeches referring to this point have undergone all sorts of later modifications. . . . All that, however, . . . does not touch the point itself with which we are here concerned. . . . Jesus promised to return into his kingdom; and now the question is, how he spoke on other occasions of his kingdom, especially whether he represented it as one which he had founded already during his human existence, or one which he would initiate only at a future return. . . . That Jesus distinguished the present as preparation, from a future as perfection, this life as a period of earning [?] from a life to come as recompense, and connected with the beginning of that perfection a miraculous change of the world to be brought about by God, appears not only in the gospels in the most decided manner, if any historical validity is left to them, but must also be assumed from the bare historical analogies. . . . But if Jesus had once held to that conviction, as of course he must have done, if he distinguished between this present earthly existence and a future one in the kingdom of God, whether in heaven or on the renovated earth, and if he conceived the beginning of the latter as a miraculous act of God, then it is indifferent in what nearer or more distant period he placed that act, and it would be nothing more than a human error if he expected it after the shortest possible delay and announced the expectation for the consolation of his followers; although we can not know whether his followers, in the troubles and distress after his passing away, may not have comforted themselves by ascribing to him such prophecies of a near approach of the better constitution of the world. In all those speeches, there is but one point that creates a difficulty for us, and that is, that Jesus is said to have connected with his own person that miraculous change, the beginning of that ideal state of recompense, that he is said to have designated himself as the one who will come with the clouds of heaven, accompanied by angels, to awaken the dead and hold judgment. The expectation of such a thing of himself is something quite different from a mere general expectation of it, and he that expects it of himself and for himself, will not appear to us as only a fanatical enthusiast, but we see also an impermissible self-exaltation in it, if a human being . . . comes to think of selecting himself to such an extent from all the rest as to put himself up as their future judge. . . . Of course, if Jesus was convinced that he was the Messiah, and referred the prophecy in Daniel to the Messiah, he must also have expected in accordance with it, sometime or other, to come with the clouds of heaven."

With that last "of course," closes that rather uncertain groping for a verdict for or against the matter. But with what impression does an unprejudiced reader take leave of that disquisition? If he is really unprejudiced, he will, I think, throw down that apologetic, even in its new dress, as worthless, and will accept as firmly established historical fact only this: Jesus told about himself that he was the Messiah, and that, in accordance with that, the expected new period of the world would begin with his appearance. He found believers, and after he was executed, the belief in him still continued, the beginning of the new period of the world was expected from day to day with his early return—he was looked upon as having already arisen from the dead. He himself may have expected that the miraculous beginning of the new period of the world would happen, without his death occurring before; with his death, that expectation changed, as stated.

And that, indeed, is all that we are able historically to establish concerning him; and it is sufficient, too, for an explanation, not only of his appearance, but also for all consequences that followed it. That historical fact must not be garbled, must not be weakened, nor must other things not belonging to it be added, lest new confusion be caused. Thus it puts the matter out of the proper perspective if it is attempted to attribute to him the belief in his being the Son of God in the eminent sense of the term, or in the Messiah being the Logos; and above all, it is pure delusion to attribute to him the character of a universal God-Man as taught by the Hegelian School. The idea that he stepped beyond national and legal Judaism must also be totally rejected, and solely ascribed to later development. Nor can the nobler religious and moral conceptions and doctrines which are put in his mouth and heart—though we should attribute them to him and acknowledge their excellence with necessary limitations—be regarded as his own in the sense that he was their author and was the first who entertained and proclaimed them, but at the utmost that he adopted them and appropriated them as he found them already made by others.

And here we have arrived at the point which to us is the starting point, but which has not yet risen into the horizon of Christian science, however necessary for a proper understanding. It not only lacks the knowledge, but also—

however heavy the charge may sound, all experience leads to prove its accuracy—the uncovetous acknowledgment of the property of others. And in this respect also, each one of our authors occupies his own peculiar position, although they meet in the same error ultimately. Mr. Renan makes a running start toward justice, does not avoid the means necessary to a clearer understanding in order—as he is pleased to assume the same of his ideal pattern—to have a serious relapse. Mr. Strauss has made up his mind at the very start; on this point he fully occupies the grounds of the ancient apologetics, repeats the old faded and exploded ideas concerning the Judaism of that time, knows nothing of recent investigations, and though he may not be charged with intentionally ignoring them, we can not but blame him for having neglected the requisite care and labor to inform himself of them.

Everyone who contemplates the origin of Christianity with a historical eye must come to the conclusion that he has to estimate and consider the three co-operating factors, viz.: Palestinian Judaism of that time, Hellenistic Judaism, and Roman-Grecian culture. It appears perfectly natural to us that former writers who, from the start ranged themselves with one side, looked at those factors through the spectacles of their party and presented them accordingly. With all of those, Palestinian Judaism fared badly. Some painted it in very black colors in order to let the picture of rising Christianity stand out in more dazzling brilliancy. Others, who admitted that Christianity had some blemishes, ascribed them to Judaism of that time; whatever in Christianity did not please them was called Jewish prejudice which had not been quite overcome at the first start but had to yield gradually as Christianity gained strength—or must yet yield. Of men who mean to consider and present the life of Jesus from a purely historical point of view, we can demand and expect a closer examination of the three factors named. They could, indeed, pass by Hellenistic Judaism and Pagan culture, both of which were unknown to Jesus, and co-operate only in the subsequent development of Christianity, and they are perhaps even forced to leave them in the background in order to avoid the error of assuming that Jesus had been influenced by those elements. But they are bound to examine the more closely, the rock from which Christianity was originally hewn, the fountain from which Jesus himself, and exclusively at that, drew his knowledge. Renan in fact distinctly denies all influence of the other two factors and abstains from further examination of both, as he could and even was obliged to do for his present purpose. On the other hand, he earnestly seeks to throw light upon the Judaism of that time, carefully informs himself of all recent researches, speedily appropriates them, and makes ready with unprejudiced and just mind, to disclose the fountain and its contents from which Jesus had drawn. If some harsh and queer opinion creeps in, some incorrect statement occurs, it happens because his aids are still insufficient. But the more deeply he enters into the history, the more embarrassing the foibles of his hero become to him, so much the more his bias gains upon him and he works himself into wrath against Judaism that much more. If it bothers him that the teacher who was at first so meek and mild "employed very harsh expressions against his opponents," he explains it by this, that "Jesus who was almost exempt from all the defects of his race, was led against his will into making use of the style used by all the polemics." "One of the most prominent faults of the Jewish race is its bitterness in controversy, and the abusive tone which it always throws into it" (p. 325). If our writer soon after (p. 334) does not deduce from Judaism the manner adopted by Jesus in controversy, it is done because he there means to make it a virtue: "His exquisite scorn, his sharply pointed challenges always struck to the heart. Eternal brands, they seared the marks into the wounds forever. The Nessus shirt of ridicule which the Jew, the son of the Pharisees, has dragged along in tatters for eighteen centuries, was woven by Jesus with divine art. Masterpieces of lofty raillery, the marks of his brush have burned into fiery lines into the flesh of the hypocrite and pretender of devotion. Incomparable pictures, worthy of a Son of God! Only a God can kill in that manner. Socrates and Moliere but graze the skin. He carries fire and rage into the very marrow of the bones." I simply quote his words, and therefore will only add his opinion on the persons who took part in the condemnation of Jesus, and on their proceeding. Of the generation of the high priests of that time, he says (p. 366): "The spirit of the family was haughty, bold and cruel; it had that peculiar and reserved malignity which characterizes Jewish politics." Mr. Renan caps the climax at the conclusion. That he calls (p. 396) the death of Jesus a judicial murder and yet designates it as legal (p. 411) and only says "The law was detestable" may be passed over. He is also kind enough to admit that the Jew of the present day should not be made to suffer on account of the application of "that detestable law" of long ago; he calls it (p. 412) "the law of ferocity" and remarks, "The hero who offered himself to abrogate it, had to suffer it before all." And then he continues, "Alas! it will require more than eighteen hundred years before the blood which he now loses will bear its fruit! In his name, for centuries, tortures and death will be inflicted upon thinkers as noble as he. Even to-day, in countries which call themselves Christian, penalties are imposed for religious delinquencies. Jesus is not responsible for such aberrations. He could not foresee that any people with disordered imagination would ever conceive him as a frightful Moloch, greedy for burnt flesh. Christianity has been intolerant, but intolerance is not an essentially Christian act. It is a Jewish act," etc.

We are weary of citing such expressions of a thinker who otherwise aspires to impartiality; the relapse appears into the old apologetics which knew to defend only by abuse. However, Mr. Havet has already exposed in the *Revue des Deux Mondes* the injustice of such a mode of proceeding, and the belletristic form in which it is presented removes the necessity of serious refutation. Against definite charges that are more than unsupported assertions, we are at all times ready to enter the arena. But it would be unjust to Mr. Renan to charge him with a considerable remnant of religious hatred. His is not the opinion of the Christian about Jews and Judaism, it is the race-jealousy between the Aryan—i. e., the Indo-European (or we call it the Indo-German)—and the Semite. Mr. Renan, as descendant of Japhet, even now, fights in the Jew, not his faith, but the son of Shem. Let us not follow him into that domain of the jealousy between races. Let us pass on to the German writer.

In my opinion, the two chapters in the book of Strauss, entitled respectively "Development of Judaism" and "Development of the Greco-Roman Culture" are the weakest part of the work. The latter part, and especially the manner in which it is treated, have really no connection with the subject of the book. As we have already stated, Grecian culture was unknown to Jesus himself, perhaps even its very name, and can not afford the smallest clue to an explanation of his character. But even into the succeeding formation of Christianity, Grecian culture entered as a fermentative agent, rather in its degenerate state than in its earlier, nobler form. But Mr. Strauss emphasizes just that earlier form and would like to ascribe to it the ennobling moral influence on incipient Christianity, while he denies such work to Judaism. An assertion of Welcker serves him as guide (p. 180) and he quotes: "Out of Hebrew supernaturalism, humanity could never have proceeded; for in proportion as its conception is earnest and exalted, must the authority and the law of the One God and Master press down human God-conscious liberty from which all energy and cheerful aspiration to the best and noblest aims emanates." Mr. Strauss may have felt the weakness of such reasoning, for he adds with a view to strengthening it, "Just because the Divinity did not confront the Greek in the force of a commanding law, he had to become a law unto himself; because he did not, like the Jew, see his life regulated for him, step by step, he was compelled to seek for a moral pattern within himself." It ought to be high time for finally dispensing with the abuse of such abstract construction of history. Whoever does not make history along the lines of such self-made categories, but derives it from the facts, and takes pains to comprehend it, will soon come to the conclusion that the moral doctrines of a people are the reflection of its conception of the Deity; the more perfect the thought of God, the more exalted the ideal towards which man aspires. As an actual fact, just that moral rottenness of the paganism of that time made it easier for Christianity to gain converts among serious thinkers; Grecian culture in its then decomposed state was a troubled, fermentative element, but never, as Strauss would like to make it, a worthy instructress.

What Strauss thus attributes and adds to Grecian culture, that he deducts in good measure from Judaism. With delight he grabs for its actual or alleged defects, and his knowledge of the Judaism of that time stands on the same plane which he occupied twenty-nine years ago. As then, so even now he ransacks Eisenmenger and Gfoerer that they may supply him through channels outside of legitimate criticism with passages from comparatively recent works, such as that of an addle-brained cabalist of two hundred years ago, Ruben Hoeschke, viz. his Yalkut Rubeni and the like. He shares that ignorance with the entire Christian science in Germany; yet he almost surpasses it in ignoring all recent researches in Jewish literature, and his delight in painting Judaism in the darkest shades is evident. His continual placing of priests and prophets in juxtaposition without divining the fundamental antagonism between the principles animating them; his presenting of priests and Pharisees as one, his outlines of the Sadducees and Pharisees, his dwelling with preference on the Essenes who were without sensible influence and of whom only the unreliable Josephus gives an extended account; his manipulation of the stenciled categories of obstinacy, narrowmindedness, one-sidedness, national rigidity, etc., exhibit the deplorable relapse of the historian into the prejudiced apologist whose phrase and verbiage but poorly veil the lack of knowledge and fathoming of the actual relation of the facts.* In that, he outdoes modern science, which still gropes in the dark with uncertain steps in this part of history, and continues to operate with

* For some particulars, compare II. Vol., pp. 295, etc., in my "Juedische Zeitschrift fuer Wissenschaft und Leben."

old, used-up material without examining it anew or increasing it, but which yet sometimes feels an impulse to gain better knowledge. Mr. Strauss seems to have stopped investigation, and thereby gives up the office of historian.

It is a very deplorable fact that men who are as highly esteemed by one side for their religious liberality as they are condemned by the other, are so little familiar with the very territory an exact knowledge of which is indispensable to a scientific examination of the subject, and that they cling with a certain tenacity to antiquated prejudices. To melt the ice of unjust prejudice may be left to the sun of progressive civilization. But the continued efforts of true science alone can succeed in overcoming ignorance. We can not clear the Jewish students of science from the charge that they have not sufficiently turned their attention to the investigation of the most important periods and developments and thereby afforded in their works, material and results to Christian investigators for correction of their opinion. But Christian science is not justified thereby. In any other department, scholars would long hesitate to pronounce a final judgment upon subjects for the examination of which the necessary premises and capacities are wanting; only as far as Judaism is concerned, they think to be at liberty to act with sovereign licentiousness. At all events, it is the right, as well as the duty, of the Jewish scholar emphatically to expose such proceedings. We hope that all sides will seriously undertake a thorough and unbiased investigation of Jewish ancient history and bring their results to the knowledge of the general public.

SECOND PART

In Twelve Lectures, with an Appendix: Open Letter to PROFESSOR DR. HOLTZMANN

Preface.

The recital in this part starts from the same basic idea, continues that of the first part, and the produced historic development can itself undertake the justification of my concept of history. The introductory and closing remarks, to which I count also the "Open Letter" (a defense against attacks on the first part), likewise contain some confirmation of it. The matter develops in this volume closer to the thread of history, and as I could not presume the events, the most important spiritual moments and carriers of the period treated, as so well known as those of the preceding one, I had to set forth more definitely the general content of the time as far as it contains the impress and development of Judaism. Accordingly, this part had to draw the essential Jewish-historical part with large strokes, and it may thereby help the larger cultured public to a better acquaintance with Jewish history without claiming to furnish a complete historical work. Yet it is to be hoped that a sharp imprint of the character of each time and the inner historic connection will be perceived so much the more easily. In the selection of the facts, the representation of which the intelligent reader will easily notice to rest upon independent investigation without requiring, according to the plan of the book, copious citations, there was no room for new, detailed examinations, and I had to be satisfied with a few short notices which treat more fully of some especially interesting particulars illustrating the general mental condition.

May this part, too, enjoy the favor of the readers. When in the eleven centuries of which it treats during an exceedingly dry period of the world's history, there is yet revealed within Judaism so much motion of spirit influencing the entire development, the superiority with which "Jewish affairs" are kept at a distance as not worth considering, might be surrendered, the impregnation starting thence be acknowledged, and the duty accepted to become better acquainted with them as influential historical factors of the world.

GEIGER.

Frankfort on the Main, May 11, 1865.

Contents.

I.

Introduction.

Judaism had not completed its mission with the end of its second commonwealth. Within itself, it had completely conquered idolatry, and had worked the idea of the unity and sanctity of God into a living conviction. It had represented to man that divine sublimity as pattern to be imitated, had exhorted him to act as a likeness of it. It had almost reduced to complete loss of importance the pretentious influence of a privileged priest-caste and an atoning sacrificial service, and had brought into prominence the equality of men and their value according to their free moral aspiration. But these foundation principles of all truly human piety, these eternal truths to which all mankind shall rise, had been worked out within a tribe which felt the necessity of forming itself into a narrow, close nation, because they had grown up amidst an environment led by vastly different convictions. The Jewish people had, therefore, to separate itself with some severity, in order not to be seized by those aberrations, while it could not, on the other hand, wholly avoid the influences from without, and many customs entered into its religious thought and life which never sprouted from its idea, but rather were intruders from the surrounding nations. Thus the mission of Judaism was not completed. It lived separate, it accepted this separation as a duty, and had to keep it up according to the condition then prevailing, while according to its true calling it shall pour out over all mankind, in love embracing all. It should guide man to walk in the ways of God, in the ways of the highest wisdom and the highest moral freedom; it should educate him to that, and it was through its exclusion, as well as through the influence of its environment, forced into many unfree extraneous formalities.

Whether Judaism with undisturbed development in its home country would have broken through those barriers, whether it would, according to the enthusiastic view of its prophets, have opened its gates wide for the reception of all humanity, whether it would have developed from within to overcome all legal formalities, is a question which the course of history does not answer for us. Nearly contemporaneous with the dissolution of the Jewish state, the attempt appeared to proclaim the entrance of the Messianic time and the dominion of Judaism as near at hand or actually in existence, but the attempt had come from an over-excited time, wrestling with despair; neither the Jewish people nor humanity was sufficiently prepared for that. Truth is not conquered by a charge; it penetrates gradually and transfigures. Judaism, indeed, sent forth a messenger who in course of time made many of its doctrines the common property of mankind; but, soon estranged from the faith that had sent him, he accepted, when he entered into the world and mixed with the heathen, also much of that world, and blended with paganism. The mission of Judaism was not accomplished by that.

It was itself to journey into the world with all its members, according to the entire form of life which it had taken. The call of the spirit directing history went out to Judaism: Go out over the whole earth, prove thy power in it, preserve thyself, purify thyself, and win over all mankind. It did not do that from free choice, nor with a heart confident of victory; sad necessity imposed the journey; shy, anxious, and timid, it stepped into a world which it regarded with suspicion. And the world growlingly turned its eyes upon it and noticed it with suspicion and gloom. Thus Judaism was cast into conditions not only foreign but hostile. Its battle had to be fought for a long time, more for mere preservation than for purification and extension. It must therefore not surprise us when we notice the endeavor for separation, for anxious preservation of every trifling differentiation, and see such endeavor crowded to the front. The indestructibility of the fundamental ideas was to be proved even under the most unfavorable circumstances, and has been proved, even when in the difficulties under which they were forced to labor, they found singular expressions. A plant that roots in darkness, works in singular twists and turns towards the light; it takes shapes and forms which are wholly strange to its nature. But he would be a poor botanist that would judge of the species according to such crooks contrary to its nature. The expert will not misjudge the normal nature and force, he will rather admire in the anomaly, the endeavor to get to the light. In the same way, he poorly judges Judaism, who attributes its medieval abnormity to its innermost nature, and does not take into consideration how it had to wind through all artificial restraints, get over unsurmountable barriers, breathe in tainted air, exist in the dark shadow of death lurking on every side, that does not rather admire the inexhaustible force of life with which it has not only preserved itself, but even worked to the light by every possible way, how it has been able to soon straighten out its crooks and has not been wrecked under all those unfavorable conditions in its process of purification and its salutary effects.

For Judaism does not present to us, even from the time when it began its journey among the nations, the picture of decay; its way is not barren; rich seeds of the spirit are scattered by it and impregnate the soil of humanity. The following chapters shall furnish the proof. Not in the sense that we are arbitrarily selecting proofs for an arbitrarily accepted result. We want to undertake our journeyings through the centuries, as far as we are favored to continue them, not with the intention of shutting our eyes before sad apparitions, spiritual deterioration and malformation, to exclusively accentuate the predominant healthy developments, to veil the other sides or even put them by artificial illumination into a blinding light and lend them a magic charm. That would be falsification of history. Let us keep far from that oblique consideration of the Middle Ages, from that forced praise of the sad aberrations of that long period of time. Let us give honor to the truth, even when it wounds us and gives us pain. We see a long period of the world's history go its peculiar ways, fight its heavy, calamitous battle, first with manifold relapses, and after frequent falls, rise by the greatest efforts to very slowly ripening results. Within this history, Judaism, which has not made the conditions, but is suffering with and by them, is producing remarkable phenomena of itself. This historic fact shines forth to us by all exact knowledge and open view, and so much the more, the more exact our knowledge and the more open the view. To bring into prominence this unmistakable truth of history is not a constraint forced upon history; it is the true expression of its innermost movement; to explain this highly remarkable fact from the deep impulse which in Judaism even under the burdensome oppression constantly stirred its forces afresh, is no far-fetched interpretation, no artificial extenuation, it is the quite simple presentation of the development which evidences itself as according to nature,

This proceeding in the contemplation of history is a truly unprejudiced objective one. The investigator who proceeds in this way does not permit his sight to be dimmed by the power gained by an opposing tendency, while Judaism had pantingly to drag itself along. The conditions of power, even if existing for a long time, are no final judgment of God in the world's history. The good and true has to wrestle long before it can rise from its insignificance and lowness and surmount the mass of opposing obstacles. Error or half-truth suits an imperfect stage better than the whole or more developed truth. The final verdict is only given at the end and when the end arrives in the course of history, who will determine that? The world's history has not yet passed over Judaism; it still stands, stands in full freshness, receptiveness, and capacity of development. He that explains it, he that reveals the reason of its endurance, is the unprejudiced investigator, not he that in his imagined superiority ignores it. Whoever judges objectively will no longer permit himself to be misled by deteriorations which sometimes were conditioned by its own peculiar circumstances and sometimes were forced from without; he will penetrate to the creative force which did not exhaust itself in those malformations, which was yet able to surmount and set them aside, and now works on their removal and on noble new formations. That is poor objectivity which sees only the particularities that force themselves to the surface, puts them together and expects to form by that a picture true to nature; a faithful picture must not only fix the momentary distortion of the features but it must render the enduring character which rules every situation, even the most disagreeable one.

From many sides, such a proceeding may again be called *apologetics*, with an insinuation of condemnation. Against the word I have no objection. To get for the misjudged good its right of which it has been despoiled, to undertake the defense of an unjustly reviled person or matter may be called apologetics, as Plato and Xenophon wrote apologies of their master, Socrates. But such apologetics is meritorious, is no blamable distortion, is no fencing trick of a pettifogger. They may always call our endeavor apologetical; we shall not be frightened by the word, but rather glory in such apologetics. To defend the weak, to awaken a minority that is gradually losing heart, to a conscious knowledge of their rights and get them their dues although they are blamed and disgraced by a public opinion which the privileged ones have produced and preserve for their self-glorification, such defense is an enterprise which had at all times more attraction for noble men than that cheap and dishonorable course of flattering the powerful and mocking the wronged and disinherited by jeers.

But let us keep far from excitement and pass on to the facts.

II.

The Dissolution of the State and Its Consequences, Divine Service, Nationality and Faith, Akiba.

The murderous fight about Jerusalem was ended; to the last moment the courageous remainder that had retreated into the Temple, defended its ruined walls. It was a hot fight in and about Jerusalem, about the Temple and within it, and long after every prudent calculation had seen the last glimmer of hope fade away, the zeal of those passionately enthusiastic for their noblest possessions could not be restrained from giving their bodies over to sure destruction. The fight was terminated, the Temple fell, it had become a ruin. Whether it was intentionally, by order of the commander, or through the blind rage of the soldiery, set afire, is not certain; at any rate, the flames consumed it. The last remainder of independence had given way, Judea was conquered, the state was shattered, and consequently there was nothing left of actual nationality and independent administration. Mighty convulsions of that kind are attended with complete transformations, but the consequences are of greatly varying kind. If they hit institutions which are already hollow and undermined, the blast shatters what had been preserved simply by force of habit, and makes room for new formations and new institutions. The effect of such convulsion is different upon arrangements and institutions which until then were yet fully alive, though needing a transformation in their root, or only leaning upon the whole and not existing by their own living force. If they have never been questioned and are now first shaken by the sudden turn of things, those who are touched thereby hold to them so much the more strongly and are more anxious, in order not to lose by outside pressure, something which they carried along as a valued possession. In this manner appeared the consequences of the dissolution of the Jewish state and the destruction of the Temple.

Up to that time, a thousand years' fight had been fought about Temple, sacrificial service, and priesthood; a fight of a thousand years, in which the noblest forces demanded a rejuvenation or a complete removal, a different expression of ideas from the manner in which they were represented by priesthood and sacrificial service. For a long time the old prophets and the later teachers had sometimes totally rejected sacrificial service and priesthood, and sometimes at least represented spiritual service as much more meritorious and rooting more properly in the essence of Judaism. In the meeting-houses of the Pharisees and their societies, a new divine service had grown up alongside and outside of the Temple service. In these meetings, prayer, contemplation, and instruction, took the place of sacrifice; it was a divine service in a smaller circle which existed by the side of the general official one, which perhaps was not considered as sufficient for the whole nation, but which still took away the best forces from that official divine service. Thus, priesthood and sacrificial service had long been outgrown; yet as existing arrangements they were too much connected with the whole life of the nation, were too closely interlaced with all institutions of the state, were so closely joined with the administration and government that their removal could hardly have been expected as long as the exterior conditions for their preservation were not absent. Now, the wind came and the withered stem fell down. Sacrificial service and priesthood were suddenly swept away, the Temple which had been their necessary basis, existed no more. If the institution had been alive, it would have been possible to look up a new place for it; but such a desire was not at all in the spirit of the time. The new divine service, prayer, took the place of the old Temple service. Prayer, contemplation, and instruction, as they already were in practice in the meeting-houses (synagogs) of the societies of the Pharisees, were now recognized as the only true worship of God, which should rule in Israel.

That was a great step, Judaism itself rose by it to a higher plane, offered a high gift to all humanity. As long as divine service consists in pilgrimage and exterior symbolical service, it remains on the plane of childhood; when the definite place gives the consecration, when the place only, gives to the assembly the possibility of approaching their god, so long worship of God remains something coming to man from without, only a dim idea of the sublimity of a higher overwhelming power is excited, it remains at the plane of obscure sensation, at childish babble that struggles for expression. Only with the step, that the place does not consecrate the assembly, but that the assembly gives the place its importance; that the clear and definite thought is pronounced and not hovering in general dim sentiment; that the manly, ripe expression takes the place of the childish babble; that man struggles to apprehend with full consciousness his relation to God and to render it in definite, clear words, to enter into himself and to securely lay down the resulting contemplations: only then man is truly religious, only then religion has produced ripened fruit. For divine service is not a religious exercise at the side of many various other ones, is not a single religious action at the side of which many equal ones have the same rank; divine service is the immediate expression of man's relation to God. Here he wants to put together all the sensations and thoughts that he is filled with towards God and which join him to God. Divine service is the expression of the common consciousness of a community of the same faith and of their religious position; in the purity and depth of divine service the truth of the religious creed is reflected in the clearest manner. The plane to which, accordingly, Judaism has risen, must be apprehended in its full importance. We have become used to divine service as an existing fact, but this fact is an acquisition of Judaism and has, therefore, only been perfectly communicated to those religions which have gone forth from Judaism or are leaning upon it. When another motive than prayer, contemplation, and instruction, presses forward, the condition of obscure sentiment recurs, mankind has suffered a relapse, religion has lost its purity and the fight must be fought anew, in order to again acquire that old genuine possession which Judaism has handed out.

That is on one side a consequence of the great convulsion which proceeded from the fall of the Temple and the dissolution of the state. In another manner those consequences are not made so clear and plain. Judaism had arisen in a people; this people was the carrier of the ideas of that faith and it could not historically be otherwise. The religion reached out far beyond the barriers of the people; it taught that it should at some time become the common property of mankind; it did not confine itself to the compatriots but joyfully accepted all who acknowledged it in true and full fidelity.

Not Jewish parentage made one a member of that nation, but the acknowledgment of the faith. The stranger and the home-born, thus it was continually repeated, were to be perfectly equal. Yet for the present, Judaism existed among definite people, the religion was interlaced with this nationality and closely interwoven with the life of its state. Where religion and people coincide, where religion and state institutions remain in constant reaction upon each other, there the state is, of course, consecrated in its laws and institutions by the religious life breathed into it; but vice versa, the religious institutions become at the same time commands of the state and popular custom, they penetrate and color the ideas of right which the state is called upon to materialize; they wear the garment of nationality which that people has to form. As long as people and religion, state and doctrine progressed within Judaism with hands joined, isolated clouds might arise out of such commingling, but the junction was a natural one. But now the people's bands were dissolved, nationality was to cease, the state was broken up, the confessors of Judaism became and should become members of that people among whom they lived and citizens of the state within the sovereignty of which they resided. How will this religion now accomplish its new task within this new position? Is Judaism really so completely permeated by nationality that it cannot exist without the same, is its real task exhausted as soon as nationality has disappeared? Or does this religion (Judaism) stand higher than nationality, will it dissolve the national ties by which it was swathed, and strive to respond to the call of becoming common property of mankind?

That question came to Judaism with precipitation; history put it without preparation. Until then a perforation of nationality had not been striven for; on the contrary, its strengthening was desired that it might be a support to the religion. What is to be withdrawn so suddenly is not surrendered so readily. Nor was the problem recognized in its full clearness at once. A people that has just been subjugated and is still bleeding from a thousand wounds is so much the less inclined to surrender the smallest particle of what has been saved of its national force. The convulsions of the organism just cut through are so mighty that it appears as the highest task to preserve the life still pulsating, and hope is yet present of quickly bringing about a complete restoration. Things were at first arranged as well as could be done. Jerusalem could no longer be the place of assembly; they removed to Jamnia to preserve coherence from there; a new magistracy was established there, the old institutions were observed as far as they were possible in life, and new ordinances and arrangements necessary for the moment were set up. It is significant that most of them proceeded from this view: "Perhaps the Temple will be rebuilt to-morrow; everything must be prepared for that, we must be properly ready to move into it at once." Thus the dissolution was regarded as a condition that would soon pass by: "All will soon be formed over, for the moment we had to give way to superior force, things will level up again, the old conditions will be renewed, let us keep prepared and ready for them."

Soon the silent longing was not enough; the convulsions took life, attempts at rebellion appeared, and barely seventy years after the destruction of the Temple, about 130, a powerful rising took place, it seemed as if the fight would be made all over again. The rebellion had wonderful fresh and new strength and kept in the field during several years against the veteran legions and the powerful dominion of Rome. Under Ben-Kosiba (also called Bar Kokhbā, "the son of the star" or "starlike"—so hailed as the star that was to rise out of Jacob) whose real name we do not even know, but is supposed to have been Simeon—under Ben-Kosiba, a courageous troop gathered and he was a brave and skillful general. He knew how to attach the scattered remnants to himself, and to breathe courage into them for resistance against the powerful adversaries. Especially in the mountain fortress Bethar, he maintained himself for a long time; the life breath of Israel was kept in anxious suspense by his enterprise; but he succumbed, and every hope of a successful rising disappeared.

Then a sad time began. So far, the Romans, if not particularly mild to the Jews, who were subjugated enemies, had, on the whole, paid no attention to their interior institutions and religious opinions, but now the conditions took another turn. Every Jewish ordinance, every custom, was considered a sign of rebellion; they no longer saw in it a religious practice proceeding from the heart, but considered them the visible marks of a rebellion which must be put down with fire and sword. "Why art thou condemned to die on the cross?"—"Because I performed circumcision."—"Why art thou sentenced to die?"—"Because I rested on the Sabbath."—"Why art thou whipped?"—"Because I observed the feast of the tabernacles." Such conversations have been handed down from that time. The most severe punishments were ordered to keep the Jew from making himself known as professing his religion; the gloomy shadows of "the time of danger, the time of repression of the faith" run through this later literature.

Yet, persecution and blood are the surest means to fortify opposing opinions, instead of suppressing them. The ancient teachers with deep historic insight said: "That for which the Israelites have given their life, has become firm and constant within them; what they have not sealed with their blood has not acquired such enduring force." Particulars that would have seemed nonessential and would never have appeared as the center, were now to attain a higher value because so much had to be suffered for them, and they even became foundations of the faith. The persecutions which, from that time on, scarcely relented, removed them from their fellow-inhabitants and threw them back within themselves; their own national memories and hopes were kept awake that much the more. The present was gloomy; to enter into and commingle with the people with whom they now resided, became an impossibility. The rulers regarded the professors of Judaism as a separate part of civil society, as a close community. They were treated as such a one and had to feel themselves so. In ancient Rome, that great world-empire, it was hardly possible that one tie should closely bind all the various countries together; each one retained its peculiarity within the loose bond. The greater part of the Jews had remained in Judea, in Palestine, and thus under pagan Rome the preservation of a certain amount of nationality resulted of itself. In the later Christian time, persecution and pressure increased, and the repelling forces from without knitted the individual members of the Jewish confession still closer together, and thus the memories of the past assumed quite naturally the colors of shining ideals and the hope of the future could consist only in this, that therein whatever the past appeared to have been would reappear. The memories heightened into religious veneration, the hopes into religious longing.

The mood was fed through the whole character of the approaching Middle Ages. Pagan Rome was verging towards its dissolution; no longer was fresh, living force circulating into its far-off members which were the component parts of the large body. Judaism, which by all fidelity to its own faith, rapidly enters into the spirit of any virile nationality, did not find such a one to which it could join itself. While pagan Rome remained without influence upon the formation of Judaism and acted only repellent, the ruling course of ideas of the Christian world which took possession of Rome's heritage, had altogether injurious effects: it confirmed and developed an oblique tendency existing within Judaism of that time, by making that tendency the ruling one within itself and for the whole world. With the rise of Christianity, the history of the world was actually completed for the Middle Ages; perfection had been reached; further development was neither ordered nor possible. On the contrary, to lean upon that ancient time, to carry that ancient ideal into the present, and when that was not possible, to hope for a future which in a marvelous way would yet make that ideal the actuality, was the inmost core of all effort of the Middle Ages. The present was ignored; it was, to use a recent form of expression, the bad fallen reality. It existed, but was unfit, useless; it appeared degenerate insomuch as it was not the counterpart of the ideal which shone over from the past, insomuch as it tried to be something of itself. Thus the world of that time had no present, it had only a past to which it looked up, and a future for which it waited. To create by their own powers of the time, to produce new formations by their own ability, that was wholly outside of the horizon of the long enduring Middle Ages. Past and present played, therefore, into each other in an exceedingly curious manner; the past times were carried along in the frame of the every-day happenings of the present, and vice versa. With such views the Christian world looked back upon the old prophets and the patriarchs; they were looked upon as men who had already had the full belief of the present, who had been full of the same longing that was felt by the world of that time; qualities were imputed to them that were now considered the best ones. Even the great ancient pagans, as far as they were known, took Christian form or were transfigured into wizards. Of historic development, of things having been different in earlier times, there was not even an inkling of an idea; consequently, they tried to bring all the past into the present and form it as a shadow into the present. What was it that really produced the great and violent struggle in the Middle Ages, what shows the only sign of life moving deeply through those times? The struggle to make a Christian-Roman world empire, attempted in two different ways, and just that difference caused mighty struggles which, after all, wrought great advantages for the world, but sapped its best forces and caused splits and division of nations, from which the present still suffers. In a certain sense, the German nation was the normal people of the Middle Ages, and its chief did not strive to strengthen the nation within itself, to soundly form by its own healthy material, to make a close junction of the individual members, but he attempted to present the succession of the Roman Empire in Christian form. He was perfectly satisfied with a pseudo-investiture, with an empty, formal acknowledgment of power that had no real strength. It was enough if only the shadow of the old ideal moved in the present across the world's stage, if only the semblance appeared that the Roman world-empire still existed. On the spiritual side also, the reality of the Roman Empire was striven for, and it was now commanded by the founder of Christianity. If he himself was not present, his shadow was to rule, he was to be represented by his vice-gerent. Even the religious idea needed his real presence at the communion table, he had to walk now as then, among his believers. Whatever else was done by the Middle Ages was esteemed ungodly; the present had merit only if it was leaning upon the past. For the future, nothing new was hoped; it should simply set up the past, perfect in all its particulars.

Can we now be astonished if that diseased tendency was also nourished within Judaism? Within it also, memory of the past and hope for the future became the chief principle of life. The national, which without this had its food by the persecutions from without, had now to permeate the religious life, the present was to be represented as a complete picture of the past, and everything that had its root in the state's existence should be preserved, even when the conditions for it were wholly lacking; whatever had been inherited, was esteemed of value, without examining its origin, was considered as law; externals grew on luxuriously without the sprout's receiving sap from the inner roots of the present life. They lived with the past in the present, they imagined the ancient devotees exactly as they beheld the devotees of the time, they wrapped the patriarchs into such masquerade as if those worthies had practiced all rules and ordinances down to the very last as they had grown up later. David and Mephiboset disputed about minor legal questions with all scholastic seriousness, even Shem and Eber had arranged schools exactly like those existing in later time. Historic sense was lacking and the different times were mixed in motley naivety; Laban was spoken of as an enemy of to-day, Haman and Amalek in like manner; Elijah was thought to be constantly at work among Israel, as present at the reception of every boy into the covenant and to have conversation with the teachers in the schools and synagogs, instructing and sometimes correcting them, often appearing in lovely manner as friend and savior, and entering every year into every house on the evening when the memories of the ancient delivery from Egyptian bondage were renewed. That delivery was, of course, an event of to-day! If our ancestors had not then been delivered from Egypt, we should to-day be subject to the Egyptians; that was repeated year by year. Past conditions were the present ones, and thus it is natural that the present ones should be the complete representation of the past ones; they strove with every force of mind and spirit to remove out of the present and to belong to a past which, in addition, they conceived upside down.

That is a strong reverse which Judaism of the Middle Ages reveals to us. It fed a life of shadows and semblances, and such a one naturally gives occasion for the most various aberrations. We must not hide that reverse if we want to estimate history justly and without bias, if we want to comprehend the task we have to work out regarding the Middle Ages. There must have been a solid sterling kernel alongside of that shadowy reverse, which could endure under the most various formations of life, under the hardest pressure of nearly eighteen centuries; there must have been an interior force which drove its sap even into those creepers. Legalism could never have preserved religion so long; religion carried legalism. Nationality could never have supplied to faith its force; faith quickened the quivering manifestations of national life, its memories and hopes. If in other religions, aberrations have been preserved for a long time, it has its cause in quite different conditions. Where rich, full life courses all its forces, when all saps that produce and nourish the planting, pour into one channel, it is natural that the movement endures, and thus all the stems that are not perfectly strong and roots that are not entirely fresh can be constantly freshened and receive new life. But when broken trunks, like Judaism, overgrown with creepers, are constantly exposed to new windstorms and yet keep alive, the root must be sound and the saps must be healthy; if they cannot, in gloomy times, appear in full beauty and noblest development, they yet have the imperturable force of self-preservation which, in spite of all overgrowth of creepers that the conditions force upon them, does not let them perish.

Therefore, even in those gloomy and difficult times, the genuine ideas of Judaism were not blotted out but always enjoyed further cultivation. We find the same men, in whom we see the founders of what we now call rigid legalism, the representatives of the most sterling truths of religion and of the deepest moral principles. Akiba Ben Joseph especially stands forth in that period. He lived at the time of the rising under Ben Kosiba, manifested in his life and teaching ardent zeal for the preservation of Israel in its inherited form. He believed in the restoration of its state and fought for it; he carried through with consistence the pharisaic principles in sharply defined externals, and contemporaries as well as posterity bow before him. The same man lays down principles that reveal a deeper comprehension than we should suppose from the author of those external ordinances. God, man, and humanity, are presented by him in the most dignified and sublime manner. He bases his sayings on verses of Scripture, interprets those in this way, as was the custom of that time. The custom had its foundation in the desire to find one's own thoughts complete in the past, designated by the same expression now in use for it. That is a method or proceeding which we may consider lacking independence and exegetically unjustifiable. But if we put aside the desire to lean upon the past and consider the views on their merits, they could not now be expressed better. "In the image of God created he him" (man), says the Scripture. Is there a shape of God and is man its image? By no means, says Akiba, the passage is to be understood in this way: God created man in a definite image, in an excellent shape; far be it that we should even in poetic expression, speak of an image of God. And again: "And the Lord God said, Behold, the man is become as one of us to know good and evil." How? Has man moved into the sphere of divinity? Should God say that? Impossible. The sense of the passage is quite different, says Akiba, and he interprets it: Man is become as one to know good and evil by himself. This interpretation is rather forced and hardly fits into the context, but it aims to remove God beyond corporeal presentation and to prevent the removal of the barrier between God and man. "For there shall no man see me and live." Is there only the death penalty against seeing God, can any man see God? Is that possible? Another misunderstanding, says Akiba. The passage means: No man sees me, and no living being, not the angels, not the holy, pure, spirits. Thus Akiba applies all the forces of his mind to preserve the conception of the spirituality of God in its purity.

In the same manner he presents man in his superiority. We have just quoted his sayings based on Scripture verses: "He created man in a definite image, in an excellent shape" and "man is become as one to know good and evil by himself." As the first saying designates man relative to his superiority above all creatures, so the second accentuates his conscience, sharp and short. Let us now quote an independent saying of his: "All is foreseen, freedom is given." These two sentences are put together which are the basis of all religion; Providence on the one side, and yet on the other side human freedom that acts of its own free will. On this metaphysical problem many religions have been wrecked. To hold fast to the sublimity and perfection of God, they pressed man deep down and made him a being incapable of acting or doing by himself. No, says Akiba, everything is forseen, but yet freedom is given. And while the former is assertion of deeper knowledge of God, the latter is assertion of true human piety. United, they form the possibility of all religiousness; united, they are of Judaism the basis which must never be shaken and has never been shaken. This capacity of man to determine for himself with full freedom, and therefore to elevate himself, to strive toward perfection by himself, and to attain it by honest endeavor, this capacity Akiba has presented in pregnant brevity as base and center of Judaism, and Judaism has steadily held fast to it. By that it has preserved the unbroken energy with which it bore and ruled the sorrowful life. Through its greatly intermingled history, this dignified conception of man runs along as the guiding line.

In recent times it has been recognized how the great poet and thinker who presented to us the struggle of the different religions, how Lessing in "Nathan" puts up, as noble representatives of the other two religions, men whose entire longing it is to withdraw from human activity. The friar would like to avoid all intercourse with men, and the dervish would flee out of the world's business to get back into his loneliness. On the contrary, the representative of Judaism is a man of the world, but at the same time a sage, a man that draws experience out of life, knows it, thoroughly apprehends its weaknesses and reverse side, but who still looks upon them with tolerance and kindness, sees in every human being a noble foundation and nourishes the joyful hope of being able to forward his development from that. Did Lessing want to glorify Judaism by that representation? By no means, but the poet in his genius has by that taken a deep look into the essence of the religions. It is true, other religions regard loneliness as the flower of all piety; they praise the withdrawal from human society, glorify celibacy and silent contemplation. The friar pronounces it with touching candor: "A hundred times a day I long to be on Tabor," and the hot-blooded dervish in his more violent manner says, "At the Ganges, at the Ganges alone, are men"—in both religions, fleeing out of the world is praised as true religiousness. In contrast to that, energetic endeavor in the world, recognition of humanity, is the basis of Judaism. A Nazarite was looked upon as a sinner because he abstained from wine; who undergoes fasting without good reason is also adjudged a sinner because he inflicts upon himself unjustifiable burdens and privations which are not approved by God. Fleeing out of the world would really have been natural to Judaism in view of its suffering and heavy trials; hermit's brooding ought to have made its appearance, and yet such doings were never recognized as worthy action. On the contrary, separation from society was reproved, labor in humanity, recognition of the goodness of God in nature and in the human world were at all times recognized and praised as the innermost kernel, as the foundation of all moral will and endeavor.

III.

Akiba, Interpretation of the Scriptures, Mishnah, Babylonian Gemara.

Let us continue the view of the period. Akiba, as we have observed, one of the foremost carriers of the tendency of that time (first half of the second century) has in brief words pronounced great eternal truths; he has presented God in pure spirituality and man in his capacity and task to develop out of himself the noblest product. Let us try to complete that representation by a few illustrations. Besides God and man separately, the question arises as to man within mankind, as to the relation of the individual within society. This question also, Akiba, in conjunction with his contemporaries, answers for us. Already the quoted saying of the excellent shape of man gives us in the form of its expression, sufficient guidance. It is, so the words run, a great preference for man to have been created in excellent shape. By that it is announced that man in general, not a separate class of men, not man under certain conditions, of a certain faith, the individual of an exclusive people, alone possesses that excellency, but man in general, all men. To leave no doubt about that meaning, he continues: For Israel, it is an excellency that they have recognized the fatherhood of God and are designated as God's children; what he said earlier of men and his high excellence, he holds to under all forms and conditions. And it corresponds to it, if he repeats the words of Hillel and pronounces: The comprehensive great principle of the law is, Love thy neighbor as thyself. In the most perfect agreement with that, is the doctrine of a little earlier contemporary of Akiba, Joshua Ben Chanania, who in general is most like Akiba. In contradiction to some other teachers, he quotes the verse of Psalms:

The wicked shall be turned into hell, and all the nations that forget God; and interprets, Only those that forget God are turned into hell, but not any that think of God; all—those outside of Israel as well—who harbor a divine idea, who strive toward higher, nobler development, even if in error now and then, who want to lift themselves toward God by honest endeavor, to all of them is due a share in eternal life, as he expresses it. That is a great thought which occurs here in briefest form, according to the method peculiar to the time, based upon a verse of the bible and without larger development of its contents, but which is of great depth and was for that period and for the long centuries thereafter, the fountain of richest and truly religious stimulation. At a time in which Judaism was forced, in order to defend itself against exterior influences, into exclusiveness, and austerely carried it through, at the selfsame time, it decidedly rejected by that doctrine, all one-sided narrowness which prevailed so mightily on the outside. It preserves to itself the recognition of all that is human, never lets go of the guiding line by which it joins the tie of peace with all humanity. We must apprehend this doctrine so much the more according to its full importance and recognize the indestructibility of the live Jewish religiousness, the more it seems to be in contradiction with the entire attitude and the efforts of the time. And this doctrine did not remain unnoticed; it became valid doctrine for all time in Judaism, even if the rigor from without, did not let it attain to its complete consequences, yet through all periods sounded the undisputed doctrine: The pious of all nations and all religions have a share in eternal life.

As to the position of the individual in society, sayings have come down to us from that time, which bear witness of the deep insight into the nature of man and his task. Everyone has value who carries within himself endeavor toward perfection, who accepts God's law and develops accordingly; he is measured by that, not according to position and rank. There are three crowns: the crown of government, the crown of priesthood, and the crown of the knowledge of the law; yet they are excelled by the crown of a good name. In every condition of life, only the faithful doing of duty which merits good repute, is the true crown. Government and priesthood are gifts of birth; knowledge of God's law can be acquired by everybody, and with it he grasps the finest crown, puts it on his head, and thereby attains true nobility. Already, at its first formation, Phariseeism had opposed priestly nobility, and all externals resting on office and birth; the value of learning and of science, as it was then understood, the value of what a man develops under all conditions, was put to the front. Akiba, like Hillel, was a man of the people, not of a higher rank, not endowed with inherited, unearned dignity; but the plain scholar, risen to the greatest importance in Israel, he stands as the hero of his time, and the builder for all times. In this, too, lies an energy of Judaism, which kept it fresh through the long period. It contained many a germ which, if it had belonged to its spiritual essence, must have necessarily developed and led to hierarchy. That this was not the case, proves that the spirit of liberty within it was too powerful for such attempts to succeed, even when they had their historic connecting links and points of departure. Induction into office by laying on of hands as sign of transference of spiritual dignity which in another religion became out-and-out endowment with the holy ghost, dates back into Judaism. Moses inducts Joshua into office in that manner. Yet, such induction never became in Israel a priestly one and was never considered to raise man to higher power. It remained an expression of acknowledgment of attained ability. It bestows the ornament of science, not the scepter of dominion; it was a testimony of the acquisition of scholarship, not a magical consecration and elevation. Therefore, at that time, as in all times, the most modest scholar without position or office, was esteemed in his circle just as much as another who had attained high position and office. This recognition of the love of the spirit and of the power of knowledge gave to Judaism strength and freshness.

Such principles, as we have learned to know them from that time, from a time in which Judaism was driven into externalism and exclusiveness, remained the living force that again gave even to the hulls some spirituality, and this endowed them with endurance; while on the other side, those hulls were necessary to guard the innermost kernel of Judaism from injuries which threatened it in such a terrible manner from that time on. Indeed, the conditions of the time demanded a tighter closing of ranks, a tangible external band, because old ties had been broken. To obtain a correct understanding of how this band was woven, which stretched around the whole life, to be able to correctly estimate the remarkable structure which then arose, we must present yet a few complementary facts which introduce us into the mental tendency that remained ruling within Judaism for a long time.

Already when the exiles had returned from Babylon to restore the state and attempted to rehabilitate the Temple, there had a certain antiquarian endeavor come back alongside of the quick and fresh spirit which they had preserved from the time of the old prophets, and which had become their real energy for overcoming all paganism. That antiquarian sentiment had prevailed in all arrangements. While yet Jeremiah, living about the time of the destruction of the first Temple, announced: "I will put my law in their inward parts and write it in their hearts;" while he, like all genuine prophets, put the emphasis upon the point that the spirit should rule, and not the letter, that not the written word but the live inner meaning should become the measure for thought and action, at the founding of the second Temple, we constantly meet the phrase, "and they found *written*." On all occasions, the books, accepted as written in godly spirit during Israel's early ages, were consulted about their opinions, and even opinions which were but temporary effusions arisen out of the conditions of a definite period, prevailed as general ordinances, valid for all eternity. It was not easy to make up the mind to admit the necessity for development and real, accomplished transformation. The spirit of tradition, which is nothing else than the creative instinct for further development, was at hand and the stream of life ran unconsciously through the whole and did the transforming—but to pronounce with full decision that a new time had arrived which must grow new products out of the old, energetic spirit, for such a decided declaration of their majority they were not ready. Even when Phariseeism arose against the priestly usurpations of the Sadducees, when it battled for the right of practical life and the vigorous body of the people, its importance against the arrogance of those who made regulations for the people as officers of the sacrificial service and the written law, it did not at first know how to give to its sound conviction and energy any other expression, and to apply for their presentation any other remedy than to transfer the letter of the law to themselves as well as to the priests, that it wrapped the whole people in priestly vestment and adjudged every possible priestly thing to them, so that they were more cramped, notwithstanding the liberal, free thought, out of which the resistance had come. In the later time, too, when mainly through Hillel, a free sentiment penetrated still farther, the endeavor was always present to compound with the letter as much as possible. That something else was ordained in the Scripture than that which prevailed in the present—to admit that, courage was lacking. They sought rather to expound one thing out and interpret another into it, to develop something different; in short, they wanted to carry the entire present into the past in order to attain the ease of mind of being really in accord with the past.

Such action was yet easier in the time of the second Temple. With the great political and religious congruence existing in those older conditions, transformations flowed in more unnoticed; the text of the old Scriptures was not as yet fixed and it was in parts treated very much at the pleasure of the copyist, never shrinking from making many changes, in the belief that it must always have read that way, since it could not be imagined to have been differently written according to then present views. The peculiarities of the Hebrew language, like those of the Semitic sister-languages, greatly favored such a change in the interpretation. As is well known, the Hebrew has in its writing, in the cold presentation by letters, only consonants—the mere skeleton of the idea, as it were—which receives its actual life only from the various pronunciations. According to the change in the unwritten vowels, sense, meaning, and importance vary greatly. Thus it was very easy at that time, when the vowels had not been written (for only much later they came to be directly indicated by little marks and points), at that time, when all punctuation was lacking, it was very easy to give new meaning to the text by other vocalization and different punctuation, joining or separating words and phrases. Such continued even when the efforts were made to fix the meaning more exact by vocalization and punctuation, and thus they have gained lasting shape in our present text of the bible. In that way, there was in that time a peculiar identification of one's own conception with the written word, a mutual accommodation, a looking up of one's own in the book which was adjudged to have exclusive validity in all its particulars, and then again a half-conscious carrying into it and soft bending of its general rules. With all veneration for the standard book, they proceeded with a certain degree of freedom; a people's life existed, which formed its wants and peculiarities independently, in which the conditions of living enforced their claims. Separate books were spoken of with boldness, they were rejected, they were accepted, according to the view held of them, according to the propriety of conviction found in them. This determination of the inner consciousness would surely have matured its fruits with a continued free nationality.

But now the time of ruin came. The tie was dissolved; if the members of this faith were to be kept together while they were scattered into the different countries, surrendering the hope of being soon again gathered; if they were not to totally fall apart, a new solid band had to be thrown around them and the spirit had to receive a lasting form by which it could be recognized. Yet the form into which it had already moulded itself was held to be the one authorized and binding for all time; it was the expression of the people to be preserved, and had to be kept with it. They believed that they must cling to the past in all its peculiarities. To ask for reasons, for occasions that might have produced this or that regulation, to measure them by the spirit within them—that seemed a wicked beginning, a presumptuous undertaking. Independence of one's own conviction could now no longer be permitted to prevail over the letter of the Scripture. Proceeding freely with the text, as had been the habit, could no longer be permitted, if everything was not to be made uncertain with the dismemberment of the national life. Accordingly, we then hear for the first time the acceptance as a firm principle (which on the one side became scientifically justified and preventing arbitrary action, had its favorable influence, but on the other side became a great hindrance): The traditional pronunciation—that is, the vocalization of the text, which was then not written but was customary in definite form—is a fence to the law; it must remain as it is now fixed and traditionally delivered to us; it can no longer be permitted that anybody should change it according to his own views.

Nothing should now be different from what the present letter of the Scripture presented, and nothing outside of it. But there were so many transformations and additions in use? That those were actually transformations and additions, could not be admitted. Clinging to the letter, they tried to interpret it as containing everything, all was to have existed as valid from the beginning, even if it was not found in the Scriptures; all should not be simply tradition as born out of the original spirit of the people and fitted to the conditions, but was to have existed in part by having been orally given in all its particulars, with the written law, to Moses, and in part by being indicated and contained in the Scriptures according to an interpretation which was regarded as perfectly justified with a divine book that chooses no superfluous word, no curious form, no irregularity, for nothing. From such seeming indications it was believed the regulations that varied from the natural meaning, and the ordinances that were outside of it, could be sufficiently proved. And thus an exceedingly dangerous method of interpretation was formed, which at first simply tried to bring the actual existing into harmony with the received text, but which, very soon in luxurious growth, created many a new regulation. Akiba and his contemporaries are patterns in this proceeding. Because Akiba demonstrated such an indication for ordinances which, without being given in the Scriptures, had become firmly established, but the validity of which was doubted by earlier teachers because they could not find any warrant for them in the written word—because Akiba demonstrated such an indication for them, he was glorified as a skillful scholar, as a man who had laid new and irremovable foundations for Judaism in its then existing form.

We have noticed a few attempts in which Akiba expounded verses in accordance with his conviction, going far away from the natural meaning. Another sample may suffice to mark the whole proceeding. It is a peculiarity of the Hebrew language that it sometimes indicates the objective case simply by the position of the noun in the sentence and sometimes by the addition of the little word "eth." That was sufficient occasion for those times to look for a particular reason why that little word or particle was used in some passages, although it might just as well have been absent, and to ask for indications in its apparently superfluous presence. That word, but derived from a different root, has the meaning "with." And that was enough for that school to expound it accordingly in that sense and call it "with" in every passage where it occurs. The proceeding grew to such an extent that the interpretation was not limited to discussion of the laws in the schools, but was carried into the bible translations. The want was felt for a new translation for the Jews who spoke the Greek language only. The ancient Greek septuagint version which represented the old position and had been made with great freedom, had lost its former authority, and thus several new Greek translations arose. Among them, the one of Aquila, a contemporary of Akiba, especially wanted to render the new position in full, and he is for that treated with great acknowledgment. It clings to the letter and in that way translates everywhere where that little word occurs as sign of the objective case as if "with" were in the text; it is rendered by the Greek "syn" although it does not fit into the connection and is repugnant to grammatical rules of the Greek language. That proceeding governed the time, and as it faces us in that translation, in the same way it was followed up by the teachers of the Mishnah—the name of the teachers of the law at that time—they expounded every sentence in which the little word was, as if something else was included. In the beginning, God created "the" heavens and "the" earth; here too, the objective case is indicated by "eth." Thence their interpretation: "the" heavens, "*with* the" heavens, all its hosts were created; "the" earth, "*with* the" earth everything produced that moves and grows upon it. Thus it is said of a contemporary of Akiba, Simon, or Nehemiah the Amsonite, that he had successfully found interpretations for all passages with that sign of the objective case, that he in fact found the mission of his life in that work. But he came across one passage at which he shied: "Thou shalt fear the Lord thy God;" here also the objective case is indicated by that particle. That besides the Lord, others should be given like fear, that another being should be named as on a certain equality with God, that he did not dare to pronounce, and he gave up any attempt at interpretation. Asked for the reason why, after so many interpretations, he abstained from finding one here, he said, "As I hope to receive reward for the interpretations which I made, so I hope to receive reward for abstaining from it in this passage." A fine sense for truth! It did not suffice to Akiba, he had more courage and was more consistent; he found an interpretation: "Besides God, you shall honor the teachers of His law."

This example may be sufficient to show with what anxiety the letter was observed on the one side, and how arbitrarily it was squeezed and pressed into service on the other side in order to interpret the most various things out of it. That anxious clamping and cramping at a given word was a sad necessity, if all was not to fall apart. The spirit could not reveal itself in its freedom. It could not in a fluid and esoteric manner have resisted a world that met it with rudeness and violence; it needed a hard, surrounding matter, a protecting hull, a sheltering roof, under which the scattered members got closer together. We learn about Akiba that he traveled far about, but we do not exactly know for what purpose. Yet it can hardly be doubted that in those journeys he did not omit to cement together the scattered members in the various countries, so that they remained parts of a whole. That endeavor was a leading principle with more or less clear consciousness. In Palestine, the old ties were dissolved, a new one was to get around them. Indeed, it gradually became a very coarse rope, but it answered the purpose; it held fast together until the time comes when the shell may be burst, and the mind and spirit can unfold freely.

The new movement with seeming convulsive clinging to the old things, effected a complete inner transformation and was decisively pressing to a close. And thus we meet, a short time thereafter, a new book worked out of that movement. It is the *Mishnah*. The word means "repetition," but is intended for "doctrine." Everything in it was then styled repetition; nothing appeared new, everything had to appear as simply repeated and renewed injunction of what the ancient time had given long ago. What the old law, so they persuaded themselves, had laid down in short words, in dim indications, that was here repeated, but expanded more definitely and more extensively. That Mishnah was closed by Rabbi Juda the Prince about sixty years after Akiba. Akiba himself appears to have started one, but it came to a close only then. It can not be our task here to enter into the particulars of it, but the spirit that rules in it is known by the matter accepted and the manner in which the material is arranged. It is in six divisions. It begins with the divine service and almost leads to the belief that this amounts to a demonstration, the presentation of the great treasure that had been gained, because divine service is the real and lasting conquest of Pharisaic Judaism against the priesthood. Priesthood is on the whole neglected and rather ignored in the Mishnah. And yet one-half of it is filled with instruction about things that had already been removed out of the present. Besides the still-valid ordinances about festivals, marriage relations, civil law matters, and the like, it treats of regulations about the soil, the dues or taxes to be paid from the crops, about sacrifices, cleanness and uncleanness. Those matters fill the greater part of the book, matters which had disappeared out of practical life and had no longer validity in the present, but were a tradition of the past. But they lived in the past and presented it.

That was the last incisive action which affected Judaism from Palestine. That country did not wholly rest during the coming centuries, forced a few sprouts, but they were without particular creative force and did not attain to governing influence upon the remaining Jewish world. The soil of Palestine had become unstable and slippery for Israel and his faith. The entire Roman empire no longer offered a safe spot for him. But a new country opened to him, or rather, a territory came again into the foreground that had once before been a refuge for Israel and in which Jewish seed had once before come up abundantly. Immediately after Rabbi Juda the Prince—that is, after the close of the Mishnah at the beginning of the third century—we find a large number of schools in Babylonia, in the country whither the scattered remmants of the first Temple had been conducted, where they were still germinating and growing, in the country whence Ezra had arisen, who undertook the restoration of the second commonwealth, and from which also Hillel, another rejuvenator of Judaism, had emigrated into Palestine to apply his fresh force to its revival. There we meet fast flourishing schools at Nehardea, Sora, Pumbeditha, and in many other places, schools that did not teach what they had received only, in the manner as it was wretchedly carried on yet for awhile in Palestine, but which took hold of their task with a fresh and live spirit. Heretofore we have mentioned the important words pronounced by a teacher there: He that emigrates from Babylonia to Palestine, commits a sin and transgresses God's command. Palestine, which was regarded as the holy land, whose soil was venerated as a holy one, which was looked upon as endowed with a certain sanctity—to migrate into that land from Babylonia should be prohibited? They felt the new spirit within themselves, felt themselves at home in a vigorous country in which endeavor could develop untrammeled. Here was the only empire into which the power of the Romans did not reach; the rough hand of the Parthians had opened a refuge for the Jews the like of which they hardly found in the remaining civilized world of that time. There were some romantics who looked toward Palestine with fond longing. It is told of such a one that he secretly withdrew from his teacher and fasted forty days, in order to forget the fresh manner and doctrine of Babylon and get used to the more sober and stunted ways of Palestine; fast days were scarcely necessary for him, because his desire indicates that the right spirit had departed from him. But those were exceptions, few and far between. The fresh spirit which moved about there, penetrated the scholars and invigorated them.

At any rate, life was not outside of the present. Many a thing was felt missing, many earnest hopes had to be deferred to a distant future, yet they did not so completely efface the present as it had become the custom on leaving Palestine. While in that country they dreamed themselves into the past and could picture the future only in order to restore the past in ideal form, a future which could not grow out of the natural course of development, they had in Babylonia a healthier realism. Between this world and the days of the Messiah, said a teacher there, there is no further difference than the pressure of the nations; the world will go on, the pressure only will cease; it is the same development, the same order of the state, only freedom enters with her reviving breath. While they in Palestine regarded the entire government of the time, as it ruled outside of Israel and pressed upon it, as illegitimate; while they recognized no verdict coming from that government machinery as legal because emanating from an illegitimate power and even put up as doctrine that it was only permissible to ask a Jewish court for a verdict and that any other should be rejected, even if the court decided according to the same principles: they taught in Babylonia that the law of the state, because founded on legitimate principles, was effective and legitimate and had religious validity. Such thoughts flow from a view which adjudges to the present its right and knows how to esteem it. Sayings along such lines are reported chiefly of a teacher Samuel, and he is also described as a patron of science. He is said to have been a physician, and learned in mathematics and astronomy. To him is attributed the saying: "The paths of the heavens are as familiar to me as the streets of Nehardea." We do not want to take that too literally and examine into the exact truth of the statement, but it shows to us at any rate, that science was studied there, and if that is especially true of astronomy, the reason is in its close connection with the fixing of the festivals.

For here again we meet a point which reveals the independence of Babylonia in a noteworthy manner. To keep the festivals according to their traditionally-fixed time, is something upon which every religious association places great importance. Many controversies were carried on in the early Christian times about the day on which Easter should be celebrated, one side insisting on the fifteenth day of Nissan, and the other side on the following Sunday. Great schisms followed out of it, and at the most various periods the dispute about the celebration of holidays has separated more than inner differences. In Israel, it was formerly the custom to send messengers out upon the high mountains to look for the new moon, and then when its appearance had been proven by their testimony, the beginning of the month, and accordingly the festivals occurring therein, were fixed by the courts, and runners of the court announced the decision to the inhabitants all around. The influence of Palestine became weaker, the ties looser, the want was felt to get out of dependence on Palestine and to order the festivals in a definite manner. That requires great resolution, to arrange a new order of fixing the religious festivals and to depart from the old proceeding of consulting the visible, natural phenomenon as it had been believed to be ordained in the letter of the Scripture and to bear the seal of divinity. Such an undertaking can arise only out of a fresh living time, and it was accomplished then. Its beginnings are hidden from us; it suddenly stands before us, a definite calendar is ordained so that the festivals are ordered according to fixed calculation, without having to observe the appearance of the new moon. With the acceptance of that ordinance, many consequences of the old proceeding fell into disuse. In the olden times, new year often had to be celebrated two days, because they did not know whether the new moon had actually appeared, and often the second day was the correct one. Those who resided far away and learned of the announcement of the appearance of the new moon only towards the middle of the month, could not know the day decided on in Jerusalem, and had to keep other holidays for two days. With a fixed calendar, all doubts disappeared, and the reason for a two days' celebration existed no longer. The two days for the new year were retained. For, said they, when the Temple is rebuilt, the former regulations about observing the appearance of the new moon will be restored, and then the cases when two days have to be kept will occur again, and therefore it is better to leave it in this way. But for the other holidays, they felt a two days' celebration to be unnecessary. Yet from Palestine a message came: "Hold fast to the custom of your fathers." Palestine felt itself injured by a transformation of the former regulation.

Thus in Babylonia a new order had arisen; and not enough, that calculation had taken the place of seeing the new moon. They shifted in some cases the day of the festival out and out. It was considered burdensome to have sabbath and a day of atonement follow each other, that the day of atonement should be on a Friday or a Sunday, as had often happened before, and is expressly shown in the Mishnah. To keep two such important rest days and holidays in succession interfered with all conditions of life; and to prevent that, it was ordained that new year should not be celebrated on Wednesday or Friday; the day was shifted if it should happen to fall on one of those days according to the calculation of the moon's course. It was a bold interference, the ordinance cut deep into the arrangements which had till then been valid, but it carried, and became the rule for all time.

In other ways they showed their independence of Palestine. In Palestine, winter is the rainy season, and for this rainy season there is in the prayer-book a fixed formula: "Give dew and rain for a blessing." In Palestine this rainy season begins in the first half of Marcheshvan, in November. But Babylonia has a different climate. The rainy season begins a month later, sixty days after the sun crosses the line in Tishri. "We pray for ourselves," said the Babylonians, "not for Palestine, for the right kind of winter and the growth of vegetation in our own country." And without hesitation, they ordered that the prayer should be made later. Consider the difference between that vigorous time and the periods of weakness following later. Then in Babylonia shortly after their removal from the soil of Palestine when the wound of its loss was still bleeding, near the land which still exerted great influence, they yet dared with decision to break away in prayer from its forms, if they did not correspond to the needs of their own country. The later time stuck to the Babylonian order. We have no rainy season, our seasons are quite different; but still we follow the Babylonian ordinance and use the formula of prayer at the time which was set for that country, with a show of fitness. Nor do we follow the rule of Palestine, which would have some justification in the mind of those who have their view upon the holy land of the future.

In every way, Babylonia had become a spiritual world-power. It had not completely emancipated itself from Palestine, had continued in its spirit, but with independent energy, with boldness and clear mind, so that its influence upon the later time remained a lasting one. A healthy, here and there, a rough realism ruled there, and the religious expressions are sometimes rough and harsh, but never sickly and weak. That rugged nature shows itself also in their tales and legends which often are very sensual, yet at the same time plastic, and proceed from a certain energy of life. Sound nature reveals itself in the vigorous moral sense that breaks through everywhere. Not only is every injustice reproved, but every action, too, which might mislead anybody into erroneous conception, even if that is not their intention. For such, the pictorial expression is used: to commit theft of the supposition of the other man. Desecration of the divine name, it is called, when a man who enjoys high regard as a teacher of religion, does not at once pay for his requirements and causes the appearance as if he would avoid doing so. It was a life of solid core, even if the stuff appears rude here and there.

Thus the schools flourished there for some time. Many a new thing was developed, even if free science could not succeed under the government of the Parthians. With all externalism, a sharp, penetrating sense is revealed so that by the collection of the local discussions Judaism was kept from stagnation. That collection was joined to the Mishnah. Yet, about the beginning of the sixth century, the schools continued in their debates, a formal closing never took place, but gloomy circumstances came in time and brought it about, and all at once completion and inactivity arrived. The Gemara—i. e., learning, completion, as that work which joined the Mishnah was called—the Babylonian Talmud, as the two works were named, was not closed; they closed of themselves. The work was never formally voted on or accepted, it gained validity and kept it until—a new spiritual, equally vigorous power arises. A complete, free development could not form itself in those times, but furrows were drawn for later seeding, the soil was kept fresh, that it may be filled with new germ.

In the meantime, the Roman empire had been moving nearer its disintegration. Roman paganism, grown weak, became at last persecution-mad in the consciousness of its impotency; it decayed gradually and could not resist new powers. Christianity in its mediation between paganism and Judaism increased in importance and respect, overcame crumbled paganism and mounted the throne. Even that new force, ecclesiastical life, was not able to rejuvenate the ageing Roman empire, so that it might have resisted the approaching storms, it did not breathe into it a full, new spirit which could have raised a dam against the floods. When the floods of the migration of nations rolled over it, all at once, the Roman empire broke down, barbarism flowed over it, perhaps necessary barbarism to bring fresh, rugged forces into the world. The Church was now the carrier of the only wretched remains of culture as far as it permitted it to be harbored. For Judaism, a hard, gloomy time had come. In comparison with that, its members had formerly only sipped at the cup of sorrows, now they were to empty it to the lees. Even the rude nations did not put up as violent resistance to Judaism, as now the councils of the Church organized it. They prohibited every intercourse with Jews; not only was marriage between them and the members of the Christian Church forbidden under severe penalties, but every tie of friendship, every intimate intercourse is represented as leading to damnation and is warned against. Thus the rudeness of the nations was paired with the refined animosity of a religion which could not pardon another for still existing and remaining among the living while it asserted to have consumed it long ago. Thus it seemed as if mankind would fall completely into barbarism. Yet the spirit of humanity never sleeps altogether; even if a part flags, if it laboriously pants along here under difficulties piled up to giant height, it rises elsewhere with unsuspected energy. All at once, day breaks within a people which had never been looked at and which until then had never been noticed. A new factor entered humanity, and it carried the light in the lead for several centuries—the Arabians.

IV.

Islam.

At the beginning of the seventh century, the world seemed in fact to have sunk into complete barbarism. Mental drouth and emptiness everywhere; nowhere a living fountain which, flowing along, fertilizes anew. Ancient Greek and Roman culture had almost completely perished; in the Greek empire, culture had shrunk together into narrow-minded formality and courtly etiquette, and the very language, once so beautiful and plastic, was barbarized. Ancient Roman culture had long ago become pithless and was no longer known by name. The Latin language, which still kept up as the language of the scholars, could hardly be recognized if tried by the measure of the old classics. In Christianity it had come so far that the knowledge of the original languages upon which the religion based itself and in which its holy books were written, had altogether disappeared. Yet in the third and fourth centuries, fathers of the church with learned mind had looked for means to spread the knowledge of the holy Scriptures and to effect understanding of them. Origines had put together all Greek translations of the Hebrew bible as they had been put forth by Jews after the Septuagint translation; namely those of the second and third centuries by Aquila, Symmachus, and Theodotion, in order to effect in that way a more correct comprehension of the text of the bible, and we now owe to his endeavor the knowledge of those valuable remains of antiquity, even if in sorry fragments, as far as the crushing ignorance has not destroyed them. Jerome had undertaken to correct, according to recent Jewish investigations, the old Latin translation as it had come out of the Greek of the Septuagint, and contained a mass of errors, and to make a new Latin translation. He was, after much resistance, followed by the Christian church, and the Latin translation which even now is canonical with Catholics and is regarded as the only valid one, the so-called Vulgata, rests mainly on the corrected comprehension received by Jerome from Jews, according to original Hebrew text. That happened in the third and fourth centuries. In the meantime the knowledge of the ancient languages disappeared entirely, and naturally the Scriptures too, lost all consideration—there was drouth and sterility.

In Judaism also, the last creative force, which had not rejuvenated, but yet worked with independence, those Babylonian schools which in the consciousness of their energy, influenced deeply and transformed, it also was dried up. The Parthian empire fell, and with its vigor the flower of the Babylonian schools went down—here too, gloomy silence soon covers everything. From the beginning of the seventh century, hardly a sound penetrates to us; at most that perhaps in Palestine an after-growth of legend-work ventured out which perhaps belongs to this time and may belong to a later one. Now a new phenomenon arises, original energy suddenly steps out among a people which till then had not been gifted by culture and which lived on its separate soil unfettered in isolated tribes. Islam arose.

The rise and course of Islam is one of the most instructive world-historical phenomena, if we do not permit our receptiveness to be dimmed for esteeming, without bias, historical events according to their true value. Since the cry, "The Turk breaks forth," no longer brings fright and confusion into the mind, since the Turk has been confined within his borders, men have in general passed on to the regular order of business. They believe that Islam is really existing only by the grace of Christianity, that it is a sick man whose dissolution may be expected at any moment, whose life is preserved but artificially, and that only the mutual jealousy of the Christian powers prolongs that artificial life and keeps it from expiring, as the faith is anyway in mortal sickness. With that conception, the present believes itself also absolved from a deeper consideration of the former importance of Islam. But if such judgment about the present condition of

Islam is one-sided and superficial, if the remarkable forces of life that are yet working within, even when they do not press so violently to the surface, are underestimated, such small consideration of its past is a gross mistake of an important historical power.

Six centuries had elapsed since a new religion had arisen. It had then full possession of the most powerful kingdoms of the world, had absorbed the saps of the entire ancient cultured world and spread to great distances. Now arises again a new religion in a cultureless people, runs a victorious race almost through the whole known world, takes the best and finest provinces of the Greek empire, spreads over Africa, takes possession of fine countries in Europe (Sicily, Southern Italy, Spain, and for awhile the southern part of France), and remains for a long time a very dangerous enemy of Europe and Christianity, becomes a feared power which for centuries has the decision of the world's affairs in its hands, and even when the original carrier of this faith grows weary and sinks down, a wild and for culture unreceptive tribe arises and freshens up the declining empire. The Ottomans came, and not only that, they offer a new stronghold, they destroy the last remains of the Greek empire, the old homestead of Christianity. Constantinople falls into their hands, and for centuries more, they stand as a threatening power. For a thousand years Islam rules over a large part of the globe, and still to-day counts its professors by millions. And not only that it rules and shows power, but during a great portion of that thousand years, it carries the torch of science at the head, culture proceeds from it, it is the refreshing fountain that prevents the spirits from going to sleep and drying up. That is certainly a grand and remarkable phenomenon.

Necessarily that religion must contain truths which helped it to so quick and long-enduring victory. But not the truths alone which it proclaimed, which were not even new, prepare that triumph, but rather that those truths were expressed in a form fitting the times and the people among whom they were spread; that was what gave to Islam such great ascendency. Islam proclaims truths which, of course, it has not created, with all energy, and they conducted the convictions to it indeed. The unity of God and the impossibility of representing Him by pictures is its emblem, the doctrine which it sustains with all decision, and every stunting of that idea is an abomination to it. That truth marched victoriously in advance of its sword and tied the power to its colors. Still another circumstance lent to Islam high meaning. It met the sickliness of the Middle Ages with a healthy feeling of the present. Islam had no ideal of the past toward which it was striving. It had no weakly longing to mirror only conditions as they had once existed; it lived in the immediate present and worked to use and enliven that. The healthiness of its essence gave it a real power in the world's history, and enabled it to pour forth encouragement for the unfolding of the living forces while they were long wasted elsewhere in sickliness. And also the defects and weaknesses even which Islam carried within itself, because they belonged to the time, because they fitted the people among whom it spread, even they were in the same degree, cause and assurance of its quick acceptance.

Islam recognizes in God, the one, the unrepresentable. It recognizes in Him the only power, the only ruler, besides whom no one can exist, besides whom nothing may be esteemed, it worships in God the almighty one. God is great, God is almighty; that is the exclamation to which it always returns with true monotony. But it does not also at the same time proclaim the holiness and purity with which He rises over all evil; that deeper recognition of the moral essence as ideal, of which the divine must be recognized, is missing from the whole elaboration of its doctrine in the multiple praises of the Koran as well as in the later writings. A deeper view into the moral order of the world, into the moral progress which proceeds from the fountain of all purity, is not found in Islam. There is hardly a word for "holy" in the Arabian language. It is true, Mohammed uses the designation "merciful" of God and it is well known that most suras of the Koran begin with the superscription, "In the name of God the merciful." But just that expression, "merciful" (*rachman*), he borrowed from Judaism; the word and the idea did not arise in and were not born of the Arabian spirit, but they were called and taken over from the source out of which it has drawn so much. Mohammed uses a word that had become customary with the Babylonian Jews who formulated "the Merciful One (*rachmana*) says" instead of the former expression, "the Scripture says." To such an extent had that become the usual expression for God. Yet, while Mohammed gladly adopted that word out of his Jewish environment and wanted to put it also at the head of his system, he found decided opposition to the designation; it remained simply Koranic, the people exchanged it for another one which means "Ruler" or "Lord of all." The deeper moral insight is lacking in Islam, as the Arabians themselves lacked it; man according to his higher worth, according to the deeper significance of his being, does not receive his full rights in Islam. "God is great," *Islam*, surrender to Him, *complete surrender*, without question, without making any claim for oneself, to expunge oneself in a measure while God alone rules: that is the whole inner core of Islam. That man carries something of the divine within him; that he has to furnish his share for the ennobling of the world; that he is the crown of creation according to his full spiritual and moral perception—that is an idea which did not reach full consciousness in Islam. Dull resignation is the highest and best that man can offer and with which he can worship God—the true fatherhood of God and sonship of man which is so beautifully expressed in Judaism and which the daughter-religion has adopted from it, is something foreign and unknown in Islam.

The real worth of man, according to its true significance, has never been recognized within the Arabian people. Every vigorous people forms out of itself a solid core which constitutes, not dependent upon the accidents of events, an almost unchangeable center around which the whole groups itself. The best ancient and modern nations had worked out of themselves such a core, old generations, families that carried their importance within themselves by merit inherited from father to son, who conceived their duties and requirements from their own worth, and who well recognized what task was incumbent upon them just on account of their social position. Such a patriciate, such an aristocracy, if it does not become fossilized, if it does not become submerged by vain pomp and claims of privileges, is such a concentration of the best and worthiest, and if it is freshened up by reception of new and healthy forces and thereby preserves its youth, forms the moral foundation of a people. It is found in all nations that have obtained world-historic importance. Greeks, Romans, Jews, and the more modern European nations show such a center within the people, which does not completely lose its worth, even when the power has been wrested out of its hands. On the contrary, people among whom even the hint of an arbitrary despot or the rumbling tramp of the mob commands, where the momentary capricious favor raises and again casts down into insignificance, are like heaps thrown together, now extending far, and again scattered apart. Such was the peculiarity of the people to whom Islam was brought first. Personal dignity of man did not exist among those people according to its full recognition, and thus Islam, which also denies it, and forces it to the rear, was particularly fitting to those nations. During the ninth and tenth centuries, there arose among the Arabians a school of philosophers who were not considered orthodox and were looked upon with suspicion; they were called Brothers of Purity. They made many scientific investigations, important for that time, and among other things there has come down from them a presentation of the dispute between man and the animals. The animals complain that man has subjugated them in an arbitrary manner and the verdict is in favor of the animals. The advantage of man above the animal, which is of course given through his reason and which he can not shake off, is not recognized according to its true justification because the moral element is beyond the horizon and not considered.

Those are dark sides of Islam, a germ of disease which was in it from the very beginning and necessarily contributed to its degeneration and enfeeblement. But for just that reason it was fitted to the taste of the people to whom it was brought. The religion of Islam spread because it was in the disposition of the people whom it was to rule. The disposition of the people, the peculiarity of the conditions of the time it is—and that is a great lesson we draw from Islam, its rise and acquisition of power—what introduces a religion into life and preserves it therein for a long time. The man who understands it to be the exponent of the mood of the time and the people, who comprehends how to wrap a general truth into the fitting garment, fitting in the eyes of the men who are to accept it, that man is the bearer of an idea shaped in keeping with the time, and he succeeds in his endeavors. Mohammed, the founder of Islam, was such a man. The religion spread so fast in Mohammed's lifetime that we are tempted to attribute to him all merit and all significance. When anywhere, in any religion from its effects a conclusion upon the dignity of the founder is justified, it should be thought to be the case in Islam. Mohammed created all, in his lifetime Islam was already a victorious power, he himself is the author of the holy book which, if he does not write it himself, he yet dictates to be written. The saying, "There is no God but Allah, and Mohammed is his prophet," has remained from the very beginning of Islam until the present day the confession of faith by which it is accepted, Mohammed is accordingly the true and full exponent of Islam. If Islam has, what can not be disputed, obtained high importance, it should be thought that its founder must have been a man that towered above the ordinary stature of men. And yet, Mohammed was not a great man. He was not a mind that, mastering and subjugating, makes the others bow before him. He was not one who, by his own importance, finds easy acceptance by the intelligent and studious, not one who, by his luminous ray, puts others into the shade. He was not a great man, had not the moral superiority, that silent grandeur to chain the minds to him. Mohammed was ignorant; he did not excel by any superiority of mind. Mohammed was a slave to his passions and to sensual greed in every way. No traits of moral nobility, of deeper sentiment, are related of him.

The Arabians are naive enough that they present his character to us in its entire nakedness, without adornment and paint. Nobody, free from bias, will count Mohammed among heroes. With this judgment those also agree who turn with preference to Arabian studies and ideas and are not influenced by any religious prejudice, and it suffices if, instead of other witnesses, I quote the words of a thorough and competent investigator. Sprenger (Moh. I, 313) says: "Burning enthusiasm, paired with low cunning, pure sacrifice for a higher aim with mean selfishness, indulgence, even dependence upon others, with obstinacy, devotion with treachery; those are a few of the contradictory psychic qualities of Mohammed's character." And yet he is founder of a religion which has exerted such a powerful influence and has it yet. He is that, because he received the truth as it lay in the disposition of his people at the time; because, filled with it, he served it, and thus he became a benefactor of mankind.

He received those truths; he was not their creator, he simply took them over out of Judaism. The rise of Islam reveals to us a fragment of Jewish history which would have remained entirely hidden from us, without it. The Jews of that country exerted no particular influence upon the inner development of Judaism as a whole; situated away off in a corner, without higher culture mentally, without learned knowledge of the law, knowing particulars only by connection with the territories which were the homes of higher culture among the Jews, they went to the rear, their whole life and existence remained out of sight. We get a knowledge of them only through Islam and the history of its rise. Jews were spread throughout Arabia from ancient time. When they first entered it, cannot be accurately determined. And, if we can not yet accord the right of historic facts to recent suppositions which want to put them back into earliest times and make them part of the original population of Arabia, so much is certain: the Jewish population of Arabia was spread in great extent through the whole country during the first Christian centuries. From the sixth century, we hear of powerful Jewish kings who have ruled in Southern Arabia, in Yemen, with courage and power, and spread Judaism afar. Their empire is destroyed by Christian Ethiopian kings, but it had impressed its memories deep into the whole Arabian existence. But in Arabia proper, too, in the northern part, where the new religion arose, there were numerous Jewish tribes who carried the complete Arabian characteristics. They move about independent, raise cattle, and carry on less agriculture, because the fertile soil offers of itself sufficient for their few wants. They carry on frequent bloody feuds among themselves and with their neighbors, and gather again in a common city, which is the meeting-place for barter, sale, and exchange, mainly in the Arabian city Jethrab, which later was called Medina, or in full, Medinath al Nabi. They were Arabian tribes with Arabian peculiarities, but at the same time with complete devotion to the faith of their fathers. I will present one man as example; he may bear witness for the ideas which ruled among those tribes, particularly in the better part of them. At the beginning of the sixth century, Samual Ben Adija was living in a strong castle on Ablak in Taima. Samual—Arabian for Samuel—was a prince of far fame in his part of the country. Mockingly, some fault-finding voices pointed to the insignificance of the Jewish tribes, to the small number of the entire Jewish nation. With manly pride, he meets the fault-finder in a song—for, like all Arabs, he was fond of poetry and song:

"If a man's honor is unspotted by disgrace,
Any garment that covers him is well-becoming.
Courageously his soul attempts the difficult,
Else his course is not directed toward fame.
They reproach: Our people's number is but small,
I say: Few are the noble ones everywhere.
A troop is not insignificant that knows to stand
As we do, striving for the best, youth as well as age.
What matters that but few we are, yet with us is honored
The refugee who, with the many, is often injured.
Ours is a mount that shields the friend in our protection,
Unscalable, it bids defy to coward eye.

Its foot fast rooted in the ground, up to the stars
Unattainable, its high, rock-front carries him."

A refugee is here mentioned, who is in his castle protected, even honored. He does not unjustly claim the glory of hospitality, that particular virtue of the Arabians toward him who entrusts himself to the house, to protect him with entire faith and devotion; he proves it in his life. He is a friend of Amrulkais Ben Hodohr of the tribe of Kend. This friend is driven from power and home; to regain it, he seeks assistance at the Greek imperial court. Before he starts on his way he entrusts his entire property, five valuable suits of armor to his friend Samual. Amrulkais has no success at the imperial court, and dies soon thereafter. Then Alhareth, an enemy of Amrulkais, appears before the castle and demands the surrender of the armor. Samual refuses and Alhareth, lays siege to the castle. It resists his wild attacks. One day the slave nurse walks outside with the youngest child of Samual; Alhareth captures her and sends to the besieged a threat that he will kill the child if his enemy's armor is not handed over to him. Samual hesitates a moment, but only a moment; then he speaks: "I can not surrender the armor and be faithless to my trust: Do as you like to do. Treachery is a collar that does not rust. My boy has brothers."

He does not hand over the armor, the child is murdered, but Alhareth is obliged to raise the siege. Again voices speak with blame on Samual's action, but he replies:

"Faultfinder, cease blaming the man
Whom you have often seen defying blame.
You should, if I am in error, put me on the right road,
Not make me err by words without understanding.
I have kept the armor of the man of the Kend.
Another may betray what is entrusted to him!
Adija, my father, long ago advised me:
Oh tear not down, Samual, what I have built!
He strongly built the fort for me in which
I did not fear to defy the besieger."

Asha, a poet of that time, glorifies Samual for it, and puts him forth as a pattern:

"Be like Samual, when the warrior prince
Pressed hard against him with all his might;
Stand between loss of child and treachery!
A bad choice which has to be selected,
But he spoke with quick decision:
Thou mayst murder thy captive, I shield my guest."

That such a man had to stand up in many a feud is natural, but he did not lose heart, and said:

"When doubtful and precarious stand affairs,
When thinking of the outcome makes one fear,
When narrow buckled armor almost breaks the chest,
When weak ones turn, unfaithful to their brethren,
Then do I avoid what to my weakness is the easier,
And act what helps to shield my honor."

And when near his end, he said:

"Would like to know, when I am on my bier
What testimony the mourners will bear of me,
If they will say: Do not leave us, for from many
A plight thou didst find means to raise us,
Thou never couldst be kept from taking thy rights,
Nor was there need of admonishing thee to give them."

There was a picture of a proud Arabian Emir, who looks with pride upon his valor and his sense of justice, upon his faithfulness and his descent. Thus were the Jewish-Arabian tribes of that time. And when Mohammed arose, we see a great number of them, the Benu Kainoka, Benu Nadhir, Benu Chaibar, and other more or less important ones as factors in the history of Mohammed himself and in the course of events. With a few individuals he had particularly intimate intercourse, like that with Abdallah Ben Salam, Pinehas, and others. From them he accepted the truths which he announced in the Koran, and they came into validity in Islam. The unity of God and the impossibility of representing Him by images, which form the basis of Islam, are taken over from Judaism, and the entire presentation of its truths is a wholly Jewish one. The principal religious ideas are borrowed from Judaism with the Hebrew words: Shekinah, as the omnipresence of God; Gan Eden as Paradise and reward of the good; Gehinnom as place of punishment of the wicked. And many other comprehensive ideas with their words have passed over from Judaism into Islam and the Arabian language without their having there an independent root; they are carried over bodily and complete. The entire presentation which he gives to his doctrine is of Jewish coloring, and he verifies and illustrates his doctrine by examples from the Jewish bible and the Jewish history. He could not read the bible, of course, but the intercourse he had with Jewish tribes, made him familiar with its tales; he completely retains the coloring of the biblical stories, the legendary ornamentation which Talmud and Midrash have wrapped around them, and thus they are related in the Koran.

Thus Judaism, if not the mother of Islam as it is of Christianity, is yet its nurse that nourished it with her best forces, yet its teacher that fitted out the pupil and raised him. Did the fosterchild treat his nurse with kinder feeling than the daughter showed to her mother? In the beginning it had that appearance. At first, Mohammed courted the favor of the Jews, did very much to please them, introduced, with a view to gain them, the fast-day Ashura (that is, the fast-day of the tenth of Tishri), he wanted to fix the Kiblah, the position to be taken at prayer, instead of the Arabian custom toward Mecca, toward Jerusalem, the holy city of the Jews. Yet he found but a small number of followers among the Jews, the greater portion could not be induced to do homage to him as a prophet. And that was perfectly natural. There was nothing new offered to them in his pretended revelations; on the contrary, they did not find in the new religion the rich treasures complete as they already had them. The more Mohammed flattered the Jews, the more offended he felt by the want of success of his condescension; and he began to persecute them as unbelievers. Violent and destructive wars broke out, and every new victory of Islam made the Jews feel its ascendancy the harder. The Koran recommends tolerance to the Jews, Christians and Sabians—probably a Christian sect of the time—as professors of the only God, while idolators are to be destroyed. But the friendly, kindly relation between Islam and Jerusalem was done away with.

Thus Islam enters without new creative impulse, rude and poor in ideas, wild, and with stormy rattling of arms. A pupil of Judaism in its religious views and sentiments, it soon turns inimically against its spiritual conductor. And yet, what breathes out of it is like fresh air. For Islam is not like a sick old man who, feeling the wasting of his force, watches the more jealously lest the power escape his hands, who punishes the more hard-heartedly every attempt at asserting one's own right as an invasion of his legitimate power, who, mean and suspicious, permits no new idea to sprout, and who spreads lingering sickliness in every direction. No, Islam was like a youth in high spirits who boldly interferes in the conditions, sometimes perhaps wasteful and destructive, but from a superabundance of energy which after all invigorates like a breath of fresh air. The living impulse, too, of building and shaping, pulsates within it, rejuvenates its entire surroundings, with new receptiveness it has also the sound sense for nobleness and high-mindedness and rapidly develops them. Islam spreads and at first esteems science and culture but little. Omar is said to have burnt the library at Alexandria with the remark: "If in these books there is something else than in the Koran, they are idolatrous; if they contain the same thing, they are superfluous." But hardly a century is past, and an ardent zeal arises among the adherents of Islam for appropriating all culture and to turn it over to the world newly invigorated. From the Syrian pagans they receive the remains of Greek culture, the treasures of the old wisdom; soon they are translated from the Syriac into the Arabic, and newly rises culture in the Middle Ages. The treasures of knowledge are again raised and are turned to good account for Moslems as well as for those living among them, and the entire Middle Ages are nourished at the reopened source of supply. Thus Islam requites, even if not with friendly, kind feeling, but yet by the new energy which it pours forth, to Judaism what it has borrowed, and partly amends the wrong done to it.

V.

Karaites, Awakening of Science.

A century had passed away after the rise of the new religion, Islam, and by force of arms it had conquered a great, wide extent of territory, and mental culture had penetrated deep into the mighty empire. The fresh youthfulness which poured forth from the new faith and the young nation from which it had proceeded, gave also to those inhabitants of the extensive lands taken by Islam, even if they had not accepted the new faith, greater liberty in civil conditions, refreshed and elevated their spirits. The newly-incited scientific endeavor penetrated powerfully also into the Jews who resided in Arabia and the countries dependent upon it. In peculiar manner this comes to the surface in a phenomenon which soon faces us. A new schism arises in Judaism. About the year 750, Anan Ben David, claimed to be of the house of David, comes forward and founds or confirms—as the old accounts call it—Karaitism, a new name, which has not appeared in history until then.

What is the essence of Karaitism? The Karaites reject the ordinances of the Talmud and their tradition affirmed by it, they cling more firmly to the letter of the Holy Scriptures. Thence also the name: Karaites, Bene Mikra, sons of the Scripture, disciples of the Scripture. What was the occasion for this new schism? The rabbis say, "Anan had been a learned but ambitious man; he had tried to obtain the highest dignities, wanted to be Chief of the Exile and the Academy, but they had no confidence in him and had refused him; driven on by his ambition, he then founded a renegade sect. How little or how much truth may be at the bottom of that account, this much is indisputable: one single man, be he ever so important, be his mental power ever so superior and his eloquence ever so overpowering, one single man gives no new direction and founds no new sect; the entire time must be fit for it. He can at most grasp the right moment, can first and definitely pronounce the word which is at the lips of all. Then a new direction is taken and a schism may result, but it does not start from the one individual as its original cause. We therefore ask again: What was the occasion for the rise of Karaitism, for the defection of the Karaites? Well, somebody may say, the ordinances of the Talmud were oppressive, their burdens could no longer be carried, it appeared unjustifiable in a freely stimulated time; the interpretations, as they had been used to confirm those ordinances, had gone too far away from the natural meaning of Scripture. The intelligent and reasonable men could not help seeing that the bolder ones came forward with contradictions and when they could not convince the community, they seceded. What a pity, might be perhaps added, that such a healthy and sensible direction was not taken, that a secession which arose eleven centuries ago and which rested on sound principles, yet could not become victorious and carry all with it.

Where we hear such mourning expressed about the course of history, mourning about expected successes that never came to pass, we may judge with certainty: History made no mistake, we are in error in our conception of the matter; the causes of which we regret that their expected effects did not appear, had never existed at all. If the result does not come out right, there must be an error in the figuring. Giving such a judgment, it is forgotten that our consideration is only in the middle of the eighth century when scientific movement existed, when many endeavored to acquire knowledge, when many a liberal idea dared to show itself, but it would be a misjudgment of the time to suppose that the idea had been so powerful that it formed a separate party and joined it together into a separate religious association. Schisms in religious life do not generally arise on the soil of science and free investigation. Science is too conscious of its general validity and of its task to take in and illuminate all mankind, to make schisms and separate itself into a sect of its own.

It has too much the full confidence of gradually penetrating into the lowest stratum, of casting the high light into the deepest nook, to seclude itself into narrow confines. Never did a religious schism come out solely from the soil of science. Only when pressure wants to bend down by force a direction that claims its justification, when power will not permit it to rise, and thus squeezes the band which has gathered around the idea to the outside; when, in addition to that, heads of the ruling religious direction show themselves unworthy and yet make claim of sanctity, yet demand to be honored as legitimate representatives of the sanctuary, when the conscience of the people is grossly insulted so that they become indignant and enraged, only then schisms enter. Toward that outcome science may have prepared, may have co-operated by breaking a way for freedom of the mind and by working the new faith into ordered, consistent and connected form. But from free investigation schism never starts. The ruling Jewish direction at that time had neither the power nor the will to persecute; its representatives were plain and pious scholars. Science was not suffering under repression and force, the moral conscience was not offended by mockery and scorn. Free investigation had no occasion to unfurl a flag of its own for its disciples in order to join them into a separate body.

Nor are the Karaites the advocates of progress or the representatives of liberal ideas. The Karaites—to state it briefly—are the corporeal and spiritual posterity of the Sadducees; they are the antiquaries of that time, although by force of peculiar circumstances many a bright ray illuminates them and many a fresh thought comes forth out of them. We have lost sight of the Sadducees; let us again look back at them. Their permanency had ceased with the destruction of the Temple. They had once been the priests, the nobility, the ruling class joined to sacrificial service and Temple, to offices and administration. All that was thrown down at one blow. The Sadducees had been crowded toward the rear in many ways by the spiritual energy of the Pharisees during the existence of the second Temple. Yet a great and powerful party does not come to an end at once.

We hear their name resound in later centuries. The Talmudical writings speak of them unwillingly. And, though they intentionally omit them, they could surely tell us more about them than they do in their scanty accounts where the name of the Sadducees often crops out, after all. Sacrificial worship and service had disappeared, the Temple existed no more, but differences as they existed in practice and life between Sadducees and Pharisees, differences in customs and ordinances did not cease altogether. The descendants of the Sadducees had kept them up quite seriously among themselves. They had no literary life by which they might refresh themselves, but they vegetated on, unnoticed, for several centuries.

They may have undergone some transformations, particularly relative to one point that was more mental and did not enter practical life. The hopes of the future had formed one point of dispute between Sadducees and Pharisees. While the latter recognized the resurrection of the dead and longed for a new time in which they would take part themselves, expecting an invigoration of the state and the nation and the whole religious existence, the Sadducees rejected it. They did not ask that conditions should undergo a transformation, they did not live in the future, the present was satisfactory, and good enough for them. But matters had changed greatly. The present was no longer joyful to the Sadducees; on the contrary they, as descendants of the Patriciate, of the ruling class, must feel it especially deeply and painfully that they had dropped from their former height. They must now, too, nourish the hope of a new future with a restoration of the old, brilliant conditions and surrender their protest against the resurrection. Thus some other transformations may have happened. In still, quiet times, when thought is not quickened and stimulated, many demarcations disappear without their being noticed, and there arises, even if not an approach, yet a grinding away of contrasts. That probably happened in the case of the Sadducees, and centuries pass while they live in their own circle without coming forth.

Then, at one stroke, a new time enters, a fresh breath

draws through them, it is as if the stiff limbs quiver, as if a spirit were to enter the dead bones to revive them. Even the scattered and wasting remnant feels the need to gather themselves for preservation from total disappearance, liberty gives them room and occasion. The convictions of everybody are respected. We learn from dark, fragmentary accounts that the calif expressly gives the Karaites permission to constitute themselves into a sect. The desire to rouse themselves into their ancient peculiarity had grown strong. The name Sadducees had, of course, become disreputable; the recollection of their variations, though many had disappeared, was still alive. Besides, it was in the time, that new names came in with almost every century, and new conditions are indicated by them. The teachers of the time of the Mishnah were called Tannaim, the teachers; those of the Gemara, Amoraim, the speakers; then followed the Saboraim, the givers of opinions; and then came the Geonim, a pompous name, probably come in with the Arabians, the Excellencies—names designating the heads of the schools as they were given under the different conditions. Thus it is not astonishing that the Sadducees, too, took a new name, because they did not want to be the same in all matters of faith, but yet desired to preserve their principles in practical life. As it historically appears, they were at first called Ananites after the name of their founder. Together with the adoption of many variations from the opinions of Anan, the name of Karaites was gradually accepted for general use.

The Karaites are spiritual and corporeal descendants of the Sadducees. The same postulates as we in part know them completely from the fragmentary accounts of the latter and in part can reconstruct them, are again found with the Karaites but with a certain accentuation and more decided consistency which then again weakens in the course of time. The Sadducees had attributed decided importance to sacrifices; the Karaites of course could no longer do that, for sacrificial service had ceased with the destruction of the Temple. But after its loss, individuals who were close to the principles of the Sadducees, arose and said, "From now on, we may not use meat nor wine for of both a certain amount must be given as dues to the Temple and as that can not be done while the altar is lacking, the use of meat and wine is prohibited." The Pharisees opposed that and won the victory. With the very appearance of the Karaites, we hear that they prohibit the use of meat while in exile. Of course, the prohibition does not last long. In the course of centuries it disappears, but just at first when the time next reveals the historic impulse, it comes forth with marked decision. But even then, when that decision weakened and the insistence on the Temple service slackened, we find that they observe the rabbinical regulations for the killing of cattle, with great severity and even go beyond them. How do they arrive at that? They who consulted the letter of the bible, found no indication of regulations for killing which have their foundation only in the Talmudical tradition and interpretation. But evidently the entire proceeding of ritual killing is taken from the custom in use by the priests at the killing of the sacrificed animals. It was a real Sadducean custom that came into use at their public repasts and which the Pharisees adopted in their struggle for priestly consecration. Of course the Karaites had to adjudge such regulations as obligatory. On the other side, it would have been natural with a schism just then appearing, to retain the element of religious life, the divine worship with its corresponding forms which, though not ordered by the bible, yet had sufficient warrant in it and had grown to fill a want of the whole community. But it does not suit the Karaites. They can not object to divine service and prayer; but they rejected the quickening, inspiring part of the accepted forms, and put together a few scanty, disconnected verses of the bible, dry and cold in that arrangement. That was because they had kept away from the labors of the Pharisees for such divine worship, and it had never become a living element with them. But cleanness and uncleanness were upheld with minute exactness by all classes who either were of the priesthood or considered themselves close to it. The Pharisees gradually modified and alleviated those regulations, and when the Temple went down, they departed from them to a very great extent and considered them inapplicable. The Karaites hold to them with tenacity in all their severity. In relation to prohibition of certain parts of the fat and the use which might be made of the meat of cattle that were not killed according to the regulations, there were disputes between the Sadducees and the Pharisees which were completely inherited by the Karaites without the letter of the Scripture indicating any decision in favor of either party.

In many customs relating to the sabbath and the holidays, Sadducees and Pharisees differed widely; the Sadducean usage being more severe and gloomy, although they may not have held such severity obligatory on themselves and their priestly functions, the Pharisean rules being to alleviate in many cases. Thus the Pharisees placed great importance upon consecrating the sabbath with bright illumination, which is sensible and fit. But they insisted so much more strongly and attributed special value to the sabbath lights because the Sadducees asserted that the verse, "Ye shall kindle no fire in your dwellings on the sabbath day," prohibited not only the kindling but also the burning of fire or lights. The Karaites followed blindly after the Sadducees and carried on a bitter fight with the Rabbinites about their using, on the sabbath, the lamps which had been lit before. The Pharisees endeavored to make the ordinances conform to the needs of actual life, often against the literal meaning of the Scripture. The verse, "No one shall go from his place on the seventh day," had formerly been interpreted that only very short journeys were permitted on the sabbath and in like manner the carrying of any burden outside of the house had been strictly prohibited. The Pharisees managed to increase the distance by fictitious joining of the spaces and to extend the "house" within which things might be carried, by the "Erub," an alleviation which of course rested on a legal fiction but which was proper for the needs of the people. The Sadducees disputed the matter; and the Karaites followed and abused the Rabbinites—as the Pharisees were called from this time, as followers of the rabbis (teachers)—for daring to get around the ordinances by cunning.

The Sadducees, or at least a part of them, the Boëthusians, asserted that the feast of weeks (Shabuoth) should be celebrated on Sunday, not seven weeks after Passover. The Pharisees oppose that with all decision; they even arrange the counting of the days from Passover until the feast of weeks so that each day there was specially pronounced: This is the day of such number, not another day, as the Boëthusians claim. The Karaites follow the Boëthusians and decide that the feast of weeks must be celebrated on Sunday. But in the meantime, as already mentioned, the divergence had been aggravated and extended over the whole calendar. The calendar had been fixed according to new principles in Babylonia, no longer dependent upon the actual visibility of the new moon, but according to calculation with the addition of some regulations demanded by practical life. New moons and festivals were fixed for all time without the necessity of sending out messengers to observe the appearance of the moon. Scripture gives no indication how new moons should be appointed, calculating them found no objection in Scripture. But it was not in use in olden time from which the custom had come down, to see the new moon and to proclaim its appearance by witnesses. It is quite in the manner of the Sadducees not to make use of calculation because it was not ancient and had been produced by the development of the times; and actually the Karaites point with all decision to the old custom and cling to it. Triumphantly they relate that the Rabbinites had once celebrated New Year's Day while the old moon was still visible. The Rabbinites pay no attention to that; they stick properly to the time fixed by calculation, which must keep its validity to prevent uncertainty. And they care nothing for the narrowminded mockery of the Karaites, those literal antiquaries. I might add many things which verify the complete agreement of Karaitism and Sadduceeism and plainly prove that Karaitism did not proceed from a want for progress, but rather from a demand for standing still. I might say, out of the needs of the reactionaries, for they felt a need of fortifying themselves for standing still and for preserving themselves against the energy of development that was moving through the time,

History always repeats itself in this, that just in times when healthy life breaks through the entire mass and quickens it, when it is to be expected that development moves victoriously through all classes, those who convulsively want to cling to the old, feel within themselves the demand to get closer together and secede, lest the new life enter their ranks. They must now group themselves more closely and insist on their principles with more marked consistency and greater emphasis than had been done. While they did not cry out before in the current and even drifted along, now they must rouse themselves, their protest must sound aloud, their resistance must be strengthened. He that should consider such noisy demonstration of reaction as a relapse of the time, is much in error. On the contrary, that shrill dissonance of reaction, that seeming retreat of the time, is the most eloquent testimony for the power of the development and progress which seizes all. Thus the appearance of Karaitism was the sign of the lively currents of the time.

Of course Karaitism contained in part also, healthier elements. Let us not forget that the development which had not affected it, may not be called a wholly clear and clean one. It had gone on in dark and gloomy times. The changes of Scripture by interpretation, as they were made by Talmudism and Rabbinism, did not agree at all with a reasonable conception of the word. When the Karaites returned closer to the letter of Scripture, they stimulated a study of the bible, which became very fertile. But they only stimulated, the fruits were not ripened by them. It is a remarkable phenomenon that just those men who looked only to the letter and regarded only the Scripture as their canonical book, who held to it to the exclusion of the later works, and should therefore be the more zealous to study and investigate it, that those men yet achieved nothing important in explaining the Scriptures, that they stand far behind the Rabbinites, have to learn much from these, and finally are weakening and wasting away. That fine peculiarity which Phariseeism and its rejuvenation, Rabbinism, show, viz., to enter always full and fresh into the course of mental and spiritual development with perfect clinging to its own principles, it appears very little in Karaitism. We find in their more recent writings only repetition of what the older ones have developed. That other fine exhibition of living energy in Judaism, to settle everywhere and to be able to feel at home everywhere, to move along everywhere where new soil becomes accessible, to draw nourishment from that soil as well as to carry there its own spiritual seed, that fine exhibition of the life of Judaism which reveals general human character—it is wanting in the Karaites; they cling to the old soil from which they can not part. They cling first to Palestine, and although they had for awhile a colony in Spain, they spread only in the Orient. They live to-day in Eastern countries and can not get loose from them. Still, now and then a new motion is noticed among them, but it seems as breathed over from Rabbinism.

Thus that new schism is of course evidence of a newly-awakened spirit, even if only by its contrast. Yet the spirit was wide awake and showed itself in the development of Rabbinical Judaism. Right in the first period when the new literature of the Arabian began, we see Jews taking part as translators, grammarians, astronomers, physiologists, physicians. In the seventh century already, in the same century in which the new religion arose, we meet Masdershvai, a Jewish scholar who translated and elaborated mathematical works; also Mashallah, who has a place of importance as astronomer and astrologer; Sahl al Taberi, and many others who appear among the first founders of the new literature and may be called the fathers of the new culture. Soon they do not remain at collaboration in which the Jews were but part in the multitude, but they carry the science over into Judaism, giving it Hebrew dress. From that time, works exist which have been rediscovered in recent times and which are now recognized as belonging to that period, breathing the Arabian spirit, and showing how active the scientific spirit was among the Jews. The astronomical work of one Samuel belongs to the ninth century. A work on mathematics and geometry by one Rabbi Nathan in forty-nine paragraphs, also called the Mishnah of the forty-nine meters, also belongs to that time.

We meet also a philosophical work peculiarly interlaced with Jewish views. Philosophy was very soon cultivated among the Arabians, at first that branch of philosophy which was more in agreement with the imagination. The neo-platonic and neo-pythagorean were the branches which were first followed with favor. Only later, Aristotle became the autocrat in philosophy among the Arabians, and during the whole Middle Ages. The neo-pythagorean branch had had peculiar charms for that time. Its fundamental element is the number as something least concrete, something belonging to pure perception without sensible wrap, an idea without a body, a contemplation without sensibility. This branch takes the Arabians, and a remarkable Jewish work of the eighth or ninth century appears wholly in such dress. The ten digits and the twenty-two letters of the Hebrew alphabet, so teaches that booklet about creation (*Yezirah*), are the instrument, the element, out of which God formed the world. They are a breath, a perception, with all their generality, yet the expression for everything physical; they are reflected in everything. As they become firm and express themselves visibly, they are the first elements of creation, of existence. These conceptions were dressed up with many more explicit Jewish definitions and worked out into a philosophical system which later gave occasion for many mystical dreamings, although that little old book is not so fantastical and chimerical. These ten digits (*Sefirahs*) were in the cabala—the later Jewish mysticism—conjointly with the twenty-two letters of the Hebrew alphabet, the thirty-two paths of wisdom in which it dreamingly promenades. Yet the little book which forms the fulcrum for this and similar fantasms is innocent of all that. It rather appears as a serious philosophical attempt, a first start for later real philosophical works.

Scientific endeavors go more closely into the real contents of Judaism. Soon after the rise of Islam, the Arabians had zealously worked at fixing their language and its grammar, especially at a visible presentation of the vowels. They had started serious labors as to how the Koran should be read in public. Like all Semitic languages, the Arabic has in its writings originally only the skeleton; i. e., only the consonants are shown by letter, the life-giving breath which gives them various meanings, the vowels, are not written originally. But when the Arabians became a literary people with a Scripture, a holy book, it soon was of importance that the sound should be definitely fixed lest various pronunciations should enter the holy book and thus obscure or even pervert its contents. Thus the Arabians acquired vowel signs which presented the three basic sounds. Grammar schools arose in different countries of the empire. The Jews did not remain idle spectators. Long ago the text of their Scriptures and of many other books had been reduced to writing, but they had been satisfied with the consonants, and the fixity of the pronunciation had been left to oral tradition. When the Arabians invented their vowel marks, the Jewish schools began to work for the same end for their Scriptures and that with a zeal and care yet surpassing the Arabians. Even the least variation of the sound was fixed by some sign and the vocalization was shaped by a thoroughgoing system. In fact, two different systems arose, one in Babylonia and the other in Palestine. The latter prevailed and is in use to-day. If we consider those labors expended upon the inherited holy treasures, they furnish the best evidence of the mental and spiritual industry and the scientific earnestness which prevailed at that time.

The Arabians are a people fond of poetry and song. But poetry among them is shown more in frequent return of the sounds than by depth of sentiment and vigor of the idea. Like children, they like the fine, full sound that comes out in their language which is rich in vowels; and thus they come to practice rhyming. In their poetic pieces the same rhyme is repeated innumerable times. One Kasside runs along with the same rhyme, even if it has a hundred strophes; and in other poems which have a diversity of rhymes, they prefer to have the rhymes repeated. They also delight in bold images. The flight of fancy in their poems often loses all measure, mocks the discipline of the thought and the clearness of the conception, the shape of the image is in a far-off fog. The Hebrew language and conception begin differently. Standing with its vocalization in the middle, between the scanty Aramaic and the richer Arabic, it does not give preference to ringing sound, it did not know rhyme at all and did not seek for a terminal ring of the sound, but rather for the rounding out of the thought. It liked to repeat the idea to be expressed, in various ways and to illuminate it on all sides. That is the parallelism of the lines, where two parts of a sentence present one idea, but in different lights, sometimes by contrast, sometimes by repetition, but always so that it comes out in sharper outline. The later prayers which we have from the first centuries after the destruction of the Temple, still carry that biblical form without using any rhyme. But now the Jews were living among the Arabians; sound bribes the ear, the flight of fancy carries along and they tried to do like the Arabians. Of course it did not succeed particularly at first. There were imitations carrying over the peculiarity of one language into the other one which, though closely related, yet has its own characteristics that may not be infringed upon. Nor was the taste sufficiently purified to find the proper mean. Rhyme was used in endless repetition in the new liturgical poems, artificial turns were purposely looked up with the intent to imitate the pomp of words. Unheard-of wrenching of words, bold, new formations which attempted something transcendant but turned out shapeless and uncouth, are surprising but lack all poetic grace.

Elasar Ben Kalir, a man in Palestine, probably of the eighth or ninth century, composed a great number of poetic prayers for the holidays containing a mass of sound figures, prayers in which the words with the same endings are constantly repeated, in which the boldest new formations are used without regard to whether they are correctly shaped grammatically or justified etymologically. A verse was considered the more poetical, the more artificial and bombastic it was. It was an effect of the time, an assumption of the character of Arabianism, without the intelligent judgment and labor which a later time applied to such adaptations as the Spanish school presents artistically. If such attempts brought no gain, nor offer any ripe fruit of mental activity, yet we perceive in them the endeavor to appropriate all mental treasures of the environment. When in our modern days, those jingling sound figures are in the houses of worship still offered to our eyes and ears, when those cumbersome prayers for dew and rain are still recited with their inharmonic rhymes, their hard words and their uncomprehended contents, it is the result of the same want of thought which keeps up a prayer in the Chaldean language for the well-being of the princes of the exile (the Geonim) who no longer exist. But for those times in which those prayers originated, we recognize in that laborious work an unconscious impulse which desires to join into the ruling culture.

The philosophical culture of the time burrows much deeper. Even doubters and critical investigators appear. It sounds rather dark but we know enough of it to be able to announce their existence with certainty. Among other names, one Chivi of Balk in Persia is quoted as a man of such bold sayings that we should hardly expect them for that time. Not only that he disputes creation out of nothing, that he asserts the world was shaped out of original matter; not only that he says about sacrifices, "Why offer sacrifices to the eternal God, for what purpose were Temple and lamps?" but also about the miraculous in the Scripture, he speaks in a manner as it was never more boldly used by the later men who attempted to explain the miracles in a natural way. Thus for instance, he explains that the passage of the Red Sea was made at low ebb; the manna he regards as a gum yielded by the trees in the desert; he does not believe that the face of Moses became shining, to him the expression appears to mean that from long fasting his skin had become hornlike. Such explanations are sober enough and do not fit the spirit of the Scriptures, but at any rate, they show a bold frankness. And this man was not the only one; it is related that his explanations were introduced into schools, which shows that he was not abused as a heretic; on the contrary, he must have passed as a respectable scholar and have found decided adherents.

That was a time of full and many-sided stimulation. Only the Talmudic schools could not properly follow the spirit of the time. At the center of the religious life there was weakness, among the Geonim there were no men of importance; their academies could not produce them. And thus a conflict between science and religion threatened to arise; it was avoided for the time.

VI.

Saadias.

About the end of the ninth and the beginning of the tenth century, the mental currents in the Eastern Arabian Empire rose high, the floods washed also around the rock of Talmudism which lay right in the middle of this movement; they did not shake it, but their roaring sound frightened all around it. Just in the interior of the Eastern Arabian Empire were the old academies as they had grown up from the Babylonian-Parthian time with the formation of the Babylonian Talmud, and had become fixed with determinative influence, Sora and Pumbeditha—the latter city quite close to Bagdad—at which the teachers had gathered numerous students and whence they spread their decisions into all countries. Under Arabian rule, the inherited Jewish constitution had reached a high importance and great regard. A Chief of the Exile, *Rosh Galuth*, invested with a certain amount of political power and the dignity of governor, presided over the Jews of the vast empire, collected the taxes from them, and enjoyed in this way, great respect. The teachers at the two above-named academies were the religious chiefs. After the close of the Babylonian Talmud, they went by the name *Saboraim*, "givers of opinions," but now in the Arabian period we find them designated by the pompous name *Geonim*, "the Excellencies," and the power of the empire as well as the liberty accorded to all inhabitants even to those not avowing Islam, gave to the academies and their chiefs higher dignity. They appeared in public with splendor, surrounded by guards who accompanied them. Their lectures, which they delivered only at stated times, were regarded as important events and were preceded by special ceremonies. Thus the Geonim were respected not only as scholars but also as spiritual dignitaries and chiefs of the entire religious union. In spite of all that, the intrinsic importance of those teachers did not correspond to the high mental movement of the time. They kept within their antiquarian, theological, Talmudical dominion, and even there they do not appear as fertile authors. We have works of Acha of Shabecha and of Simon of Cahira, but they never held the office of Gaon. Of the Geonim we have little to show; mostly decisions, answers to questions which were addressed to them from all countries. Only a few individuals stand out. We learn of one Judai Gaon who attempted to fix *Halachoth* (conclusions or customs); and of Zemach Ben Paltoi who made a weak, pioneer attempt to compose a kind of Talmudical dictionary. Amram Ben Sheshna sends a complete liturgy to Spain with the regulations to be observed at prayer. Those are about all the scanty literary products from the academies. The schools were weak, and became so low that even in the Talmudical branch, the most important men did not head them. Ambition had cast its eye upon those spiritual dignities and many a rich dilettante aspired to occupy that position and succeeded in getting it.

Thus the gaonate decreased in value and importance, but the times demanded something else. It was felt that the whole structure would break down if, while science was rising everywhere, religion should remain in its old shape and waste more and more. And a man was looked for who, as a son of his time, could also be accepted as an able scholar, learned in the Talmud. Such a man was found about the first half of the tenth century, near 930, in Saadias Ben Joseph, called Said in Arabic. He did not belong to the Babylonian schools and had not resided in Babylonia, but was an Egyptian, born in Fasum in 892. He had become known in many ways. He was of a virile nature and full of a desire to reconcile the differences, yet at the same time to oppose his whole force to any obstinate opinions that tended to prevail, with rigor and determination. As a young man of twenty-three he appears to have composed an argument against Anan, of which we have not even a fragment. Possessing little mentally creative power, he was a man of broad and wide knowledge, eager to bend aside the points in order that the varying tendencies might tolerate each other and cause no wounds. Saadias himself, in some of his writings, places before us the principles which determine the course of his ideas.

Scripture, tradition, and reason, are the sources of knowledge and these three have their full validity and form complete unity. Scripture is to him the complete expression of reason and he not only finds nothing contradictory to reason in it, but on the contrary he goes so far as to propose the question, for what purpose revelation was given, since it completely corresponds to reason, and its announcements could and must be found as well by reason. His answer is: "They correspond perfectly to each other, their contents coincide, but revelation had the purpose to bring the contents which reason could but slowly dig out, sooner into reality. Long periods would have to elapse before mankind would have been led up by its own reason. Revelation hastened the process of thinking. Scripture, tradition, and reason, are, accordingly, the three sources of knowledge and are in complete agreement with one another, because they are born out of the same divine mind. They are simply shaped in different modes of expression, but are alike in their real contents. Accordingly, Scripture must agree perfectly with reason, and such objections as are made by bold rationalists as we have heard them from Chivi of Balk, he rejects in different ways.

According to Saadias, it is not at all repugnant to reason that God should miraculously interfere with his almightiness. Miracle, as emanation of divine power, is in his opinion not in contradiction with the otherwise general and regular operations of the laws of nature and therefore not in contradiction with reason. If he solves that question, which is still pending nine centuries after him, in such manner, we must not consider him for that, an opponent of knowledge by reason. But there are some miracles which contradict all reason and natural law with a certain directness, as when the serpent speaks to Eve, or the ass to Balaam. Such a miracle changes the whole nature of those animals; there is not a momentary interruption but a complete upsetting of the laws of nature and reasoning power. When in modern times a representative of liberal tendencies points to such examples for his assertion that Scripture should be read, not according to the letter, but according to its spiritual meaning, and addresses to his adversaries the question whether they really believe that Balaam's ass had spoken, and they answer with a loud and vigorous *yes*, Saadias had no such courage to subject reason completely to faith. "No," he says, "the serpent never spoke, but an angel pronounced the words so that it appeared to Eve as if the serpent had spoken. In like manner, God caused a voice to be heard which Balaam thought came from the ass." All divine revelation he takes, not as a visible appearance of God (for everything corporeal must be kept out), but rather as hearing a voice created by God, or seeing a glimmer of light produced by God, therefore momentary creations for the definite purpose of being audible and visible to the prophet. He had therefore no difficulty in assuming a similar proceeding in those miracles. But how is it with the witch of Endor when she conjures up Samuel for Saul? How does a witch acquire such power? What God may do for accrediting his prophet should not happen for the benefit of a witch. But he stands by his opinion. Saul had provoked confirmation of his superstition so that God caused the appearance of the shade of Samuel to become visible to him at the time of the witch's conjuration, but not *by* that.

In the prolog of Job, Satan appears as the accuser of Job. We find in that highly poetic representation no difficulty. We know how to take poetry as poetical, and Goethe did not know how to introduce his Faust more fittingly than by imitating the prolog of Job. That old time had no proper conception of the poetical; for it, that poem was a historical fact. How is a Satan, a bad spirit, to be imagined? The superior spirits must be pure and perfectly sinless, a bad spirit is to Saadias a contradiction in itself. Therefore Saadias transfers the event from heaven to earth. In a company of excellent men who admired Job for his virtue, there was a doubter who found fault with Job's purity and thus became his accuser. To disprove him, the divine trial of Job is made that he may prove himself true. We may consider such attempts at explanation weak and insufficient and yet they have been repeated in similar manner in the course of the centuries.

Saadias holds decidedly fast to freedom of human will, and where an expression occurs to endanger that freedom and seems to indicate interference by God, he is not satisfied to say simply that the expression should not be taken too literally, but he rather attempts to so twist it that the threatening meaning disappears. For instance, if we read, "The king's heart is in the hands of the Lord as the rivers of water, he turneth it whithersoever he will," this sounds as if God puts the thoughts into the heart of man. "No," says Saadias, "such is not the meaning; rather, the king's heart is in divine power; i. e., when the fear of God fills it as water and rivers, he has his heart and his passions under control and can turn his heart whither he will."

As Saadias tries in this manner to make Scripture and reason agree, so he proceeds also in regard to tradition. Here it was important, especially in opposition to the Karaites who emphasized the variation between the word of the Scripture and the development of law as it was shaped in Talmudical Judaism, to prove that such variation was but a seeming one, that on the contrary, tradition and the word of Scripture express the same thing. The admission that a historic development had taken place which produced a removal from the word of the Scripture and transformed its regulations, was repugnant to the spirit of the time, in spite of the fact that the impulse and its justification were deeply inherent in Judaism. In earlier times there had been no hesitation to announce that the court has the right to tear up by the roots any ordinance which was no longer fitting for the times even if written in the bible. It had been acknowledged that custom and practice have the power to acquire validity even if opposed to ordinances, which means nothing else than that the development of the time as it shapes itself has well-grounded validity as against the dead letter. That could be announced without hesitation at a time when the fight against it had not been started and things were moving in still self-confident unconsciousness. But when the Karaites came forward with their contradictions and denied the right of shaping ordinances against the divine letter, the leaders shied, and Saadias attempted to bring all ordinances, as they had been shaped by development and were considered traditional, into agreement with the word of the Scripture, even to find them in it. Let us consider a single example.

The Scripture says, "When two brothers reside together, and one of them dies without leaving children, the surviving brother shall take the widow as wife, and the oldest son produced of this marriage shall take the dead brother's place and inherit his possession." The ancient Sadducees and the Karaites like them, took no offense at this regulation, because it permits marriage of the brother's wife, which is forbidden elsewhere; and they applied the law exclusively to the betrothed woman, but not to the married one. Pharisees and Rabbinites were closer to the letter, when they contended that in such a case it was permitted to marry the wife of the deceased brother. But in course of time, practice among the Rabbinites had changed the law. If the bible says, "And it shall be that the first-born which she beareth shall succeed in the name of his brother which is dead" (i. e., he should inherit by right of primogeniture), the actual practice had become that such a marriage was no longer considered a mere continuance of the old one, but an entirely new one; the husband took possession of the inheritance and all children proceeding from this marriage had equal shares, the first-born had no advantage above the others. But upon the first-born, the oldest one of the surviving brothers, the obligation of marrying the widow was to rest. The Karaites objected to this as an innovation and declared it contrary to Scripture and unjustifiable. Saadias does not hesitate to attempt to carry the new practice into the word of the bible; he translates: "That the first-born to whom she beareth, he shall succeed in the name of his brother"—so that the word "first-born" does not mean the first son of the new marriage but the oldest of the brothers, to whom the widow bears children, and he takes the inheritance.

We have before mentioned the hot fight between the Karaites and the Rabbinites about the regulation of the calendar. Saadias finds here also a way out, though rather a forced one. He asserts that the calculation is not a new thing; that both calculation and observation of the new moon had been in use in the earliest times, and if both are not plainly expressed in Scripture, he seeks to figure them out from some slight indications. The violent dispute into which he enters with the Karaites about this matter is not a particularly successful one. Later Rabbinites admit that Saadias leant upon a broken reed. But at the time, Saadias could not make any concession; he had to gather all forces together to support the customary practice in a rational manner and to concede the proper right to reason without divesting usage of its sanctified character. Saadias is a theologian of reconciliation, and thus a perfect son of his time which is to develop a stronger period.

That he was a man of his time, he shows also by this, that he wrote all his works in the language of his country, in Arabic. So long as religious subjects are elaborated and treated in the customary language of the scholars, in which they first arose, the conceptions are the customary ones and remain the old ones. They are like the coins which pass from hand to hand, the value of which is accepted according to their determined coinage without questioning what their actual value might be. Religious conceptions, too, pass for what they were formerly claimed to be and appear in a certain independence as long as they are pronounced in their ancient language. It is something quite different when the language elaborates from the home, if it comes forth quick and alive from the pure fountain of the temper and spirit with which the entire life is in connection; then thoughts are rejuvenated. It is not sufficient that the conceptions be customary, they must be in harmony with the entire mode of thinking as it runs along constantly fresh in life. When Thomasius, at the end of the seventeenth century, first delivered his lectures in German instead of the Latin, he effected by that as much as by his fight against the belief in witches; and when Saadias wrote his works in the Arabic language, he essentially broke the way for a union of the consciousness of the time with religious custom, even if he did not effect it completely. But he did more yet, he made an Arabic translation of the bible.

A new translation of the bible—if it does not proceed from purely literary endeavor, if it is worked out in times when the activity of authors is not a trade and every work comes forth in response to an actual demand—every such translation of the bible is the revelation of a changed consciousness of the time, the expression of a newly recognized desire for better connection of the derived religious life with its source. It always comes forth at the threshold of a new period of time. When the Greek-Alexandrian Jews wanted to bring their ancient religious inheritance into a certain unison with the Greek ideas which flowed around them, the Greek Septuagint translation came forth and gave the impulse to a new culture in Egypt. When Talmudism had acquired firmness and spread afar, the Chaldee translation received its final touches and became fixed and standard. When science attempted to penetrate into the church of the Middle Ages, which, sunk into ignorance, was moving along by sheer momentum and had lost all acquaintance with its source—when science dared the attempt to throw its rays into the tightly-closed portals of the church, Luther arose with a new translation of the bible which became the banner of the new time and the new tendency grouped itself accordingly. When in Judaism a new time of redemption and illumination arrived, after long and hard oppression had enslaved the minds and custom, and want of taste had held dominion, Mendelssohn inaugurated that new period with his translation of the bible and gave it a definite impression. Such a translation of the bible is, therefore, the work of the time, and he that undertakes it, is the man of the time and the carrier of the thought and the mental forces which are moving the time. Such a man Saadias was too.

Translations of such a kind do not proceed from a purely scientific impulse, but from a religious instinct, from the endeavor to arrange a union of the new thought with the traditional religious conceptions and views. They are, therefore, not built on strictly scientific principles. And if the translation can not stand up in all regards before the judgment-seat of science, it has great importance in that it is the mirror of a newly awakened consciousness, and as it arises from attachment to the faith which it wants to reconcile with arising opposition, so it is, on the other side, the product of a new culture for which it becomes a strong support, and which spreads and sanctions it.

In addition to all that, Saadias was very busy as Gaon, labored in the Talmudical field, had to send into many countries answers and decisions upon questions addressed to him, and composed a considerable number of small polemical writings. He was mixed up in many disputes. Of a virile nature, he was not easy to bend, and thus had to fight out a long quarrel with the Chief of the Exile, David Ben Saccai, who wanted to force him to confirm a decision which he (Saadias) considered unjust, so that he was divested of the Gaonate during seven years, and had to keep in hiding. A man of compromise and reconciliation, and yet of unbending sense of justice! And all that, he accomplished in a life which lasted but fifty years. Such a man is well worthy to be glorified, a man of valiant, untiring endeavor, of unbroken energy, and a mind filled with general knowledge. He did not carry the new endeavors to completion, but he gave stimulus in all directions and thus laid the foundations for a new period.

Yet in general, the Arabian Empire in the East was entering its decline. As the sun rises in the east but moves toward the west, so too in the history of mankind, culture starts in the East and spreads toward the West to be completed there in higher development. The califate of Bagdad paled gradually. The califates subordinate to it acquired their independence and developed into superior powers, and power is followed by mental elevation. We soon see in Northern

Africa, rich culture arise. Saadias, too, had been from Northern Africa, from Egypt. Cairo had become an important gathering place of intellect. There flourished the contemporary of Saadias, Isaac Ben Solomon, also called Israeli, who lived nearly a hundred years, from the middle of the ninth to the middle of the tenth century—one of the most fertile authors. His works were translated from the Arabic into the Latin, and retained their supremacy through the entire Middle Ages. Physician, philosopher, mathematician, and astronomer, he had accomplished and produced much, judged by the condition of the time; but he also labored in the theological field and he also attempted to explain that neo-pythagorean philosophical little book, "Of the Creation," in a natural, rational way. He busied himself, too, with interpretation and explanation of the Scripture and probability indicates that he is the "Isaaki" in whose name many critical opinions are quoted. Among other things, Isaaki asserts that the passage, "And these are the kings that reigned in the land of Edom before there reigned any king over the children of Israel" (Genesis xxxvi, 31), after which eight generations are named, was written at the time of Josaphat, one of the later kings of Juda, and not by Moses. And consider that the man lived nine centuries ago.

Another man of decided literary attainments is Juda Ben Koraish who did solid work in comparative philology. It was natural to him; he had a good knowledge of Hebrew, Arabic was his mother tongue, Chaldee, which he calls Syrian, he had in the Targum (the bible translation). He compared those three Semitic sister-languages and recognized that they are closely related dialects, derived from a common root; that they are in essentials determined by the same laws, even if they diverge again in their complete development. The science of comparative philology has only in most recent times again found intelligent treatment. The nine centuries between Juda Ben Koraish and the present are almost entirely void in that field. What ventured to show up as comparative philology is fantastic and confused dreaming. It is the more gratifying to meet among the Arabian Jews of that early time with a man who with clear, sober view and scientific certainty correctly recognizes the basic laws of comparative philology and knows how to present them. But the richer land deserves our fuller attention, and we pass over to Spain.

VII.

In Spain.

There are periods in the world's history which cast their illuminating rays into the late centuries. They are like a mighty fountain which, when the grounds through which it had formerly wandered have been covered by drifting sands or laid waste, breaks forth somewhere else and starts growth there, a fountain from which the late comer yet eagerly dips refreshing drink. Such is the biblical-Hebrew period, such the Greek-Hellenic time, and such is, even if not in the same high degree, the Jewish-Spanish-Arabian period. Already in early times, Spain had not been entirely unknown to the Jews, but it was regarded by them as a far distant country. It is not named in the bible, and Sepharad, as the Spanish Jews called their country in Hebrew, is not Spain in biblical language. But the Mishnah mentions it and knows the fine fish from there which are served on the tables of gormandizing Romans as dainty dishes. It is also spoken of as the province of the sea, the land of the West, and as the farthest limits of the world. The time when Jews first settled there can not be fixed with certainty. But while all the ancient nations—Phoenicians, Greeks and Romans—visited Spain and founded colonies there, Jews may have come along with them; and when the Romans conquered the country and held it as a pearl of their empire, it may be accepted as certain that Jews went and settled there. In the first Christian centuries we find them there in large numbers and as long as Christianity existed there in milder form, as long as the Arians who were less dogmatic, ruled in Spain, we find the Jews in friendly intercourse with the rest of the population. But when the more severe tendency of the trinitarian faith gained the supremacy and councils of the church convened frequently, ordering the suppression of so-called heresies with rigor and violence, the Jews were treated as the worst unbelievers, Judaism was adjudged the most criminal heresy, and severe measures were employed against them. To the fanaticism of the church, West-Gothic brutality became joined, and the lot of the Jews was a very sad one as long as the West-Gothic church government remained unshaken down to the eighth century. The names Reckared, Sisibut, Receswinth, Erwig, Erika, are written in blood into the history of the Jews. The most severe laws were ordered against them, so that toward the last, they were considered and treated as slaves and bondmen.

Then a storm swept along, convulsing and purifying. Hardly a century had passed since Islam had arisen and its adherents had spread over Northern Africa, reached the Pillars of Hercules and now crossed the narrow strait which separates Africa from Europe and quickly took possession of the whole of Spain. Spain turned over a new leaf. Arabianism, Islam, kept itself on Spanish soil from the beginning of the eighth century for over seven hundred years and gave to the country splendor and glory and noble civilization. Merry song, elevation of mind, flourishing science soon prevailed in the country; amidst battle and clanking of arms the minds became strong, and yet mild manner did not disappear. A peculiar life arose there. Two nationalities wrestle for exclusive possession; to each nationality attaches different speech and faith. Here is the old-Spanish-Roman population with Roman-Castilian language and Christianity; there is the Oriental population with musical Arabic language and Islam. A fight for life starts. Who speaks Arabic professes Islam; who speaks Roman is an adherent of Christianity, and both languages flourish with that mutual emulation. At the side of both populations and languages there exists a third nationality, the Jewish, with Judaism for faith, and also with the desire, natural under the circumstances, to revive the Hebrew language. The Jews are said to have assisted the Arabians at their invasion of Spain. If they did so, no fault should be found with the slave who had been robbed of his country for eagerly seizing the means offered to break his chains. They were not deceived. Their fetters were struck off and they who carried many scars and marks of wounds in body and soul, breathed again anew.

Almost two centuries passed before the country entered more quiet conditions, before the rapid conquest changed to peaceable possession, and the mental elevation could attain its proper development. At the beginning of the tenth century, a ruler arises to whom it is permitted to spread the culture of his tribe over the whole of Spain and to establish its power therein. A reign of fifty years gives endurance to his labors. Abdorrahman III. reigns from 911 to 961, a wise and mighty prince, who with his son and successor Al Hakim, represents the time when Arabian dominion in Spain was in flower. The Spanish califate had become separated from the supremacy of Bagdad and was independent. The calif of Spain also took the title of Ruler of the Faithful and made treaties independently with other powers. At the side of Abdorrahman stood a Jew who is named everywhere as his faithful adviser and agent of his enterprises, viz., his physician, Chasdai Ben Isaac Ben Ezra Ben Shaprut. Chasdai belongs to those eminent, grand natures who everywhere operate creatively, whose appearance commands confidence and reverence so that the mean and narrow does not dare to come near them. He was a statesman of genius, of that genius which does not delight in daring conceits, but which completely overlooks the road to be taken with clear view before beginning, keeps his eye constantly on the goal, and knows how to move toward it wisely and without ceasing. A man of that kind acts stimulating and elevating even where he can not and will not move independently. Whether Chasdai held a political office besides his position as physician to the calif, if he was minister (secretary) of Abdorrahman, is not certain. He is not designated as visier, but in any case he was his prince's faithful adviser and confidant who took the most difficult tasks in hand and executed them. He directed the foreign relations; the negotiations which Abdorrahman entered into with foreign powers were made through him. Abdorrahman considered it very important to be on good terms with the realms which bordered on the Eastern Arabian Empire, especially with the Greek Empire, in order to be secure against the sovereignty which the calif of Bagdad did not want to relinquish. On this account he sent a deputation to Constantinople, which was returned with presents. That was done through the agency of Chasdai, who turned the legation to the advantage of science because he obtained the botany of Dioscorides and procured a learned Greek monk, with whose assistance he made the book the property of the Arabians and of Europe. Abdorrahman made also connection with the German Empire. Between 953 and 956, a deputation went to Otto I., who was then German emperor, and it was answered by letter in the hands of a German legation, of which John Von Goertz was the leader. His biographer relates that the calif had at first been suspicious and full of doubt lest the letter might contain something insulting to Islam as similar expressions about Christianity had greatly delayed the reception of the Arabian deputation at the German imperial court. He therefore entrusted the first steps to a Jew Hasdeu (Chasdai) and, he adds, our men testify that they never saw a wiser man. He knew how to manage that he learned the contents of the letter, and as there were really some expression in it which might wound the calif's feelings, he made great exertions to have the letter changed for another one, and succeeded in having it done. If such arrangements served only to raise the glory of the court, there were others of essential advantage, especially as they were made with small, still existing Christian principalities in Spain. Don Sancho, the son of Ramir, was ruler of Leon, but he was considerably objected to by his people; in Navarra, a relative of his with his grandmother Tota held sway. Through the diplomacy of Chasdai, Abdorrahman succeeded so well that the two princes came to Cordova and requested the calif to act as arbitrator. As Don Sancho was sick, Chasdai gave him medical treatment, and then as diplomat, succeeded in getting him to yield. From the Slavic kingdoms, too, delegations came of half-savage tribes and as among the other legations, there were among those Slavish ones also isolated Jews who understood best how to effect the approach. From them Chasdai heard the confirmation of a rumor which had reached him before, that in that eastern part of the world, a Jewish kingdom existed, a realm of which a Jew occupied the throne. It was the realm of the Chazars.

It had been founded in the eighth century in the Caucasus and the present Crimea formed a part, in those regions where wild mountaineers dwelt who retain their character till the present time. There a realm was formed with Chakanes at the head; these professed Judaism since the eighth century. The realm presents a picture the like of which we hardly find again in the Middle Ages. A great number of Jews lived there and they left their traces deeply marked in the history of those lands. At the present time the fragments of that ancient Chazar-Jewish culture are yet to be found in the Karaites residing there who in part are their descendants and antiquities have been and are discovered which reach back into early times and permit us to get a deeper view into the development of many a Jewish quality. The Chazar-Jewish rulers did not force the population into acceptance of their faith; the realm was governed by a council of state, composed of members of the various faiths prevailing in the land. In the tenth century when Chasdai heard of it, the empire of the Chazars had already passed the time of its flower; the wildly crowding, half-savage populations of the frontiers had somewhat shaken the throne, and shortly thereafter, the Moscowites put their hands against the realm, when the Mongols destroyed it. Chasdai was greatly affected by the news; he could not rest until he should have communication with that Jewish monarch, this time not by order of his master, but to satisfy his own heart. After much trouble and several unsuccessful attempts, he succeeded. As his messenger, Jacob of Nemez is named, which in the Slavonic languages means Germany. A copy of the Hebrew letter which Chasdai addressed to the King of the Chazars has been preserved and is in many regards a valuable document from that time. After high-flown, pompous beginning,

Chasdai explains his position in the Western Empire, how God raised him up, gives an account of Sepharad, now called Andalusia, its location, character, government, and relations with other countries. Yet he was always grieved by the jeers that the government had been taken from Israel, and he had rejoiced the more upon hearing of a Jewish-Chazar kingdom. He therefore prays for more exact information, and it would be a great comfort to him to behold it with his own eyes. The pompous introduction is an acrostic showing the name Chasdai Ben Isaac Ben Ezra Ben Shaprut. The king of the Chazars, who had the Hebrew name Joseph, answered in very smooth Hebrew, gives information about his realm, its extent, borders, and connections; he derives the descent of the Chazars from Japhet, and tells that his ancestors had been converts. He would be glad to see Chasdai and wishes him health and prosperity. If that intercourse has had no further consequences, that exchange of letters has preserved to us a historic fact, illustrating the position of Judaism in the East at that time. Out there where the power of Greece and Rome had not penetrated, it hung long in the balance which religion would prevail. Even the Moscowite ruler was in doubt as to which one he should incline to and Christianity owes its acceptance there almost to chance. That exchange of letters without consequences, the Chazars washed away without deeper effects upon world-historic development like so many other kingdoms, was for a long time overlooked and then doubted. Only recent time has proved the letters genuine and the actual existence of the Chazar realm with its Jewish kings. Now we also find more and more remains of ancient Jewish culture in those parts, which give us revelation of deep effects of Judaism upon that time and at the same time throw remarkably strong light upon the entire inner course of Judaism, revealing ancient inner developments which without that, had been completely covered up, and showing points that fit into the whole process as necessary parts.

But let us return to Chasdai. He also put himself into communication with the academies at Sora and Pumbeditha, aimed to get learned Talmudical writings in return, corresponded with Dosa, the son of Saadias, and sought to complete his knowledge of the conditions in the country which was acknowledged as the land of the birth of Judaism. In that an event came to his aid which he seized eagerly. Four Jewish scholars—probably residents of the Greek Empire—had undertaken a journey by sea, the ship was captured by a Spanish-Arabian admiral, the crew and passengers were made slaves and sold. Of the four Jewish scholars, Shemarjah was sold to Alexandria and redeemed by Jews residing there, Chushiel went to Cairo, and Moses with his son (who was probably the fourth one) whose wife preferred death in the sea to the embraces of the lascivious admiral, came to Spain and was sold to Cordova. He was not recognized at once, but his true character was soon revealed. Chasdai joyfully seized this opportunity to appoint him chief of an academy, to dissolve the dependence in which Judaism had been on Eastern Arabia, and to make Spain independent in Talmudic scientific relations, just as his master had dissolved the dependence of Spain from the Rulers of the Believers at Bagdad.

Such grand efficacy on all sides—and he was in communication with the learned polyhistor Isaac Ben Solomon in Cairo—had to exercise an important influence upon the mental elevation of the Jews in Spain. All later authors are full of his praise and proclaim that through his patronage Jewish thought had first moved glad and new, all science had flourished, and song and poetry had begun among the Jews. In the days of prince Chasdai—says Abraham Ben David about 1160—began a merry chirping, and later, under prince Samuel, clear song resounded. The later literary critic, Charisi, himself at the beginning of the thirteenth century a straggler after the eminent poets, gives in a Hebrew poem extravagant praise to Chasdai for his influence and liberal patronage of Hebrew poets and scholars. In another short passage, he acknowledges that the beginning of culture had started then, but that those beginnings had been weak in comparison with the later, higher accomplishment: "Formerly there was a number of poets—the crowd grew wild and rank—now their songs are forgot—nobody wants to hear them—Menahem Ben Saruk, Dunash Ben Librat and others alike their songs have dropped out of sight—they were weak and empty and light."

Charisi, an aesthetician, characterizes the periods almost exclusively by the poetic attempts made and executed, but he mentions in that passage names that are important in other fields. Menahem Ben Saruk was an industrious scholar and exerted great influence through his quiet work. He was born at Tortosa, made his living as a merchant, but lived for science. Chasdai induced him to remove to Cordova. There he composed the first Hebrew dictionary with an introduction containing the principles of grammar. As a first attempt, that book has its faults and weak places. The proper insight into the structure of the language had not yet been attained; Menahem did not yet know the law of the three-letter roots, which is the basic law for all Semitic languages and especially for the Hebrew, and upon which alone grammar and dictionary can be scientifically constructed. But he placed everything known up to his time properly together, and broke the road for further progress by the general survey of what had been done. He looks with clear and sober comprehension upon the phenomena of the language, and his explanations of the numerous passages quoted by him are sound and preparative for his successors. Menahem's dictionary remains even later a guide for that part of the Jews in the Middle Ages who, ignorant of the Arabic, worked along the lines of his book which was in Hebrew. For even that was an important step in advance, made by Menahem; he composed his work in the Hebrew language and founded a new scientific style which put aside the degeneracies and mixtures customary till then, and strove for linguistically correct as well as elegant expression. If just in Spain we meet such an attempt to renew the youth of the Hebrew language, the reason for it is probably in the battle of languages going on there. In the fight between Islam and Christianity, the Arabic wrestled with the Castilian tongue for the prize, and thus Judaism might be incited to to take part in the struggle and attempt to revive its language. The enterprise could not succeed with a language that no longer prevailed in practical life. If excellent results were yet achieved, it is a strong proof of the noble zeal and the high gifts applied to it, and the aesthetic culture acquired by it effected a purification of the taste in the explanation of the Scriptures. Menahem made an important advance in that. With clear, often sublime expression, he has a fine sense for the characteristical of the presentation, and does not permit his eye to be dimmed by the customary interpretations. As far as science can be his guide, he follows it. Of course, Menahem was no poet. If he had to make an effort now and then to celebrate his patron Chasdai in a poem or to sing of some event in his house, he did not make a great success at it. It probably did not suit his upright, honest mind to follow the Arabian fashion of climbing the ladder of praises and placing extravagant homage at the feet of a patron. He may have thought with a later maker of proverbs:

> Who likes to make songs of praise for the men on high
> Must know how to flatter and understand how to lie.

With all his thoroughgoing, scientific activity, Menahem recognized and appreciated the work of others, and as much as he excelled the labors of his predecessors, he yet abstains from any detracting remarks even where he cannot avoid contradicting their opinions, and on the contrary, tries to keep any blame away from them.

A man of such sterling and gentle character deserved a quiet life and reverential recognition, and yet he did not receive what his modest claims entitled him to demand. The times were crowding and stormy. A younger contemporary, Dunash Ben Librat, also known as Adonim Ha-Levi, a native of Bagdad, had made his residence at Fez. Whether he removed to Spain, attracted by the glory of Chasdai, is not certain although probable; at any rate, he was in close communication with Spain. Of a nature very different from that of Menahem,

Dunash pitches with youthful impetuosity into his learned contemporaries. At first he attacks Saadias and does not confine his remarks within decent limits, eagerly seeks for small faults, and points his criticisms into little epigrams which he adds effectively to each critical remark. He does not belong among the strongest, yet he tells the highly respected Gaon, "Notice who is behind, and who the right does find." His egotism is not altogether without reason, for he has a better insight into the peculiarities of the language and has suppositions which later students form into scientific certainties. Aben Ezra says of him correctly, "Dunash awoke somewhat out of the sleep into which the earlier ones had dropped, and his explanation of the Scripture strives for greater objectivity." — But his fight against Saadias was merely a skirmish which he soon ceased. He appears against Menahem with greater severity. He annotates the dictionary with cutting glossaries which now and then hit correctly, but treat the meritorious scholar with arrogant contempt and he attempts to violently strip him of the pioneer's honor. Those criticisms he hands to Chasdai, who accepts them favorably, so much the more as they are accompanied by a poem that praises Chasdai to the sky.

Dunash belongs to the first ones who introduced Arabic verse metre into the Hebrew language. Exact metre is foreign to the biblical Hebrew, although a natural rhythm prevails in its poetical portions and especially a rhythm of thoughts. If they aimed at that time to introduce an exactly constructed metre in poetry, such was of course not in the character of the Hebrew language but was an imitation of the Arabic which used various metres and rhymes. The kinship of the Hebrew with the Arabic facilitated the carrying over of the peculiarities of the latter and they did not sound foreign. The sensation of euphony was heightened and the severe discipline of fixed laws kept out the prolixity of unlimited prose. Although that taking over of Arabic poetic forms into the Hebrew did not revive it anew, nor could acquire a lasting or scientific property for it, it was yet a good educational remedy which did not miss its aim.

Dunash was one of the first to compose by the Arabic metres, and he plumes and prides himself on that account. When he lays his poem at the feet of Chasdai, he does not omit to remark that it is constructed in compliance with the new art of versification. He addresses Chasdai:

In song, cast into metre-mold
(Better than it was made of old,
Perhaps it might seem bold,
    I made the great improvement,)

I sing the honor and glory
Of the gallant man's story
Who knows well how to parry
    Against foreign foes' intent.

He towers above all men,
Skilled both with sword and pen
He took strong cities, ten,
    And forced the foes' consent.

Oh, how he has close-mown
The weeds so overgrown
When Ramir's son was thrown
    And had to be content.

With prayer, and in bad plight
Without heart for a fight,
That king came in to write
    His name to th' agreement.

Tota, the king's grandmother,
She, too, just like the other,
Surrendered with small bother
    To diplomatic argument.

Our faith he makes secure.
Though 'gainst the evil-doer,
He cares for many poor
    And helps them to ascent.

To poets does his hand
With gifts and cheer expand,
Like waters o'er the land
    By clouds in rain are spent.

And in the Diaspora
He glorifies the Torah;
To th' academy in Sora
    Rich presents he has sent.

We do not want to find fault with the extravagant praise which his poetic verbiage renders to the great statesman and gracious patron, but it wounds our feelings when he tacks to that pompous halo of glory mean and cutting attacks upon the meritorious scholar Menahem. For, without further ado, he continues:

The false Scripture explainer,
The word- and meaning-sprainer
I meet as strong retainer,
As safe and proven guard.

And when he thus continues in many rhyming lines, we regret such impassioned invective, which can find its excuse only in the stormy youthfulness of the age. What effect that homage, joined to the abuse of Menahem, may have had upon Chasdai, we do not learn. It can not be supposed that Menahem was by it crowded out of his heart. And when we read the surprising account in papers which have recently been found, that Menahem had once suddenly fallen into disfavor with Chasdai, that the latter had even permitted or himself ordered Menahem's house demolished on a Sabbath day, there must have been some other circumstance to excite Chasdai's ill-will to such a degree. The writings do not reveal the incident. We simply learn that Menahem asserts his innocence and feels convinced that Chasdai will also recognize it, if he will only quietly hear him and read his words properly. A first address which has not come down to us, seems to have borne the introduction:

Thou great pillar of honor,
A very fountain of fairness,
I adjure thee by the law
Of Moses the Korahite.

Oh, take notice of my excuse,
A hearing do not me refuse,
By answer return good news
To a soul that suffered deeply.

It very often happens in history, and specially in the history of literature, that events of importance are not even mentioned, and that we can only grasp at them by a tip that has been preserved on account of its oddity. The letter to which those uncouth verses were the introduction, has been lost, but that introduction has survived the centuries on account of its oddity. The strange designation of Moses as Korahite—i. e., as attacked by Korah—has caused the preservation of the lines. If the letter has not come down to us, it certainly reached the hands of Chasdai, for we learn the hard answer he gave to this or a later one: "If you did wrong, the punishment has made it right; if you are innocent, I have increased your reward in the next world." A bitter word, with which a proud magnate thinks to square things. Menahem complains of this in a fine letter still existing, which keeps within the proper bounds in spite of the full indignation of the injured man and the just consciousness of his own innocence, and does not fail to appreciate the merits of the man whom he accuses to himself. He represents to Chasdai whether he may be judge in his own behalf without examination or investigation, and execute such verdict; whether he, a human being, could penetrate into the heart and mind of another and make himself the judge of his intentions. It seems that the former friendly relations were re-established and history had spread reconciliating silence upon that dissonance. And yet curiosity incites us to lift the veil. What was it that could goad Chasdai to such severe proceeding?

Where sure facts depart from us, supposition attempts to take their place. And if we can not clear Chasdai of passionate irritation, we may guess that wounded vanity blinded the man. We know that Chasdai addressed an epistle to the king of the Chazars, which carried the acrostic of his name in the introduction. Chasdai did not write the letter himself. He was a man of general scientific acquirements, but not specially learned in Hebrew, though he had the title of Chief of the Academy. If he had been such a scholar, he would hardly have established the liberated Rabbi Moses as chief of an academy with such glad haste, and contemporaries and posterity would have also celebrated his achievements in that branch beyond the proper dues, while there is perfect silence on the subject. He was a physician and statesman, loved science and promoted it, without taking actual, productive share in it. Surely, as he generally employed Menahem in such matters, he made use of him for the epistle to the Chazar king, and the letter was composed and made up with the acrostic by that scholar. When we consider the matter further, we find that the introduction does not end with the acrostic, but the verses run on with the same rhyme. If we examine those closely, very plain fragments of another acrostic, "Menahem Ben Saruk," appear, and it is very easy to restore the whole name by a few small changes which correspond to the expressions and the meaning more than they would disturb it, and the presumption is near, that Menahem actually indicated his name in that way. Will you call that literary vanity? It may have been, yet at any rate pardonable, and it corresponded to the fashion which permitted to the writers of even hymns and liturgical poems such indication of their names as authors. Yet, Chasdai himself, or the flatterers around him, may have thought differently about it. Envious and mean, they may have seized the occasion to cast suspicion on Menahem and represent him as ambitious to share or even dim the glory of his patron of whom he was simply the servant. And thus probably the sensitiveness of Chasdai was aroused. The fragmentary condition in which the name of Menahem appears in the letter now, is very likely the result of intentional changes.

At any rate, the spirits were reconciled long ago, and from Chasdai's memory, too, that dim shadow has moved away. Chasdai, Menahem, and Dunash, shine in pure lustre. They are the men of the beginning and promise; they deserved to have their lives and their work considered more at length. The rich Spanish-Arabian period begins with Chasdai, who worked half a century to the honor of his country and for the ennobling of Jewish culture. His name and those of his contemporaries are graven into history, and their monuments are the more complete and finished achievements which follow upon their time.

VIII.

First Half of the Eleventh Century.

Whenever intellectual culture is about to begin a new flight, whenever the endeavor is renewed to advance from the plane of naive consideration to a higher point of view, the students lean upon two ancient cultured nations and avail themselves of their literatures; namely, the Hebrew and the Greek. Different in their points of view, Hebraism and Hellenism mutually supplement each other. Islam availed itself of those resources and formed connection with them. The Koran had drawn from Judaism and its bible the best and noblest contents. The literature of the Moslems following thereafter leaned especially upon the monuments of Greek literature which came to them in translations. For Islam was able to direct into its territory only the brooklets draining out of those streams of life, it could not draw directly out of the source. Hebrew and Greek remained entirely unknown to the professors of Islam, they drew only from translations which interpreted the Greek originals to them, and from that which was communicated to them from Judaism. In that way they received a culture that was brought to them at second hand as it were; the actual spirit of the well, moving and living in those fountains, did not touch them. If the culture is to be a truly refreshing one, it must go up to the fountain itself. Thus we see in later times, when men at the resurrection of science dived with real eagerness and youthful enthusiasm into the rediscovered languages of Greek and Jewish antiquity, how again in the last century, after the fountain has been roiled for a time, people crowded more closely up to it and drank mental health out of the limpid waters.

While every foreign language remained unknown to the professors of Islam, the Hebrew language and literature were never wholly sealed up to the Jews, and whenever a fresh breath moved them, endeavor awoke to dive into the Hebrew language and acquire a deeper insight into it, lively and youthful, not simply as scientific impulse, but as dim consciousness that it would bring fresh life and rejuvenation. Philology appears at such times, as history teaches us, as the queen of sciences; humanism, study of humanity, is then the name for knowledge of antiquity; with this knowledge, the truly humane is cultivated. The labors expended on that study pass, therefore, not as purely academic inquiries, but are considered problems of the entire mental existence. Immensely high value is attributed to linguistical discussion which we now consider insignificant; then, they are an issue of the mental life's current.

Thus it occurred also within Judaism during that period; the awakening culture revealed itself in the great attention given to the Hebrew language. We have become acquainted with that zeal in Menahem and Dunash. If the fight becomes hot between them about something peculiar and insignificant, that inflammability of temper finds its explanation in the immense value which they necessarily had attributed to those subjects that were to them more than mere learning. What they had begun, their successors continued with the same zeal to happier success. One pupil of Menahem is the celebrated Juda Chayug with the Arabian name Abu Sakaria Jachia, the most important grammarian, who first penetrated into the inner nature of the Hebrew language and first revealed the triliterality of the roots, thus gaining and communicating clearness in the whole view of the grammatical structure of the language. The double names with which we meet among the Jews of Spain consist of an Arabian, besides the Hebrew name, and that is a mark of the period. As Jews, they have their Hebrew names, but they lived so much within the people and the language of their country, in its manners and customs, that they had to bear an Arabian name as well, for general use—a sort of double nature, repeated in later times. A successor of Chayug, who immediately follows him, correcting and completing, and with whom science of biblical grammar and lexicography of that period closes, is Jonah, Abulwalid Mervan Ben Ganach. He was a physician and philosopher and created an epoch as philologist by elaborating a complete Hebrew grammar and a Hebrew dictionary in the Arabic language and laid enduring foundations in that science. He was master of the entire material, showed deep insight into the structure and the fundamental traits of the language and knew how to prove systematically and put into order all its fine points. All later writers drew on him, and though his works were hidden from those who were not masters of the Arabic and are in part yet unprinted in the Hebrew translation because later works, made more to the taste of the time, seemed to make them superfluous, the most generally accepted books of instruction have all drawn from Abulwalid and the most recent time has gladly turned to him again to profit from his unexhausted wealth, and to receive instruction out of the depth of his views.

With him we have entered into the first half of the eleventh century, into the period that shows great numbers of men of culture and scholars of every kind. In all branches of science, men appear who reveal the profound and many-sided mental movement; astronomers like Hassan Ben Hassan, also known as Jekuthiel, numerous Talmudists, although that science was then in Spain at an early stage and rose only later into greater perfection, workers in the most various philosophical branches, as also men who entered more deeply into the essence of human life and endeavored to know man himself according to his moral requirements. As such a one, I want to particularly mention Bachia (Bechai) Ben Joseph Bakuda, a man of an amiable sincerity, who introduces us into the depths of the human heart, who deeply feels and examines its true religious and moral requirements, so that, putting aside the outer rubble, he dives into the stream of mental and sentimental life, permits it to rush through himself and presents the refreshing waters to others. There is a certain trait of pietism in him, not altogether free of tenderheartedness, but otherwise of such cordiality that he knows how to break through the fetters of the prescribed credence and manner of action and puts mere naked doing behind fresh, living conviction. The name of his work is sufficient to show by what tendency the man is ruled: "Duties of the Heart." He wants to present what the heart feels as obligatory and what it requires for its ennobling. He lets man descend into himself that he may become conscious of his advantages and abilities and strive to cultivate and develop them, but also to recognize his shortcomings and finiteness and humbly labor towards perfection. "Duties of the heart," he says, "surely precede duties of the limbs as the compliance with a mere commandment. Works, that are outside of me, which I can thoughtlessly practice with hands or feet, are not the highest goal of man; such is rather the awakening within himself of the consciousness of the duties of the heart to gain strength by them." And this man was *Dayan* (judge), by office and calling, a religious leader of the community, and thereby his time is yet more distinctly characterized by the circumstance that men of his position place disposition and conviction higher than ritual performance and learning. It surprises him, he said, to see how many raise the most remote questions and make searching investigations about particulars relating to ceremonies which occur but rarely. Upon such a question once addressed to him, he replied: "My dear, you must surely have advanced very far in the culture of your heart. Have you actually achieved so much along that line that you have leisure to investigate such rare matters?" A beautiful period that holds such a man.

Song and poetry in the Hebrew language were cultivated with particular enthusiasm. As scientific knowledge of the language stood high then, they wanted to have full possession of it, sing in it and make poems in it. Such an undertaking could not succeed; a language that has departed out of everyday life is not fitted for song welling forth from the heart. And yet the attempt was natural, and we see it come out at all periods of awakening culture. With the revival of the sciences and the resurrection of classic antiquity, men dived into the Latin and Greek languages and attempted to make poems in them as if they were the speech of head and heart.

To the Jews, the Hebrew was much nearer; for it was the language of their religious life, of their divine service, and seemed thus to be well fitted for the expression of deepest sentiment. Therefore, while scientific works were written in Arabic, poetry was composed in Hebrew. Two men in particular attract our attention; one more by the wide compass of his knowledge, the wealth of his effectiveness, and at the same time, the many-sided attempts in various branches of literary activity to which his poetical works also belong. I mean Samuel Ha-Levi, surnamed Ha-Nagid, or the prince, with the Arabian name Ibn Nagdilah.

Samuel is an elevating character. Of plain station, he rises to the visierate at the court of the calif of Granada. He was born at Cordova, but persecutions occurring there drove him out of that city. For even in that time, shining to us in the poetic shimmer of distance, violent cruptions were not infrequent. Rebellion against one dynasty broke forth, and it was crowded out by another; incursions of the Berbers from North Africa threatened to suffocate the flowers of culture and, at any rate, frequently shook the secure position of the thrones. Thus, that period must not appear to us too ideal; it did not enjoy undisturbed evolution; civil welfare and mental progress were often interrupted by rough blows. Only they were passing convulsions, not the constant pressure, almost enacted into law, as it was the rule in the Christian Middle Ages. By such a convulsion, Samuel was driven out of Cordova. In Malaga, where he went and where the calif of Granada had established his seat for awhile, he became known to his visier and used by him. And before his death, that officer recommended Samuel to the calif as his successor, perhaps because he had recognized him as a well-cultured, adroit and reliable man, who was master of the Arabic language up to its most artistic, pompous forms. Samuel obtained the visierate and remained in that place in the empire for a long succession of years; his sincerity and good sense, his ability joined with modesty, caused him to surmount all difficulties arising on numerous occasions. While he thus showed himself thoroughly equal to his position as statesman, he shines to posterity also as one of the most important scholars in many fields. He was head of the academy, an important Talmudist, author of scholarly works, entertained a lively correspondence with scholars in various countries and left a large number of Hebrew poems which, if they do not exhibit special genius, yet are not without skill and fine expression in their language. He died highly honored in 1055, and left the visierate to his son, who is also greatly praised, but who, grown up in position and affluence, did not possess the modesty of his father, and lost his life during a riot.

A man of different kind, and towering high above his time, is Solomon Gabirol, also named Aba Ajub Suleiman Ben Gebrol. Sublime is the poetic tale of antiquity, how the men of the days of yore shake at the bars of their finite power and endeavor to acquire their full independence. The Titans pile mountain upon mountain to storm the heavens; the men of one language and one speech want to build in Babylon's wide plain, a city with a tower the point of which shall reach into heaven, in order that, relying upon their own power, they may have a guarantee of endurance and preservation. Such bold aspiration of man fails on account of his weakness, and results in punishment and fall. Yet more sublime is the poetic conception that presents man in his mental strife, how he wants to break through the narrow confines that surround his mind, by penetrating the darkness of the moral order of the world. Job carries the consciousness of his virtue and purity with a certain intrepidity into the fight against the mishaps of life; he calls eternal justice to account: "Why all this to me? Do I not rate higher than my fate? And yet such things happen to me?" In that strife of moral indignation with the afflictions of life lies an elevation and dignity that we feel ourselves lifted up with the wrangler in spite of his afflictions. Composed, we enter with him again into the subjection to the higher spirit of God, who reveals Himself to him in His infinite sublimity. Still more profound and ingenious is it, when the poet of modern times presents Faust to us, as he tries to penetrate into the depths of knowledge, see the veil lifted from the secret of creation, descend into the web and woof of the source of force and spirit, work with them, and thus solve the riddle of all existence, impatiently wants to become master of his mental finiteness and limitation. Deep is his fall when he sinks from that presumptuous height into sensuality to suffocate his high endeavor in it. Only through the naivety of an innocent, pure being that becomes chained to him, he is saved. Such a Faust-nature, but without any mixture of sensuality, without desire of exhausting the enjoyment of life at one time and of draining the cup to the lees, such a nature is Solomon Gabirol. A man whose life is an uninterrupted wrestling to descend into the deepest secrets of existence, to apprehend the driving wheel of mind and life and of the forces which bind the universe together.

Such men are driven by a constant unrest; they are never satisfied within themselves, because they never reach the goal for which they strive without ceasing. The ideal appears to them from afar in its full grace and beauty, they rush after it, they think of seizing it, and it disappears. Yet they never weaken, they begin the race anew, they rise with the bold flight of enthusiasm to come near to the last reason of things, they weaken in their flight but still rise again. Deep gloom surrounds such men, a world-pain, or rather a knowledge-pain, goes through their soul, and yet it is like the cloud that veils the divine glory and reflects it at the same time. When they enter into the reality, it appears naked and bald to them, they do not find their ideals materialized. The idea, as it enters the material, visible world, appears to them broken, dishonored, profaned, and they run over with complaints about the insusceptibility of their contemporaries for the grand and sublime, complaints which appear to us often very bitter and unjust. They throw their whole contempt upon their own time especially; the former times, they think, may have been better. The difference between the ideal and the actual is with them too great, so that a just verdict can hardly be expected from them. They would like to join in close communion with individuals, their heart longs for a mind of like tone; sometimes they think of having found one to whom they may pour out their impulse, but alas! it was an illusion. Some come to them with the self-complacency of a Wagner, admire and praise their great knowledge without surmising the depth of their soul. From the other ones with the practical understanding who in addition think themselves far superior to such noble souls, they turn away with the same indignation as from the serfs of sensuality. And thus they remain lonesome and alone.

Such a man is Solomon Gabirol, a poet whose poems are consecrated, full of thought, a thinker whose thoughts are poetically transfigured. When Charisi, the later poet and æsthetic critic, gives his verdict upon the various earlier poets, it seems as if the flight of Gabirol's muse had lent him wings, as he characterizes him with a few words:

> A king he stands, sublime and grand, alone;
> The song of songs is made by Solomon.

Sublime, high, is with him both thought and word.—Who goes up into heaven and brings them from there?—His songs for fast-days are beautiful—wonderfully powerful—his prayers for repentance hours give odor like beds of flowers —incomparable is his figure's force—unattainable the word as it powerfully roars.

Legend loves to glorify the childhood of great men. It is spared the trouble in Gabirol's case, for he stands out finished, scarcely beyond the years of childhood. At the age of sixteen, he says of himself:

> A boy of sixteen years
> In experience of gray hairs.

In experience, not in the sense of having lived many years and gained knowledge of the world, but experienced in the painful sense that the dissonance between the ideal and the actual had then already sounded within him, and that he felt it as if a rent had set his heart a-trembling. He punishes himself for breaking out into such painful complaints at so early an age and for not overcoming them, because he can not quit his high aim:

Does plaint fit one of sixteen years
Bemoaning disappointment in his life?
With cheeks like the morning's ray
With the youngsters I ought to play.
But no; my heart so old in manner
Enrolled me under wisdom's banner,
And thus my youth has disappeared,
And the road for pain was cleared.
Sighing and groaning close to me keep,
If I see pleasure, I have to weep.
What profits the tear? Vain conceit!
What promises hope? Pale deceit!
They say some balsam will make me sound;
Me? who is down with mortal wound.

It may have once been better, but what use is that to him?

What use my plaint, my pine,
That the world is not perfected?
No doubt it once was very fine—
My coming's time's too late selected.

He lived at first at Saragossa, whose inhabitants certainly were not the worst among the Jews of Spain; Bachia too, whom we have mentioned before, seems to have been a resident of that city. Of course they did not come up to Gabirol's ideal.

With this bad generation I am in sore plight,
What I call left, they call that right;
Lonesome like a grave it is all around,
My house feels like a coffin, I am so bound.
Yet I must sit in their council's assembly
And must hear their senseless babble,
For around me are fools and hinds
Who think themselves giant minds.
They would give me wormwood to sip
With smiling mien and flattering lip
And bitter hatred in their heart.
When I hear them speak, it makes me start.
It seems as if they're whispering Latin apart.
What profit to me if poet I am,
To sing for that kind of rabble?
'Tis better I loose every latchet,
And chop them up with my tongue for hatchet.

He entertained at times very friendly relations with Samuel Ha-Levi. The noble prince probably liked to see the excellent man in his neighborhood, recognized his worth and valued him accordingly, but he was a poet himself and perhaps felt a rival's jealousy. Gabirol sang the fame of Samuel now and then, but we catch discords too, which sound through their relations. A short verse of Gabirol's, preserved by chance, reveals the tension. It says:

I feel so cold, I am chilled most stiff and tight
As if I heard a song by Samuel the Levite.

Such sharp scorn sounds through other poems. Epicurean worldlings approach him to be wise, to live like others, to apply the world's pleasures against melancholy, and to drown his pain in wine. But he opposes that with that deep, nobler pain which mocks at such remedies:

With tears thy grief thou dost bemoan
Tears that would melt the hardest stone.
Oh, wherefor sing'st thou not the vine?
Why chant'st thou not the praise of wine?

But I: Poor fools the wine may cheat,
Lull them with lying visions sweet;
Upon the wings of storms may bear
The heavy burden of their care;
The father's heart may harden so
He feeleth not his own child's woe.

No ocean is the cup, no sea,
To drown my broad, deep misery.
It grows so rank; you cut it all,
The aftermath springs just as tall.
My heart and flesh are worn away,
Mine eyes are darkened from the day.

The lovely morning red behold
Wave to the breeze her flag of gold
The hosts of stars above the world
Like banners vanishing are furled.
The dew shines bright; I bide forlorn,
And shudder with the chill of morn.

There is but one thing by which he can overcome his pain,

that same which produces the pain—investigation, striving for the goal of his desire:

Endowed with the strength, never shall I cease
Until I finish what I swore to do.
If Time does melt me up, as fire melts gold,
Yet shall I faithful be to wisdom, ever true.
If Time for me would not put saddle on his racer
Yet did I dare the ride, as long as life does last,
I'll not surrender, and shall yet succeed;
My heart is strong, courageous, too, indeed.
I've often wrestled hard with fate:
I have not conquered it, it has not mastered me.

The same decision breathes through another song:

My soul, thou'rt whirring, the thoughts
Are tottering restless about,
As clouds of smoke are curling aloft
When flames are starting up.
Perhaps thou art a wheel, circling the earth,
A sea in which the cares are heaving,
A maelstrom in the swirl of which
The earth's foundations are a-sinking?
The world thou didst not court, and it knows
How to richly requite thee with trouble.
Quit wisdom's path, and that same world
Will hand to thee its festive garments.

This is what makes me full of sorrow,
Who'll cure me of this pain so sharp?
I'm looking for a man of mind and spirit—
In vain! My chase has no result.
And if the world has but illusion,
I'll spit at its deceptive image,
I want it not if to my light its
Eye is dimmed and veiled and blind;
And yet, how I should love it,
If kind and friendly face it would show me.

Enough of wickedness has been accomplished.
Face right about, O world, and turn thy wheel;
Full long enough the wise and honest
Thou hast selected to do slaves' work.
'Tis long enough that noble cedars
Have been esteemed like useless brush;
Oh take away the wicked wights
Who, because hollow, are puffed up so much.

If by justice, thy award is made,
They should not harvest all the joys,
Nor choose the daughters of the sun
To propagate their folly.

Is it your quarrel, O thorny labyrinths,
That I descend into the depths
Of wisdom, dig her treasures?
Because you can not see, you ask
That I be blind to all her lustre,
And dissolve my covenant with her
Ordained by God's own power.
How could I leave thee, lovely mother,
Who kindly bendest to thy child?
How could I cast away the soul's treasures,
Tear from my head thy glorious diadem?
While her Eden's streams are running
Mighty, yet so clear and mild,
O sweetest pleasure, heart's refreshment
Which all along their shores I find!
Therefore, my soul, get up and rise,
At her sun, get your fire,
And swear it loud and firm:
I'll search until I find the Source.

Thus does Gabirol's spirit wrestle boldly titanic in many grand poems in which his true sentiment is expressed more deeply than in the many religious ones which do not deny his wrestling but still follow the customary views more closely. And a peculiar force is in those, too. A few out of the great plenty which are yet in use in many of our houses of worship may serve as proof.

At dawn and in the evening
I seek Thee, rock and lord,
To give my heart an opening
And speak a praying word.
Afraid I stand, and anxious;
I know Thine eye has caught
The most secret of my thought
Before the word can sound.
Withal, what is the force of thought
What does the word avail,
Howe'er it boldly soar aloft
Or try a pleading, soft?

Yet Thou art pleased with praise
And thanks in songs of men to Thee,
And so I'll sound it merrily
As long Thy breath's in me.

Another:

Before mine eyes, three things stand firmly founded
Of which each one Thy name has sounded:
I see Thee when the high *heavens* I regard
Which 'round the earth, proclaiming Thee, is wound.
The *earth* itself, my dwelling place, incites the mind,
That in its structure, the master it may find.
And my *soul* praises my God in glee,
When by introspection it finds itself of Thee.

Entering still deeper into Jewish life, and joining more closely to customary manner, his muse sounds in accords no less gracious and strong:

Judge of the world, take a pleasure
In our morning prayers' measure,
As of old, in the Temple's time,
When the priest yet did the pleading,
When he did the interceding
With the sacrificial odors rising.

Mercy and pity and grace is Thy name,
Merit of our own we can not claim,
Kindly remember our forefathers' deeds,
Accept it if their memory for us pleads
For their sake accept our supplication
As at the sacrificial odors rising.

Thou always lettest mercy prevail,
When we tremble in balancing scale.
Impress with Thy grace's bliss
The loving, fatherly kiss
On the forehead of all Thy children
As at the sacrificial odors rising.

Remember Zion, once so praised!
Let the mild light now be raised
O'er the minds of all mankind,
That Thy laws' truth they may find
As once from the Temple's court
With the sacrificial odors rising.

God alone can be your stay;
If you walk along His way
He turns the threatened wrath
Mildly into pardon's path,
Lets repentance be advising
As at the sacrificial odors rising.

No wonder when his word sounds also cutting and gloomy against the oppressors, against Christians (Edom) and Moslems (Ishmael):

The foe's triumphant. I am down, exhausted,
To wild and rough, untamed hordes a prey;
Plaint of my pain in words I dare not say;
A trembling lamb, a beggar by the way.
O God, when will relief come to Thy throng!
When will this end? O Lord, how long!

Babel oppressed me down to its very fall,
Then Persians, Greeks, and Edom's nations all,
Till, fugitive, I roam from land to land,
Ishmael, too, strikes me with heavy hand,
Four hundred sixty and one years* so strong—
When will this end? O Lord, how long!

The first redemption to Abram was revealed,
The second was to Jeremiah's word fulfilled,
The third was told in enigmatic writ
To Daniel, but its solution deeply hid,
No clue to questioner's mind, however strong—
When will this end? O Lord, how long?

After such serious poems, let us listen to a merry song. He had been invited to a banquet by a certain Moses; the wine provided was but a small quantity and soon drunk up. The guests had to be satisfied with water. With mock mourning and comical indignation, Gabirol complains of the misfortune and laughs at the miser who causes the wine (Hebrew *yayin*, the letters used as numbers equal to 70) to be crowded out by water (*mayim*, equal to 90):

Gone is the wine!
Oh torture of mine!
My eye overflows
With water.

* The year 461 of the Hegira: 1169 A. C.

The Seventy is full of the fire of youth
Banished is he by the Ninety-Monster uncouth.
    Now quit your singing,
    The glasses stop ringing,
Full of water, and water, and water.

From the bread has parted its flavor,
From the meat, too, has fled all savor;
    I am not even myself
    When cups come from shelf
Full of water, and water, and water.

By Moses were dried up the sea and its showers,
The Nile's flood changed. But this Moses of ours
    O Heavens! makes drip,
    O Heavens! makes sip
But water, and water, and water.

To a frog to turn me he'd like,
To croak like a frog by the dyke,
    He never tires quite
    To shriek and invite
Quaff water, and water, and water.

Turn hermit, if you live ever so long!
May drink ne'er refresh you, enjoy never song,
    And the children when near,
    May cry in your ear:
Bring water, and water, and water.

As Gabirol reveals as poet his desire to apprehend the first cause, so he attempts as philosopher such a mental flight with the full fervor of his soul and the energy of his will. The work which contains the results of his thoughts was composed in the Arabic language and is no longer extant in the original and exists only in translations. Its name is "The Source of Life." The Neoplatonists are undoubtedly his instructors. Like them, he uses the method, not to get up to the infinite and unfathomable by gradual rising from the comminuted actuality, but to sink into the all-sun with intuitive view, in order to recognize how all is illuminated by its rays, to seize the absolute in genial flight and to comprehend how it penetrates with creative necessity into constantly lowering circles. His doctrine is a doctrine of emanation, divine omnipotence pours out in its plenty and inexhaustibility, and thus gradually arise weaker mental formations which close together into constantly narrowing forms until it arrives at our sober world in which we must breathe, but from which we can lift ourselves up to the first cause, the all-spirit, the impregnating stream of all existence. Yet the divine creative energy is not blind necessity; it is the mighty Will which freely emanates from Divinity to form and sustain its creations through the times.

We can not follow that system further here. But it is recognized that Gabirol in the boldness of his thought reminds us of Spinoza to whom he has been frequently compared in recent times, even if he does not approach him in plastic quiet and consistency, while he towers above him in fervor and poetic talent. His theory of the will reminds us of Schopenhauer, who stands far below him in moral enthusiasm and depth of investigation. Like both, he went lonesome and alone through the world, recognized during his life and in later times as a great man but yet not fully estimated according to his high importance. After eight centuries, let us put the wreath of honor on the head of Gabirol. Like one descended from unapproachable heights, unrecognized, he ran his race in life's arena. Rubbish and gravel soon piled up around his writings. His philosophical work, translated into Latin, was much used by the scholiasts of the Middle Ages, called by a name that hardly makes Gabirol known; viz., Avizebron or Avencebrol, which is nothing else than Aben Gebrol. A later Hebrew translation, rather abbreviated, remained altogether unknown. After the middle of the thirteenth century, history is almost silent about the laborious work of his thoughts. Of his best poems, many have been lost, many were long covered up, only a few of his religious pieces have preserved the name Gabirol to recent times. And only now he has in a certain way been again discovered and properly estimated. We are far removed from him. A long interval of time, development broadly swollen in the meantime, separates us from him, in strange garb and in distant views he appears before us. Yet the high and deeply furrowed forehead of the thinker bids us reverence, the fervid eye of the talented poet flashes toward us, and thus we repeat after Charisi:

> A king he stands, sublime and grand, alone!

IX.

The Orient, Spain from 1070 to 1140.

The first half of the eleventh century in Spain reminds the observer of the time of maturing youth. To the able and aspiring youth a new mental world is opening; his enraptured eye rests upon it, he dives with pleasure into it, endeavors to enrich and deepen his knowledge in all directions. In that occupation he is so happy, and he is so taken up with it that he hardly takes notice of the world around him; he does not bother about the contradictions which stand in the actuality against his ideals; and pursuing these, he lets the other be and merrily enjoys what is offered to him. The man who has arrived at his conclusions and lives no longer within himself, takes offense at the actuality much more easily; the fight between that which he has formed within himself and strives for, and that which exists and which he can execute and complete, comes to him nearer and more oppressive. The time of that age was a period of youth and men dive into the great mental treasury which they elaborate farther. Culture grows up richer, it completely fills minds according to their different bents; each one cultivates his own branch, tries to make himself feel at home in it according to his condition and occupation and to complete his knowledge through the progress made elsewhere. Whatever was valid in actual life was left alone without taking offence at it. The contradictions between the results of thought and the existing ordinances remained yet covered and did not come forward with great distinctness so that they would have come into collision. Everybody was too busy with himself for entertaining any desire to start a fight between the external actuality and the pressure for transformation. Spain's development went on happily natural. It had no fixed ancient learning against which the new culture arose as an alien thing. The Jewish population had passed over out of plain conditions into the new culture, and that spread equally in all directions, philosophical, linguistical, Talmudical, each peaceably communicating with the others.

It was different in the empire of the Arabian East. There, an old Talmudic learning had become already fixed since the Babylonian time. There was the seat of the Gaonate, those Talmudical excellencies who were acknowledged as the highest religious authorities, who sought and found their importance in their Talmudic learning. When the new culture arose with Islam, the contradiction was soon felt, and the attempts at compromise and reconciliation were not sufficient, especially as the culture in the East was soon dimmed, and fell into decline. So we meet at that period with a man who at the last yet vigorously upheld the Gaonate, and imparted to it a rich glory like a fine sunset on its sky. It broke down soon after him. The Gaon at Pumbeditha, Hai Ben Sherira —his father too, had been Gaon and had acquired great fame as such—was justly considered a great Talmudic authority. He possessed rich, many-sided knowledge, but was not favorably inclined toward science and especially toward philosophy. In a letter of his to his influential contemporary in high position in Spain, whom we know already, prince Samuel Ha-Levi, who probably had announced to him his appointment as visier and head of the academy, and asked advice of the older authority, he writes impressively, warning against surrender to tempting science, and exhorts him to avoid the snares of logic which catch everything in the net of reason and rules of thought. He says science had been given entry for a time in Bagdad and permitted to influence the religious life; there too the assertion had been made that true knowledge of religion could only be attained by investigation and philosophical study. But it was soon shown that it only leads away from compliance with the commandments and ordinances and brings unbelief. Gaon Samuel (Ben Chofni, Hai's father-in-law in Sora) had cultivated science but had given it up after he found out that it led into error.

In fact, we learn of Samuel many bold sayings. For

instance, when Saadias—and Hai concurring with him—had said of the witch of Endor, that she could not have conjured Samuel up through her own power, but that God had made an arrangement by which Samuel appeared at the same time when the conjuration took place, Chofni rejects that conception as an improper one: "Nothing is to be accepted as true, that contradicts reason." The tale should rather be considered a vain pretence of the witch who fraudulently said that she saw Samuel, when there was nothing to see. Hai does not rise to such boldness.

The Talmudical writings contain legends of many kinds. They are products of the people's poetic imagination, folk-lore, brought forth by the people when on the child's plane, bearing its mark. One hardly knows whether they are a merry play of poetic fancy or arise with a claim of full belief; such twilight of opinion corresponds to the child's plane of culture. But when time has progressed, people become serious and want a decisive verdict upon them. Talmudical scholars who cultivate science, leave such legends aside or treat them as dreams, visions that appeared to one or the other teacher, or they give them symbolic interpretation. Hai would not accept such expedient, he sticks to the plain, natural conception and, even if he does not want to place the most decisive importance upon the matter and find the center of faith in them, he yet asks what objection there be to believing that the heroes of a later time were also glorified by divine apparitions and that extraordinary things had haphapened to them.—Thus in the East.

In North Africa we meet yet excellent scholars whose ideas were more for compromise, but who occupied a strict Talmudical stand and acquired important fame. Hai enjoyed great respect in Spain; he was honored and when he died (1038), he was deeply mourned and celebrated for his great poetic merits. And yet his tendency did not carry the day. Prince Samuel, to whom the above-mentioned letter was addressed, as practical statesman may have kept away from high-flying metaphysical speculations, but he was a man too highly educated and too much of a bel-esprit to run against the fruits of culture as they had matured in Spain. On the contrary, the general cultivation of learning increased continually and scientific labors expanded. Great Talmudists also appear in the succeeding generation. Five men are named to us, all bearing the name Isaac; four of them born in Spain; all of them, in addition to being excellent teachers of the Talmud, were well versed in the various sciences. One was an astronomer, another a poet, the third was a philosopher, and the fourth a linguist, and thus science and religious discipline went together, hand in hand. The fifth Isaac, a very famous Talmudist, Isaac Alfasi, was not born in Spain but came from North Africa and was head of the most important school at Lucena. We know him as important only in his field, the Talmudical literature. But with what clearness he treats that; what soft, cultured breath wafts through that dry work which puts the results of the Talmud together. Nowhere appears rude bluntness, there is no hard word against science; on the contrary, many a point is bent and many an edge is smoothed.

In all branches of knowledge men arise who promote investigation and define the results. They are again crowded out by men of the succeeding generation, so that we know their names but only few of their works; and thus it may suffice if I name only one; Moses Ben Samuel Gikatilia, who belongs to the second half of the eleventh century and stands very high as grammarian, as linguist of fine feeling and as explainer of the bible. By the few fragments which have come down to us of his works, we recognize the independent thinker and critic who acts in the explanation of Scripture with bold frankness, lays hold of the problems with clear view and presses them toward their solution.

Even with an uninterrupted, quiet development, the contrasts would gradually sharpen and the inner, undimmed joy could not last. But in the first half of the twelfth century, events were preparing that must effect a change. The power of Islam in Spain began to decline. The realm was divided among several small dynasties which lost in respect and importance. From North Africa more and more Berber tribes forced an entry, savage, refractory hordes, who soon acquired the ascendency over the effeminate Arabians of Spain. After having made their conquests, the intruders were yet slowly civilized, but the stability of state and of culture were threatened by them. The time was long past when the mighty arm of Abdorrahman III. united nearly the whole of Spain under his califate and held down every resistance of the original population. But now the old Romanic Christian population arose in opposition to the divided principalities which weakened themselves still more by mutual feuds. It was especially Castile where the Romanic or Christian element erected a bulwark. There the church of the Middle Ages first founded its power firmly, and from there the excursions constantly penetrated, conquering deeper into Spain.

The influences upon culture in general and upon Jewish culture in particular were of a wholly different kind from those proceeding from Islam. Islam is poor, has few religious principles, bases itself altogether on the belief in the unity and omnipotence of God and takes little account of all other aspects of God and man. It therefore offers few points of support for speculation, but on the same account it opposes fewer obstacles and barriers to a free development of reason and science. Culture within Islam perished through the brutality of the tribes that surged over it, not through inner contradiction which Islam itself raises against culture. It was different with the church of the Middle Ages. According to her origin she made it her task to unite Judaism and paganism within herself. Judaism offered the pure spirituality of God, His unity, His infinity and perfection, the unlimited in God which therefore can not be attained by any physical representation, to whom no image can correspond, for which even the word remains insufficient, the all-comprehending, unseizable, impalpable to which thought can not rise perfectly, and so much less, the senses. On the contrary, paganism elaborated its ideals to the senses. Its divinities were not perfect beings, they were only more perfect than men, they were seizable ideals, could be copied in individual appearances, art could approach them and present them to view. The church of the Middle Ages had the endeavor to unite those two contrasts within herself. The infinite, limitless, and spiritual on the one side, and yet on the other side again, the individual, corporeal, palpable, appearing in human shape, and representable to human senses. In the expression "Godman," those contrasts are forced together into a word which language attains by side-by-side position, without designating a clear thought by it. But the church strove to reconcile those two contrasts, or rather, to push and slide them into each other and thus to assert them as an actually existing unity. She fought against every tendency which placed one of the sides in the background and did not permit in that union either the divine in its ideal unity, or the human, to come forward sufficiently. Either was heresy. The two natures of equal power, the human and the divine in their union, in perfect mutual penetration, that was fixed as the only true faith.

That desire, to slide the corporeal and the spiritual, the sensible and the infinite supersensible into each other, resounds everywhere as supreme principle in the church. From that follows the other desire, that in certain corporeal apparitions, the fullness of the spirit should be recognized as perfectly indwelling. In the host, divinity itself was to be; from the relics or fragments of saints' bodies, spiritual mercies were to proceed. The individual, ecclesiastical actions did not pass as simple means serving for consecration and religious uplift; they became sacraments, including within themselves a fullness of divinity and mercy which pours out upon the performer. Such a religious tendency prescribes certain results to philosophy, it does not remain passive about the product of speculation, it dictates where the striving must arrive and what its goal must be. It commands—as it actually happened during the long period of the church's dominion over the minds—that the greatest efforts be made to comprehend and unify those contrasts. Truly astonishing resources of mind have been exhausted and wasted without the Middle Ages arriving at anything beyond formulas and skeleton scholastics. At a later period, the church itself fought against the consequences of that basic tendency. Protestantism put aside the most glaring parts without, however, surrendering the root out of which they had naturally sprouted, and thus the contrasts are now, as then, unreconciled in their existence. Whether a solution may yet be attained, can be left to the future. The church of the Middle Ages put the contrasts side by side without permitting them to be considered contrasts; they should rather be recognized as perfectly united and mutually penetrated.

Where the church dominated, that tendency was the mental air that was breathed by all, even those who did not profess Christianity. Its influence upon the development of Judaism within the Christian countries can not be misunderstood. Its full measure appears only later when the undisputed domination of the church asserted itself. The later Jewish mystic is a product of that influence; the cabala with its effort to prove how divinity limits itself to let the terrestrial proceed from it, how the terrestrial beings on their side affect the spiritual order of the universe by the practice of the several ceremonies, and how thus a mutual penetration and interweaving arises. But even at that time and especially in Castile, that basic tendency of the church could not fail to have a partial effect upon the conception of Judaism, especially upon such men as felt the want of a fervent heart and had a poetic temperament. While fully rooted in Judaism, they took a certain coloring from the church, because just for poetic temperaments such a tendency has great attraction. For as it put fetters on speculation and liberty of philosophical and clear thought, the heart and fancy love to pour out all their riches upon the singular, to reverse the individual and palpable as something higher, to embrace with all fervor and to spread the whole glory of the divine over it.

We meet a thinker of poetic geniality who remains an ornament of Judaism for all times and yet appears with the designated coloring of his views in Juda Ha-Levi, Arabian name Abul Hassan, born about 1080 in Castile, died about 1140 in Palestine. Juda is an amiable character and important man. Not satisfied with that speculation which feeds on philosophic generalities, he demands something more personally seizable upon which he can lean his warm heart and which he can take into his poetic breast. To recognize God, the proof which rises from full actuality into constantly attenuated abstraction, does not suffice to him; that is not sufficiently alive for him, is nothing individual which one may love, worship and revere. Of course he carries Him within, in his heart, in his longing, as he so often sublimely expresses it in his religious poems; yet more vivid He is recognized by him in history, especially in that of Israel. Here God appears, personally causing effects, shows Himself as the power which rules everywhere and leads to definite ends. In general the influence of God upon individual men appears with him in the foreground, for full life is only in the individual and personal. The revelation of God, he says, was first addressed to the first man, upon him the full, immediate influence of God was poured out, the fullness of the divine spirit entered into him. From him the inspired divine disposition goes over into his descendants by corporeal propagation. In some, that divine afflatus is veiled, sometimes by their own fault, sometimes by a chain of unfavorable circumstances, is dimmed and condensed in the descent more and more into gloomy materialism. But in others it appears through favorable conditions or through self-ennobling efforts with unlimited enlargement and becomes true divine illumination. Thus the divine spirit entered into the patriarchs, from them into Israel, especially into the prophets, and thus it is inherited on and on in Israel, even in its dispersed individuals. It is an inheritance, interwoven in body and soul, and indestructible.

As through the persons, so the divine spirit runs through the ordinances, even if they are not comprehended in their deeper meaning, yet carrying ennobling force and cementing the ties to divinity. While the ancient teachers say of many ordinances that they are to be observed as commandments issued by God and to be practiced in pure obedience, without entering into reasons for them, Juda's deeper sentiment was not satisfied with that, neither did he want to look for forced reasons which would deprive them more of consecrative character than add to their illumination. No—and here it is especially where the influence of the church becomes visible—no, he says, those ordinances are imbued with the divine spirit, they effect ennoblement and spirituality of themselves, the consecration placed in them by God pours out upon those who practice them. He gets into a tight squeeze with a few ordinances; with all his visionary, enthusiastic tinge and yet plain, unsophisticated sense he finds it difficult to attribute to them consecrating force. He does not mistake that many a Talmudical ordinance looks too much like a cunning evasion or an artificial shift. It is plain how he is troubled by that view because he returns to it several times, yet he finally shakes off his hesitation. If it is prescribed in the bible, he says for instance, that a greater distance should not be traveled on the Sabbath nor a burden carried outside of a narrow limit, how can the long road he squeezed together and outside territory be turned into one's own by an artificial arrangement, *erub*, in contradiction to the actual conditions, fancifully changing and getting around the prohibition? But the force of the system gets over such scruples also. Such arrangements, too, carry a consecration which we cannot recognize but is still hidden within them. If you want to inquire, he adds, and seek after reasons only according to your intelligence, then you shake all firm foundations; you must surrender yourself to the influence of the outpouring consecration and subject your reason to it.

What he asserts of the several practices holds good also of the places. The ancient teachers have especially accentuated the peculiar sanctity of Palestine. There was the Temple; there was the dwelling place of the independent realm; there only, the ordinances could be practiced in proper completeness. Yet there is but a very weak indication that perhaps Palestine or Jerusalem pours out sanctity or spreads greater consecration even at a time when the Temple was destroyed, the realm dissolved, and Israel no longer gathered there. The Babylonians asserted the contrary with all decision: It is sinful to emigrate from Babylonia to Palestine. With Juda we first meet the idea of the sanctity of Palestine even in its devastation. According to him, the grace of God has located there for all times, there the junction of the divine and the corporeal is lastingly established, there was the place of full revelation, those localities have received the stream of sanctity, it never dries up from them, they bear the indelible mark of holiness. Therefore, for him the grace of God was still pouring forth upon the ruins of Jerusalem, the gates of heaven still communicated with the broken gates of the holy land, from there a transfigured and transfiguring light was still going out over all.

Those views Juda Ha-Levi presented in a religious-philosophical work of which the introduction is characteristic enough. Beginning with the realm of the Chazars, the rulers of which professed Judaism, he lets that king appear before us, who first accepted Judaism. A devout, thinking man, as reverential toward God as benevolent toward his subjects, he lived in natural religion. In dreams there appears to him several times, an angel who speaks to him: "Thy disposition is pleasing to God, but not thy actions." Troubled by such exhortations, he sends for the priests and teachers of the different religions. Since Islam and Christianity point to Judaism as the mother religion, he turns to Judaism, and thus Juda develops in the dialogue between the king and the Jewish teacher, his own views, the basic thought of which we have given, with instructive fullness of thought and powerful fervor of sentiment. At the close, when the Jewish master thought to have accomplished his task, he announces his resolution to go to the holy land. "How," says the king, "what do you want there now? It is laid waste, the Temple stands no more, dangers of various kinds surround you, what good will staying there afford you? Can you not lead a devout life anywhere?" "Well," replies the teacher, "if we are prevented from going there, if our settling there is impossible, God will accept my sentiments and my actions in any other country; but if there is any possibility, heart and duty call me there. If the land is but a place of ruins, then I must journey over the rubbish; if I can not perform my devotions in the Temple, the ruins and remaining fragments are so consecrated that the heart finds noble nourishment and greater uplift in them." And the king lets him go.

The teacher is Juda Ha-Levi himself. He has not talked the matter over with a king of the Chazars, but weighed it seriously in his mind, and it pressed him on and on more irresistibly. His countrymen meet him with decided opposition, for the tendency of the Arabian Jews of that time was nothing like that of Juda. He is not understood, he is reminded with sober admonitions, he is almost a subject of mockery. But he can not do otherwise, his poetic longing must find satisfaction in the journey.

For Juda Ha-Levi was a poet, a poet of the noblest kind, of the most fervid depth of heart, of the most brilliant presentation. He appears perfectly ready in early youth, and when he is a mere boy, sends a poem to a famous man and poet; the latter designates the effusion with the following words:

"A writing like the morning's glow,
A song—a wreath of spirit's bloom,
Of sound so strong, tender and soft,
Of noble sense, deep and aloft.
Yet still a lad, my dear young son,
How comes it that you are so wise?
Such diving in the depths of knowledge,
Such rising to the heights of view?"

His poetic force is revealed in all his pieces as it pours out over the most various subjects, especially wherever his tender elegiac sentiment can come forward—in religious hymn and in longing for Palestine. A few samples may be enough as proof.

"God, I've plainly heard Thy call,
Thee I'll faithful serve in all,
Shall not question, shall not scan
Nor be so bold to grasp Thy plan.
Thou art my refuge, rock and shield,
Thou art the light that goes through all,
Each soul to Thee in praise does yield,
My own heart, too, breaks forth in song.

"The heavens in fear and trembling
Proclaim Thy honor and glory.
Thy messengers, angels assembling,
Bear witness to the old story.
How without tiring or slumber
Thou sustainest beings without number:
Angels on the ether's flow,
Creatures of the earth below.

"Who the hidden God can find?
Yet in His all-gracious mind
He to all His sons descends,
Shows Himself in holiness.
And the prophets do behold
Him, not as figure, not a face,
Yet as ruler, high, sublime,
Great in wisdom, full of grace.

"His working! Who can fully trace?
But, O man, do not delay
To render homage unto Him whose place
Is all the suns and worlds and space.
Unto Him give all the honor!
Without change or pretense
Reverence what He may dispense
And give thanks to the donor.

"Know thyself! and wonder
What you are and who's your founder.
Upon God's handiwork ponder,
It announces to you His grandeur.
Inquiring too much is but sinning,
Entertain no bold pretenses,
Impenetrable has been from beginning
What is hidden from our senses."

Juda was a physician of great practice and highly honored. He had an only daughter who bore two grandsons, Juda and Asarel. He was fond of and bound up in his house, his home and his family; and yet he tears himself away, leaves his home; he must go to Palestine, to Zion, which shines to him from afar and which he glorifies in song:

"For my God's dwelling I am forced to depart,
Where the anointed throned, there is my heart.
No longer I find joy, my loved ones to kiss,
My longing prevents me the garden to miss

Which I planted and worked as a pleasant pursuit.
Oh how I cared for its growth and its fruit.
Of Asarel and Juda I dare not even think,
Though they be of my family the most beautiful link,
Nor of Isaac whom like a son I did hold,
And at my sun he did to manhood unfold.
The place I forget where in prayer I stood,
Where in searching for God my soul found its food,
The joy of the sabbath that filled the whole house
The festival's rest which freshened us all;
All those I give up of my own free will
And trust to the sea for a voyage until
My eye will behold where God's glory was shown
And, with satisfied look, may claim it its own.
There I shall sit, cooled by that heavenly air,
And daily bathe in Jordan's flood so fair;
There shall I praise and sing and cheer.
Hasten, ye months, to bring that glorious time near."

He tears himself away. He goes by the way of Egypt. There too, friends besiege him with doubts: "You want to go to Palestine? Alas, the soil there is waste. Remain with us. In Egypt too, there was a revelation of God; it was the first place where the wonderful appearance of God brought help and redemption to Israel." But he cannot. They try to keep him with bonds of love, but he breaks away:

"How? May body's wants then set at naught
The heart's imperative word: You ought?
What is still left to me in life,
For what can I yet plan and strive,
Than to behold thee, noble soil,
Sacred by high-bred priests' and prophets' toil?
In pain I broke the family ties
And miss my Spanish ground and skies,
And cross the seas, traverse the plain,
Repel the friends who would retain,
Make company with savage throng,
Their moan and howl to me is song,
No lure to me is Egypt's sight,
Canaan attracts me with irresistible might.

"For that I'm blamed by their cold reason
Which simply thinks of present season.
I suffer still and dumb; I'll overcome; and—
What use to speak? Thou wouldst not understand.

To them appears the only thing of worth
Serving the great ones of this earth.
A bird in the hand of young boys
I was, with which they had fun and joys.
No day appeared to me fair,
Meat and drink fed but my care,
Exhausted, pressed down to the sod,
Serving but men, removed from God,
My heart burns like the desert sand—
I travel forth to holy land.

"There in the land of revelation,
I look for pardon and acceptation;
There my eyes behold Mount Sinai,
Abarim's hill with Moses' blessing,
There needed rest for body I shall find,
There is peace for weary spirit and mind,
There is the blessed promised land
Where seers received their high instruction,
There at the graves of all my saints,
There I shall weep, pour out my plaints,
Where they lived and worked and now rest,
There I shall be with the blessed.
Therefore hasten, sail fast, O my ship,
To where the law came from God's lip.

"Yet I fear for my youthful transgression
Which on Time's page has left its impression.
Mature age too, escaping so fast,
Has it all without errors passed?
I do not claim freedom from fault,
Not always I warded off sin's assault.
And yet, my heart, what will you offer
While my soul such pain does suffer?
If the heart carries a heavy load,
It still appeals to the pity of God
And gains strength by confession
And quiet by Mercy's intercession.
Recompense, reward or punish; I trust
Thy judgments are always just."

And he moves on. How long he remained there, whether his soul found the deep refreshment and satisfaction, whether it was sobered by the ruins, we know not. No message reaches us, yet legend knows how to decorate the end of Juda with proper dignity. It has invented a trait that is drawn from a deep understanding of his character. The tale runs, that when he entered Jerusalem, an Arab came galloping along and rode him down, and Juda's last breath was his Zion's song. His longing was satisfied, his task was done; arrived at the goal, the legend has him finding life's end, too. With poetic spirit, Juda anticipates the tendency of a later time; his contemporaries did not entertain it. Culture in Spain progresses further, problems and conflicts rise with greater distinctness and press for solution. Full of deep, mental seriousness, men attempt the task in a manner which towers high above the fine labors of the Spanish time thus far.

X.

Aben Esra and Maimonides.

Firmly and deeply rooted culture is not readily shaken even when it has to wrestle with great difficulties and is met by obstructions not known thus far. As if driven by an interior mental necessity of nature, it keeps working toward its height even under unfavorable circumstances. Only then when its task is accomplished and it has reached its goal, it may decline in weakness and quickly succumb to the storms which break over it. In Spain, the sad events which were to burst in over that land and especially over its Jewish population, were already casting their gloomy shadows before; the sky was already covered with dense clouds and yet the sheaves of the mind were ripening apace. The incursions of the Berbers from North Africa were increasing in threatening rapidity. Those tribes, rude and uncivilized, filled with wild fanaticism, founded a few disconnected kingdoms; and the sciences found no patrons in them. About the middle of the twelfth century, the Almohades arose, those fanatical bands who first satisfied their blind zeal in North Africa, in order to carry on similarly in Spain. They acted as if driven by the instinct of declining Islam, and to ward off the weakening which culture caused to it, they proceed with fire and sword against science, and in addition, persecute the other religions with rough violence. Christians and Jews were to be tolerated only when they ceased to be Christians and Jews by conversion to Islam. Both confessions could be adhered to only in secret. The more serious minds, the men of higher culture gradually sought to leave the country in order to live publicly elsewhere according to their convictions. Islam does not carry on the work of such persecution persistently; it does not inquisitorially invade houses and hearts and the effect does not slink destructive and enervating into the marrow of the mind, but anyway, that persecution is like a mildew that falls upon the growing crops.

At the end of the eleventh century those circumstances had not yet reached their full severity and the mental movement was not disturbed in the regularity of its progressive development. Even the influence of the Romanic-Christian element which grew stronger and spread more and more with the disruption of the Spanish-Arabian power, was in general little to be noticed, although individual soft hearts, like Juda Ha-Levi, were not entirely proof against its impressions. Castile was Christian, and yet Jewish culture within it was Arabian through and through. The Jewish inhabitants of that part of the country were always in closest connection with the Spanish-Arabian Jews, and were drawn by their mind and sentiment toward the place where they found higher mental development. A number of highly cultured men meet us about that time, men who excelled in the most various ways, yet without adding any new element or elaborating any old one with greater distinctness or clearness.

Only two men tower above the others in such manner and deserve our careful consideration. A younger contemporary and fellow-Castilian of Juda Ha-Levi, Abraham Ben Meir Aben Esra, born at Toledo in 1093, died in Rome in 1167. A man of extraordinary versatility, an acutely penetrating mind and a pliable cleverness. He possessed the Arabian culture and the Jewish learning of that time in all directions to perfection, and yet the place of his birth seems to have exercised a certain disadvantageous influence upon him because, as I think, although familiar with the Arabic language and perfectly at home in the Arabian literature, he had not become so fully master of the Arabic as to become an author in it. He lived among the Romanics, his mother tongue accordingly was not the Arabic, and the supposition lies close that he learned it but was not able to handle it for literary work. Else it would be surprising in the highest degree that we have no work of Aben Esra in Arabic written during the period when he lived in Spain; that is, while in his youth and vigorous manhood—the smaller ones said to be of that time are dubious—and that no work of his has appeared in Arabic. That circumstance weighed down the entire Middle Ages and in the same manner heavily handicapped the Jewish scholars of that time, namely, that they had no speech in which they conversed and thought and wrote, but had to translate their thoughts into a dead language, had to cast their feelings into standing forms, which detracts liveliness from the course of thinking, and freshness from the presentation. Only about 1140, when Aben Esra as a matured man had attained the age of forty-seven years, the first larger work of his appeared and, from thence, work rapidly succeeds work. Nearly everyone gives, in addition to the date, the place of composition; they are written outside of Spain. As it seems, he went by way of North Africa and Egypt into the Christian countries where we see him in Rome, Lucca, and Mantua; then into the Provence where he stays at Narbonne, Beziers, and Rhodez; then into Northern France where the scholars receive him with reverence as everywhere. At all those places as well as at those of his later residence, he elaborates works for patrons and friends, of which he rewrites a few repeatedly. From there he goes to England and does some literary work there during several years. Then he makes the return trip, probably along the same route, until he passes away from earth at Rome in his seventy-sixth year.

His life must be called a disrupted one. A man with the complete Spanish culture, living in the Arabian atmosphere, breathing its free mental air in full drafts—he is driven about in countries the tendencies of which he did not share, whose language was strange to him, communicating with men who occupied other points of view, everywhere at home, yet nowhere enjoying a home. He himself expresses his pain in many places about that restlessness:

> "Aged, in foreign land I wander without rest
> Like the birds that anxiously coo for the nest."

He longed for his native country and yet dared not enter it. The disturbances which had broken out there, the fury of the oppressors as he says, had driven him forth, and so he was wandering about and found nowhere a lasting home. He was honored everywhere, the scholars know how to estimate his importance; and yet he had to experience insults and carry on fights with the illiberality and narrowmindedness among the Jews in the Christian countries. He himself occasionally gives us an account of such happenings. Somewhere in Italy, he met with a Jewish scholar from the Byzantine Empire, who with the narrowmindedness of his home and imbued with the Talmudical spirit, looked down with contempt upon every scientific endeavor. That man corresponded more to the mental attitude of Italy than Aben Esra, and this one had to hear how the other abused all the important Spanish scholars, and yet was treated with all respect. He pours out his pain at that to a friend in a poem:

"My youthful hopes are under the ground,
My mouth and tongue in chains are bound
My mind is sore with serious wound,
And restless roving strain.

"O friend, here I am rated vile,
Around me are madness, folly and guile,
My mind is now in double exile
By scorn, with grief and pain.

"How lucky if I had but died,
While fortune yet with me did abide
Before this rabble began to deride
And treat me with grievous disdain.

"In Edom* is neither honor nor praise
For sages from Spain or one of their ways,
Where ignorance rules all of the days,
Contempt is their only gain.

"Yet if there comes in a cricket from Greece,
Of all dignity he is given a lease,
And in his mind he does increase
To a giant on uppermost plane.

"See the winks and the nods of the hypocrite,
What bows he makes, how he tries to fit,
How he presses their hands and does never omit
To press hands for money to gain.

* Edom means the Christian countries.

"And then he swells up, abuses the blessed
The great spirits now gone to their rest,
While the empty heads who feather his nest
With laughter are bursting in twain.

"O masters and men! ye that spread the light,
Our teachers and poets, heroes in the fight
'Gainst folly and wrong! Does this requite
The work and stress of your brain?

"And now he makes his voice resound
So loud, it must be heard all around;
He pretends the Talmud to expound,
And yet he is weak in that domain.

"Ask him who does so glibly converse,
Ask out of the bible but for one verse,
Known to a child from the mouth of his nurse,
'I do not know' is his refrain.

"To make of such a fool a god,
To tremble at his wink and nod!
Yet fill they him with meats and wash
Them down with best champagne.

"So feed him up lest he grow less,
Get him purple and linen for his dress,
Maids for his service also press,
Perhaps absolution may be your gain.

"Well, keep on with serving his weight,
Procession and pray at his gate!
We shall stay true to the word of God
And true in the spirit's domain."

Deep pain goes through Aben Esra during his restless wandering, and the pain is reflected in all his works. Pessimism and melancholy shine through everywhere. Just as he is at home in every land but without a home in it, so he is at home in every mental field and yet finds no rest for his soul in any. Aben Esra is grammarian, elucidator of Scripture, philosopher, astrologer, mathematician, poet, important in every branch, and yet he is wanting in the union which ties the whole together; he lacks the penetrating idea which brings peace into all. An unceasing digression dominates him, his mind hurries disquieted from one subject to another; we notice that he never finds full satisfaction in what he works and cultivates. I said that Aben Esra is an astrologer. That is a disease of an unsatisfactory time and dissatisfied minds. Times and men who feel uneasy in the present would like to lift the veil of futurity and look into the mysterious growth in order to get a glimpse of the fulfillment in the future of hopes the realization of which they despair of for the present, and thus to gain peace by that view. They would like to solve the riddle of the reason of the contradiction between their fate and the ruling of justice. They try to recognize in the stars a solution of the riddle of futurity and also the power which guides terrestrial conditions and to which all must submit without resistance.

Aben Esra is the first humorous Jewish author. Humor as literary manner is a beauty-patch of modern literature. The ancients did not know it, and it really only has its justification if it enters as a merry joke, as a graceful wrap for a harmless thought; or vice versa, if it arises from deep, bitter earnest, tacking itself to the mean, revealing it in its complete ridiculousness, pouring sharp lye over it, if it works decomposing in its vitals and tears it with a certain pleasure. But when it enters as a surprise into serious investigation, when it is wound as artistic drapery about the thought without clinging to it naturally, when it dashes in like a flash as something extraneous, then it is uncalled for and unjustifiable. It always seems to me of an author to whom humor has become his manner, as if he was not fully alive to the subject he treats of; a foreign subjective moment leaps into the center and tears him out of the objective consideration of the matter before him. His presentation is not the faithful picture of the thought produced by the object, but he calculates it for the future reader from whom he wants to gain a smile. He looks to him, enjoys his surprise, and listens for the admiration which the striking turn produces. Aben Esra was the first humorous Jewish author, and he may perhaps owe his greater favor to his spicy manner of presentation at a time when taste was declining. Yet we must acknowledge that with Aben Esra, humor is not artificially joined to the thought. It rather pours out from within and is the expression of his mental restlessness, the dissatisfied digression from his subject; he must break violently through the fetters that confine him, he must roll away the pressure that hinders the full free expression of his opinion, sometimes by fine irony, sometimes by a merry turn.

For Aben Esra is a man of depth and acuteness of mind, and even though he illuminates all fields through which he travels, with bright rays, yet he makes you guess much more than he reveals. He is especially great in explaining Scripture. There he could treat the most various branches in motley changes, join thoughts in sharp points without systematic arrangement, and use and disseminate, stimulated by the variety of the themes, a mass of scattered ideas. In that branch, Aben Esra feels himself particularly at home; here he works with the greatest pleasure and with the greatest success. Here too, he acts with a boldness such as had hardly been heard before him and has for a long time been totally silent since, but also again with that mocking caution which veils the bold expression or assumes the air of taking it back. Aben Esra is the Jewish exegetist who mostly uses biblical criticism and who gathers for us the accounts of the more ancient teachers who worked in like manner at the Scriptures. No difficulty escapes his eye, and he has the courage to confess the difficulty and call attention to it. For instance, if he finds that places the names of which owe their origin to later events are mentioned with those names in the older writings, in the Pentateuch, he says, "Here is a mystery, or," he adds at once, "this is here so designated by prophetic foreknowledge." As in this case, so in other matters that belong to a later time and yet are in earlier accounts, he points to a mystery which he reveals while he covers it. In one place he puts a number of such passages together, of which he asserts that they belong to the same category, but that a wise man keeps quiet about them. Of course, the mystery, which consists in the fact that such passages can only have been written at later times, was not hidden from intelligent teachers, and the judgment about that bold indication was very different according to the position of the judge. For instance, Nachmanides says about it, "Rabbi Abraham says there is a mystery; well, I shall be the traitor and make the mystery known." And then he abuses Aben Esra in severe, unseemly terms. On the other hand, a later writer of the middle of the fourteenth century, a great admirer of Aben Esra and yet fully convinced of his orthodoxy which he wanted to save against all attacks, says in naive sincerity, "Aben Esra says there is a mystery here;" i. e., these passages cannot have been written by Moses, they must have been added by later prophets. Does that matter? Whether written by Moses or by later prophets, they remain prophetic words.

Aben Esra is an expounder who enters deeply into the natural and plain sense of the text and therefore perceives that in accordance with such proceeding he is often obliged to differ from the interpretation which the Talmudists and the Rabbinists following in their footsteps give to them in order to find a foundation for regulations. He gives the natural exposition full, circumstantial, and clear, but adds: "We should explain thus, if it were not for tradition, but tradition is valid, and the insight of our teachers was deeper and clearer than ours; we have to stand by it." But, is it not enough if he cast the flashes of lightning into the dark night of the Italian, French and English sky of that time? Was he not forced to cautiously cover the points which, if inclined or intended to pierce more deeply into those regions, would certainly have been turned against him? It might also be explained psychologically, if his clear view were sometimes dimmed within that stiffened environment where thought found no receptive soil and proper words no echo, that he thus sometimes lost confidence in himself. With all such necessary imperfections, Aben Esra is one of the clearest minds, one of the most talented thinkers of the rich Spanish development. The sparks which he emits are not simply momentary crackling sparks of wit, but thought sparks that give steady light for all times. He possesses inextinguishable force, so that the most important minds gladly accepted his support and were instructed by him.

That which Aben Esra lacked, namely, complete tendency to reconciliation with his own mind and therefore a systematic rounding out, a younger contemporary possessed, and through that he became the maker of an epoch. Moses Ben Maimon, with the Arabian name Abu-Amran Musa Ben Abdallah, and generally known as Maimonides, was born at Cordova on March 30, 1135. His father Maimon, was a pupil of the highly esteemed Joseph Ben Migash, pupil and successor of the famous Isaac Alfasi at Lucena. Maimon was *Dayan* (judge) in his native city of Cordova, then one of the most flourishing cities of Spain.

He was an able Talmudist and at the same time—which was a matter of course with the men of his kind in Arabian Spain—a thoroughly educated man in science. His son Moses received his education from him and was initiated from his early youth into the various branches of science. He soon became as well versed in the Talmud as at home in the other scientific training. As Saadias, the pioneer of the Jewish-Arabian tendency, tried to acquire the entire field of knowledge, just as he, when Gaon, as representative of the prevailing Talmudical-Judaism and at the same time as philosopher, linguist, and expounder of Scripture, took the initiative for the new foundation of a united scientific and Jewish-religious development of thought, so we find in Maimonides the full possession and domination of the two separate mental fields. While among Spanish scholars in general, one tendency prevails, some being able Talmudists with only moderate general acquirements, and others, men of science with but general Talmudic knowledge, we find both equally united in Maimonides. He dominates the various branches, which formed the learning and the mental ornament of the Jewry of the times, with equal excellence. As a practising physician his studies, theoretically as well as practically, must have produced a much wider expansion of his mental sweep.

The life of Maimonides falls just into that period which threatened the most danger to Jewish-Arabianism in Spain. When he was yet a boy, the Almohades invaded Spain with the rallying cry, "Confess Islam or die!" Maimon and his family for a short time conformed with the enforced conversion, but soon made their escape into Northern Africa. There too, in Fez, the Almohades were masters, and the stay there could only serve as a point of passage until they might get, by way of the sea and Palestine, to Egypt where they could again live as Jews, under a high-minded ruler, Saladin. But even during the time of repression as well as later, when Moses again breathed in liberty, the activity of his mind was not interrupted. Already in Spain, he began to elaborate his first larger work, the commentary to the Mishnah, in which he revealed the intention which he pursued through his whole life, and the impulse which forced him from writing to writing. He first wanted to master the immense mass of discussions as they are put down in the Talmud and spread more and more so that a whole life is hardly long enough to go through it—that mass he wanted to master, form into a well-ordered digest, and clearly sum up the result in order to save future generations the labor of making their way through the dialectic thickets. His commentary to the Mishnah is short, intelligible, and clear. He attempts to present the results of the entire Talmudic-practical life, and thus to offer to the disciples of that science an abstract which, he believed, would be sufficient for them.

But he soon found that he had not yet exhaustively elaborated the whole material, and he undertook that grand, Titanic work, the code, which bears the name Mishne Tora, repetition of the law, or *Yad Chasakah* (the strong hand); the latter, because it is divided into fourteen books, which number corresponds to the numerical value in Hebrew to *Yad*, hand. In that codex he knows how to gather the different subjects and the immense material in intelligible, clear order, so that a general view over the whole is gained, and with the exclusion of the discussions, everything is taken up and put into proper connection. He says in the preface frankly and sincerely, for which he was afterwards blamed by many: "I have here composed a work so that if you have read the bible and made yourself familiar with this work, you can do without the Talmud, for you will have complete knowledge of the doctrines of Judaism as it has grown up Talmudically." That such an undertaking—because it presents the whole like a finished structure in which stone is fitted upon stone as an inseparable totality which, if a part is taken out, falls to pieces—that such an undertaking injures or prevents the historic conception, just because it makes everything appear as if moulded at one casting without giving a chance to suppose how the times have long labored at it and have only gradually put together very various matters; that it also cuts off the possibility of giving entry to the breath of coming times for bringing new life into the torpidity by solving, completing, or reforming action: such disadvantages Maimonides could not consider. For the idea of looking at things in their historic development was wanting in him as in the entire Middle Ages. To them, whatever existed, appeared as having always existed and as lasting forever.

Already in both of these works, Maimonides shows that —even if their contents were purely practical—theological and the whole matter of precept and dogma of Judaism as it was contained in the Talmud, was to be clearly put together —he yet had a higher motive in the background. For wherever a chance offers, he strays over into religio-philosophical subjects, attempts to illustrate, takes pains to show the deeper bases of Judaism and to present the thoughts which give it life and support it, as the most essential thing to be achieved. Thus he had used in his first work the treatise of the "Fathers" to elaborate a moral code along Aristotelian principles and prove their harmony with Judaism. Thus, among other things at the passage which speaks about the exclusion of individuals from a share in the world to come, he seizes the chance to prove the bases of Judaism and designate them as eternal and inviolable as he lays them down in thirteen articles of faith. In the same manner he shows in his larger work, not only in many separate passages how to point to the deeper proof in the moral-religious idea which dwells in the precepts, but he gives also, introducing in popular espression a philosophy of religion as essential basis of the dogma, philosophic-practical rules of life and other matter that can be joined to it. But all appears as developed out of the Talmud, artificially based on passages which he brings into connection and groups systematically. Yet small space only could be given to those philosophical discussions, and they had to come in as an occasional side issue. The work itself was chiefly to serve to open Talmudical knowledge to the student and at the same time, as he hoped, to conclude it. But his final goal was not attained by it.

Maimonides cultivated philosophy with a noble passion, metaphysics was a matter of heart to him; in the confirmation of the recognition of the pure spirituality of God and His perfection he saw the true task of his life and that was not completed in the works he had written thus far. As a man who had already attained the zenith of life and as a physician in extensive practice, he went at his chief work which, like his first one, the commentary to the Mishna, he wrote in Arabic—while for the code he had used a pleasing and easy Hebrew. That work to which he gave the Arabian title *Dhalalath Al-Hajirin*, Guide of the Perplexed—better known by the name in the Hebrew translation—*Moreh Nebuchim*—has the exclusive aim to reveal the deeper principles of Judaism, to prove its complete harmony with philosophy, to adjust the opposing difficulties and to consummate its reconciliation with science. Bible and Aristotle are for him two infallible sources. He draws from them, they are the two basic books of wisdom which teach the same thing in different expression. The pure spirituality of God, the perfection of His being which may not be limited by anything even in thought, is to him the deepest principle of Judaism; even those attributes which are spoken of God as good and glorifying ones appear to him a limitation. An attribute does not perfectly inhere to the being, it only approaches it in a certain sense. But nothing is added to God, all is indivisibly united in Him, while an attribute of qualities presupposes a certain division and asserts a composite unity, not one perfect within Himself as God must be thought. Accordingly, because nothing individual can be predicated of God, in order not to limit the conception thereby, we may only speak of negative qualities: that *no* fault is in Him, that *no* defect can be thought of Him, so that all limit is removed and only the complete separation of all concrete and the most high abstract may be considered as the only idea approaching Him.

But if there occur so many corporeal expressions about God in the bible, they are corporeally sounding designations for spiritual things. Maimonides is not satisfied to say by that, that they are paraphrases, pictures, naive ways of expression as they have to be used for the understanding at a low plane of culture. And when he supposes that, he is not satisfied with it, because then the word of the bible would not be significant enough, he rather asserts that there is in those corporeal expressions also a spiritual meaning. The words, he says, express different conceptions related to each other, of which one more accentuates the corporeal and the other the spiritual moment. For instance, when we read, "God stands," it means he is constant, unchangeable; if the bible says, "He descends," it means His effect upon worldly matters; if the throne of God is spoken of, that means the higher sphere which is more spiritual because it receives the nearest effects from God; and so on. He also thinks, in general, that the ancients purposely express themselves in a manner which has an external sense suitably for those of an immature understanding, while the intelligent comprehend the deeper signification of it; that the men of the bible and the Talmud had, like the ancient philosophers, sometimes purposely chosen expressions and forms of presentation which say also something for the ordinary human, without that he recognizes the complete truth, but which disclose the deeper wisdom for the thinker. Such declarations, he says, are golden apples in perforated silver shells. To him that stands afar, like to a near-sighted person, only the silver shells are visible, the more valuable contents within are hidden from him; he that approaches nearer, like one who has sharp eyesight, recognizes the golden apples through the silver shells. Therefore, the intelligent must look deeper into such corporeally sounding expressions of the ancients, to apprehend the truth hidden deeper in them.

Of course God in His spirituality can not be perceived by the senses; therefore revelation can not be an appearance which is seen with the eyes or heard with the ears. If former philosophizing theologians, avoiding such a conception, express themselves in effect that God causes an appearance of light to become visible and creates a voice that may be heard, Maimonides does not want to contradict such a solution straight out, it satisfies him if everything corporeal is kept away from God, but such a conception does not correspond to his real thought. For him, revelation is exclusively a purely spiritual act, it is the rising of the human spirit to the Divine Spirit, which act can of course take place in very few men in full measure, and is therefore the property only of select individuals in very different degrees. While one can rise only once in his life to that complete height as if a flash of lightning illuminates the horizon only for a short time and all sinks back into darkness, thus in another one the flash is repeated several times. In a third one it occurs still oftener and with greater clearness and completeness, and in another one, as in Moses, it lasts through life. This spiritual height of man is to him revelation, because through it man comes into closer touch with the spirit of God.

In general, according to his conception—which dominates the entire Arabian philosophy and is by it considered as Aristotelian, while it is really a neoplatonic modification—the whole universe is inspirited by degrees through the overflowing of the Divine Spirit. There are various heavenly spheres which are inhabited by heavenly spirits; the stars and the spheres are for him, as for all philosophers of his age, living beings of a higher kind. Thus the Divine Spirit next influences the highest spheres, from them it descends and permeates the lowest earth sphere; the inspiration of which is designated as the effective reason, we are tempted to say, as the spirit of the earth which illuminates and guides all terrestrial beings and things. The man who endeavors to raise himself to that all-spirit of the earth, who is able by his deep thinking and by his pure morality, by overcoming sensuality, by liberation from limitations and prejudices, to purify and spiritualize himself, enters into closer connection with the spirits, he continually rises higher on the scale of the spheres; the prophets attained to the highest point. The concept of divine providence also signifies to him nothing else than the junction of the Divine Spirit with the human spirit, so, that the enlightened and higher standing one stands during his whole life in closer connection with God and receives stronger effusions of His omnipotence.

In such sense the reward of men is also to be apprehended. The man who has arrived at a higher development of his mind, who has purified his spirit, who has steeled his moral force, retains such lasting gain firmly and approaches God and the eternal blessed spirits. In his system there is of course no room for a bodily resurrection, a reviving of the body of the dead. For him the future world is a purely spiritual life, and in his first work already, in the commentary of the Mishna, he reveals that view by a beautiful and significant comparison. He says, he that wants to instruct men and to urge them towards the good, must use different ways of proceeding according to the stage in which they are, just as it has to be done with children with whom advance is made gradually. If it is desired to spur the young, unintelligent child to diligence in study, sweetmeats are promised to him as reward; when he grows older, such a reward produces no longer any effect with him; other things are promised which have greater influence. With one of a larger growth, ambition is aroused; he is told, My son, if you are diligent, you will be called a master in Israel, you will occupy a high position. All those matters are without him, by which he may be allured. But when he has attained mature age, then he can finally be led to a recognition of the importance attained by the development of the spirit within him, of the value with which the endeavor for the culture of his soul endows him. In similar manner the representation of rewards and punishments in the Scriptures is to be apprehended as means of education. The true reward is and remains the eternal life of the mind and spirit; as to the resurrection of the dead, we have already developed it—and nothing more. And yet he puts it up as one of his thirteen articles of faith. For Maimonides pays due regard to public opinion, "give honor to general acceptance." He does not break the thin thread which joins him to the community, he does not destroy the bridge which keeps him in communication with the mass. He, too, uses, as he presumes it of the ancients, here and there a form of presentation which assumes a popular wrap but reveals his views perfectly to the truly intelligent. Gradually it may have happened to him as to many other thinkers who chose the same proceeding that the reader can not judge with full decision what is form of presentation and what is true inner intention. And so it gradually becomes unclear in the mind of the thinker himself, he sometimes grasps at the form and designation chosen by him, in order to hold it fast as essential and of deeper values.

Even about the view of Maimonides of the creation of the world, we are therefore, not quite clear. He acknowledges that philosophy asserts that creation proceeded out of existing matter and that the Divine Spirit only shaped that matter. Thus says his highly revered Aristotle; yet, he thinks, this is the only point in which he must disagree with him. The natural meaning of Scripture would by no means force him to that, for they may be interpreted in many ways, "the gates of explanation are not closed;" but on the other side, the proofs of original matter are not all-convincing, and the general acceptance in Judaism of creation out of nothing is preponderating, and thus he joins that general religious view, especially because, if it should be set aside, the possibility of miracle would disappear. If everything has not come out of God, if matter has its own independence, the miraculous influencing of the course of things cannot be explained. He recurs also upon miracle at the resurrection of the dead which he will not admit to have contradicted. The passages in the bible which are referred to for that dogma, he thinks, all permit of different explanation, only one passage in Daniel uses a more definite expression; but the general acceptation is so unanimous that we must follow it. It is a miracle, can only take place in miraculous manner, and we must accept it as such.

But what is his opinion of miracle itself? Here, too, we meet that double presentation which retains a certain twilight. Already in his earlier works, he pronounces: The ancient teachers say, the world goes its regular course; whatever arises as miraculous is put into the movement of the world as condition together with its creation, so that it must appear at the given point of time; the miracles are therefore not a sudden event, not a breaking through the eternal law, but they are part of the law put into matter from the very beginning. But with that, what appears as miraculous ceases to be a miracle. The Israelites, he says in his second work, did not believe in Moses on account of the miracles he performed, for we meet miracles performed by wizards; but they believed him because they themselves had seen and heard, they had a revelation themselves. Thus the miraculous is substituted for the miracle without denying it straightout. Its force as proof is set aside, and an appeal to it is to be adjudged as nothing but popular presentation.

But even in that he attempts to effect many diminutions of the miracles. Individual revivals of the dead, as they are related of Elijah, he explains as cures only in cases of trance, or severe sickness which brought the patient near death but did not produce actual death. Many other miracles he considers dream-visions, seen in a trance, not actual events; others he weakens, if he can not do away with them altogether. The first men lived many centuries, then suddenly the high age ceases and the duration of life corresponds to ours. Such an extreme age is plainly an exception to the laws of nature. With individuals of whom it is expressly mentioned in Scripture, as in the case of Adam, Seth, and others, it must certainly be admitted; but the other contemporaries, "the sons and daughters" begotten by those patriarchs, whose ages are not plainly given, attained the ordinary age only. Later opponents think that a very insufficient solution; for if there be one exception to the law, there might be others.

The resurrection at some future period is a miracle, he pronounces several times; but let us not be too extravagant in the provisions of that miracle. The dead rise, but they will then not live forever, they rise and die again, after having enjoyed a long and happy life. The true goal remains the eternal life, the immortality of the soul. A younger contemporary replies to that, not indelicately:

> " 'Pon resurrection follows second death?
> What good to me this second loss of breath?
> Out of the grave I rather would not rise,
> Than have death to suffer twice."

With such discussions Maimonides transgresses beyond the proper scientific-philosophical field, and he does not hesitate to penetrate still farther into the conceptions and the arrangements of every-day life; he wants to explain also the practical religious ordinances and place them in their proper position. To take them simply as precepts to which we have to submit without further ado as having proceeded from the highest lawgiver, that would not agree with his general view. They must be effluences of the highest wisdom, means which guide us toward a higher conception of life; if we do not comprehend them, they have no value. Accordingly, he attempts to prove deeper reasons for a part of the precepts, and of others he thinks that they were measures of protection against former erroneous conceptions and idolatrous customs. The sacrificial service, for instance, has no value for him, but the Israelites were to be weaned away from the sacrifices which they brought to idols, and since a complete abolition could hardly have been effected, they were to consecrate them to the eternal God, by which they were led away from the most injurious error. With many other precepts he believes to have historically found the superstitious ideas of ancient time to which they should make opposition. Of course, here the highly uncritical manner which in his time dominated the entire consideration of history, crops out. Maimonides with all his contemporaries, seriously accepted the intentional and legendary forgeries which were handed around of an aboriginal nation of Sabians. Biblical and pagan data, thrown together promiscuously, fitted that alleged aboriginal nation out wonderfully, and Maimonides uses them to explain by them the precepts of Scripture and partly those of the Talmud, and thus prove their justification. Evidently this part of the proof of the pract'cal-Jewish precepts is the weakest of his work and system. Such proof may at the most induce the admission that they may be considered admissible and not contradictory to reason, without furnishing any evidence for recognizing in them an essential religious motive or establishing their necessity and inviolability or possessing intrinsic force of moral and spiritual elevation. With all that, it must be admitted that the existing precepts of practice are considered as forever obligatory by Maimonides himself, in spite of his poor proof.

For Maimonides occupies the point of view of the Middle Ages, out of which no man of that time could escape. The Middle Ages gave to the individual no complete justification, no independent freedom; the individual was a member of a corporation, not only of the state and the nation, but rather of the narrow circle within which he moved. That circle has its fixed manners and usages, its rights and liberties, its privileges, its charter, but also its perfectly defined formation within which he has to keep himself. The guild, like the feudal system, the city, like every close corporation, in which the population of the Middle Ages were divided,—all had their definite precepts and customs; whoever did not hold to them was suspended in air. The Jew had to hold to that which designated him as Jew and made him known as such, which assigned him his definite position as Jew in the articulation of the whole. Wanting to free oneself from it was to remove the ground from under one's feet. Maimonides feels that condition quite correctly when he considers the precepts as ordered for the preservation of the world, as part of the proper social conformation and strengthening of the social tie. The Middle Ages can not get out of that circle; even if his mental culture rose to the greatest height, the line of limitation, within which the individual and the circle to which he belonged, remained fixed and impassable. Thus Maimonides was necessarily more interested in a purely philosophical conception than in a transformation of life. If that generally offered barriers which the Middle Ages could not break through, we must also not forget that Islam had become fanatical in the time of Maimonides and did not at all favor free, independent action of the individual. Averrhoes (Ibn Roshd) was a contemporary, a little older than Maimonides, an Aristotelian philosopher who represents the height of that tendency in Spanish Islam, a philosopher who enjoyed great esteem through the entire Middle Ages. Averrhoes, too, had to bend and submit to the most customary conceptions and practices. Yet a few unguarded, incautious, and very innocent but for the time bold expressions brought him under suspicion and exposed him to great persecution.

Thus Maimonides actually attained the greatest height which it was possible to attain in Judaism at that time. He was a man of the holiest and purest zeal for deeper knowledge of Judaism and for general, scientific, thoroughgoing culture, a man who certainly paid regard to public opinion and gave honor to what had been accepted, without, however, permitting his fervor for truth and the spreading of truth to be dimmed. He does not misjudge the doubts which oppose the publication of his religio-philosophical work, he himself calls attention to the considerations and the form of presentation which he thought necessary, and yet he knows that he could not avoid offense. "In short," he says, "I am so constituted. If a thought presses me, and I can present it only in a manner that satisfies and aids one thinker among ten thousand men, while it perhaps appears insufferable to the great mass, I boldly and openly pronounce the word which illuminates the intelligent one, even if the blame of the ignorant crowd is cast upon me." Maimonides was a man of thought, but at the same time, of the purest and most serious intent. If pure knowledge, theoretical culture, was the highest to him, that was yet in closest connection with pure moral action and ennobling of character as the indispensable condition for mental elevation. Without presumption, he is always busy with self-examination. Modesty and benevolence mildly shine through every one of his words, and in this way even his Talmudic-legal works—a few dogmatic-metaphysical severities excepted—are full of a gratifying moral warmth. For that he stood highly honored as a man of mind and noble deed in his own time and in all later periods.

We have now arrived at the summit of the Spanish development. It could not go higher. Even if conditions had remained favorable, weakening would have followed; unfavorable conditions hastened the fall. Yet before we close with the highest development of Jewish-Spanish Arabianism, let it pass before us in short review. Let us imagine as present, the three brilliant centuries as they passed before our eyes. What magnificent results that period offers to us! Science is not only nurtured, it is enriched in every relation. Knowledge of the Hebrew language rises into science and attains a degree which has not been passed until the last century. Interpretation and explanation of the Scripture enter deep into its meaning and stimulate the greatest problems. Philosophy becomes common property, and though it is not creative, it is yet ennobling and enlightening. The Jews did not walk alongside, they stand in the front ranks of the mental movement. Gabirol is one of the few who arise as genuine masters of philosophy in Spain, Maimonides is the contemporary of Averrhoes, who are not mutually dependent, but only at later age the labors of either become known to the other. Both are the rulers on the throne of philosophy through the entire Middle Ages. The Jews remain the lasting intermediaries in all sciences, for the Arabian writings would have perished completely and remained without influence for later times if they had not been saved for us in Hebrew translations, because they would have remained unknown in Arabic and many of the originals were completely lost. We owe it only to the zeal of the Jews that they exist yet to-day as monuments of a time of fine culture. Islam rendered great service to Judaism by leaving to it room; it did not go in advance of it in everything and could not offer everything to it, but it gave it room for the development of its powers. And thus we look back upon that illustrious time as a brilliant period of Judaism. We shall honor that Spanish-Arabian development of Judaism. It produced men who have remained bright stars at all times. On Aben Esra, Spinoza grew up. Maimonides was the teacher of the whole Middle Ages, and every enlightened mind that arose later, drew eagerly from him, found stimulation in him, and gladly acknowledged himself his pupil.

XI.

In Germany and France.

From wide, high-vaulted halls, permitting the freest movement of the mind, I now lead you into low, narrow chambers, affording very limited distance to the view. The position which the Church of the Middle Ages occupied toward culture and the use of reason in general, was a quite different one from that which Islam held. Islam left reason wide, free room, did not prescribe the results of its investigation and made no demands contradictory to its natural impulses and tendency. Its deepest principle, the unity and omnipotence of God, carried no opposition against the demand of reasonable thought, and consequently in its best days it always showed itself favorable to the cultivation of science and philosophy. It was different with the Church of the Middle Ages. From the beginning, that Church had attempted to unite opposite principles within itself and to make such union the basis upon which it sought to erect the entire superstructure of faith. Having thus planted within its own vitals an irritating contradiction, the irritation became more acute with the awakening of study so that every attempt to heal the wound, caused it to gape more widely. It had put up, before reason, certain results which were to be esteemed as inviolable and unassailable and which yet could not be comprehended by it, and were in fact in complete opposition to reason. Thus in the development of the Church, the repugnance toward the use of reason and all science had to be nourished more and more. In that mental atmosphere as it was wafted out from the Church, mental health within Judaism could not prosper as we have seen it appear so finely in the realms of Islam. The flower of true culture, deeper entrance into the meaning of Scripture and into the principles of Judaism as well as progress in science could not be maintained as among the Spanish Jews.

The position of the Church toward Judaism and Jews was also a wholly different one from that of Islam. This permitted Judaism to walk by its side, and did not think it necessary to undertake a fight against it. Relying upon its power, it looked proudly down upon it; its superior domination was sufficient warrant for its truth. It formed no contrast to Judaism. The unity and omnipotence of God, upon which it based its whole system of faith, its pure spirituality, so that divinity might not be represented in image or picture, the moslem heard accentuated with equal decision by Judaism and he felt in that a kindred spirit. On the whole, there was a certain trait of kinship between Islam and Judaism; both carried the unmistakable imprint of their Oriental origin, even the languages being closely related. Thus they went side by side, even if not in perfect harmony, yet not repelled by each other, but on the contrary tied together by similar traits. Even in the customs and precepts of practical life, there was a certain agreement. For Islam has taken over from Judaism many legalities which he observed as seriously as Judaism and its adherents. The moslem practised circumcision, the use of pork was prohibited to him, and in Islam many other things are found which it has borrowed from Judaism and has in common with it. They could remain quietly side by side without troubling about each other, so much the more as each had its own source and basis which the other left untouched. The moslem had his koran, which he esteemed as the only infallible authority. He was perfectly satisfied with it, without going back to its source, the Hebrew bible. He ignored that, and since it remained strange to him and he did not understand it, he left its treatment to the Jews. These, on their side, were wholly taken up with the bible, either knew very little of the koran or paid no attention at all to it. Thus, each had its own particular ground.

The position of the Church toward Judaism and the Jews was quite different. The contrast between them both could not be covered up; it came always clearly forward. To the powerful Church, it was a thorn in the flesh, that Judaism kept up at all; its very existence appeared unjustifiable to it; like a mockery, every Jew was a walking protest against its truth. If the Jew emphatically asserted the indivisible unity of God, it was a wicked attack upon the trinity; his abstention from every corporeal presentation of God appeared a denial of the human incarnation of God. The belief that by proper acting, even after having sinned, he might by repentance regain God's favor and accordingly could obtain forgiveness by his own force, was negation of original sin and necessity of redemption. His hope of a better time, on the coming of the Messianic Kingdom, was a blasphemous assertion that the redeemer had not yet appeared. Thus the entire contents and the whole appearance of Judaism, even if it kept perfectly still, was an eloquent contradiction of Christianity. At the same time, they stood on the same original ground, and the Church could not tolerate the idea that Judaism should claim that ground as its own. They both stood on the bible. The Church asserted it was its property. Its doctrine was contained in it and whoever deviated from that was a heretic, an enemy of the Church, and a perverter of Scripture. And since Judaism did so with that certainty which the exact knowledge of the contents of the bible and the superiority which the familiarity with the language of the original gave it, the hatred was inextinguishable and had to be so, according to the manner of that time. The Israel of which the bible speaks, the Church asserted, was the Church itself, although its confessors were not bodily descended from Israel, yet all promises were given to it. If the Jews asserted the contrary, it was an invasion of the sacred rights of the Church, a wicked attempt to cut the nerve of the Church. The interpretation of the bible was, accordingly, a field of constantly waging battle on which they moved. What did Islam care how any verse in the bible was explained? The Church was greatly interested: everywhere, indications of Jesus should be found, everywhere the doctrines of the Church should be expressed or typically indicated.

In this way the position of Judaism and the Jews within the territory of the Church was necessarily a far more unfavorable one than within the realms of Islam. Of course, the three centuries which we have seen passing before us as the time of fine, rich culture of Jewish-Arabian-Spanish civilization, namely from the beginning of the tenth to the end of the twelfth century, those three centuries form the advance period of the real degeneracy of the Middle Ages. In that time the medieval stagnation within the Church itself, as well as among the Jews, had not reached its full perversity. At that time there was yet a certain freshness of nature in the nations that then were yet novices in Christianity. The nations of Western Europe had then been converted to Christianity, but were still natural, still possessing plain, fresh, original sentiment, not yet artificial in thinking and feeling, not yet scholastically entangled. Of sound, even if uncultured sense, the population was not yet filled with hatred of the Jews as it was in later centuries of the Middle Ages. It is true, persecutions, fanatical ebullitions, of course through artificial spurring, took place in those centuries, as the crusades belong to them too. But that was more a wild outburst of momentary passion, a running over of brute force, not the uninterrupted refinement of petty cruelty which pricked with needle points into the healthy and then into the sore flesh and could never cease to spitefully practice its petty malicious tortures. That entire time shows yet a sound energy, the leading persons in the state as well as in the Church show aptitude, freshness, and a forceful endeavor which was stimulating, even if science in the true and full sense of the word, could not prosper within that circle.

The Jews had come in early times already into Western Europe. On the banks of the Rhine, in the Vosges mountains, in Germany, in France, we meet them in early centuries, we find them at the courts, as members of embassies, as physicians. Their position in general was, on the whole, that of a well-liked, often influential class. The suspicious tension between them and the people did not yet exist. Of course, we hear nothing of a special culture among them, and just as little of Talmudic learning. They lived in a certain state of nature like the people in whose midst they abode; enough that they were firm and constant in their faith. Zealous princes of the Church made violent opposition to them, like Agobard of Lyon in the ninth century, but his voice dies away and has no effect on the position of the Jews. An emperor Charles is said to have brought along a learned Jewish family from Lucca in Italy, to Germany, and some wanted to trace from them the Talmudic learning which later spread in those countries. But such fugitive notice is not confirmed by the historic course, at least, as to any influence upon learning.

There were very old, important congregations, but before the tenth century we learn even within them, nothing of any particular mental movement. The congregations at Speyer, Worms and Mainz are especially named to us as old, firmly organized communities, and they soon come into the foreground by a rich number of learned men in their midst. But even in them there are no traces of learning before the period which we are now considering. With the tenth century, all at once Talmudic learning meets us quite independently and fertile. Where did it come from? Everything points to the fact that Talmudic learning came directly from the Gaons in Babylonia to Germany and France. If the distance seems to you too great under the difficulties of communication at that time, such really wonderful action is repeated through the entire Middle Ages that, in spite of the great impediments opposed to communication, a lively intercourse is going on between the Jews of the most distant countries, and that an exchange of learned letters is carried on from Occident to Orient, from Spain to Bohemia, from France to Bagdad. This shows us how a serious mental striving knows how to overcome all barriers of space. Enough! In France at first a man appears who is named as propagator of Talmudic learning, but of whom we know nothing more than that he had a great pupil whom we shall now consider. Rabbi Leontin is named to us as teacher of Gershom Ben Jehuda. The name given to the latter, "Light of the Exile," announces sufficiently the regard he enjoyed and the mighty influence he exerted.

Gershom, who flourished at the end of the tenth and the

beginning of the eleventh century and who, it seems, taught principally in Mainz, was a comprehensive Talmudic scholar. The whole, widely branching field lay perfectly open before him. He cultivated it, made various commentaries on Talmudic tracts, was occupied in like manner with the bible down in its detail, and we learn to know in him, even though not much of his writing remains, the sober, clear, intelligent mind, who does not rise boldly, does not dive speculatively nor lose himself in fantastic dreaming, does not bring strange presumptions to his investigations, goes objectively at what is before him and apprehends that with simple, sound sense, keeping close to the thought and expression. We recognize also by him, how in healthy times, even without higher culture, the general custom of the country and its pecularity exercise an important influence upon religious views. Gershom was a scholar with European sentiment, with German views, and formulates them in important decisions when they deviate from the Oriental view.

Judaism, according to its deepest base, knows well how to recognize the dignity of woman. It, therefore, according to its character, demands marriage of one man to one wife. It does not favor polygamy, even if it does not prohibit it straightout. The entire history bears witness to that—the history of the bible and of the Talmud—so that all examples of a different kind are to be considered exceptions, tolerated only, while the sacred custom demands monogamy, without being fixed as law. Even under Islam, which in that point allows the Oriental custom in full extent, Judaism held fast to its basic character, and we meet among the Jewish-Spanish poets, poetical products which bear testimony to the sincerity between husband and wife, bearing a wholly different character from the Arabic erotic poetry. A peculiar Jewish trait, for instance, is an entire class of poetry which, quite strange to the Arabians, is made only by Jews, as we have some excellent ones by Juda Ha-Levi, namely, wedding songs, which express the sacredness of marriage and the cordiality of the relation between husband and wife full of deep sentiment. Thus the fixed custom, which is mightier than law, has sanctified that relation. If the custom was not shaped into law so that exceptions, even though occurring rarely and with general disapproval, could not be proscribed, it was because the conditions did not force toward it and the authorities did not think themselves justified in fixing a law for which there was no support in the letter of the Scripture. It was different in Western Europe. There also, outside of Judaism, monogamy was the general custom; a deviation from it, even if it happened only seldom, must violate the popular sentiment. Accordingly, Gershom, in connection with learned contemporaries, met in a synod, to sanction the custom as law from now on, and polygamy was put under the ban. Thus we owe to this convention of rabbis the legal fixing of a principle which has root in Judaism and grew out of it naturally, but which yet until then had not found legal authority and recognition. We owe it to the freshness of those men who understood the needs of their country and had no hesitation in giving them expression. A later, narrow-minded orthodoxy would have found imitation of foreign custom in such action, and would have wrapped itself into sickly fear, abusing the name of piety, to throw blame upon the preceding ages by such an innovation, if something was put under the ban, that had been tolerated before. Of such narrowmindedness or refined pietism, Gershom had no idea. A like narrow liberalism would in that well-timed regulation have feared the hierarchical interference by a synod of rabbis. That healthy, naive time did not know such weakly fears.

In close connection with that view are yet other decisions of Gershom. One of them relates to divorce. According to the Oriental view, which by the way is shared by all Antiquity, divorce is entirely in the power of the husband. Already the prophet Malachi designates the putting away of the wife as an action hated by God, and Judaism as it was shaped about the beginning of the second Temple under the rule of the Sadducees and the old custom, made divorce more difficult; it was to be permitted only in case of adultery committed by the wife. By that, the power of the husband was limited, but the remedy ending marital discord was also withdrawn.

Phariseeism in its more consistent development, as represented by Hillel and Akiba, made divorce more easy and again put it completely at the pleasure of the husband. But even then the living impulse of Judaism was better and mightier than the law. Divorces did not increase in number and improperly as some had expected. If in general, marriages were cordial and peaceable, many difficulties in married life were patiently borne, too; and the teachers give us fine examples how by mildness and quiet resignation, even the fate of being tied to a quarrelsome wife may be borne. It is an old saying: "Even the altar sheds tears at him that puts his wife away." Yet, according to law, the matter was always only in the hands of the husband. The wife was provided for according to his financial condition; the right was even granted her, of which the bible contains nothing, to demand divorce under certain circumstances and to obtain it by judicial proceeding. But anyhow there remained to the husband the unlimited power to put away his wife, and the inclination to make use of such legal right even for small cause would now—Gershom felt that very well—gain fresh strength if he lost the possibility of marrying a second wife besides the one looked upon with disfavor. Well considering the wife's position in his country as deviating from that in the Orient, Gershom ordained that divorce cannot take place without the consent of the wife. A very important transformation of the legal ordinances.

Yet, a similar case expresses his recognition of the greater independence of the wife. According to biblical order, at the death of a childless man, his wife shall be married by the brother, the leviratical marriage shall take place. Only if the brother-in-law refuses the marriage, the liberation of the wife from her obligation to him is effected by a judicial proceeding according to a fixed form. Accordingly, the leviratical marriage was the rule; its refusal by the brother-in-law was considered a blamable action and a disgracing of the widow, and in its stead the so-called Chalizah took place. In Talmudical times already, that relation between leviratical marriage and its neglect with subsequent Chalizah was no longer understood in that way. Many voices asserted Chalizah to be preferable to marriage of the brother's widow; that this should be omitted and the Chalizah be performed under all circumstances. Yet the matter was not settled and under Islam the opinion again prevailed which had the letter of the bible and the most important Talmudical teachers on its side, that the leviratical marriage held the first place, while Chalizah was but a makeshift. Here, too, Gershom acted in conjunction with his colleagues, in correspondence with the character of his time and country and demanded that Chalizah should take place under all circumstances and the leviratical marriage should cease. Those are expressions of a mind, bearing witness to his complete independence and a thorough entrance into his time and its view. By those settlements, Gershom towers far above that rigid legalism which covers itself with the brazen shield of the inviolable law against many a remainder of antiquated views, which deafens its ear against the lamentations of the broken heart of a woman and mocks its desiccation without sympathy with such suffering caused by the rigors of an antiquated law as weak sentimentality.

On the whole, Gershom's tendency was a mild, natural, healthy one. Gershom had to make a sad experience. His son abandoned Judaism and joined the Church. When the young man died, Gershom kept mourning double time, fourteen days instead of the prescribed seven. As long as his son was alive, he thought that he would return to his father. That hope was now gone; now he must fear that his son was lost to him in the next world too, and his mourning was doubled. A later stunted orthodoxy will not permit to a parent's heart that expression of his sorrow; it demands that no mourning be done or worn for such a son, for his passing away ought to make no difference.

Of other learned contemporaries in France and Germany, little information has come down to us. Gershom's brother Machir is named and his attempt at a dictionary, his "Alphabet," is mentioned. Joseph Tob-Elem (Bonfils) at Limoges seems likewise to belong to that period, a man of wide Talmudical knowledge, who earned particular merit by spreading the products of Jewish literature brought over from the Orient. At any rate, Gershom's light outshines them all, and numerous pupils spread his fame everywhere as they make the products of his learning common property. The school at Worms is especially praised, where Jacob Ben Jakar, Isaac Ben Jehudah, and several others appear as excellent scholars of that time, although they have left no writings, they fitted out a pupil who has exercised an influence the more lasting upon the entire Judaism of the Middle Ages, who does not rise above the character of the Jews in the Christian countries of the Middle Ages, but is still an appearance as amiable as he is important. Solomon Ben Isaac of Troyes in the Champagne, who falls into the second half of the eleventh century, from about 1040 to 1105, generally called Rashi after the initial letters of his name, was, like Gershom, a man of sober, clear sense, at home in his field and dominating it, of amiable modesty. His own personality almost completely recedes behind the objects which he treats. Solomon Ben Isaac wrote a commentary to the entire Talmud, the whole bible, and a part of the Midrash. He composed also penitential hymns, which, like all penitential hymns and similar poems of the French-German Paitanim (liturgical poets) have no other value than that they furnish a sad illustration of the conditions then existing. He carried on an extensive, learned correspondence, inquiries being addressed to him from all directions. In his commentaries, the clear view of the commentator is recognized, who feels the least difficulty which might arise in the passage for a reader not so well versed. With short words, keeping close to the text, he knows how to remove the difficulty and clear up the darkness. He keeps off every digression and avoids every discussion not strictly belonging to the subject. He wants to be commentator only, and he is that completely. Of course he appears to us as such, first in his commentary of the Talmud. There he is perfectly on his home soil and moves in his manner of view and thought. In his commentary of the bible, his endeavor is similar, but here the mighty current of the Talmudical way of explanation, legends and far-fetched interpretations have overpowered him to such an extent that he thinks himself obliged to give their results briefly, so that by such proceeding the natural sense and meaning is obscured. He feels that himself, and joins to the artificial Talmudical and Midrashic interpretations his own simple explanation and seeks, as far as it is possible for him from his standpoint, to investigate the meaning of the passage of the Scripture and to explain the construction by the grammatical aids at his command. Of course, as far as they are at his command, for the French school of that time had not got beyond the degree reached by Menahem Ben Saruk and Dunash Ben Librat, whose works, because written in Hebrew, were accessible to the French scholars, while the later works, written in Arabic, remained unknown to them. Thus they stayed limited to the childhood of linguistical knowledge and were not able to penetrate to the depth of the simple meaning. As stated, Rashi was dependent upon the whole interpretation as delivered to his hands by the old Talmudical writings, so that his explanation often leads more away from the simple meaning than up to it. Under the conditions and influences of that time, the appearance of a man can not surprise us, who on the one side never denies clear, undimmed view and sound, sober sense, and who yet, on the other side, quite harmlessly agrees with all legends and miraculous stories, accepting them as perfectly valid and indisputable as if there were nothing strange in them. Such is Rashi, and such is his School.

Among his contemporaries and successors, of course, there were men who ventured upon simple explanation of the Scriptures with far more decided earnestness and consciousness. One of Rashi's contemporaries who later, because the age had no longer an organ for his sober conception of the bible, received but little attention, was Menahem Ben Chelbo, whom we may designate from the quotations of his pupils as the father of a reasonable exegesis in France. A nephew of his, and probably grown up under his tutorship, was Joseph Ben Simon Kara. A later dark age has almost buried him, too, under its rubbish, until he was again discovered in our days. Kara had a bright mind, was a sober expounder of Scripture who came close to critical results by his clear way of looking at things, although he was without philosophic culture and scientific guidance. A grandson of Rashi, as famous as Talmudist as he was meritorious as expounder of Scripture, Samuel Ben Meir, known by the appellation of Rashbam, was a man of very fine linguistic sense and happy mode of interpretation. Yet he lacked his grandfather's skill in expression, so that he becomes too prolix at times and at other times too brief and dark. If his clumsy way of expression is overcome, a treasure of sound interpretation is revealed which may be used even to-day in many directions. Rashbam is fully conscious of the opposition in which the natural manner of interpretation stands to the Talmudic one. He himself tells us how he had many discussions with his grandfather and how that famous old man had with his admirable modesty admitted to the mere youth that if time were granted him, he would completely rewrite his biblical commentaries and shape them more according to the simple conception. Samuel Ben Meir handles that manner with all decision and there is no escape from his view for critical problems which he solves with fine, tracing tact.

Yet the same man appears to us again as expounder of the Talmud, diving into the most isolated and petty discussions, perfectly naive in his views, and we scarcely comprehend how the clear soberness in his biblical works can be made to agree with his proceeding in those upon the Talmud, how it is possible that in the latter he goes into the queerest things without hesitation. The Spaniards had kept themselves either on the parry against such matters or were satisfied to ignore them. But those clear Frenchmen walk into them without distrust. One example may suffice, and we may as well quote it here as the same passage will come up again in the course of our historical review.

The Talmudic legend to which we refer, belongs perhaps to the queerest, even if similar ones occur. Of course, it is not characteristic of the whole Talmud. Legends are, as already mentioned, children of the people's poetry, fabulous presentations, of which one hardly knows how the childish mind conceives them, whether simply as a merry plaything or if it lays claim to a serious belief in them. The legend runs thus: "Rabbi Banaa marked the grave caves, and came to the one in which Abraham and Sarah are entombed. Elieser, Abraham's servant, stood before it, and replied to the question of Rabbi Banaa whether he might go in, that Sarah and Abraham were in private, but he would ask. He returned with the answer to enter, because in that world no sensuality exists." The Spanish scholars passed that legend, like all similar ones, in silence; they avoided it. The great contemporary, Isaac Alfasi, had not admitted it into his work. And when asked how it should be taken, he said that it might have been a dream of Rabbi Banaa's. Samuel Ben Meir expounds the tract in which that passage occurs. He has not the least doubt about the truth of the story, he makes only isolated remarks: "Only to a man like Rabbi Banaa, who was so devout and learned, it might have been conceded to enter the grave caves of the blessed; also, Elieser, Abraham's servant, belongs to the seven persons who entered Paradise alive and had an eternal life; and thus he is Abraham's servant in that world as he had been in this one." The Tosaphists (makers of additions), as the later teachers are called, who proceeded from the School of Rashi and others, have another question to join to the story; they say, "Rabbi Banaa probably marked the grave caves only to designate the places where there were bones of the dead which have to be considered unclean. But as Abraham and Adam, to whose grave Rabbi Banaa comes also, had lived before the revelation on Sinai, and the law about uncleanness had its origin only then, it could not apply to those patriarchs. And then they grope for a solution of that difficulty.

Jacob, surnamed *Tham*, the brother of Samuel, also was a man of great literary activity, famous on account of his great Talmudic learning and ingenuity, and he was not without sympathy for other scientific knowledge. A few later Spanish grammatical works had reached him in translations. He had a short, personal intercourse with Aben Esra, wrote a reconciliation between Menahem and Dunash, in which, in the manner of that time, he took the side of the older Menahem, and is on the other side out-and-out the beginner of that method which, grasping the particular, esteems the discussions higher than the result and raises the legends above their basic idea. From those men, a school arises, called the Tosaphists, which enters with a great expenditure of ingenuity into all particulars of dialectics, discovers contradiction and attempts to reconcile them, without caring for the result but simply to execute a maneuver of ingenuity and mental activity. We must not pass over one of Jacob Tham's pupils who deserves to be assigned a very important position as a simple expositor of Scripture. I mean Joseph Behor Shor who, in the ways of Samuel Ben Meir, furnishes a very meritorious work in his commentary of the Pentateuch, a work which the centuries had also long buried, because they did not know how to estimate its value, until it was again dug up in our times. We meet yet industrious scholars with very useful works. Thus, *Tobia Ben Elieser* at Mainz, plainly after a residence for a long time in the Orient, puts together a Talmudical collection to the Pentateuch; and similar but more comprehensive, *Simon Darshan*, to whom, on the title-page of his repeatedly printed work, "Yalkut," Frankfort on the Main is assigned as birthplace, for which I would not undertake a guarantee. If those and men like them do not represent an independent tendency, if they do not work with creative and stimulating effect, they are yet worth our esteem as being useful, collecting together from partly remote works the material referring closely to passages in the bible.

In that way, all those men and their activity bear witness of devoted, earnest, and mental freshness as far as it could exist in that surrounding. They all are not dry scholars; all their sayings are borne by enthusiastic, deep faith, breathing loving fervor, and revealing pure, sound, moral sense. The simplicity of the manners, the naivety of the benevolent heart reconciles us with their mental conception, sometimes so narrow, so that when we approach them, we are forced to say,

"We have entered gloomy, narrow huts, the mind's light could not shine bright in there, and yet it was not extinguished, and still the heart was fresh and sound."

That was in Northern France and in Germany.

XII.

Italy and Provence.

An essential difference between the Middle Ages and Antiquity, among others, is the following: In Antiquity, a single people always stands in the foreground, deploys its full power toward the outside and appears as surpassing the rest of the world with its mental culture; the other nations either follow its lead or remain in their dark, dreaming life. In such solitary prevalence, the Egyptians, the Assyrians, the Babylonians, the Persians, the Greeks, the Romans, take their turns. In the Middle Ages, the relation shapes itself differently. Several nations live side by side, remaining on the same plane, even if dissimilar and differing among themselves in power and mental progress, but representing together in general a certain division of the world relative to power and mental effect. That is to be ascribed partly to the influence of the ruling Church. Antiquity produced everything out of the people; mental culture and religion were its own full property as it grew out of it, and for that reason it had to shape itself to a power dominating the less developed nations. In the Middle Ages, the Church was a universal power, it represented itself as such, standing above all nations, acknowledging the life of no single nation, or rather, no national life at all, as justifiable. It did not permit that the individuality of a nation should become a creative energy which might produce something out of itself. It wanted to be the only power to which all mankind must do homage, out of which they must draw all their force. Civil life was considered subordinate, the whole worldly activity was adjudged vain, null and void, and accordingly, each people might carry on their affairs, but the Church alone was the institution which contained the mental and spiritual treasures for all and dealt them out equally to all. Thus the mental life was separated from the popular life, the state had no inspiration, religion and science were without real life, without the energy which, rooting in the innermost impulses of the people, constantly receives new nourishment out of the soil of actuality. And both religion and science, became mere shadows or rigid shapes which did not live in the innermost heart of the people. Thus the intermediate link which joins popular life with higher popular culture was missing too; viz., the cultured language which, through the nobility of the thought that science puts into it, elevates even the ordinary relations of life, talked about in it, and keeps scientific investigation in connection with practical life. The affairs of daily life belonged, in the Middle Ages, to the popular language, uncultured and barbarized, which increased the rudeness of the manners and the want of taste in modes of conception. The affairs of science and religion were the property of a language of scholars, which remained remote from the people, and being dead, did not draw out of the constantly running fountain of life and rejuvenate itself. In addition, that language of scholars, Latin, was not permitted to lead back to its classic products. Being works of Paganism, they were proscribed and only the degenerate, fossilized manner of monkish expression was permitted. A long barrier to a free development of the mind among Christian humanity.

On the other side, that arrangement of states was prepared by the Church which permitted the existence of different nations, side by side, and gradually brought forth a group of formed states, that arrangement of states which later prevailed as a political axiom under the name of European balance of power, and strives now for acknowledgment as the right of the nationalities. Thus we see during the Christian Middle Ages, several nations, side by side, painfully working themselves up out of the mental stagnation and equally taking interest in the higher affairs of mankind, according to the plane which they occupied. In the same way, we meet within Jewry of that time in the different countries with the contemporaneous and equal endeavor of learning, and we see men arise everywhere who unite in themselves a great amount of knowledge as the exponents of the time. As in Germany and France, we meet the same phenomenon in the other countries which had at that time reached a certain degree of culture. In Italy too, learning developed at first on the Talmudical field only.

Italy, that land in which so many fragments of old culture were scattered about everywhere, in which it should be expected that the immediate succession to Antiquity should produce a deep effect upon the whole life, Italy stood at that time no higher than any one of the other countries. There, too, science was in its infancy, befogged by the spooky shapes which the religious tendency of the times had conjured up. Accordingly, we find in Italy within Jewry also, although it had gained a home in that soil for centuries, no appearance of anything to attract attention, down to the eleventh century. Out of the first half of the tenth century, a long-forgotten man has been awakened in our days into historic life. Physician, astronomer, astrologer, active also in the field of Jewish knowledge, *Shabthai Donolo,* or *Donulus,* stood on the summit of the science of the times, but what that summit means, is well enough known. Medical knowledge at all times was not strange to the Jews. It was a free science, which yet offered a secure position for living. Accordingly, as we find everywhere and at all times, even in countries and periods where science and culture were at a low ebb, Jewish physicians and medical authors, so Shabthai was also active as physician, astrologer and as commentator of the booklet on the creation (Yezirah), in a certain sense also a philosophical author. If we put him beside his contemporary and acquaintance, St. Nilus, it would be difficult to deny him the preference in real human culture, scientific intelligence and purified devoutness. When St. Nilus became sick, Shabthai offered him his services. But the former declined them; he feared that his cure by a Jew might injure the position of the Church.

Only about the end of the eleventh century—he finished the work in 1101—we make the acquaintance of a Talmudical scholar who has attained importance as an author. *Nathan*

from the persecutions of the Almohades increased the population of the Provence by settling there; they brought along from their former home the entire rich culture and the treasures of their science and literature, and tried to make another home for them in their new country.

Before that, we meet in that country beginnings of learning, Talmudic and Midrashic authorities, like Moses Darshan of Narbonne, who flourished there about the first half of the eleventh century, and others who were teachers and propagators of Talmudic science. In the twelfth century, the group of men is numerous, who, provided with all aids of Talmudic spirit and knowledge, made an excellent record, practically and theoretically. In Lunel, *Meshullam Ben Jacob* lived with his learned sons, also his pupil *Serachya Ben Israel Ha-Levi*, who is described as of Spanish descent, a man of great self-consciousness, decided power, and great intelligent youthfulness, who provided glossaries to the works of earlier Talmudic scholars and asserted his own, independent view in opposition to them. His fight against a great teacher, he even defends in the preface with the words, "The old sages say, 'Dear is Plato to me, dear is Socrates,' but dearest to me is truth." That is an assertion of independent conviction against the belief in authority by words of Greek wisdom. There in Posquieres lived Abraham Ben David, a man of vast Talmudic learning, of bold mind, but in ill humor at every opposition, and looking gloomily upon Spanish tendency and dissatisfied with the Talmudic work of Maimonides, which was the only work of that author he was acquainted with. There was also *Isaac Ben Abbamari* at Marseilles, author of a learned Talmudic work, "Ittur," and many others.

The Provence is yet more important as go-between, between the Northern-French and the Spanish views, or rather by the labor of bringing the Spanish-Arabian works, which would later have been inaccessible to the Jews, to the knowledge of those who did not understand Arabic, in Hebrew adaptations and translations, and thus spread them all over. Already in the first half of the twelfth century we notice the individual appearance of men of science coming over from

Spain; among others, *Abraham Ben Chiyah*, a mathematician, who appears as an authority to the mathematicians of the Middle Ages under the mutilated name Savasorda. Two families gained excellent merit in the second half of the twelfth century and exerted a peculiarly great influence upon succeeding times. They are Kimchi and the Thibbon families, *Joseph Ben Isaac Kimchi*, the father, and his two learned sons, *Moses* and *David Kimchi*, as imitators, brought linguistic knowledge, grammar, lexicography, sober explanation of the bible, from Spain over into the Provence. Joseph Kimchi composed commentaries to many biblical works, adapted and translated some philosophical and poetical pieces of literature of Spain, and thus became one of the new founders of scientific life for the entire Middle Ages. Moreover, the influence of the new home upon the linguistic treatment of the Hebrew appears in Joseph Kimchi in a remarkable manner. The Jewish grammarians among the Arabians had, according to the peculiarity of the Arabic language, put up also for the Hebrew three principal vowels; namely, a, e, o. Joseph Kimchi was the first one who, influenced by the Romanic languages, carried the division into five vowels also into Hebrew, and that, with double marks for long and short vowels. Both of his sons followed his way. Of greater importance than the older son Moses who perhaps attained greater fame than he merits, David, known everywhere under the name *Redak*, was the teacher of the entire Middle Ages by his grammar, his dictionary, and his commentary on the bible, and honored as almost indisputable authority. That scholar well merits the fame and the respect he enjoys, by his exact carefulness and his intelligent industry as collector, even if he was not a creative energy. Just by not striving for originality, by only desiring to present plainly and to transmit comprehensibly, his effect was more lasting and he became the reliable guide of the entire Middle Ages until the past century; and even to-day, his writings are properly much esteemed and offer instruction much material that has not yet been exhausted.

The other family, the Thibbons, followed the Spaniards

much more closely. While the Kimchis worked more independently, the Thibbons were satisfied to make translations and closely followed the tracks of their predecessors and masters. *Juda Ben Saul Thibbon,* also at the beginning of the second half of the twelfth century was a physician, possessed an exact knowledge of Arabic, and was a man of high general culture. He not only translated grammatical books, like the works of Abulwalid, which thereby became also accessible to the younger Kimchis who, as it seems, did not understand Arabic, but his greatest merit consists in having made translations of the works of the Arabian-Jewish philosophers. He translated the religio-philosophical works of Saadias, the "Duties" of Bechai Ben Bakuda, the religio-philosophical book Cusari of Juda Ha-Levi, and other things. Those works, if they had remained in Arabic only, might perhaps in our days have been found again and appeared as monuments of boldly striving, mightily wrestling and investigating minds. But they would have had no effect, would not have illuminated the long darkness. We owe it to Juda Thibbon that those works were not only preserved through the entire Middle Ages but that they flowed as a stream of life through their sandy desert and impregnated it in many ways. The oppressed spirit was refreshed by them, the hearts bowed down were raised by them. Juda Thibbon had an only son, Samuel. It is something peculiarly pathetic, if we are introduced into the close domesticity and the little cares of a scholar of merit, and that is permitted to us by Juda Thibbon. We have a writing from him to his son which contains a sort of scientific testament. Samuel, being an only son, seems to have been somewhat spoiled. His father cared for him with the greatest tenderness, took every means to expand his mental power in the best manner, kept for him the most excellent instructors, encouraged him in every way, and on that very account, Samuel was peevish and the petty pedantic guidance of his father made him unwilling. In this testament, Juda complains of that and exhorts his dear son, against whom he could not make any other complaint, who was well endowed by nature and possessed praiseworthy moral sentiment, to respond more to his care. He had put up so many fine book-cases for him, procured expensive works, all books were beautifully written, bound excellently, and kept in good order. He had advised him to write a fine, neat hand as he had noticed he could do, had encouraged him in the study of Arabic and all sciences and smoothed the way for him; in all books he would find notes made to facilitate the understanding. What he had so far done sluggishly, he ought now to attend to seriously, as he would soon have no guide. He should take good care of the books, take the unbound Hebrew ones out of the cases and dust them once a month, the Arabic ones once in two months, and the bound ones every three months, and thus he continues with similar exhortations. I hardly think that such well-intended and tender anxiety or benevolent torture could have effected much; it might rather have set the son still more against those studies than guide him up to them. But the sun of Maimonides arose. That work, "The Guide of the Perplexed" made a striking impression on the spoiled youth by the fullness of the thoughts, the boldness and power of conviction and the rounding out of his system. He needed no further spurring to study. Samuel went at it with a will, and resolved to translate the work. He opened communication with the author and sent him his translation for approval and correction, piece by piece. The correspondence between Samuel and Maimonides is as fine as instructive. Thus, taking no account of some other translations made by him, and his own literary attempts, Samuel executed a very meritorious work by his translation of the "Guide." To him we owe it that later times came into its possession and received its fructifying effect.

By their translations, the Thibbons became the creators of the peculiar philosophical, Hebrew style. Neither the language of the bible, nor that of the rabbis was sufficient to render all philosophical terms according to their speculative development. The careful endeavors of the Thibbons have created a philosophic-Hebrew language which is not elegant but has the advantage of definiteness and exact expression of the thought. It gained adoption into Jewish literature and became generally comprehensible in spite of its occasional strange new formations. It grew into a pliant instrument for the expression of philosophic ideas for later authors, and thus again a new germ for rich growth of culture in succession. The Provence had become a store-house for the manifold treasures of learning, a gathering place for minds very differently developed and separate. Will they have peaceable communication together?

We have come to the summit of the Middle Ages. With the end of the twelfth century an important period closes for the history of the Middle Ages in general as well as for the history of Judaism within it. History has passed through twelve centuries. We have kept company with it, and we began the journey with two great events; the entrance of Christianity into the world's history and the dissolution of the Jewish nationality. In the course of those twelve centuries, the Church has constantly extended its power and has become dominant afar. Its first home, where its cradle stood, it was soon forced to leave, and it has never carried any fructifying life there. Palestine has never attained a flowering growth through the Church; though the land was at one time in possession of the Church, it did not remain so. Its second home was the city and the empire where the Church mounted the throne. In Constantinople, in the Eastern Roman Byzantine Empire, it attained domination in the fourth century. It did not bring the blessings of a rich development to that new home either. The Byzantine Empire shrank together within itself, its power and mental culture became empty formulas, stunted into quarrels about etiquette, until that home in course of a later time was also taken from the Church. But it has founded a third home for itself and spread from there the fullness of its whole power over the Occident. From Rome, which has not yet lost the old right of possession to be the center of the world and all political dominion, the Church has extended its influence afar, has constantly increased its power in the course of those centuries, and has attained its summit at the end of the twelfth century. Yet it was not able in the first centuries to penetrate the Roman people, the Italian state; it could furnish no resistance to the submersion by barbarism. Pressure of barbarism can overcome and throw down only there where it strikes against inert, mindless masses, against effeminate people with hollow, pseudo-culture. The living spirit, awakened consciousness of the people, a refined mind, opposes a powerful dam to the attacking flood, to the raw, natural force. The migration of nations did not destroy Roman culture, Roman culture was already collapsed, the Church had not breathed a new, healthy spirit into it, and therefore the migration of nations could force in without hindrance. The Church, being carrier of higher ideas, tamed those savage hordes; that is its greatest merit. Yet it did not prove itself a higher intellectual power to which free minds willingly do homage, which brings all noble impulses in the character and life of the people to development; it became a spiritual power that bent down the enslaved minds under itself. In the course of those twelve centuries, there arose no new science, no popular literature fed by the fresh forces and matter. There is a long desert with scantily wrung fruits, a dried-up scholarship, torturing dissection of uncomprehended ideas. Facing such impressions and phenomena, Judaism had no inducement to withdraw from the stage of the world, it did not hear the urgent admonition of the world's history: "Cease, a new living force has arisen which accomplishes your task in higher manner." At the side of those phenomena, Judaism had the complete right to preserve and present its truth.

If in those twelve centuries, Judaism had to pass through difficult times, worse were yet to come. With the beginning of that period, a wholly new life commenced; no longer carried by a closely secluded nation, its scattered individuals sent out into widely different directions, the doubt might well arise: Can such a cleft people preserve itself? Can a religion joined so closely with the life of the state, continue without it? History has banished such misgivings. Those torn-apart members have accomplished a great work. Well considering the circumstances of the time, they built manifold bulwarks and walls around about themselves, in order not to succumb to the pressure from without, and yet have shaped themselves by great intrinsic force of preservation and evolution out of national life into a fellowship of faith. They have elaborated their system with mental abundance, have fortified and made themselves more and more unassailable in the truths of the faith, but have also imbued life with the views which, if in part, forcibly retaining a passed away time, yet in part impressed upon it true consecration and spiritual elevation. Thus they have faithfully preserved their intrinsic property, even if yielding here and there to the pressure that bore upon them from without and led them to malformations; they have elaborated their system to its depth and in all directions, and have taken a lively part in all higher interests of life, especially of intellectual life, as far as they were given room. In the meantime, Judaism has impregnated the Church with a knowledge of the Hebrew bible, has nurtured Islam in its cradle, has matured new linguistic knowledge, has graven deep marks in the development of every science in times when mental elevation was possible.

What gives it its charter of nobility, is that during that entire period it never lost the benevolent, genuinely humane sentiment toward its own members as well as toward outsiders. No proof is needed for the delicacy of feeling which Jews have shown at all times toward their fellow-believers; it is a well-known fact. But also toward other religions which had only the word of damnation against men of other faiths, Judaism held fast to the word which we already heard in the Talmudic time, that the righteous of all various nations and religions have a share in the future life. That had penetrated all circles and strata of the Jewish popular life. When a Moslem, convert to Judaism, heard from his teacher the harsh word, that he had been an idolator before, and directed an inquiry on that point to Maimonides, he was answered: "Such a sentence is to be doubly disapproved, when coming from one who should serve as teacher and pattern. If professors of Islam tell falsehoods about the Jews, that does not give professors of Judaism the right of judging Islam more severely than it merits. The professors of Islam make pilgrimages to Mecca and pray at the Kaaba, that old black stone which had been idolatrously worshiped during pagan times among the Arabs. But that could not be counted idolatry, it being merely an old custom, while the belief in the one God is and remains the basis and center of Islam." That corresponds perfectly to another Talmudic saying, that the nations outside of the holy land were not idolators and had simply preserved the customs of their fathers, without idolatry taking root in their heart. That doctrine had at all times the force of law in Judaism, in spite of the fact that from its point of view, the religion of the surrounding nations must have appeared to it a second edition of heathenism.

During that entire period, the teachers and carriers of Judaism shine by learning and purity of morals. In the Church, it is not rare that even highest dignitaries are deeply sunk in ignorance. The pride of Judaism was the fostering of learning. Only the scholar enjoyed lasting honor; everyone considered it a holy duty to have a knowledge of the doctrine according to his power and opportunity; his joy was in intercourse with scholars, and it was a raising of his own value, to esteem science in others. In other faiths, cases of demoralization just in the places where we should expect virtue and justice, love and benevolence, are not rare; with the Jewish teachers, sense of justice, sentiment of fairness, and mild disposition prevail, and an exception could hardly be found. From all those centuries, we possess opinions and legal decisions upon the most various relations in life, and in all of them, sound sense and a clear conception of life are joined to most severe impartiality, unbending sense of justice, most serious care for preservation of morality and promotion of the common weal. All honor to those men, able of mind and heart, even if many among them could not pass beyond the low standard of their time and country.

Judaism of the Middle Ages also reached its summit about that time. From now on, the course is downward in the history of the Middle Ages, as in that of Judaism. Within the Church, decompositions and frictions take place, the nationalities want to work up, science wants to attain liberty —but the Church draws the reins tighter, to prevent that. From time to time, a mortal combat arises, but the power of the Church is not broken, free movements are watched with more suspicion and persecuted more severely. Then from all sides arises the rallying cry: "Reform all through, reformation of morals, views, faith and life!" Again it almost seems the call will be choked in blood and the flame of the pyre. But no! A part secedes, but the old Church retains its power over the greater part. About the second half of the sixteenth century the nations wrestle up and are still wrestling with the old view which has not fully lost its power, which still to-day sends out the fulminations of excommunications even if they no longer set afire, and which still to-day comes forward with the same, or even increased wrath against all science and political formation.

Judaism has, during the course of that time, a doubly difficult position for contrary reasons; it is persecuted by two enemies, hostile to each other. The old animosity of the Church is not decreased, but even the new rising nationality looks no less unfriendly upon Judaism. People and state have not yet the full consciousness of their power, they do not yet possess the confidence in themselves that they can also receive strange matter into their body, work it up and divest it of its strangeness. To the just awakening and easily vulnerable nationality, Judaism and its believers appear strange material that must be excluded and kept off. Thus, persecuted by both parties, crushed from without and within, Judaism leads a sad existence for several centuries till in the middle of the last century. Then a new time begins for it also, a new light illuminates mankind, shines through the wide spaces of the world, and penetrates also into the dark chambers of Jewry.

How the time will develop farther, how mankind will form itself in that wrestling, is not in doubt for the presentient eye, spying into the distance. The mind of mankind is striving upward, the nations altogether as individual members of one great body of humanity will be illuminated by the real, divine spirit, all mutually promoting, strengthening, and purifying each other, and religion will appear as the energy of life, rejuvenated as the noblest flower of wisdom in the minds. Whether it will be that religion which has inherited the power, whether it will be able to work up to the full height of accomplishing its reconciliation with the live, political spirit and with science—to render a final verdict on that, may be left to the future. At any rate, Judaism, since it is permitted to enter into the full movement of the world's history, has rejuvenated its spirit, received science, and has partly broken through the bars which excluded it as mere national faith from the rest of mankind. That change of form and mental transformation of Judaism is a fact which it has already accomplished during the narrow, only gradually widening opening of its jail gates, a fact out of the history of the last, painful century which is graven with shining lines into the tablets of history.

Animated by the breath of complete liberty, constantly more and more imbued with the spirit of science and widening and deepening the view, Judaism of the present will steadily become more and more conscious of its task and strive for its accomplishment, a task which corresponds as much to all deeper endeavor of the present as it is deeply rooted in its own basic essence: *to become the religion of mankind. Only that religion which is reconciled with free thought* has the justification, but at the same time also, the *guarantee of its continuance.* On the contrary, every religion which makes battle against the right of the mind will be crushed under the wheels of time. *Only that religion which carries the guarantee of its future within itself, which considers it its task to spend its blessings to all mankind, and therefore presents itself to the totality in a form fit for it,* not one that confines itself to a narrow circle, withdraws into a cell, bars itself from the rest of mankind as if that were a soulless or alien body and is absorbed by preference into its own petty interests. Judaism will always bear in mind that it is called to strive for the goal, even if that can not be brought about by us alone, that *God will be acknowledged as one, and His name as one.*

Notes.

1. To 7 (Page 298)

These words are quoted in the Hebrew original by Abulwalid in Rikmah C, 21 end page 140. The last word is to be read מרויחי according to the manuscript, instead of מרוחי as it appears in print. That Menahem is the author of the verses and that they are addressed by him to Chasdai is a supposition which experts will approve.

2. To 7 (Page 299)

As the verses now appear, the acrostic אנחא בן נרוק is given. That the beginning of one verse should be read בזורי (with Beth), instead of פזורי Luzatto has already shown from the first edition (Kerem Chemed VIII., page 86). He then also recognized (ibid, page 188) that the name Menahem Ben Saruk is in the acrostic, he having indicated himself thereby as composer of the epistle. But how about the three wrong letters? Luzatto supposes that Menahem had been afraid and had hidden his name by exchanging the letters. No proper reason can be imagined for such a game of hide-and-seek which would have served no purpose and would have destroyed the aim of the acrostic. I rather suppose that Menahem had originally shown his name in full and that his words appear now before us in changed form. The sentence: ארכו העתים ונמשכו הימים may have been originally: משכו העתים וארכו הימים as he uses later on in the letter the expression: עד אשר משכו העתים and by that, the first Mem in Menahem would be established instead of the Alef. At the beginning of the sentence אל אל איילותי אפרש כפי the fitting word מרום may have dropped out, perhaps אשא עיני stood in place of אפרש כפי; that will restore the second Mem in Menahem. The words נצח קרית מלך רב were probably preceded by סלה which all ancients, and Menahem too, render "forever" (compare his dictionary, Edition Filipowsky page 120); and hereby the Samekh in Saruk would be restored. If my supposition is correct, that the acrostical indication of his name at the side of that of his patron excited the ire of Chasdai against Menahem, it is also very explicable that he caused the destruction of that acrostic, which was easily attained by the omission of the first word of the last two verses, and by transposition in the first one, which was then closer to the biblical language because in the bible ,מֹשֶׁךְ , used of time dragging along, occurs only in Niphal, while Menahem here, where the Mem demanded by the acrostic might induce it, but also in the body of the letter where nothing forced it, uses the Kal in that sense. So much, to support the position given in the text, which I want to be considered a supposition only.

3. To 10. (Page 335)

It does not matter who was the Greek Talmudist whom Aben Esra inveighed against so violently in that poem, and we shall hardly be able to fix particulars about him, as Aben Esra himself gives but dim indications about his person. Luzatto, who was the first one to publish the poem (Kerem Chemed IV., page 138), thought by one verse of it, that the man's name was Shimei (page 139, Note 6). But that rests on a misunderstanding. The words from which Luzatto concludes that name, are (page 140):

כמו שמעי כשמו והיחש עמו וחשבון עם טעמו
דברים עתיקים: יוני בחם שים יחי שקוץ מעשים

To that, Luzatto very correctly annotates (Note 8) that if " יוני " (the Greek), in numerical value of the letters = 76 is added to שמעי = 420, the sum, 496, corresponds to the word שקוץ (abomination). But the preceding words clearly indicate a play with the numerical value of the name, and that the man's name was not Shimei. They are to be rendered (בשמו) with Beth is probably better): "As much as Shimei is in his name if his surname is added; the agreement of the numerical value with the meaning of the word is an old, well-proved matter." Then he continues in the same manner: "Add to them (the given name and the patronymic), יוני , and it becomes שקוץ . Accordingly, the man's name was not Shimei, but his two names, of which one is surname, equal Shimei in numerical value; by which Shimei Ben Gera, who cursed and abused David, is indicated (2 Sam. 16, 5, etc.), and the Greek is compared to him because he attacked great teachers in like manner with curses and abuse. But the real name is not given by Aben Esra, and we can only guess at it by calculation. That makes one suppose—without guarantee for its correctness—that the Greek's name was משה כהן which two names, given name and surname, together have the numerical value 420, just like שמעי . Of course, there is little gained by guessing the name, as there is no Moses Cohen in Greece of that time known or mentioned elsewhere, and as Aben Esra described him, he would not be worth further search. But other arbitrary suppositions that have been made with such great assurance in this matter, are hereby shown to be erroneous.

Open Letter

To Professor Dr. H. I. Holtzmann.

DEAR SIR:

You have honored the first volume of this book by such a circumstantial discussion* that I feel obliged to return the attention by entering into an examination of the views you have put up in opposition to mine. What we have to discuss between ourselves, are questions of general interest; personal position can place no weight into the balance. If my assertions are correct, it does them no detriment that they "come from the mouth of a Jewish rabbi," a man of whom you presume "that the questions treated of here with such frankness about religion, revelation, Scripture, biblical history, have already been decided in advance and that in a sense which admits of no variations." That presumption only proves that within Christian-theological scholardom there is no idea of the mighty spiritual movement which has ruled at all times in Judaism and has prevailed with renewed vigor during recent years. It is therefore not surprising that you now, in me, "meet a Judaism which you have not known thus far, at the sight of which you look in vain for traces of Semitism, reminiscences of *Eisenmenger*, and even for echoes of the language of Canaan."

Such opening words might really spoil all desire of reading on; to such degree they raise the presumption of mental narrowness. Something like musty odor sticks to them and they come close to the manner with which the anonymous correspondent of the *Augsburger Allgemeine Zeitung* reviews my book, whose entire proceeding makes the impression of a half-knowing dilettanteism. In fact, it is highly surprising to me how you lean upon him in such dependence, copy his

* Protestantische Kirchenzeitung, 1865, No. 10, pp. 225-237.

disgusting pretenses of humorous allusions to Shylock and become so captivated by them that you turn Shylock yourself and ironically address me as "wise judge." So much as passing remark. But do you really believe that in the presentation of Judaism reminiscences from Eisenmenger must rise up to you? Is it possible that such is *your* knowledge of Judaism, especially of biblical Judaism, which was principally treated of in the first volume? Against such poorly stocked knowledge, it is hardly worth while to dispute. You looked in vain for traces of Semitism and even for echoes of the language of Canaan. My German style should abound with very rude Hebraisms and bad errors of speech, to be acknowledged as Jewish by you. For what other purpose should the language of Canaan serve here? Has every presentation of Christianity to carry the imprint of the poor Hebrew-Grecian dialect in which the earliest Christian writings are composed, to be permitted to lay claim to fidelity? You look in vain for traces of Semitism? With that word, a very wicked game is played in recent times. The generic notion of Semitism primarily expresses the gathering of a number of nations with speech of the same family of languages and to whom therefore it is believed to be proper to ascribe a common descent. In the former conception, which can not be doubted, as well as in the latter, which arises from analogy, a certain common mental disposition of those nations, a certain view of matters common to all, is acknowledged. That, too, may be called Semitism. But the mental peculiarity clinging to such a family of nations is difficult to grasp, and still more so to characterize so definitely that such character could everywhere with certainty be proved in their products. Such classification has led into great errors in recent times. Sometimes taking all Semitic nations together, a monotheistic instinct has been attributed to them, while not one Semitic nation outside of the Jews professed monotheism and that belief is not original with the Arabs, but was accepted by them. On the other hand, all philosophic disposition was denied to those nations, while those of the Aryan or Indo-German family were put forward as endowed with especial philosophic profundity. As if all European nations had not been philosophically educated solely through their contact with Hellenism—which in part was brought to them by Arabianism and Judaism—while they were not able to produce by themselves any other culture nor any philosophic one. Susceptibility was shown by those nations by accepting the influence of Hellenism; but was that not shown by the Arabians and the Jews too, if it is still determined to estimate them apart according to their descent? Of course, to you, seems "the entire Alexandrian philosophy of religion to have value and significance of a great curiosity only, particularly their most prominent representative (Philo), with whom the figures of the Old Testament have to act such queer roles upon Greek boards and before a Platonic background." But, my dear sir, is not the entire conception of Christianity as it is expressed in the gospel of John with its Logos, the whole Greek patristic with its symbolism, solely a fruit of that "great curiosity?" And now admit frankly, does not Schelling's and Hegel's philosophy of religion, when it wants to join itself believingly to the Christian facts, come very close to that "great curiosity?" You seem to have no idea of a speculative development within Judaism after Alexandrianism. Perhaps this second volume instructs you that it was never interrupted, perhaps you may now become better acquainted with the influence upon the speculative development of Christianity exerted by the entire Jewish mental history, especially by several Spanish thinkers, like Avicebron, Maimonides and others. You will hardly say of those men that "they had grown beyond the specific-Jewish world of conceptions and had then taken big portions out of the contents of the modern Christian mind." Yet you assert that of "the few names of modern culture which are connected with the Old Testament." You surely have Spinoza *not* in mind, you certainly do not count him among the modern ones, although he furnished the most prominent impulse to the modern conception. But of a few more recent ones who may appear before your mind in that connection, you say that they became what they were only by having grown beyond the world of Jewish conception and having taken big portions out of the contents of the modern Christian mind. For the present, that growing beyond may be left aside, but the expression "modern Christian" which is so much used in certain circles, deserves a serious word.

Of course, we have become accustomed, long ago, to meet within Christendom with a combination of words which are in most decided opposition to each other and which are yet so put side by side or even compounded together as if the contradiction were removed thereby, in the habit of seeking a very peculiar profundity of thought in the welding together of contradictory terms and conceptions and in the belief that such profundity is formed in the lack of clearness and perspicuity (compare above, pp. 322, etc.). Used to such out-of-joint compounds for centuries, the expression "modern Christian" passes, although under other conditions its component parts would quickly be recognized as completely dissolving each other. For, to speak plainly, the modern is not Christian, and the Christian is not modern. Christianity has closed up eighteen centuries ago, has kept away every further movement, fought it at all times and still fights it to-day, not only in its greater part, Catholicism, but also in the smaller part of Christendom which has granted some room to historic development, Protestantism, where in theological circles the ruling so-called orthodoxy fights the modern as its worst enemy. Modern culture leans in religion upon Jewish monotheism and in science and arts on Hellenism, while it either ignores or rejects the specifically Christian. Where attempts appeared to really create something "modern Christian," from Ezechiel's Vision by Raphael to Klopstock's Messias, from the lucubrations of Jacob Boehme to Schelling's philosophy of revelation and the like, I am almost tempted to use your expression, that we meet here "great curiosities." I do not misjudge the estimable effort of the human mind to reconcile the contradictions revealed thereby. And if no healthy fruit resulted, thinking was practised and the mind was exercised. The modern nations have called up the modern mental development and Christianity has been forced to yield, even if unwillingly, to its influence. That is an effect exercised upon Christianity, and it is not the cause thereof. To that general movement of culture, Judaism has not closed its doors, it rather has willingly given itself to it and has taken part to the extent of its powers. It is therefore wholly unjustifiable to say the Jews have "taken big portions out of the contents of the modern Christian mind." They have willingly given ear and mind to modern culture; Christian matter they have not discovered in it, and as far as found therein, have decidedly kept away from themselves.

In general, there is a very dangerous error to which Christian theology yields, and which produces very serious confusion of thought. All earlier history it considers solely as preparation for Christianity; all mental labor of Jews and Greeks is only a preparatory school, education toward Christianity; it does not even hesitate to lay claim to all pithy and juicy elements in them as Christian property. Every new humane development since the origin of Christianity is considered as its product. I have already acknowledged the world-historic influence of Christianity; history can not be erased unpunished. But want of careful consideration should teach modesty. The first six centuries of Christianity are times of mental decay, moving with impetuous rapidity; there the effects of Christianity could be but latent. In the succeeding six, Islam stands at the head of national and mental life; is that an aberration of the history of the world? Then two centuries enter in which the mental movement within Christendom is revealed by its trying to get rid of the fetters which the existing Christian arrangements form, and ending without result. The efforts may be considered as steps leading toward a new plane of Christian culture, at any rate the fight against the prevailing Christian ordinances predominated and that fight received its weapons from other mental powers than Christianity. In the succeeding time again, liberation does not proceed from Christian thought, but from the newly resuscitated Hellenism; that shakes violently at the Church, partly bursts it, and breaks its omnipotence. Because now for three centuries the nations with Christianity as their officially ruling religion stand at the head of culture, just like the nations of Islam in former centuries, Christianity claims itself entitled to proclaim all modern culture as its work, without taking the earlier or contemporaneous factors into consideration, and brags on what has been forced from it and accomplished in spite of its resistance, as if it were its work.

In like manner you prove to me what I owe recent Christian authors. "What is said about the relation of revelation and tradition that *might*, if Christianity is read instead of Judaism, be inserted verbally into the famous part of *Moehler's* apology." Of the first lecture, "The Nature of Religion," you say: "It does not demand separate proof that that language has not come out of the Talmud, that those ideas are not borrowed from Rabbi Hillel or any other one of those teachers who are praised by the author so much beyond all measure, . . . but that both, thought and expression, were possible only in a time in which at one side *Schleiermacher* had spoken on the essence of religion, and on the other side there is the endeavor to see the mental patterned in nature. . . . At any rate those are ideas which are and remain transcendent to the genuine Jew." After quoting a few sentences from the third lecture on revelation, you say with the same inexorability: "There is hardly more particular proof required that we can consider these sentences as Jewish only if the speculative philosophy of the Hegelian school deserves that name. We are out-and-out reminded of Strauss, if the sentence is emphasized and elaborated with such great energy that the Jewish people, not individuals, had been the vessels of that revelation. . . . The idea does not pour its contents upon individuals, but upon the totality. As the Greeks were the people of artistic geniality, but not all artists, but as a nation alone capable of producing great masters, so the Jews are the people of revelation from which came the favored organs. With such views the author steps still more decidedly beyond into a circle of thought and presentation which has been drawn neither by Jewish hands nor by Jewish instruments. And when the author disregards sundry facts which disturb his construction, and comforts with the sentence that the idea is also in Judaism mightier than the vessel in which it develops, we may recall that already *Herder* wants to find the key to the whole history of Judaism in this, that it had been a vessel too narrow and confining for the contents poured into it, and that it had perished through that contradiction in capability and task. (Compare Allg. Ztg., page 5247.)"

Thus, according to you, they are everywhere "modern and not rarely straight-out Christian ideas of which the author lives and with which he operates," and I only remain in this, "genuine Jew," that I have "by no means got over the last remainder of the inveterate deep grudge against the victorious daughter-religion." My dear sir, you might have extended my borrowing much farther and would have been sure of my complete approval. Continue and pronounce that I have not myself made the German style used by me, have not drawn it from the troubled waters of the Jewish-German literature of the Middle Ages, have neither formed myself only by Mendelsohn and his school nor by Boerne and Heine who were of Jewish descent, still less exclusively by our contemporaries Riesser, Berthold Auerbach, and others, but that I have drawn eagerly from the German classics and have endeavored to purify my esthetic sense by their artistic presentation as far as my capability reaches. But what does that prove? Only so much, that average men as we are, dear sir, have to accept the treasure of thought stored up by the men of great genius and that it is meritorious if we work it up, make it our own, and then know how to employ it independently or even to enrich it. If I had stupidly passed by those great treasures of the centuries, just reproach would apply to me; on the contrary, it is queer that I am blamed for being filled by the thoughts of all promoters, even of those of the most diverging tendencies and for having in a particular manner joined into an independent presentation the new thoughts and mental turns with which they have corrected and enlarged our view.

For as little as I want to deny the influence of the heroes of our time upon my whole manner of thinking, as naturally as that works upon everyone who does not live outside of his time, just as little can it be proved in the external manner as you attempt it, and just so much are you mistaken in your endeavor to divest me of my borrowed ornamentation. Thus, the newer Jewish literature has not waited with the definition of the conception of its tradition for *Moehler;* thirty years ago it has designated it as the fitting expression for the uninterrupted development and its justification. That conception has become the common property of the whole recent Jewry, even of that portion calling itself conservative. You deny the truth of that conception, you call Moehler's Catholicism "idealized, showily decked out with ideas and moments of the consciousness of modern times." —That you may fight out with Catholicism. Judaism has at all times preserved its liberty, its unchecked mental movement is therefore expressed in its whole formation. It is therefore perfectly immaterial whether what I say about the relation and tradition might be inserted verbally into Moehler's apology; it has grown on Jewish soil. If my definition of tradition can be applied in any manner to Catholicism, it is only natural, because it contains the conception the same as Judaism, but it has naturally shaped itself in the latter, it can not be said to have been borrowed of Moehler. The "Protestant ideas and moments of the consciousness of modern time" with which it is said to be patched up, belong again to that favored side-by-side position of contradictions which is so much less justifiable in the case because Protestantism rejects tradition.

If you find in the religio-philosophical views, echoes of *Schleiermacher* and *Hegel,* you sufficiently admit by the mere joining of those two diverging tendencies—which with you has become second nature—that I must have formed my views independently. But as little as I hesitate to confess that I have listened to the words of those masters and that, without surrendering to them, I gladly accept from them what I find correct thought, yet they are violently pulled in at my touch upon the philosophy of religion. The problems I treat of belong to thousands of years, Judaism has accomplished their solution in a very definite manner, the mounting of those thoughts is modified, the influence of the progressing mental development upon it is bound to show. And yet, even the mounting is found in the works of the earlier, unprejudiced minds only in different shape, sometimes not as clear and sharply defined, and then again with surprising clearness and brightest illumination. He that knows the works of the ancient Jewish philosophers is often surprised at the agreement in the conceptions down to the particular elaboration and presentation, even if in the expressions of their time.—Yes, you are out-and-out reminded of *Strauss*, and to clearly prove the borrowing of the thought down to the very expression, you attribute the following words to me: "The idea does not pour its contents upon individuals, but upon the totality." Well, that is the famous saying of Strauss in full, which was to dethrone the single God-Man, in order to put the entire God-Humanity into his place. And so I should of course be caught with the goods on me—if I had said that or something like it. But thought and expression were far from me. I did not and do not dispute the height of the individuals, consequently not that of the individual prophets, but simply emphasized that they, like other great men of genuis, whose sublimity I do not attempt to drag down, arise only in a nation which likewise has that even if latent undeveloped disposition, that they are the center and focus of a widely spread mental hearth. That thought lays no claim to originality, even if its strong emphasis on the particular subject should not find approval everywhere. But it does not touch the meaning of Strauss at all, just as Judaism has no occasion for any dispute like that made by Strauss. That the fullness of divine life is not poured into one individual, that even "Moses and Aaron died on account of their own sins" is something so well admitted in Judaism that it would be ridiculous to go a-begging at Strauss' for that idea.

Christianity is so intergrown with that theory which Strauss disputed, that just that sentence pressed out the most violent screaming, so that Strauss for awhile felt like beating a retreat on that point, instituted the "Cult of Genius" and had the air of placing genius so high that it stands only and alone, unattainable, as if elevated above all influences of its time and nation. That is it which forced him against his will in his new presentation: "For the People" to detach special matters from the totality of history and to stamp them as eternal, incomparable deeds. About that remainder of an even very much weakened apologetic, I have not failed to express my doubts. You as well as your "Allgemeiner Friend" have honored my verdict upon Renan and Strauss with great praises and it is astonishing if "such a logical, trenchant critic," a man who "in few sentences, so sharp and fitting"—of course, "with sharp, Jewish sense," you say, which I accept with thanks while others may refuse it at their pleasure—has "scored up" two such important works and is then again in other parts treated in a degrading manner with proud superiority. In fact, that praise arises from a peculiar position; it is, as the Talmudists say of Harbona, not the product of love of Mordecai, but of hate of Haman. You have real, malicious joy at seeing those acute critics shown up in certain points as apologists, which is a just reproach to them, as you admit from your point of view. But when I enter into that weakly apologetic remainder, when I especially reduce the estimation of "the rich collection of sentences or maxims" to their proper modest measure, the "Allgemeine" is quickly ready with the verdict that my criticism "shows less of integrity than of hypercritical subtlety." You yourself quote that verdict of your "Allgemeine friend" with pleasure, yet pass by this "hypercritically subtle" dissection of mine very quickly. You say only one thing: "Those synoptic parallel passages of the new patch on the old garment must undergo a rigorous examination, the result of which consists only in that, what has been known long ago, every parable limps." How queer! About every sentence and every parable, innumerable long dissertations have been written, which treat of every sentence and every word, of every relation and every possible application with the greatest circumstantiality, and now my short discussions, because they are incommodious to you, are to be all at once hypercritically subtle, are to put up for the poor children of thought an unjustifiable, rigorous examination, because they do not glorify? But it has no other result than, etc., etc. Is that true? I prove that the whole sentence with its comparison "is very loosely, even contradictorily attached to the preceding reply," that it occupies a very different and later attained point of view, and that it therefore "does not belong to Jesus at all." All that you are silent about with innocent air! If, as it seems, you know of nothing to say against it, you have no right to shrug your shoulders in pity. Yet, you pretend that the whole result consists in the proof that every parable limps. Have you well considered what you express by that? An admission as great as I can possibly demand. Those are comparisons and parables, perhaps no worse, yet no better, than hundreds of others, in no case "imperishable sayings, for in them truths that are every day getting fresh corroboration, are put into a form that plainly fits them and is at the same time universally intelligible." I disputed that, and proved how such claim and all pretension founded on it are unjustifiable; you admit it, and say: "Well, the parables are limping, *as they all do*." By what right do you then adopt the words of your "Allgemeine?" Yet do not believe that I assert not to have learned anything from all recent labors, whether done by Christians or Jews, and especially not to have received anything from Strauss. I acknowledge every instruction thankfully, and Strauss, as well as the mental current of which he was and is the expression, has certainly had its effect on me. As there are defects clinging also to favored minds, as I believe, I assert that in opposition to one-sided conception the other view should be shown for correction. With this, my respect for the great carriers of culture remains, I gladly accept their mental impulse. Yet in that external manner where you look for the effect, it is not to be found.

It is yet worse with being reminded of *Herder*. Herder's flashes of mind have illuminated us all, even if we have always to be on guard against being wrapped into the often quickly succeeding darkness. He would undertake a meritorious work, who succeeds in fixing such a bright moment and would elaborate the thought often thrown out by Herder, loosely, without further connection. The idea which you quote here, following your "Allgemeine" has so little kinship with my consideration of history, that in this connection it has only now become known to me through both of you. Therefore, I simply keep to your quotation. Judaism, Herder says—according to you—contained in a too narrow vessel a great idea which had to burst the same, in order to be able to reveal itself in its fullness, and so should be added, that happened by Christianity. As far as that figure is applicable, it suffers from a certain obliquity which produces a squint. The idea forms its vessel, its carriers; it transforms them according to the needs of its growth; the hulls which were formerly fitting, grow with it, become looser, and shape themselves otherwise according to the inner ideal requirements. Vessel and idea are not in opposition, they are correlates that bear the fate of mutability together. The vessel breaks only when the idea has finished its life. As long as the latter retains its vitality, the former is also preserved, only that it has to go with the other through the entire process of formation. When Hellenism had exhausted itself, the nation of the Greeks collapsed; when the national energy of the Jews lost its vitality, the Jewish state ceased, but therewith Judaism did not collapse, but it kept on forming its vessel according to requirement.

The great chasm that separates us is not in that wherein I agree as alleged, with the sentence of Herder quoted by you, but in that wherein I differ with him. You and your colleagues have to admit on the one side that the complete, pure idea of religion was alive in Judaism, even if it necessarily appeared in the form conditioned by the time, and yet, on the other side, you would like to save for Christianity something new, something hardly guessed at before, and you can not do so in any other way than by again placing Judaism low down, not only in the temporal expression of its appearance but also in its essence and its deepest sentiment. In that I find contradiction and injustice. You do not see with materialism in the corporeal appearance, in the momentary stage of the individual man, the complete exhaustion of his being, you recognize that rather in the living, overtowering spirit which impels him to higher development. Neither do you find in the past of Christianity, nor even in its present, the full formation of its soul, you rather assert a deeper endeavor and its further formation from within to be hoped for and you represent many a temporal expression thereof as malformation not chargeable to it; you separate ideas from appearance with all decision. But you stand up against Judaism with flat sobriety and assert that it, which pronounced its idea from the very beginning so often with such decided emphasis, with such unclouded clearness, is so imprisoned in the individual, temporal, limited expressions that it cannot free itself from them, you shut your eyes before the profundity and the compass of its spirit, and would represent that also as narrowminded. That is the contradiction which clings to the entire confessional narrow theology.

You think: "Serious Christian science will, in view of so many labors to throw light upon the genesis of the Hebrew conception of God, only smilingly shake its head, if right here in the second lecture, that conception of God drops in finished, without all traces of national limitation, without any anthropomorphic gift at its birth." I do not begrudge to the seriousness of Christian science that smiling, I grant to it that knowing shaking of the head, but if you would know my "Urschrift"* and my other labors not simply by their name, but according to their actual contents, you might have even caught me in a flagrant contradiction, as I have uncovered those temporal expressions and the endeavors of later times to cover up and blur those expressions leading to error, more than any earlier author. Of course, then you could no longer have smiled and shaken your head with "Christian seriousness" at my "Jewish learning." You would rather be obliged to acknowledge that I do not clear the Jewish holy scriptures of national and anthropomorphic presentation of even the conception of God, just as no human expression can at any time rise above it, just as it appears in naive times

* Urschrift & Übersetzungen der Bibel. Geiger. Breslau 1857.

with the most natural harmlessness, but that yet the truth in its inmost profundity shines through the defective expression, that the clearest light breaks through the slight clouding and even gilds it. God is one, without form, is lord of heaven and earth, is ruler of all fates—that is the conception proclaimed loud and unambiguous, even if it may be pronounced in the most childlike expression. What you say of the "many labors to throw light upon the genesis of the Hebrew conception of God" is but phrase. That conception of God has its sole genesis in the secret depth of the Jewish spirit and it is present as soon as that finds its expression, it is undisputed in its *entire* literature, that mouthpiece of a nation, it comes out "finished," if you so desire, from that place of its birth, like the child, even if it does grow up to manhood, it has not put itself together out of component parts, blown together from the most various points. You may call that "dropped in." I know of no genesis, God Himself is its father and Israel its mother, and you can not find for its parents, nor even nurses, wheresoever you may look for them. It has had its history and has it yet farther on, but it is independent according to its inmost essence, always accepted for its development only what was homogeneous to that essence and what could not grow into it as foreign substance, it owes at most the stimulation to more rapid growth to external impulses. Neither is there any occasion for you to smile, if all Parseean influence upon Jewish consciousness is denied. Whatever opposed Jewish basic disposition in Parseeism was decisively rejected with the clearest feeling of the opposition, and what agreed with the former, was as modification of its own not kept out, just as it happened later with Hellenism and Islam. Even the Parseean doctrine of the resurrection of the body could intrude only as a complement of national longing, first as party shibboleth, then as general comfort during national distress, and with the existence of that as with the whole national tendency, it stands and falls.

"It is something *entirely new* to you" if you read: "The idea of Judaism is one embracing all mankind, but it needs at first an individual people for introduction into life," "something *entirely new*, the consciousness to encompass mankind and to labor for it" forms the real germ of the Jewish spirit which we, poorly informed, have thus far held to be the expression of the toughest and most rigid particularism and of unconquerable narrowmindedness." You were really poorly informed, if that is something entirely new to you, if you do not know one word of all biblical passages that announce it, from the account of the creation of *man* in the image of God, from the promise to Abraham that in him and in his seed all nations of the earth should be blessed, to the announcement by all prophets, how all the world would be united in knowledge of God and peace, down to the sayings of all later teachers who under the heaviest pressure did not part with that spirit nor lose that consciousness. Yes, the Jewish spirit is tough, it does not bend nor break; rigid and particularistic it was made only by the peculiar opposition. Why is there such a great fight made by the other side, when it is divesting itself of that particularism forced upon it? You are greatly incensed if I say of animal sacrifice, that it "had not sprouted from the root of Judaism," that it "had been tolerated, and only tolerated;" you think, "ordinarily the difference and prominence of Judaism over paganism is placed in this, that its sacrificial service had originated from a more deeply conceived need of expiation and reconciliation than the pagan one," with that, you opine, I "might be satisfied." It is just that, that I am not satisfied with the crumbs thrown to us from the table of Christian theology, that I investigate Judaism, not from the New Testament, but from its own sources, and if I have therein prophets and poets of psalms pronounce a unanimous verdict of rejection against sacrificial service, if I observe its complete crowding out in later history, if I see that many thinking leaders do not dive into petty sacrificial symbolics, but step higher above the whole conception of sacrifice, then I know that the ancient sacrificial service was but tolerated. If you reply to me on that point as well as in regard to the "law" lugged into the dispute by you and the "Allgemeine," that I can not hide to myself, that in the documents of the Old Testament sacrificial service and priesthood are very often and for only tolerated matters, much too often spoken of, your side is keeping with improper preference to the Pentateuch, about the origin and final completing of which criticism is as yet very defectively informed. I have not hesitated to enter that difficult field in learned works and shall try to further my contributions. But where one should appear with sure results, the unfinished must remain in the background. Here only this much! The "law" is frequently a product of fights and compromises with the external conditions, and those drag along through the entire history of Judaism from its origin down to the present; yet its inmost energy arises always anew and pierces even the bars of the compromise. The most instructive example is furnished by the very history of priesthood in Israel, an institution without which mankind does not believe to be able to get along, which also in Judaism made efforts to adapt itself to all formations and to rule them thereby, and yet had to fall because in opposition to its essence. Yes, "the traits of dissatisfaction with priesthood, which are communicated to us are," as I say, "nothing isolated;" and if you point to Numbers 16 and 17, to represent "what the relation of the Jewish spirit is to such traits of dissatisfaction," you mistake the condition of the individual event that is related for the Jewish spirit. In the same way, if you say later, with fine irony, "If David has the enemies of God's people sawed to pieces and baked in furnaces, it may be comprehended by the economy of the materializing idea, and if a curse is uttered against the Babylonian mothers (?) that their children may be dashed against the stones, that is a wise accommodation because the idea must not at once appear too ideal, if it is to find admission." What does the outburst of wrath of the individual concern me, even if his name be David, or even if he be a poet whose song, pressed out of him by deepest woe, has been received into the book of psalms? That belongs to the essential differences between Judaism and Christianity, that the former is not founded upon a personality, but carries its base within itself. "Doubtless thou art our Father," says the prophet, (Isai. 63:16) "though Abraham be ignorant of us, and Israel acknowledge us not: thou O Lord, art our Father, our Redeemer is thy name from everlasting." With the finally achieved preponderance of Judah, David, as founder of the Jewish dynasty, was highly extolled, and yet, the traits from the old accounts, which in part proceeded from the opposition, have not been wholly obliterated from his history. That is a question of historic criticism. In spite of many confessed defects, he and Solomon were ideally glorified, David himself (as it reads in Ezechiel) or "a son of David," as he was named in popular imagination, was again to become the savior, the hero of the glorification. Take no interest in the "son of David," divest David himself of his ornamentation, do just as you please. Only in the interest of historic truth, a protest might appear from my side against an unfair verdict, never in the interest of Judaism which has not represented him or his son as a sinless saint.

This is and remains the kernel of the difference between us. We do not base our truth upon persons and do not limit it to determined times; you and your colleagues tie it to a single personality which you elevate to the accomplished ideal and make superhuman and close with his time as the time of the realization of the ideal. By that you put yourself into contradiction to history and yet would like to let history testify for itself. You would like to make believe that you alone had remained standing on the plan of the world's history, you can not help getting angry if Judaism also makes claim of not yet being dead as a factor in the world's history. Then a remnant of those old faded phrases of Jew hatred comes shuffling along. On such a road I do not follow you. I am doing enough if I copy your sentences which you again clamp to the "Allgemeine:" "Tough Judaism, indeed, struggles and twists through all sorts of obstacles, and where a new culture is produced, it grapples on, to work it up." (What an outrage!) "But that it will find a new home anywhere" (who could join a clear thought to this?) "and enter in really productive manner into the course of the mental development of mankind and become merged with it" (that it does not do you the small favor of perishing!) "that nobody will hardly be able to assert in general." (Why screwed down so carefully?)

But for what purpose should those phrases be quoted farther? It is useless to enter into dispute about them. Fleeting time calls for better use, There are still enough of scientific problems that claim the force of every honestly striving person. I shall always be glad to meet others, you too, on that road; but that superior looking down upon the Jew journeying alongside does not make the least impression upon me, perhaps may only make me smile at the vain pride. It is better if we move along together in mutual esteem!

Frankfort on the Main, May 11, 1865.

www.ingramcontent.com/pod-product-compliance
Lightning Source LLC
LaVergne TN
LVHW011159110826
845150LV00006B/1263

* 9 7 8 1 4 2 5 5 7 3 2 6 3 *